Course	Introduction to Theatre
Course Number	**THEA 100**
	Richard Wesp
	SUNY GENESEO
	Dept. of Theatre and Dance

http://create.mheducation.com

ISBN-10: 1308555776   ISBN-13: 9781308555775

Contents

Credits

The Theatre Experience

The Theatre Experience

THIRTEENTH EDITION

EDWIN WILSON
Professor Emeritus
Graduate School and University Center
The City University of New York

THE THEATRE EXPERIENCE THIRTEENTH EDITION

Published by McGraw-Hill Education, 2 Penn Plaza, New York, NY 10121. Copyright © 2015 by **Edwin Wilson**. All rights reserved. Printed in the United States of America. Previous editions © 2011, 2009, and 2007. No part of this publication may be reproduced or distributed in any form or by any means, or stored in a database or retrieval system, without the prior written consent of McGraw-Hill Education, including, but not limited to, in any network or other electronic storage or transmission, or broadcast for distance learning.

Some ancillaries, including electronic and print components, may not be available to customers outside the United States.

This book is printed on acid-free paper.

1 2 3 4 5 6 7 8 9 0 DOW/DOW 1 0 9 8 7 6 5 4

ISBN 978–0–07–351427–7
MHID 0–07–351427–6

Senior Vice President, Products & Markets: *Kurt L. Strand*
Vice President, General Manager, Products & Markets: *Michael Ryan*
Vice President, Content Production & Technology Services: *Kimberly Meriwether David*
Brand Manager: *Sarah Remington*
Director of Development: *Dawn Groundwater*
Marketing Manager: *Kelly Odom*
Director, Content Production: *Terri Schiesl*
Content Project Manager: *Lisa Bruflodt*
Buyer: *Jennifer Pickel*
Cover Designer: *Laurie Janssen*
Cover Image: © *Michael J. Lutch*
Design Elements: Dynamics of Drama: © Ingram Publishing/Alamy RF; Playing Your Part: © Digital Vision/Getty Images RF; In Focus: © Brand X Pictures/PunchStock RF
Compositor: *Aptara®, Inc.*
Typeface: *Adobe Garamond Regular 10.5/13*
Printer: *R. R. Donnelley*

All credits appearing on page or at the end of the book are considered to be an extension of the copyright page.

Library of Congress Cataloging-in-Publication Data

Wilson, Edwin.
    The theater experience/Edwin Wilson, Professor Emeritus, Graduate School and University Center, The City University of New York.—Thirteenth Edition.
        pages cm
    ISBN 978-0-07-351427-7 (acid-free paper)—ISBN 0-07-351427-6 (acid-free paper)
    1. Theater. I. Title.
    PN1655.W57 2014
    792—dc23

                                          2013039856

The Internet addresses listed in the text were accurate at the time of publication. The inclusion of a website does not indicate an endorsement by the authors or McGraw-Hill Education, and McGraw-Hill Education does not guarantee the accuracy of the information presented at these sites.

www.mhhe.com

About the Author

Edwin Wilson, as a teacher, author, critic, and director, has worked in many aspects of theatre. Educated at Vanderbilt University, the University of Edinburgh, and Yale University, he received a Master of Fine Arts degree, as well as the first Doctor of Fine Arts degree awarded by the Yale Drama School. He has taught at Yale, Hofstra, Vanderbilt, Hunter College, and the CUNY Graduate Center. At Hunter he served as chair of the Department of Theatre and Film and head of the graduate theatre program. At CUNY he was the Executive Director of the Segal Theatre Center. He was the theatre critic for *The Wall Street Journal* for 22 years and edited and wrote the introduction for *Shaw on Shakespeare.* He is the author of *The Theatre Experience* and a coauthor, with Alvin Goldfarb, of *Living Theatre, Theatre: The Lively Art,* and a coeditor of *The Anthology of Living Theatre,* all published by McGraw-Hill. He has served as president of the New York Drama Critics' Circle, as well as a member of the selection committees of the Pulitzer Prize in drama and the Tony awards. He is currently on the board of the Susan Smith Blackburn Prize and the John Golden Fund, and for many years was on the board of the Theatre Development Fund, of which he served as president. Wilson served as assistant to the producer for the film *Lord of the Flies* directed by Peter Brook and the Broadway play *Big Fish, Little Fish* directed by John Gielgud, was resident director for a season at the Barter Theatre in Virginia and the executive producer of the film *The Nashville Sound.* He co-produced the Broadway play *Agatha Sue, I Love You,* directed by George Abbott.

To my wife, Catherine

Contents in Brief

Contents

PART 2

The Performers and the Director   66

PART 3

The Playwright and the Play   120

PART 4
The Designers 194

Preface

ACTIVE AUDIENCE PARTICIPANTS, ACTIVE CLASS PARTICIPANTS

The Theatre Experience prepares students to be well-informed, well-prepared theatre audience members. With an audience-centered narrative that engages today's students, a vivid photo program that brings concepts to life, and features that teach and encourage a variety of skill sets students master core concepts and learn to think critically about theatre and the world around them. As a result, students are better prepared for class, and better prepared for theatergoing.

Engage with Your Role

- True to its original vision—to focus on the audience's experience of attending a live theatre performance—the 13th edition of *The Theatre Experience* **opens with three chapters that focus on the student as an audience member**. Topics include: the difference between being at a live performance and watching a dramatic performance on film, TV, or an electronic device; the enhancement of the experience aided by the proper preparation and background; and the awareness of the role of the audience in live theatre.

- **Dynamics of Drama** features illustrate some of the more challenging theatre concepts in a way that is easier for beginning students to understand and apply as audience members. For example, topics include realism and nonrealism (Chapter 1), and climactic and episodic forms (Chapter 7).

- **NEW Play Links**, a feature in *The Theatre Experience,* 13th edition, allows you to read many of the plays mentioned in the text online. Any play referenced in the text that can be found online is highlighted in blue typeface when first mentioned in a chapter. Should you want to read one of these plays, you can refer to the list that precedes the Glossary at the end of the book and find its URL. Titles are listed alphabetically.

The plays can be used to highlight key concepts and to complement the discussions found in *The Theatre Experience,* 13th edition. In addition, many of the new Thinking about Theatre and Experiencing Theatre exercises can also be supplemented and enhanced with examples from these plays.

Master the Basics

- **Parts 2, 3, and 4 cover the important elements of theatre**: acting, directing, playwriting, and design. The authors' efficient structure and succinct style set students up for a clear understanding of the basic concepts, freeing up valuable class time for deeper discussions and more personal engagement with course concepts.

- **Photo Essays and a dynamic art program** allow students to visualize the core theatrical concepts introduced in each chapter. Topics include modern domestic drama (Chapter 8), forms of comedy (Chapter 8), costumes and masks (Chapter 10), uses of stage lighting (Chapter 11), and others.

Think Critically and Engage Actively

- NEW "Playing Your Part" is a feature in each chapter that includes two distinct sets of questions and activities that emphasize thinking and engaging critically.
  - "Experiencing Theatre" activities help students actively to engage with the concepts of the text. These exercises ask students to undertake activities within the classroom or to understand how aspects of their everyday lives connect to core concepts discussed in the text.

PLAYING YOUR PART: EXPERIENCING THEATRE

1. If you were to write a play about your life, what would you choose as your opening scene? What would some of your complications be? Would there be a climactic moment?

2. If you were to write a play about a family you know (your own or another), what point of view would you take? Why? Are there strongly opposed forces or balanced forces in this family?

3. If you were told you were going to have to attend a play that lasted over four hours, what would your reaction be? Why? What are your traditional expectations about the space and time of a play?

4. After watching a popular film, describe how the opening scene aids in setting the action. Describe one or two of the complications in the film. Can you discuss the film's point of view?

• **"Thinking about Theatre"** questions challenge students to analyze and examine elements of a theatre experience.

PLAYING YOUR PART: THINKING ABOUT THEATRE

1. Think of a play you have read or seen where the main character encounters one impediment or roadblock after another. Describe the various obstacles that must be overcome before the end of the play.

2. Think of a play or musical you have seen or read where two major characters are in conflict with one another. Describe the two characters and explain the source of their conflict. How does it play out?

3. Think of a situation some people saw as very serious, but another person viewed as humorous. Explain what you believe led different people to see it so differently. What was your own feeling—was the incident funny or sad?

• NEW **"In Focus"** features include two categories:
  • "Global Connections" present the global reach and influences of theatre from various cultures. Topics include Augusto Boal's "Theatre of the Oppressed" (Chapter 1), Asian influences on the playwrights Brecht and Wilder (Chapter 6), and global influences on Julie Taymor (Chapter 12).
  • "Historical Perspectives" features bring relevant topics about the past to life: women in Greek and Elizabethan theatres, performers' status at different points in time, the evolution of the director.
  • NEW Marginal Definitions For the first time in The Theatre Experience, definitions of boldface words or terms in the text are provided in the adjacent margin.

Selected Chapter-by-Chapter Changes

Chapter 1 begins with a new section on the great diversity of contemporary theatre, first in terms of the variety of places in which theatre can be viewed: from the largest auditoriums or Broadway houses to regional, college, and community theatres, as well as small, informal spaces, and second, in terms of the extraordinary range of subject matter as well as ethnic and cultural material. The chapter then turns to the unique experience of live theatre that differentiates it from all other media. In this and all subsequent chapters, when a play is mentioned for the first time, it is set in blue type to signal its inclusion in the new "Play Links" feature. This indicates that the script of the play can be retrieved by means of a URL, which is provided at the end of the text.

Chapter 2 retains the core content about audience involvement, including background information and preparation that makes attending the theatre more meaningful and enjoyable. The chapter's coverage of critics and reviewers has been extensively updated, now including new discussions of bloggers, social media's impact on audiences, and audience behavior.

Chapter 3 has a new Dynamics of Drama feature, "Popular Performance Spaces," which extends the coverage of venues where live performances take place. Material on stage spaces has been edited and updated.

Chapter 4 features minor updates to keep the content as current and engaging as possible. Information on the training, preparation, history, and techniques of acting have been retained from previous editions.

Chapter 5 expands anew the auteur director and the postmodern director. The material on the artistic director and managing director of nonprofit theatres has been revised.

Chapter 6 features a new introductory section on the playwright's role in the creation of a script, explaining the playwright's relationship to ancient storytellers. Also, information has been added on the context in which the playwright works, the demands and challenges of developing a script, and the unique requirements of a work for the stage.

Chapter 8 has been substantially edited and revised. There is a new opening section on the mood, tone, and point of view of a production that are conveyed to an audience in the opening moments of a production.

Chapter 12 features a new discussion of recent trends in stage musicals, together with up-to-date examples.

Chapter 13 features refined listings of playwrights and plays, updated with the latest names and productions from around the world. Material that was previously in Chapter 1 has been incorporated into this chapter.

TEACHING AND LEARNING RESOURCES

Support for Instructors

The Theatre Experience offers a wealth of supplemental materials to aid both students and instructors. The Online Learning Center at www.mhhe.com/wilsonte13e is a resource for students and faculty. Instructors' resources are password-protected and include:

- Instructor's Manual.
- Test Bank.
- EZ Test Computerized Test Bank: McGraw-Hill's EZ Test is a flexible, easy-to-use electronic testing program that allows instructors to create tests from specific items in the text. It accommodates a wide range of question types, and instructors may add their own questions. Multiple versions of the test can be created, and any test can be exported for use with course management systems. The program is available for Windows and Macintosh.

Student Resources

The Online Learning Center at www.mhhe.com/wilsonte13e is a robust tool for students, providing a wide range of material to enhance learning and to simplify studying. Resources are keyed directly to this edition and include the following:

- Chapter-by-chapter quizzes for testing students.
- Essay Quizzes that can be e-mailed directly to instructors.
- The Theatre Goer's Guide is an excellent introduction to the art of attending and critiquing a play. This guide will assist students in everything from making theatre reservations and knowing when to applaud to evaluating a performance and doing web research.
- Detailed explanations and examples of Major Theatrical Forms and Movements.
- Synopses of Plays.
- Select Bibliography.

Craft your teaching resources to match the way you teach! With McGraw-Hill Create, **www.mcgrawhillcreate.com**, you can easily rearrange chapters, combine material from other content sources, and quickly upload content you have written, like your course syllabus or teaching notes. Find the content you need in Create by searching through thousands of leading McGraw-Hill textbooks. Arrange your book to fit your teaching style. Create even allows you to personalize your book's appearance by selecting the cover and adding your name, school, and course information. Order a Create book and you'll receive a complimentary print review copy in 3–5 business days or a complimentary electronic review copy (eComp) via e-mail in about one hour. Go to **www.mcgrawhillcreate.com** today and register. Experience how McGraw-Hill Create empowers you to teach your students your way.

Anthology of Plays

Anthology of Living Theater (978-0-07-351413-0) offers 18 plays for use with *The Theatre Experience.*

CourseSmart ebook

The Theatre Experience is available as an eTextbook at www.CourseSmart.com. At CourseSmart, students can take advantage of significant savings off the cost of a print textbook, reduce their impact on the environment, and gain access to powerful web tools for student learning. You can view CourseSmart eTextbooks online or download them to a computer. CourseSmart eTextbooks allow students to do full text searches, add highlighting and notes, and share notes with classmates. Visit www.CourseSmart.com to learn more and try a sample chapter.

ACKNOWLEDGMENTS

First and foremost I wish to thank Professor Alvin Goldfarb for his invaluable contribution to this edition of *The Theatre Experience*. My coauthor on *Living Theatre* and *Theatre: The Lively Art*, Al's ideas, his research and writing skills, his originality and imagination, and his persistence have been indispensible in completing this, perhaps the most audience-oriented and insightful version of *The Theatre Experience* of the entire series.

I first developed many of the ideas in this book while teaching a course in Introduction to Theatre at Hunter College of the City University of New York. To my former students and colleagues at Hunter, I express my continuing appreciation. Also, to those professors and other experts who have contributed importantly to prior versions, I express my deep appreciation. They include Alexis Greene, Naomi Stubbs, Susan Tenneriello, Donny Levit, and Frank Episale. In addition, I express my gratitude to Professor Jeff Entwistle for his prodigious contribution to the chapters on design, and I also thank Professor Laura Pulio for her helpful suggestions on acting. A special thanks also to Professor Oliver W. Gerland and his fellow teachers at the University of Colorado. I would also like to thank Professor Scott Walters, University of North Carolina-Asheville, for developing the first teacher and student study guide materials for Theatre Experience and Professor John Poole, Illinois State University, for his revisions that are now found on the On Line Learning Center.

James Bell, Grand Valley State University
Scott Boyd, Middle Tennessee State University
Chris Gray, Illinois Central College
Richard Hansen, Middle Tennessee State University
Ethan Krupp, Bloomsburg University of Pennsylvania
Jeannine Russell, Wichita State University

Through twenty-six editions of my three textbooks published by McGraw-Hill, my colleague Inge King, the incredible photography expert, has discovered every photograph that has appeared in every edition of every text, including this edition of *The Theatre Experience*. Inge is amazing as well as being an irreplaceable colleague. As I pointed out previously, through the years Inge has discovered thousands upon thousands of photographs from which she has helped select the ones that make up our extraordinary illustration program. There is no way adequately to acknowledge her taste, persistence, abiding loyalty to the project, and her creativity.

At McGraw-Hill I express my gratitude to the following editors:

William Glass
Sarah Remington
Dawn Groundwater
Thomas Sigel
Kelly Odom

Lisa Bruflodt
Jennifer Pickel
Laurie Janssen
Brenda Rolwes
Jenny Bartell

The Theatre Experience

THIRTEENTH EDITION

Preface

ACTIVE AUDIENCE PARTICIPANTS, ACTIVE CLASS PARTICIPANTS

The Theatre Experience prepares students to be well-informed, well-prepared theatre audience members. With an audience-centered narrative that engages today's students, a vivid photo program that brings concepts to life, and features that teach and encourage a variety of skill sets students master core concepts and learn to think critically about theatre and the world around them. As a result, students are better prepared for class, and better prepared for theatergoing.

Engage with Your Role

- True to its original vision—to focus on the audience's experience of attending a live theatre performance—the 13th edition of *The Theatre Experience* **opens with three chapters that focus on the student as an audience member**. Topics include: the difference between being at a live performance and watching a dramatic performance on film, TV, or an electronic device; the enhancement of the experience aided by the proper preparation and background; and the awareness of the role of the audience in live theatre.

- **Dynamics of Drama** features illustrate some of the more challenging theatre concepts in a way that is easier for beginning students to understand and apply as audience members. For example, topics include realism and nonrealism (Chapter 1), and climactic and episodic forms (Chapter 7).
- **NEW Play Links**, a feature in *The Theatre Experience,* 13th edition, allows you to read many of the plays mentioned in the text online. Any play referenced in the text that can be found online is highlighted in blue typeface when first mentioned in a chapter. Should you want to read one of these plays, you can refer to the list that precedes the Glossary at the end of the book and find its URL. Titles are listed alphabetically.

The plays can be used to highlight key concepts and to complement the discussions found in *The Theatre Experience,* 13th edition. In addition, many of the new Thinking about Theatre and Experiencing Theatre exercises can also be supplemented and enhanced with examples from these plays.

Master the Basics

- **Parts 2, 3, and 4 cover the important elements of theatre**: acting, directing, playwriting, and design. The authors' efficient structure and succinct style set students up for a clear understanding of the basic concepts, freeing up valuable class time for deeper discussions and more personal engagement with course concepts.
- **Photo Essays and a dynamic art program** allow students to visualize the core theatrical concepts introduced in each chapter. Topics include modern domestic drama (Chapter 8), forms of comedy (Chapter 8), costumes and masks (Chapter 10), uses of stage lighting (Chapter 11), and others.

Think Critically and Engage Actively

- NEW **"Playing Your Part"** is a feature in each chapter that includes two distinct sets of questions and activities that emphasize thinking and engaging critically.
  - **"Experiencing Theatre"** activities help students actively to engage with the concepts of the text. These exercises ask students to undertake activities within the classroom or to understand how aspects of their everyday lives connect to core concepts discussed in the text.

PLAYING YOUR PART: EXPERIENCING THEATRE

1. If you were to write a play about your life, what would you choose as your opening scene? What would some of your complications be? Would there be a climactic moment?
2. If you were to write a play about a family you know (your own or another), what point of view would you take? Why? Are there strongly opposed forces or balanced forces in this family?
3. If you were told you were going to have to attend a play that lasted over four hours, what would your reaction be? Why? What are your traditional expectations about the space and time of a play?
4. After watching a popular film, describe how the opening scene aids in setting the action. Describe one or two of the complications in the film. Can you discuss the film's point of view?

- **"Thinking about Theatre"** questions challenge students to analyze and examine elements of a theatre experience.

PLAYING YOUR PART: THINKING ABOUT THEATRE

1. Think of a play you have read or seen where the main character encounters one impediment or roadblock after another. Describe the various obstacles that must be overcome before the end of the play.

2. Think of a play or musical you have seen or read where two major characters are in conflict with one another. Describe the two characters and explain the source of their conflict. How does it play out?

3. Think of a situation some people saw as very serious, but another person viewed as humorous. Explain what you believe led different people to see it so differently. What was your own feeling—was the incident funny or sad?

- NEW **"In Focus"** features include two categories:
  - "Global Connections" present the global reach and influences of theatre from various cultures. Topics include Augusto Boal's "Theatre of the Oppressed" (Chapter 1), Asian influences on the playwrights Brecht and Wilder (Chapter 6), and global influences on Julie Taymor (Chapter 12).
  - "Historical Perspectives" features bring relevant topics about the past to life: women in Greek and Elizabethan theatres, performers' status at different points in time, the evolution of the director.
  - NEW Marginal Definitions For the first time in The Theatre Experience, definitions of boldface words or terms in the text are provided in the adjacent margin.

Selected Chapter-by-Chapter Changes

Chapter 1 begins with a new section on the great diversity of contemporary theatre, first in terms of the variety of places in which theatre can be viewed: from the largest auditoriums or Broadway houses to regional, college, and community theatres, as well as small, informal spaces, and second, in terms of the extraordinary range of subject matter as well as ethnic and cultural material. The chapter then turns to the unique experience of live theatre that differentiates it from all other media. In this and all subsequent chapters, when a play is mentioned for the first time, it is set in blue type to signal its inclusion in the new "Play Links" feature. This indicates that the script of the play can be retrieved by means of a URL, which is provided at the end of the text.

Chapter 2 retains the core content about audience involvement, including background information and preparation that makes attending the theatre more meaningful and enjoyable. The chapter's coverage of critics and reviewers has been extensively updated, now including new discussions of bloggers, social media's impact on audiences, and audience behavior.

Chapter 3 has a new Dynamics of Drama feature, "Popular Performance Spaces," which extends the coverage of venues where live performances take place. Material on stage spaces has been edited and updated.

Chapter 4 features minor updates to keep the content as current and engaging as possible. Information on the training, preparation, history, and techniques of acting have been retained from previous editions.

Chapter 5 expands anew the auteur director and the postmodern director. The material on the artistic director and managing director of nonprofit theatres has been revised.

Chapter 6 features a new introductory section on the playwright's role in the creation of a script, explaining the playwright's relationship to ancient storytellers. Also, information has been added on the context in which the playwright works, the demands and challenges of developing a script, and the unique requirements of a work for the stage.

Chapter 8 has been substantially edited and revised. There is a new opening section on the mood, tone, and point of view of a production that are conveyed to an audience in the opening moments of a production.

Chapter 12 features a new discussion of recent trends in stage musicals, together with up-to-date examples.

Chapter 13 features refined listings of playwrights and plays, updated with the latest names and productions from around the world. Material that was previously in Chapter 1 has been incorporated into this chapter.

TEACHING AND LEARNING RESOURCES

Support for Instructors

The Theatre Experience offers a wealth of supplemental materials to aid both students and instructors. The Online Learning Center at www.mhhe.com/wilsonte13e is a resource for students and faculty. Instructors' resources are password-protected and include:

- Instructor's Manual.
- Test Bank.
- EZ Test Computerized Test Bank: McGraw-Hill's EZ Test is a flexible, easy-to-use electronic testing program that allows instructors to create tests from specific items in the text. It accommodates a wide range of question types, and instructors may add their own questions. Multiple versions of the test can be created, and any test can be exported for use with course management systems. The program is available for Windows and Macintosh.

Student Resources

The Online Learning Center at www.mhhe.com/wilsonte13e is a robust tool for students, providing a wide range of material to enhance learning and to simplify studying. Resources are keyed directly to this edition and include the following:

- Chapter-by-chapter quizzes for testing students.
- Essay Quizzes that can be e-mailed directly to instructors.
- The Theatre Goer's Guide is an excellent introduction to the art of attending and critiquing a play. This guide will assist students in everything from making theatre reservations and knowing when to applaud to evaluating a performance and doing web research.
- Detailed explanations and examples of Major Theatrical Forms and Movements.
- Synopses of Plays.
- Select Bibliography.

Craft your teaching resources to match the way you teach! With McGraw-Hill Create, **www.mcgrawhillcreate.com**, you can easily rearrange chapters, combine material from other content sources, and quickly upload content you have written, like your course syllabus or teaching notes. Find the content you need in Create by searching through thousands of leading McGraw-Hill textbooks. Arrange your book to fit your teaching style. Create even allows you to personalize your book's appearance by selecting the cover and adding your name, school, and course information. Order a Create book and you'll receive a complimentary print review copy in 3–5 business days or a complimentary electronic review copy (eComp) via e-mail in about one hour. Go to **www.mcgrawhillcreate.com** today and register. Experience how McGraw-Hill Create empowers you to teach your students your way.

Anthology of Plays

Anthology of Living Theater (978-0-07-351413-0) offers 18 plays for use with *The Theatre Experience*.

CourseSmart ebook

The Theatre Experience is available as an eTextbook at www.CourseSmart.com. At CourseSmart, students can take advantage of significant savings off the cost of a print textbook, reduce their impact on the environment, and gain access to powerful web tools for student learning. You can view CourseSmart eTextbooks online or download them to a computer. CourseSmart eTextbooks allow students to do full text searches, add highlighting and notes, and share notes with classmates. Visit www.CourseSmart.com to learn more and try a sample chapter.

The Audience

1

The Audience

THE AUDIENCE

The basic encounter in the theatre is the exchange, the chemistry, the electricity between the audience and the actors performing on stage. The presence of the audience sets live theatre apart from all other forms of dramatic entertainment. Here the audience is gathered for a production of *Treasure Island* at the Colorado Shakespeare Festival in the Mary Rippon Outdoor Theatre on the University of Colorado, Boulder, campus. (© Steve Mohlenkamp/stevemohlenkamp.com)

1 **The Audience:**
Its Role and
Imagination

2 **The Background**
and Expectations
of the Audience

3 **Theatre Spaces:**
The Audience
Views the Stage

Part One

The Audience

We may not realize it, but when we attend the theatre, we, as spectators, are essential to the experience. To be complete, each one of the performing arts—opera, ballet, symphony concerts as well as theatre—requires an audience. Whether watching a classic like *Romeo and Juliet,* or a modern family play, for most of us, it is likely that our first encounter with a dramatic work was on film, television, or a handheld electronic device. No matter how impressed we were with seeing a play or a musical in this way, however, it

must be remembered that the experience of watching television or a movie is quite different from attending the theatre. With TV or movies, we are looking at a screen on which there are no live people but only images of people. And the experience of being in the presence of a living, breathing person makes all the difference. Another way of putting this is to say that the audience is not an incidental factor in a theatrical performance; if we are audience members, we become an indispensable element in what is occurring.

At a theatrical performance, we become keenly aware of the actors onstage. What we may not realize is that the actors are just as aware of our presence. Laughter at a comedy or a deep silence at a tense moment in a serious drama is communicated directly to the actors and has a very real effect on their performance.

In a number of events other than the performing arts, spectators often play a key role. For example, most sports contests—football, baseball, basketball, soccer, tennis, NASCAR races—elicit huge

Fans cheering at the NASCAR Sprint Cup Series auto race in Martinsville, Virginia. (© Don Petersen/AP Images)

President Barack Obama greeting the crowd after the oath of office was administered during his inauguration for his second term. (© Ann Hermes/The Christian Science Monitor via Getty Images)

4

interest from fans. This is true whether the sports event is at the high school, college, or professional level. In other spheres as well, the participation of viewers is crucial. Political conventions and political rallies depend on large, supportive crowds to be considered successful. A good example is a national nominating convention. The hall where the event takes place becomes a giant stage set, with a stagelike platform, backdrops, and carefully arranged positions for entrances and exits. The programs are carefully scripted to build to a climax, with a finale consisting of stirring music and literally thousands of balloons dropping from the ceiling.

Despite the similarity between theatre events and sports events, there is one unmistakable difference. Theoretically, a sports contest could take place in an empty stadium and still be considered complete: though the thrill and the excitement would be missing, the results would be entered in the record book, and the won-lost statistics would be just as valid as if the game had taken place before a large crowd.

This is not true for the performing arts. Each theatre, ballet, or opera performance, each musical concert, is intended specifically to be presented in the presence of an audience, which is an absolutely essential part of the event. Of course, any of these can be recorded digitally or otherwise, but listening to or viewing one of these is not the same as attending a live event. In a very real sense, a theatre performance at which no audience is present is actually *not* a performance. It may be a rehearsal of some kind, but the performance occurs only when the actors perform in the presence of an audience.

In Part One we will explore who makes up the audience, how audiences are created, how they differ from one another, how they respond to what is happening onstage, and how they interact with performers.

The audience at a performance of *The Two Gentlemen of Verona* at Shakespeare's Globe in London. (© Gideon Mendel/Corbis)

The audience watching a 3-D movie. (© Image Source/Corbis RF)

6

The Audience:
Its Role and Imagination

Live theatre: The performance of a dramatic event by a group of actors in the presence of their counterparts, the audience members.

For the past 100 years there have been persistent and dire predictions that live theatre would soon be dead. It has been argued that each one of a succession of remarkable technological innovations would make theatre obsolete. First there was radio, then silent film, talking film, and television, followed by video on computers and a myriad of handheld devices. Each one, it was pointed out, was far less expensive and far more accessible than live theatre. How could any art form survive this onslaught of continuously more and more advanced entertainment media?

[handwritten note: how has theatre lasted through technology]

Miraculously, theatre has not only survived, it has thrived. One measure of the amazing health of live theatre today is the astounding range of opportunities we have of attending theatre, with more locations, not only in the United Sates but throughout the world, presenting a greater variety of theatre offerings perhaps than ever before. For a long time Broadway was the fountainhead of live theatre in the U.S.A. Though it is still thriving and touring Broadway shows are regularly seen in major and mid-size cities throughout America, theatre that originates on Broadway is not as predominant as it once was. At the same time, performing arts complexes in all parts of the country, not only present Broadway shows, but often have other spaces which feature live theatre. These might include 1,000 seat, 500 seat, or 200 seat theatres that offer new plays, revivals, intimate musicals, and other types of dramatic entertainment.

[handwritten note: so many locations to watch theatre]

In addition, during the last half century there has been a burgeoning of what are known as "regional theatres." These are permanent, professional, nonprofit theatres that offer a season of first-class productions to their audiences each year. Their association,

[handwritten note: nonprofit theatres]

◀ **THE ROLE OF THE AUDIENCE**

The audience and the performers are the two essential elements of theatre: both are required for theatre to occur. The presence of the audience sets theatre apart from the experience of watching a theatrical presentation on film, on television, or in any other electronic medium. Here the audience gives the cast of Newsies *a standing ovation in New York. (© Benjamin Norman/The New York Times/Redux)* the League of Resident Theatres, lists a total of 74 high-caliber such theatres scattered across the country. Added to the above are approximately 120 Shakespeare theatres found in virtually every state in the United States which feature, especially in the summer months, high-quality productions of Shakespeare and the classics as well as modern plays.

 Colleges have theatres

Another important component of today's theatre landscape is the many college and university theatres found in every one of the fifty states, as well as Canada and elsewhere. Many colleges have not one but perhaps two or three theatre spaces in which students and guest artists perform. There might be, for instance, a 500 or 600 seat theatre, a smaller 200 seat theatre with a different configuration, and a 100 seat "black box" for more experimental or intimate productions.

Finally, in every corner of the United States, there are an astonishing 7,000 so-called community theatres. These are semiprofessional and experienced amateur groups who present a series of plays each year to local audiences. It might surprise people to learn that these several thousand theatres present roughly 46,000 productions each year to audiences that number in the millions. Obviously, taken together, the total number of theatre events presented each year in the United States is a staggering, almost unbelievable figure.

It is not, however, just the vast range and number of annual productions that is surprising, it is the diversity of offerings. It begins with new plays and musicals, and moves to classics, revivals of old plays, and then encompasses experimental and avant-garde offerings. There are top-flight theatres that specialize in each of these types of theatre. Some theatres, like regional and university theatres, often encompass all of them. Still a different category encompasses site-specific theatre and performance art. The former are presentations offered in nontraditional theatre settings, such places as warehouses, churches, firehouses, street corners, and public parks. The idea is that the unusual locale together with a different approach in the material will make audiences conscious in a different way of what they are seeing and experiencing. Performance art is usually highly individual and presented by only one person but never by more than a small number. The content is usually quite personal, and may be combined with art, dance, film, or music.

Today, along with diversity in types of theatre and where it is presented, there is an incredible mix of ethnic and multicultural presentations. In addition to Anglo-American theatre, there is a rich mix of work from many other traditions and cultures. These include African American theatre, Hispanic theatre, Native American theatre, Asian theatre, Arabic theatre; in fact, virtually every type of regional, cultural, and national theatre imaginable. Contemporary theatre is also widely diverse, socially, politically, and culturally, and includes Gay and Lesbian theatre and Feminist theatre. One could argue that it is as inclusive and multicultural as can be imagined.

In addition, today's theatre, as we will discuss more fully later, is truly global. There are theatre traditions unique to nations across the world as well as international theatres that tour the world and integrate cross-cultural techniques and styles.

How can we explain all this? Today, not only are there movies in every neighborhood and television in all of our homes, there is ever-growing use of pads, tablets, and cell phones on which digitally transmitted theatrical presentations can be seen. In the midst of this why would any of us bother with theatre? How would we have the time or make the effort to see actual performances? The answer lies in the nature of live theatre—it happens at a given moment before our very eyes. We are there watching it and we are actually participants in the event. The drama critic Walter Kerr (1913–1996) explained what it means for audience and actors to be together:

> It doesn't just mean that we are in the personal presence of performers. It means that they are in our presence, conscious of us, speaking to us, working for and with us until a circuit that is not mechanical becomes established between us, a circuit that is fluid, unpredictable, ever-changing in its impulses, crackling, intimate. Our presence, the way we respond, flows back to the performer and alters what he does, to some degree and sometimes astonishingly so, every single night. We are contenders, making the play and the evening and the emotion together. We are playmates, building a structure. This never happens at a film because the film is already built, finished, sealed, incapable of responding to us in any way. The actors can't hear us or feel our presence; nothing we do, in our liveness, counts. We could be dead and the film would purr out its appointed course, flawlessly, indifferently.[1]

THE CONTRAST BETWEEN THEATRE AND FILM

As Walter Kerr suggests, one way to explain the special nature of live theatre is to contrast a drama seen in a theatre with one shown on film or television. Both present a story told in dramatic form—an enactment of scenes by performers who speak and act as if they were the people they represent. The same actress can play Juliet in *Romeo and Juliet* by William Shakespeare (1564–1616) on both stage and screen. Not only the dramatization and the acting but also other elements, such as scenery and costumes, are often similar on stage and screen. In fact, many films and television specials have been based on stage productions: *A Chorus Line, The Phantom of the Opera, The Importance of Being Earnest, Les Misérables,* and numerous plays by Shakespeare. Also, one can learn a great deal about theatre from watching a play on film or television, which can also give us many of the same feelings and experiences that we have when watching a theatre performance. Moreover, the accessibility of film and television means that they play a crucial role in our overall exposure to the depiction of dramatic events and dramatic characters.

As important as the similarities are, however, there is a crucial difference between experiencing live theatre or watching it on television or on film. We are not speaking here of the technical capabilities of film or television, the ability to show outdoor shots taken from helicopters, cut instantaneously from one scene to another, or create special effects such as those in the *Lord of the Rings* trilogy, *The Hobbit,* or *The Avengers.* No, the most significant—in fact, the overriding—difference between films and theatre is the performer-audience relationship. The experience of being in the presence of the performer is more important to theatre than anything else. With a film or with television, we are always in the presence of an image, never a person.

The American playwright Jean-Claude van Itallie (b. 1936) has explained the importance of the actor-audience relationship in theatre, and how theatre differs from films and television:

> Theater is not electronic. Unlike movies and unlike television, it does require the live presence of both audience and actors in a single space. This is the theater's uniquely important advantage and function, its original religious function of bringing people together in a community ceremony where the actors are in some sense priests or celebrants, and the audience is drawn to participate with the actors in a kind of eucharist.[2]

In an interview in 2013, playwright Richard Nelson (b. 1950) put the experience in these words:

> Theatre is a place where human beings can come together in the same room, in the same space, and in the same time to talk to each other, or to listen. I think theatre fills a profound need.[3]

THEATRE IS TRANSITORY AND IMMEDIATE

A theatre performance changes from moment to moment as the audience encounters a series of shifting impressions and stimuli. It is a kaleidoscopic adventure through which the audience passes, with each instant a direct, immediate experience.

The transitory nature of theatre—a quality it shares with all the performing arts— sets it apart in a significant way from literature and the visual arts. A painting, a piece of sculpture, a novel, or a book of poems is a fixed object. When it leaves the artist's hands (or, in the case of a book, when it leaves the printer's shop), it is complete. In a world of change and uncertainty, these objects remain the same. The Winged Victory from the island of Samothrace in Greece is today almost the same majestic figure that was fashioned 2,200 years ago. When we see this statue, we are looking at a soaring figure, facing into the wind, which is essentially what the Greeks saw at the time it was created.

The essence of literature and the visual arts is to catch something at a moment in time and freeze it. With the performing arts, however, that is impossible, because the performing arts are not objects but events. Specific objects—costumes, props, scenery, a script—are a part of theatre, but none of these constitutes the art. Bernard Beckerman, Shakespeare scholar and director, explains the difference:

> Theater is nothing if not spontaneous. It occurs. It happens. The novel can be put away, taken up, reread. Not theater. It keeps slipping between one's fingers. Stopping, it stops being theater. Its permanent features, facets of activity, such as scenery, script, stage, people, are no more theater than the two poles of a generator are electricity. Theater is what goes on between the parts.[4]

Plays are often printed in book form, like literature, and many novels and short stories contain extensive passages of dialogue that could easily be scenes in a play. But there is an important difference between the two forms. Unlike a novel, a play is written to be performed. In some respects a script is to a stage production as a musical score is to a concert, or an architectural blueprint is to a building: it is an outline for a performance.

Drama can be studied in a classroom in terms of imagery, character, and theme, but with drama, study of this sort takes place *before* or *after* the event. It is a form of preparation for or follow-up to the experience; the experience is the performance itself. Obviously, we have more opportunities to read plays in book form than to see them produced; but when we read a play, we should always attempt to visualize the other aspects of a production in our mind's eye.

HUMAN BEINGS—THE FOCUS OF THEATRE

Books often focus on people, but they can also focus on science or nature; music focuses on sound; abstract painting and sculpture focus on shapes, colors, and forms. Uniquely among the arts, theatre focuses on one thing and one thing only—human beings. This is true even though different plays emphasize different human concerns, from profound problems in tragedy to pure entertainment in light comedy. And even when the performers play animals, inanimate objects, or abstract ideas, theatre concentrates on the human concerns involved.

In the modern world, human beings have lost the central place they were once believed to occupy in the universe. In the Ptolemaic view of the universe, which prevailed until the sixteenth century—when Copernicus theorized that Earth revolved around the sun—it was assumed that Earth was the center of everything. In science, we have long since given up that notion, particularly in light of explorations in outer space and other transformative discoveries regarding our universe. Human beings have become less significant, and less at the center of things. But not in theatre, where the preoccupations of men and women are still the core, the center around which other elements orbit.

THE CHEMISTRY OF THE PERFORMER-AUDIENCE CONTACT

The fascination of being in the presence of a famous person or observing firsthand a special occasion is difficult to explain but not difficult to verify. No matter how often we have seen a favorite star in the movies or have seen a singer on television or listened to their songs on a handheld device, we will often go to any lengths to see him or her in person. Probably, at one time or another, each of us has braved bad weather and shoving crowds to see celebrities at a parade, a political rally, or a concert. Even a severe rainstorm will not deter many of us from seeing our favorite star at an outdoor concert. The same pull of personal contact draws us to the theatre. At the heart of the theatre experience, therefore, is the performer-audience relationship: the immediate, personal encounter whose chemistry and magic give theatre its special quality.

As suggested above, during a stage performance the actresses and actors can hear our laughter, can sense our silence, and can feel our tension as audience members. In short, we, as audience, can affect, and in subtle ways change, the performance. At the same time, as members of the audience, we watch the performers closely, consciously or unconsciously asking ourselves questions: Are the performers convincing in their roles? Will they do something surprising? Will they make a mistake? At each moment, in every stage performance, we, as fully participating audience members, should be looking for answers to questions like these. Actually two experiences are occurring almost simultaneously: our individual experience, which is highly personal; and the group experience, which we will discuss below.

actors feed off each other

THEATRE AS A GROUP EXPERIENCE

Certain arts—such as painting, sculpture, and literature—provide solitary experiences. The viewer or reader contemplates the work alone, at her or his own pace. This is true even in a museum: although many people may flock to look at a single painting and are with each other, they respond as individuals, one by one. In the performing arts, however, including theatre, the group experience is indispensable.

The performing arts share this trait with other communal events such as religious services, spectator sports, and celebrations. Before the event can take place, a group must assemble, at one time and in one place. When people are gathered together in this way, something mysterious happens to them. Though still individuals, with their own personalities and backgrounds, they take on other qualities as well, qualities which often overshadow their independent responses.

Psychology of Groups

Not all crowds are alike. Some are aggressive, such as an angry mob that decides to riot or a gang that terrorizes a neighborhood. Others are docile—a group of spectators on a sidewalk

crowds are different

THEATRE AS A GROUP EXPERIENCE
In theatre, the size, attitude, and makeup of the audience affect the overall experience. The theatre can be large or small, indoors or outdoors, and the audience can be people of similar tastes and background or a collection of quite varied individuals. Depicted here is the audience giving the cast of *Elizabeth Rex*, facing the viewers on a thrust stage, a standing ovation at Chicago Shakespeare Theater's Courtyard Theatre. (© 2012 James Steinkamp)

observing a juggler, for example. A crowd at a football game is different from a congregation at a religious observance; and a theatre crowd is distinct from any of these. In spite of being different, however, the theatre audience shares with all such groups the special characteristics of the *collective mind*. Becoming part of a group is a crucial element of the theatre experience. For a time, we share a common undertaking, focused on one activity—the performance of a play. Not only do we laugh or cry in a way we might not otherwise; we also sense an intangible communion with those around us. When a collection of individuals respond more or less in unison to what is occurring onstage, their relationship to one another is reaffirmed. If there is a display of cruelty at which we shudder, or sorrow by which we are moved, or pomposity at which we laugh, it is reassuring to have others respond as we do. For a moment we are part of a group sharing an experience; and our sorrow or joy, which we thought might be ours alone, is found to be part of a broad human response.

How Audience Composition Affects the Theatre Experience

Although being part of a group is an essential element of theatre, groups vary, and the makeup of a group will alter a theatrical event. Some audiences are general—for

IN FOCUS: GLOBAL CONNECTIONS

Augusto Boal: The Theatre of the Oppressed

If ever there were an international theatre figure in recent times, it was Augusto Boal (1931–2009). Born in Brazil, Boal (pronounced Bo-AHL) attended Columbia University in the United States. Returning to Brazil, he began working in the Arena Theatre in São Paulo. At first he directed conventional dramatic works, but Boal was a man with a powerful social conscience. During his early years he began to develop his philosophy of theatre. He concluded, for example, that mainstream theatre was used by the ruling class as a soporific, a means of sedating the audience and inoculating it against any impulse to act or revolt. In other words, conventional theatre oppressed ordinary citizens, especially the underprivileged.

Boal also became fascinated with the relationship of actors to audience members. He established a partnership between them, and he felt strongly that spectators should participate in any theatre event, that a way must be found for them to become performers, and a part of the action. In putting these theories into practice, he began to present *agitprop* plays, that is, plays with a strong political and social message. He experimented with several versions of such plays. One was the Invisible Theatre, in which actors, seemingly spontaneously, presented a prepared scene in a public space such as a town square or a restaurant. Another was his Forum Theatre, in which a play about a social problem became the basis of a discussion with audience members about solutions to the problem.

Considered an enemy of the authoritarian government in Brazil for his work in the 1960s, he was jailed in 1971 and tortured. Released after a few months, he was exiled from his native land. Following that he lived in various countries: Argentina, Portugal, and France. He decided along the way that his approach should be less didactic than it had been, that he would be more effective if he engaged audiences in the theatrical process rather than confronting them. This was the basis of his Theatre of the Oppressed, which became the cornerstone of his lifework from then on. He wrote a book by that title, which appeared in 1974.

Augusto Boal (© Sucheta Das/AP Images)

In 1985 Boal returned to Brazil. From that point until his death, for the next quarter century, he traveled all over the world, directing, lecturing, and establishing centers furthering the Theatre of the Oppressed. He also wrote other books, which were widely read. His approach to theatre found adherents in more than forty countries. Wherever the Theatre of the Oppressed was established, its productions challenged injustice, especially in poor and disenfranchised communities where citizens are often without a voice or an advocate. In his later years he was looked upon by many as the most inspirational person of his time in propagating socially oriented theatre.

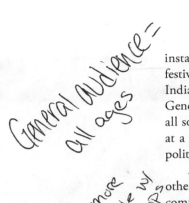

General audience = all ages

You can be more comfortable w/ certain groups

instance, the thousands who attend outdoor productions such as the Shakespeare festival in Ashland, Oregon, and *Unto These Hills,* which is a play about the Cherokee Indians presented each summer on a Cherokee reservation in western North Carolina. General audiences include people of all ages, from all parts of the country, and from all socioeconomic levels. Other audiences are more homogeneous, such as spectators at a high school play, a children's theatre production, a Broadway opening night, a political play, or a performance in a prison.

Another factor affecting our experience in the theatre is our relationship to the other members of the audience. If we are among friends or people of like mind, we feel comfortable and relaxed, and we readily become part of the group experience. On the other hand, if we feel alien—for example, a young person with an older group or a liberal with conservatives—we will be estranged from the group as a whole. The people with whom we attend theatre—their relative homogeneity and our relation to them—strongly influence our response to the total event.

THE SEPARATE ROLES OF PERFORMERS AND SPECTATORS

It is important to note the difference between *observed* theatre and *participatory* theatre. In observed theatre, as audience members, we participate vicariously or empathetically with what is happening onstage. Empathy is the experience of mentally or emotionally entering into the feelings or spirit of another person—in this case, a character onstage. Sometimes we will not be in tune with the characters onstage but will react vehemently against them. In either situation, though, we are participating empathetically. We might shed tears, laugh, pass judgment, sit frozen, or tremble with fear. But we participate through our imagination while separated from the action.

There are also times when observers and audience members participate in a theatre event. In rituals and ceremonies in parts of Africa and among certain tribes of Native Americans, those attending have become, in effect, participants, joining in the singing and dancing, for instance. At a number of contemporary theatre events spectators have also been urged to take part. For example, one of the chief aims of the Theatre of the Oppressed created by Augusto Boal was to eliminate the distinction between audience members and performers. In Boal's philosophy, every spectator could be and should be an actor, and he developed a number of strategies to bring this about.

How Should the Audience Be Involved?

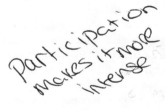

Participation makes it more intense

The attempt to involve audience members directly springs from a desire to make theatre more immediate and intense, and such work can be innovative and exciting. It remains, however, an exception to the kinds of theatre most of us are likely to encounter. The theatre most of us will experience requires a degree of distancing, in the same way that all art requires a certain perspective. Imagine trying to get the full effect of a large landscape painting when standing a few inches from the canvas: one would see only the brushstrokes of a single tree or a small patch of blue sky. To perceive and appreciate a work of art, we need distance. This separation, which is called *aesthetic distance,* is as necessary in theatre as in any other art.

In the same way that we must stand back from a painting to get its full effect, so too, as theatre spectators, we must be separated from the performance in order to see and hear

Aesthetic distance
Physical or psychological separation or detachment of audience from dramatic action, usually considered necessary for artistic illusion.

need to create distance & not have too much participation

what is happening onstage and absorb the experience. If an audience member becomes involved in the proceedings or goes onstage and takes part in the action, as often occurred in a Boal production, he or she reverses roles and becomes a performer, not a spectator. The separation between performers and spectators remains.

Audience Participation through Direct Action

Today a range of educational or therapeutic activities employ theatrical techniques. The aim is not a performance viewed by an audience, as such. Those who take part in such activities are not performers in the usual sense, and there is no attempt to follow a written script. Rather, the emphasis is on education, personal development, or therapy—fields in which theatre techniques have opened up new possibilities.

DRAMA THERAPY

Theatre techniques can be used for educational and therapeutic purposes. A group called the Geese Company, for example, visits prisons and has convicts reenact scenes from their own lives. Here, the actress Pamela Daryl (right) is listening to a prisoner unburdening himself of painful memories of childhood. (© Steve Liss/Time Life Pictures/Getty Images)

In schools, for example, creative dramatics, theatre games, and group improvisations have proved invaluable for self-discovery and the development of healthy group attitudes. By acting out hypothetical situations or giving free rein to their imagination, children can build self-confidence, discover their creative potential, and overcome their inhibitions.

[handwritten margin note: hypothetical situations help kids]

In some situations, creative dramatics can teach lessons that are difficult to teach by conventional means. Playwriting, too, has often proved to be an invaluable educational tool. Students who write scenes, whether autobiographical or fictional, find the experience not only fulfilling but enlightening. In addition to creative dramatics, a wide range of other activities—*sociodrama, psychodrama,* and *drama therapy*—incorporate theatrical techniques. For adults as well as children, these activities have come to the forefront as educational and therapeutic methods. In sociodrama, the members of participating groups—such as parents and children, students and teachers, or legal authorities and ordinary citizens—explore their own attitudes and prejudices. One successful approach is *role reversal.* A group of young people, for instance, may take the part of their parents while the adults assume the roles of the children; or members of a street gang will take the roles of the police, and the police will take the roles of the street gang. In such role playing, both groups become aware of deep-seated feelings and arrive at a better understanding of one another.

[handwritten margin note: Roleplay to help understand]

Psychodrama uses some of the same techniques as sociodrama but is more private and interpersonal; in fact, it can become so intense that it should be carried out only under the supervision of a trained therapist. In psychodrama, individual fears, anxieties, and frustrations are explored. A person might reenact a particularly traumatic scene from childhood, for example. In participatory drama, theatre is a means to another end: education, therapy, group development, or the like. Its aim is not public performance, and there is little emphasis on a carefully prepared, expertly performed presentation before an audience; in fact, just the opposite is true. In observed drama, on the other hand, the aim is a professional performance for spectators, and this requires a separation between the performers and the audience—the "aesthetic distance" described earlier.

[handwritten margin note: Not always for public entertainment]

THE IMAGINATION OF THE AUDIENCE

The audience and the performers are the two essential elements of theatre: both are required for theatre to occur. One aspect of the audience's participation is the use of its imagination. For a production of *War Horse*, which originated at the National Theatre in London, the audience was called on to imagine that a large puppet operated by actors was actually a real horse. The horses were created by the Handspring Puppet Company. (© Marilyn Kingwill/ArenaPAL)

THE IMAGINATION OF THE AUDIENCE

For those who create it, theatre is a direct experience: an actress walks onstage and impersonates a character; a carpenter builds scenery; a scene designer paints it. For these people the experience is like cutting a finger or being held in an embrace: the pain or the warmth is felt directly and physically. Members of a theatre audience experience a different kind of pain or warmth. As spectators in a theatre, we sense the presence of other audience members; we observe the movements and gestures of performers and hear the words they speak; and we see costumes, scenery, and lighting. From these we form mental images or make imaginative connections that provoke joy, laughter, anger, sorrow, or pain. All this occurs, however, without our moving from our seats.

We naturally assume that those who create theatre are highly imaginative people and that their minds are full of vivid, exciting ideas that might not occur to the rest of us. If we conclude, however, that we in the audience have only a limited theatrical imagination, we do ourselves a great injustice. As we saw earlier, theatre is a two-way street—an exchange between performers and audience—and this is nowhere more evident than in the creation of *illusion*. Illusion may be initiated by the creators of theatre, but it is completed by the audience.

In the eerie world of William Shakespeare's *Macbeth,* when three witches appear out of the mist or when Banquo's ghost interrupts the banquet, we know it is fantasy; witches and ghosts like those in *Macbeth* do not appear in everyday life. In the theatre, however, we take such fantasy at face value. In Shakespeare's own day, for instance, a convention readily accepted by audiences was that women's parts were played by boy actors. Shakespeare's heroines—Juliet, Desdemona, Lady Macbeth—were not acted by women, as they are today, but played by boys. Everyone in the audience at an Elizabethan theatre knew that the boys were not actually women but accepted without question the notion that a boy actor was presenting an impression or an imitation of a woman. The film *Shakespeare in Love* (1998) afforded a fascinating glimpse of this: the actress Gwyneth Paltrow plays a young woman portraying a boy actor (in secret), while her acting partner is a young man playing a young woman portrayed by a boy (in the open).

Along with fantasy, we, as audience members, accept drastic shifts in time and space. Someone onstage dressed in a Revolutionary uniform says, "It is the winter of

Audience is just important as creators

Old days, boys played women parts, and audience must accept that

PLAYING YOUR PART: EXPERIENCING THEATRE

1. Watch a scene from the film *Les Misérables.* Now try to imagine why it would be different as a live theatrical experience.

2. Read aloud the balcony scene from Shakespeare's *Romeo and Juliet.* What is realistic about the scene? What are some nonrealistic elements?

3. Discuss your favorite current nonrealistic film or television show. What fantastic elements are most appealing? Why?

4. Discuss a recent film or television show that you felt was realistic. What was real about it? What wasn't real?

5. Read a speech from a play (or a paragraph from a novel) aloud in class. How did your classmates affect your reading? How would you describe your class as an audience? Homogenous? Heterogenous? Explain.

1778, at Valley Forge," and we do not question it. What is more, we accept rapid movements back and forth in time. **Flashbacks**—abrupt movements from the present to the past and back again—are a familiar technique in films and television shows such as *Looper* and *Dexter;* but they are also commonplace in modern drama. A similar device often used in drama is *anachronism.* An anachronism involves placing some character or event outside its proper time sequence: for example, having people from the past speak and act as if they were living today. Medieval mystery and morality plays frequently contained anachronisms.

The medieval play *Abraham and Isaac,* for instance, is set in the time of the Old Testament, but it makes several references to the Christian trinity—a religious concept that was not developed until centuries later. The medieval audience accepted this shift in time as a matter of course, just as we do in theatre today.

In his frequently revived play *Angels in America* (1993), Tony Kushner includes a number of bizarre and fantastic characters or events. For example, a character in the play called Mr. Lies is an imaginary person created in the mind of Harper, a housewife who is addicted to pills. Near the end of part 1, Mr. Lies takes Harper on a fantasy trip to the Antarctic. At the very end of part 1, an angel crashes through the ceiling and speaks to Prior, a man ill with AIDS. In the theatre, then, our imagination allows us to conceive of people and events we have never seen or experienced and to transcend our physical circumstances to the point where we forget who we are, where we are, or what time it is. How is this possible? It happens because in the theatre our imagination works for us just as it does in everyday life.

Tools of the Imagination: Symbol and Metaphor

We can understand this process better if we look closely at two tools of our imagination: symbol and metaphor.

Functions of Symbols   In general terms, a **symbol** is a sign, token, or emblem that signifies something else. A simple form of symbol is a sign. Some signs stand for a single, uncomplicated idea or action. In everyday life we are surrounded by them: road signs,

Flashback In a narrative or story, movement back to a time in the past to show a scene or an event before the narrative resumes at the point at which it was interrupted.

Symbol A sign, a visual image, an object, or an action that signifies something else; a visual embodiment of something invisible. A single image or sign stands for an entire idea or larger concept—a flag is a symbol for a nation; a logo is a symbol for a corporation.

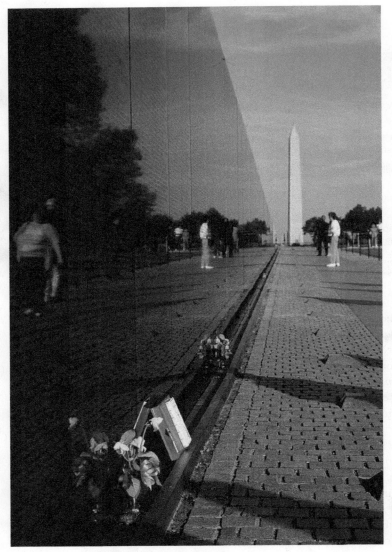

THE POWER OF SYMBOLS
Symbols and metaphors, though not real in a literal sense, have enormous power to influence our lives; in that respect, they become "realer than real." A forceful symbol of the bravery, tragedy, and losses of the Vietnam War is the wall designed by Maya Lin in Washington, where the names of those who died are etched into the side of the memorial. (© R. Morley/PhotoLink/Getty Images RF)

such as an S-shaped curve; audible signals, like sirens and foghorns; and a host of mathematical and typographical symbols: $, 1/4, @, &. We sometimes forget that language itself is symbolic; the letters of the alphabet are only lines and curves on a page. Words are arrangements of letters that by common agreement represent something else. The same four letters mean different things depending on the order in which they are placed: *pear, reap, rape.* These three words set different imaginative wheels in motion and signal responses that vary greatly from word to word.

At times, symbols exert incredible emotional power; a good example is a flag, embodying a nation's passions, fears, and ambitions. Flags are symbols: lines, shapes, and colors that in certain combinations become immediately recognizable. Like flags, some symbols signify ideas or emotions that are far more complex and profound than the symbol itself. The cross, for example, is a symbol of Christ and, beyond that, of Christianity as a whole. Whatever form a symbol takes—language, a flag, or a religious emblem—it can embody the total meaning of a religion, a nation, or an idea.

Functions of Metaphors   A similar transformation takes place with metaphor, another form of imaginative substitution. With metaphor we announce that one thing is another, in order to describe it or point up its meaning more clearly. (In poetry, you will remember, a simile says that one thing is *like* another; metaphor simply states directly that one thing *is* another.) The Bible is filled with metaphors. The psalmist who says, "The Lord is my shepherd," or who says of God, "Thou art my rock and my fortress," is speaking metaphorically. He does not mean literally that God is a shepherd, a rock, or a fortress; he is saying that God is similar to and has qualities like these things. Just as with symbols, metaphors are part of the fabric of life, as the following common expressions suggest:

"How gross."

"He's off the wall."

"It's a slam dunk."

"Give me the bottom line."

"That's cool."

DYNAMICS OF DRAMA

Realism and Nonrealism: A Contrast

The distinction between realistic and nonrealistic techniques in theatre becomes clearer when the two approaches are examined side by side. This distinction is present in all aspects of theatre.

Realistic Techniques	Nonrealistic Techniques
STORY	
Events that the audience knows have happened or might happen in everyday life: Blanche DuBois in Tennessee Williams's *A Streetcar Named Desire* goes to New Orleans to visit her sister and brother-in-law.	Events that do not take place in real life but occur only in the imagination: in Kushner's *Angels in America,* a character in a housewife's mind takes her on an imaginary trip to the Antarctic.
STRUCTURE	
Action is confined to real places; time passes normally, as it does in everyday life: the hospital room setting in Margaret Edson's *Wit* is an example.	Arbitrary use of time and place: in August Strindberg's *A Dream Play,* walls dissolve and characters are transformed, as in a dream.
CHARACTERS	
Recognizable human beings, such as the priest and the nun in John Patrick Shanley's *Doubt.*	Unreal figures like the ghost of Hamlet's father in William Shakespeare's *Hamlet* or the three witches in *Macbeth.*
ACTING	
Performers portray people as they behave in daily life: the men on a summer holiday in the country house in Terrence McNally's *Love! Valor! Compassion!*	Performers portray animals in the musical *The Lion King;* they also engage in singing, dancing, and acrobatics in musical comedy or performance art.
LANGUAGE	
Ordinary dialogue or conversation: the two brothers trying to get ahead in Suzan-Lori Parks's *Topdog/Underdog.*	Poetry such as Romeo speaks to Juliet in Shakespeare's play; or the song "Tonight" in the musical *West Side Story.*
SCENERY	
Rooms of a real house, as in Edward Albee's *Who's Afraid of Virginia Woolf?*	Abstract forms and shapes on a bare stage—for example, for a Greek play such as Sophocles's *Electra.*
LIGHTING	
Light onstage appears to come from natural sources—a lamp in a room, or sunlight, as in Ibsen's *Ghosts,* where the sunrise comes through a window in the final scene.	Shafts of light fall at odd angles; also, colors in light are used arbitrarily. Example: a single blue spotlight on a singer in a musical comedy.
COSTUMES	
Ordinary street clothes, like those worn by the characters in August Wilson's *The Piano Lesson.*	The bright costumes of a chorus in a musical comedy; the strange outfit worn by Caliban, the half-man, half-beast in Shakespeare's *The Tempest.*
MAKEUP	
The natural look of characters in a domestic play such as Lorraine Hansberry's *A Raisin in the Sun.*	Masks worn by characters in a Greek tragedy or in a modern play like the musical *Beauty and the Beast.*

We are saying one thing but describing another. When someone describes a person or event as "cool," the reference is not to a low temperature but to an admirable quality. The term "slam dunk" comes from basketball, but in everyday parlance is applied to a wide range of activities that have nothing to do with sports. We can see from these examples that metaphors, like symbols, are part of daily life.

The "Reality" of the Imagination

Our use of symbol and metaphor shows how large a part imagination plays in our lives. Millions of automobiles in the United States can be brought to a halt, not by a concrete wall, but by a small colored light changing from green to red. Imagine attempting to control traffic, or virtually any type of human activity, without symbols. Beyond being a matter of convenience, symbols are necessary to our survival.

The same holds true for metaphor. Frequently we find that we cannot express fear, anxiety, hope, or joy—any of the deep human feelings—in descriptive language. That is why we sometimes scream. It is also why we have poetry and use metaphors. Even scientists, the men and women we are most likely to consider realists, turn to metaphor at crucial times. They discuss the "big bang" theory of the origin of the universe and talk of "black holes" in outer space. Neither term is "scientific," but both terms communicate what scientists have in mind in a way that an equation or a more logical phrase could not.

Dreams provide another example of the power of the imagination. You dream that you are falling off a cliff; then, suddenly, you wake up and find that you are not flying through the air but lying in bed. Significantly, however, the dream of falling means more to you than the objective fact of lying in bed. Theatre functions in somewhat the same way. Though not real in a literal sense, it can be completely—even painfully—real in an emotional or intellectual sense. The critic and director Harold Clurman (1901–1980) gave one of his books on theatre the title *Lies Like Truth*. Theatre—like dreams or fantasies—can sometimes be more truthful about life than a mundane, objective description. This is a paradox of dreams, fantasies, and art, including theatre: by probing deep into the psyche to reveal inner truths, they can be more real than outward reality.

THE IMAGINARY WORLDS OF THEATRE

Realism and Nonrealism

As theatre audience members, we are asked to accept many kinds of imaginary worlds. One way to classify these imaginary realms is as *realism* and *nonrealism* (or *departures from realism*). At the outset, it is essential to know that in theatre the term *realistic* denotes a special application of what we consider "genuine" or "real." A realistic element is not necessarily more truthful than a nonrealistic element. Rather, in theatre, realistic and nonrealistic denote different ways of presenting reality.

Realistic Elements of Theatre   In theatre, a realistic element is one that resembles *observable* reality. It is a kind of photographic truth. We apply the term *realistic* to those elements of theatre that conform to our own observations of people, places, and events. Realistic theatre follows the predictable logic of everyday life: the law of gravity, the time it takes a person to travel from one place to another, the way a room in a house looks, the way a person dresses. With a realistic approach, these conform to our normal expectations. In realistic theatre, we are called upon in our imaginations to

Realism   Broadly, an attempt to present onstage people, events and scenery corresponding to those in everyday life.

Nonrealism   Also known as departures from realism, means all types of theatre that depart from observable reality.

Symbols & metaphors help w/ imagination

REALISTIC AND NONREALISTIC THEATRE CONTRASTED

These scenes illustrate some of the differences between two approaches to the make-believe of theatre. At the left we see Gabriel Brown as George Murchison, Edena Hines as Beneatha Younger, and Susan Kelechi Watson as Ruth Younger in the Westport Country Playhouse production of Lorraine Hansberry's *A Raisin in the Sun.* In contrast, the scene right is from a revival of an avant-garde production presented at the Brooklyn Academy of Music of *Einstein on the Beach,* directed and designed by Robert Wilson. Note the abstract setting, the eerie lighting, the symbolic characters. This kind of theatre contrasts sharply with realism. (© T Charles Erickson, © Sara Krulwich/The New York Times/Redux).

accept the notion that what we see onstage is not fantastic but real, even though we always know we are in the theatre and not watching an actual event.

We are quite familiar with realism in films and television. Part of the reason is mechanical. The camera records what the lens "sees." Whether it is a bedroom in a house, a crowded city street, or the Grand Canyon, film captures the scene as the eye sees it. Theatre too has always had realistic elements. Every type of theatre that is not pure fantasy has realistic aspects. For example, characters who are supposed to represent real people must be rooted in a human truth that audiences can recognize. When we are so readily able to verify what we see before us from our own experience, it is easy to identify with it and to accept its authenticity. For this reason, realistic theatre has become firmly established in modern times, and it seems likely to remain so.

Nonrealistic Elements of Theatre Nonrealistic elements of theatre include everything that does not conform to our observations of surface reality: poetry instead of prose, ghosts rather than flesh-and-blood people, abstract forms for scenery, and so forth. Again, we find a counterpart in films and television. The extremely popular vampire and zombie films and television shows, such as *True Blood, The Walking Dead,* and the *Twilight* series present us with fantastic characters and situations. All of the *Star Wars* films had intriguing computer-generated characters and effects, which is one of the reasons audiences are so looking forward to the recently announced new additions to the series.

In theatre, the argument for nonrealism (or *departures from realism*) is that the surface of life—a real conversation, for instance, or a real room in a house—can never convey the whole truth, because so much of life occurs in our minds and imagination. If we are depressed and tell a friend that we feel "lousy" or "awful," we do not even begin to communicate the depth of our feelings. It is because of the inadequacy of ordinary words that people turn to poetry, and because of the inadequacy of other forms of daily communication that they turn to music, dance, art, sculpture, and the entire range of symbols and metaphors discussed earlier.

A wide range of theatrical techniques and devices fall into the category of nonrealism. One example is the **soliloquy**, in which a solitary character speaks to the audience, expressing in words a hidden thought. Another example is **pantomime**, in which performers pretend to be using objects that are not actually present, such as drinking from a cup or opening an umbrella. Many aspects of musical comedy are nonrealistic. People in the streets or in an office building do not break into song or dance as they do in musicals like *Guys and Dolls, West Side Story, Mary Poppins, Wicked,* or *The Book of Mormon.* One could say that any activity or scenic device that transcends or symbolizes reality tends to be nonrealistic.

Soliloquy Speech in which a character who is alone onstage speaks inner thoughts aloud.

Pantomime A form of theatrical presentation that relies on dance, gesture, and physical movement without speech.

Theatre has mixture of real & nonrea!

Combining the Realistic and the Nonrealistic In discussing realistic and nonrealistic elements of theatre, we must not assume that these two approaches are mutually exclusive. The terms *realistic* and *nonrealistic* are simply a convenient way of separating those parts of theatre that correspond to our observations and experiences of everyday life from those that do not. Most performances and theatre events contain a mixture of realistic and nonrealistic elements. In acting, for example, a Shakespearean play calls for a number of nonrealistic qualities or techniques. At the same time, any performer playing a Shakespearean character must convince the audience that he or she represents a real human being.

To take a more modern example, in *The Glass Menagerie* by Tennessee Williams (1911–1983), and in *Our Town* by Thornton Wilder (1897–1975), one of the performers serves as a narrator and also participates in the action. When the performer playing this part is speaking directly to the audience, his actions are nonrealistic; when he is taking part in a scene with other characters, they are realistic.

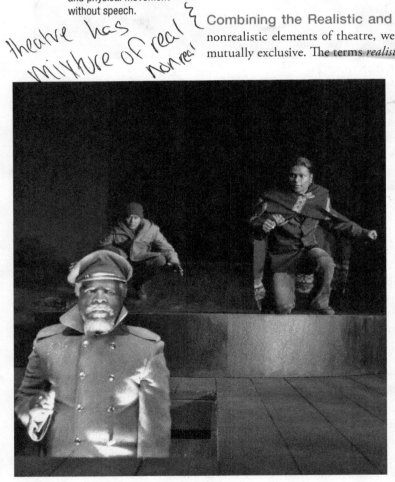

NONREALISTIC ELEMENTS

Realism has been a major approach to theatre since the late nineteenth century, but for hundreds of years before that, theatre incorporated many unrealistic elements. One example is Shakespeare's use of ghosts and various otherworldly creatures. Shown here in a Royal Shakespeare Company production of *Hamlet* is Vaneshran Arumugam in the title role (right background) encountering the ghost of his dead father, played by John Kani (left foreground). (© Geraint Lewis)

Distinguishing Stage Reality from Fact

Whether theatre is realistic or nonrealistic, it is different from the physical reality of everyday life. In recent years there have been attempts to make theatre less remote from our daily lives. For example, plays have been presented that were largely transcripts of court trials or congressional hearings. This was part of a movement called *theatre of fact,* which involved reenactments of material gathered from actual events. Partly as a result of this trend, theatre and life have become intertwined. Television has added to this with *docudramas,*

FACT-BASED THEATRE
A popular form that has emerged in the past half century is theatre based on facts. This includes documentary theatre taken from court trials, congressional hearings, and interviews. Shown here is Demosthenes Chrysan as one of the refugees in *Aftermath,* a documentary drama based on interviews with Iraqi victims forced by the war to live in exile in Jordan. Their stories are both harrowing and haunting. *Aftermath* was developed by Jessica Blank and Erik Jensen. (© Sara Krulwich/The New York Times/Redux)

dramatizing the lives, for example, of rape victims, convicts, and ordinary people who become heroic. There has also been a vogue for what is called "reality television," in which real people are put in stressful situations with a presumably unplanned outcome.

This kind of interaction—and sometimes confusion—between life and art has been heightened, of course, by the emergence of television and film documentaries, which cover real events but are also edited. In addition, today we have "staged" political demonstrations and hear of "staged news." In politics staged events have become commonplace: a presidential or senatorial candidate visits a flag factory, an aircraft carrier, or an elementary school for what is called a "photo opportunity." When news becomes "staged" and theatre becomes "fact," it is difficult to separate the two.

These developments point up the close relationship between theatre and life; nevertheless, when we see a performance, even a re-creation of events that have actually occurred, we are always aware, on some level, of being in a theatre. Most of us have seen plays with a stage setting so real we marvel at its authenticity: a kitchen, for instance, in which the appliances actually work, with running water in the faucets, ice in the refrigerator, and a stove on which an actor or actress can cook. What we stand in awe of, though, is that the room *appears* so real when we know, in truth, that it is not.

PLAYING YOUR PART: THINKING ABOUT THEATRE

1. Think of an event you have recently attended in person, a rock concert, a circus, a dance or musical presentation, a religious or memorial service. Explain what it meant to you to be present, in the same space at the same time as those performing or officiating. What was the feeling, the emotion, the stimulation you experienced that would not have been the same if you had watched the event on television?

2. During a performance you may observe a puppet or group of puppets who appear as real as people we deal with every day. Or you may see on a bare stage two or three props (a tree, for example, or a throne) and you assume you are in a forest or a royal palace. Why do you think during a performance we are able to let our imaginations take over? Is this something we also do in everyday life?

3. While watching a performance you may dissolve into laughter or cry real tears. The whole time, on some level, you know what you are observing is not "real." But does this matter? In some sense is the experience real? What is the relationship between a theatre experience such as this and an experience in daily life?

We admire the fact that, not being a real kitchen, it looks as if it were. We are abruptly reminded of the distinction between stage reality and physical reality when the two lines cross. If an actor unintentionally trips and falls onstage, we suddenly shift our attention from the character to the person playing the part. Has he hurt himself? Will he be able to continue? A similar reaction occurs when a performer forgets lines, or a sword falls accidentally during a duel, or a dancer slips during a musical number.

We remember the distinction, also, at the moment when someone else *fails* to remember it. Children frequently mistake actions onstage for the real thing, warning the heroine of the villain's plan or assuming that blows on the head of a puppet actually hurt. There is a famous story about a production of *Othello* in which a spectator ran onstage to prevent the actor playing Othello from strangling Desdemona. Most people, however, are always aware of the difference; our minds manage two seemingly contradictory feats simultaneously: on the one hand, we know that an imagined event is not objectively real, but at the same time we accept it completely as fantasy. This is possible because of what the poet and critic Samuel Taylor Coleridge (1772–1834) called the "willing suspension of disbelief." Having separated the reality of art from the reality of everyday life, the mind is prepared to go along unreservedly with the reality of art.

SUMMARY

1. During the past 100 years, theatre has been challenged by a succession of technological developments: silent movies, radio, talking movies, television, and electronic handheld devices. It has survived these challenges partly because of the special nature of the performer-audience relationship.

2. The relationship between performer and audience is "live": each is in the other's presence, in the same place at the same time. It is the exchange between the two that gives theatre its unique quality.

3. Theatre—like the other performing arts—is a group experience. The composition of the audience has a direct bearing on the effect of the experience.

4. Participants and spectators play different roles in the theatre experience; the role of spectators is to observe and respond.

5. There is a difference between participating in theatre by direct action and by observation. In the former situation, nonactors take part, usually for the purpose of personal growth and self-development. In the latter, a presentation is made by one group to another, and the spectators do not participate physically in the experience.

6. For the observer, theatre is an experience of the imagination and the mind. The mind seems capable of accepting almost any illusion as to what is taking place, who the characters are, and when and where the action occurs.

7. Our minds are capable of leaps of the imagination, not just in the theatre but in our everyday lives, where we use symbol and metaphor to communicate with one another and to explain the world around us.

8. The world of the imagination—symbols, metaphors, dreams, fantasies, and various expressions of art—is "real," even though it is intangible and has no objective reality. Frequently it tells us more than any form of logical discourse about our true feelings.

9. Theatre makes frequent use of symbols and metaphors—in writing, acting, and design— and theatre itself can be looked upon as a metaphor.

10. Theatre calls upon audiences to imagine two kinds of worlds: realistic and nonrealistic. Realistic theatre depicts things onstage that conform to observable reality; nonrealistic theatre includes the realm of dreams, fantasy, symbol, and metaphor. In theatre, realism and nonrealism are frequently mixed.

11. In order to take part in theatre as an observer, it is important to keep the "reality" of fantasies and dreams separate from the real world. By making this separation, we open our imagination to the full range of possibilities in theatre.

26

The Background and Expectations of the Audience

You are soon going to attend a theatre performance, either for personal enjoyment or as a class assignment. As a soon-to-be audience member is there a way you can prepare so that the production will be more entertaining or more meaningful? Are there steps you can take beforehand that will enhance the experience, make it more rewarding, and make you a more engaged audience member? The answer to these questions is "yes."

In a sense, this entire book is a preparation for going to the theatre. Chapter by chapter it explains the various elements of a production—the acting and directing, the script, the scenic and costume design—and how all these fit together in the final stage presentation. But initially, before getting to these specifics, there is information and preparation that will make attending a specific production more exciting and pleasurable, as well as make you a more informed, engaged, and knowledgeable audience member.

For one thing, when we attend a theatre event, we bring more than our mere presence; we bring a background of personal knowledge and a set of expectations that shape the experience. Several important factors are involved:

1. Our knowledge and personal memories.
2. Our awareness of the social, political, and philosophical world in which the play was written or produced—the link between theatre and society.
3. Our knowledge about the play and playwright.
4. Our personal expectations concerning the event: what we anticipate will happen at a performance. As we will see, misconceptions about what the theatre experience is or should be can lead to confusion and disappointment.

◀ THE AFRICAN AMERICAN EXPERIENCE
Members of a theatre audience come to a performance with individual, personal backgrounds, which can make the experience more meaningful. An example would be an African American audience member seeing The Piano Lesson *by August Wilson. Set in Pittsburgh, the play is about a brother and sister who have different ideas of what to do with the family's piano. The brother, Boy Willie (Brandon J. Dirden), standing, wants to sell it to buy a farm in the South. His sister, Berniece, wants to keep the piano because it is a family heirloom. The man playing the piano in this photo is a family friend, Wining Boy (Chuck Cooper), in a production directed by Ruben Santiago-Hudson at the Signature Theatre. (© Joan Marcus)*

BACKGROUND OF INDIVIDUAL SPECTATORS

A background element that each of us brings to a theatre performance as an audience member is our own individual memories and experiences. Each of us has a personal catalog of childhood memories, emotional scars, and private fantasies. Anything we see onstage that reminds us of this personal world will have a strong impact on us. When we see a play that has been written in our own day, we bring with us also a deep awareness of the world from which the play comes, because we come from the same world. Through the books we have read, through newspapers and television, through our discussions with friends, we have a background of common information, values, and beliefs. Our shared knowledge and experience are much larger than most of us realize, and they form a crucial ingredient in our theatre experience.

The play *A Raisin in the Sun* by Lorraine Hansberry (1930–1965) tells the story of an African American family in Chicago in the late 1950s whose members want to improve their lives by finding better jobs and moving to a new neighborhood. But they face a number of obstacles put in their way by society. Any African American—or, for that matter, any person who belongs to a minority or to any group that has lacked opportunities—can readily identify with this situation. Such a person will know from personal experience what the characters are going through.

BACKGROUND INFORMATION ON THE PLAY OR PLAYWRIGHT

Often to enhance our experience of attending a theatre production we need additional information about a play or a playwright. For instance, a play may contain difficult passages or obscure references, which it is helpful to know about before we see a performance. As an example, we can take a segment from Shakespeare's *King Lear:* the scene in the third act when Lear appears on the heath in the midst of a terrible storm. Earlier in the play, Lear divided his kingdom between two of his daughters, Goneril and Regan, who he thought loved him but who, he discovers, have actually deceived him. Gradually, they have stripped him of everything: his possessions, his soldiers, his dignity. Finally, they send him out from their homes to face the wind and rain in open country. As the storm begins, Lear speaks the following lines:

> Blow, winds, and crack your cheeks! Rage! Blow!
> You cataracts and hurricanoes, spout
> Till you have drenched our steeples, drowned the cocks!

In the first line, the expression "crack your cheeks" refers to pictures in the corners of old maps showing a face puffed out at the cheeks, blowing the wind.[1] Shakespeare is saying that the face of the wind should blow so hard that its cheeks will crack. In the second line, "cataracts and hurricanoes" refers to water from both the heavens and the seas. In the third line, "cocks" refers to weathercocks on the tops of steeples; Lear wants so much rain to fall that even the weathercocks on the steepletops will be submerged. If we are aware of these meanings, we can join them with the sounds of the words—and with the rage the actor expresses in his voice and gestures—to get the full impact of the scene.

In contemporary theatre, playwrights frequently use special techniques that will confuse us if we do not understand them. The German playwright Bertolt Brecht (1898–1956), who lived and wrote in the United States during the 1940s, wanted to provoke his audiences into thinking about what they were seeing. To do this, he would interrupt a story with a song or a speech by a narrator. His theory was that when a story is stopped in this manner, audience members have an opportunity to consider more carefully what they are seeing and to relate the drama onstage to other aspects of life.

If we are not aware that this is Brecht's purpose in interrupting the action, we might conclude that he was simply a careless or inferior playwright. Here, as in similar cases, knowledge of the play or playwright is indispensable to a complete theatre experience.

BACKGROUND OF THE PERIOD

Even when we identify closely with the characters or situation in a play and we have knowledge about the play and the playwright, often in drama from the past there are elements we cannot understand unless we are familiar with the history, culture, and philosophy of the period when it was created. This is because there is a close connection between any art form and the society in which it is produced.

AUDIENCE MEMBER'S PERSONAL BACKGROUND
The personal background of individual audience members will affect their experience in attending a theatre production. Young people from diverse ethnic and cultural backgrounds who have worked together on a project or other undertaking will have a better understanding than others of a theatre piece such as *Emotional Creature* by Eve Ensler, shown here. In the play, six young actors from different countries around the globe develop an involvement in their mutual social problems that inspires them to express their feelings in song and dance. (© Carol Rosegg)

Theatre and Society

Art does not occur in a vacuum. All art, including theatre, is related to the society in which it is produced. Artists are sometimes charged with being "antisocial," "subversive," or "enemies of the state," and such accusations carry the strong suggestion that artists are outsiders or invaders rather than true members of a culture. To be sure, art frequently challenges society and is sometimes on the leading edge of history, appearing to forecast the future. More often than not, however, such art simply recognizes what is already present in society but has not yet surfaced. A good example is the abstract painting that developed in Europe in the early twentieth century. At first it was considered a freakish aberration, an unattractive jumble of jagged lines and patches of color with no relation to nature, truth, or anything human. In time, however, abstract art came to be recognized as a genuine movement, and the disjointed and fragmentary lines of abstract art seemed to reflect the quality of much of modern life.

Art grows in the soil of a specific society. With very few exceptions—and those are soon forgotten—art is a mirror of its age, revealing the prevailing attitudes, underlying assumptions, and deep-seated beliefs of a particular group of people. Art may question society's views or reaffirm them, but it cannot escape them; the two are as indissolubly linked as a person and his or her shadow. When we speak of art as "universal," we mean that the art of one age has so defined the characteristics of human beings that it can speak eloquently to another age; but we should never forget that every work of art first emerges at a given time and place and can never be adequately understood unless the conditions surrounding its birth are also understood.

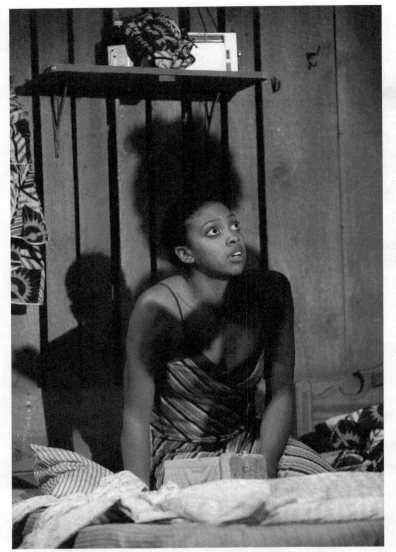

THEATRE REFLECTS SOCIAL ISSUES
Theatre can be a powerful tool in calling attention to social and political injustices. A good example is Lynn Nottage's *Ruined*, directed by Kate Whoriskey, jointly produced by the Goodman Theatre in Chicago and the Manhattan Theatre Club in New York. The play is set in the Democratic Republic of Congo in the year 2000 and tells the story of Sophie (Condola Phyleia Rashad) and her horrific experiences at the hands of men. She crosses paths with Mama Nadi, a sharp businesswoman who helps such women but at the same time exploits them and profits from them. (© Liz Lauren)

Greek Theatre and Culture

A study of theatre in significant periods of history confirms the close link between art and society. In ancient Greece, for example, civilization reached a high point in Athens during the time of Pericles, the latter part of the fifth century BCE. This was the golden age of Greece—when politics, art, architecture, and theatre thrived as they never had before, and rarely have since. As the Athenians of that period gained control over the

THE SYMMETRY OF A GREEK TEMPLE
The formalism and sense of order of Greece in the fifth century BCE are reflected in the Parthenon, on the acropolis in Athens. All art, including theatre, reflects the attitudes and values of the society in which it is created. (© Adam Crowley/Getty Images)

world around them and took new pride in human achievements, they developed ideals of beauty, order, symmetry, and moderation that permeated their entire culture, including theatre.

By the fifth century BCE, standard forms of drama had emerged in Greece, both for tragedies and for comedies. One convention limited the number of scenes in a play: usually, there were only five scenes, interspersed with choral sections. In addition, the drama took place in one locale—often in front of a palace—and within a short span of time. Another convention reflected this society's sense of balance and order. Though bloody deeds occurred often in the myths on which most Greek plays were based, in the plays that have survived these deeds almost never took place in sight of the audience— murders, suicides, and other acts of violence usually occurred off stage.

Elizabethan Theatre and Culture

Another example of the strong link between theatre and society—an example that stands in contrast to the classical Greek period—is the Elizabethan age in England. Named after Queen Elizabeth I, who reigned from 1558 to 1603, this period saw England become a dominant force in the world. Under Elizabeth's rule, England became a unified country; trade and commerce flourished; and with the defeat of the Spanish Armada in 1588, an age of exploration for England was under way. England was expanding confidently on all fronts, and these characteristics were reflected in the drama of the period.

From medieval drama the Elizabethans had inherited stage practices that made it possible to shift rapidly in a play from place to place and from one time period to another. Using these techniques, as well as others they perfected, Shakespeare, Christopher Marlowe (1564–1593), and their contemporaries wrote plays that are quite different from the more formal drama of the Greeks. A single play might move to a number of locations and cover a period of many years. Rather than being restrictive, Elizabethan plays are expansive in terms of numbers of characters and in terms of action, and there

IN FOCUS: HISTORICAL PERSPECTIVES

Women in Greek and Elizabethan Theatres

Did women attend theatre in ancient Greece? In Elizabethan England, why were women forbidden to appear onstage? These are only two of many significant and intriguing questions that arise when one examines the role of women at various times in theatre history. And of course, they are inextricably linked to larger questions about the treatment of women in society in every age.

In Athenian society of ancient Greece, only male citizens had the right to participate in politics. Although women counted as citizens, they were generally excluded from the institutions of government. They were thus also excluded from appearing onstage in the annual spring theatre festival called the City Dionysia. The plays were written and acted by men, even though many feature important female characters. A broader social question is whether women were allowed to attend the dramatic festivals as spectators. There appears to be no conclusive answer, and the question continues to perplex classical scholars. Even if a select number of women were at performances—after all, men brought their male slaves to the theatre—the plays primarily address a large male audience. Contemporary sources supporting the view that women attended theatre are fragmentary and inconclusive; for instance, a character in the *The Frogs* by Aristophanes (c. 447–388 BCE) remarks ironically that all decent women committed suicide after seeing one of Euripides's plays. Later commentaries, such as an often-repeated story that a few women who saw the chorus of Furies in *The Eumenides* by Aeschylus (525–456 BCE) had miscarriages, are discounted because women did attend theatre after the classical period.

One argument for the attendance of women is the important role women often played in other aspects of the cultural life of the city-state. They contributed to civic life,

for example, by playing leading roles in religious ceremonies, celebrations, and other ritual activities. In fact, they were creatively involved in theatre at other festivals. Because the public activities of women were regulated in order to protect their reputation, female entertainers came to be associated with indecent behavior. Even so, popular entertainments included female performers as singers, dancers, acrobats, and musicians.

In the sixteenth century, actresses appeared onstage in continental Europe. Also, women had appeared in medieval theatre productions in England, but in the English public theatres in the time of Elizabeth I (r. 1558–1603), women were forbidden by law to appear on the stage. Although some actors rose to become celebrities, actresses were often associated with "public women" or prostitutes—particularly by Puritans who viewed theatre as an immoral profession. Female roles therefore were played by boys, notable for their ability to imitate feminine beauty and grace. An exception to the prohibition of actresses was the appearance of Italian singers and French actresses who performed in England for both the nobility and commoners. Outside the public theatres, historians identify a vast, hidden tradition of female performance gleaned from private documents, such as letters and diaries. At court and in manor houses aristocratic women took part in extravagant spectacles called masques; parish dramas and pageants included female members of the community; other women worked as traveling entertainers. The disapproval of women performing in public changed with the restoration of the monarchy in 1660, when actresses were finally permitted to appear in licensed theatres.

Prepared by Susan Tenneriello, Baruch College, CUNY.

is no hesitancy whatsoever about showing murder and bloodshed onstage. At the end of an Elizabethan play, corpses frequently cover the stage in full view of the audience. This expansiveness and this sense of adventure mirror the temper of the age in which the plays were written.

Modern Theatre and Culture

Moving to the contemporary period, we find once again a link between theatre and society. Modern society, especially in the United States, is heterogeneous. We have people of different races, religions, sexual orientations, and national backgrounds living side by side. Moreover, the twentieth century was marked by increasingly swift global communication. By means of television, computers, and the Internet, an event occurring in one place can be flashed instantaneously to the rest of the world. Text messaging and social media, such as Facebook and Twitter, now make us aware of events instantaneously. By these means, too, people are continually made aware of cultures other than their own.

When cultures and societies are brought together, we are reminded of the many things people have in common but also of the differences among us. At the same time that we are brought together by immediate global communications, other aspects of life have become increasingly fragmented. A number of institutions that had held fairly constant through many centuries—organized religion, the family, marriage—have been seriously challenged in the century and a half preceding our own day. Discoveries by Charles Darwin (1809–1882) about evolution, by Karl Marx (1818–1883) on economics, by Sigmund Freud (1856–1939) about the importance of the unconscious, and by Albert Einstein (1879–1955) on relativity questioned and threatened long-established views of the universe, of religion, economics, psychology, and science.

Similar changes in viewpoint and discoveries about nature have continued to the present, the cumulative effect of which has been to make human beings much less certain of their place in the cosmos and of their mastery of events. Today, in the early twenty-first century, life appears much less unified and less ordered than it once did. We must add to these developments the effect of the horrific events that have occurred over the past 100 years: the two World Wars, the second of which saw the Holocaust, the extermination of millions of Jews and others by the Nazi regime; the highly controversial Vietnam War; the effects on our society of the events of 9/11; more recently, the Iraq and Afghanistan wars, and natural disasters such as the deadly typhoon in the Philippines on November 8, 2013, in which thousands of people were killed. All these global and historical developments are reflected in our theatre today, which is an inclusive theatre, fragmented and *eclectic*, and embracing different styles and traditions. The theatre productions we attend today come from around the world, and range from the darkest of tragedies to the lightest of comedies to the highly experimental, created by dramatists who write on many subjects and in many diverse styles,

A typical theatre company today performs a wide range of plays. In a single season, the same company may present a tragedy by Shakespeare, a farce by the French dramatist Molière (1622–1673), a modern drama by the Spanish writer Federico García Lorca (1898–1936), a play like *Eurydice,* by Sarah Ruhl (b. 1974), a young American playwright, as well as a one-person show by a performance artist.

The three periods we have looked at—the Greek, the Elizabethan, and the modern—are examples of the close relationship between a society and the art and theatre it produces. One could find comparable links in every culture and period. It is important to remember, therefore, that whatever the period or culture in which it was first produced, drama is woven into the fabric of its place and time.

To sum up, for our purposes it is important to realize that when we go to the theatre, it is extremely helpful to be aware of the period and circumstances in which a play of whatever sort was created. These are things our professors and instructors can teach us, but things we can also learn ourselves by going online or checking reference books.

BROADWAY THEATRE
Productions in the major theatres in New York City–collectively known as Broadway–are usually characterized by elaborate scenic elements, first-rate acting, and scripts with wide appeal: either new works or revivals. Shown here is a scene from the award-winning *The Book of Mormon*. It concerns a group of Mormon missionaries who visit the African country of Uganda and much of the humor arises from the clash of cultures. Written by Trey Parker and Matt Stone, the music is by Robert Lopez. The actors are (l-r:) Rema Webb, Andrew Rannelis, and Josh Gad. (© Sara Krulwich/The New York Times/Redux)

EXPECTATIONS: THE VARIETY OF EXPERIENCES IN MODERN THEATRE

If we have not often been to the theatre, we might expect that all theatre experiences will be much alike. In fact, most of us go to the theatre for entirely different reasons. Some of us enjoy the escape offered by movies and television and are interested primarily in light entertainment. If we attend a dinner theatre or a Broadway musical, we do not want to be faced with troublesome problems or serious moral issues. Instead, we are looking for something that will be amusing and perhaps include music, dancing, and beautiful scenery and costumes.

On the other hand, some of us want to be stimulated and challenged, both intellectually and emotionally. It must be remembered, too, that many of us like both of these kinds of theatre. At times we may seek light entertainment and at other times, meaningful drama. Not only do performances vary in the type of theatre they offer, they also take place in a variety of settings, and this too has an effect on the nature of the experience. In the mid-twentieth century in the United States "the theatre" was largely synonymous with one kind of experience: Broadway. In the last several decades this has changed radically—further evidence of how diversity in theatre reflects the overall diversity in contemporary life. In the opening chapter we mentioned different places where the great variety of theatre events might be experienced today. In the pages that follow we examine these opportunities in more detail.

Broadway and Touring Theatre

Broadway is the name of the oldest professional theatre in New York City: it refers specifically to plays performed in the large theatres in the district near Times Square in New York City. From 1920 until the early 1950s, most new plays written in the United States originated there, and productions in other areas were usually copies of Broadway productions. Productions sent on tour from Broadway to the rest of the country are exact replicas of the original. Scenery is duplicated down to the last detail, and performers from New York often play roles they had played on Broadway.

Because our society is diverse and complex, however, and because theatre reflects society, no one form of theatre today can speak equally to all of us. As if in response to the complexity of the modern world, in the second half of the twentieth century people began searching for new forms in theatre, and for alternative locations in which to present theatre.

Resident Professional Theatre

One significant development, which began in a few cities in the 1950s and has since spread across the country, is resident professional theatre, sometimes known as *regional theatre.* Theatre companies have been formed, and theatre facilities built, for the continuing presentation of high-quality professional productions to local residents. The performers, directors, and designers are generally high-caliber artists who make theatre their full-time profession.

Most cities have developed theatres that present a series of plays over a given span of time, with each play being performed for about four to twelve weeks. Among the best-known of these theatres are the Arena Stage in Washington, D.C., the Long Wharf in New Haven, the American Repertory Theatre in Boston, the Actors Theatre of Louisville, the Alley Theatre in Houston, the Goodman Theatre in Chicago, the Milwaukee Repertory Theater, the Guthrie Theater in Minneapolis, the Seattle Repertory Theatre, and the Mark Taper Forum in Los Angeles. Among African American theatres, examples are Towne Street Theatre of Los Angeles,

THEATRE AWAY FROM THE MAINSTREAM
In addition to traditional mainstream theatre, there is an important active theatre such as off-Broadway, off-off-Broadway, and avant-garde, not only in major cities but in many other places around the world. One example is *All in the Timing*, a collection of provocative, darkly comedic vignettes by David Ives presented at 59E59 Theatre. Pictured are (l-r:) Matthew Saldivar, Carson Elrod, and Liv Rooth, who appear to hear, see, and speak no evil. (© Sara Krulwich/The New York Times/Redux)

the North Carolina Black Repertory, and the Black Repertory Company of St. Louis. A season of plays in these theatres will usually include both new plays and classics, and theatergoers are encouraged to buy a season subscription.

In addition to resident companies, there are now a number of permanent summer theatre festivals and Shakespeare festivals throughout the United States and Canada. Among the best-known are the Shakespeare festivals at Stratford, Ontario; San Diego, California; Cedar City, Utah; and Ashland, Oregon.

Alternative Theatre: Off-Broadway and Elsewhere

In New York City *off-Broadway theatre* began in the 1950s as an alternative to Broadway, which was becoming increasingly costly. Off-Broadway theatres were smaller than Broadway theatres—most of them had fewer than 200 seats—and were located outside the Times Square area. Because off-Broadway was less expensive than Broadway, it offered more opportunity for producing serious classics and experimental works. Off-Broadway itself, however, became institutionalized in the 1960s and 1970s, and small independent groups developed *off-off-Broadway*, which produced a wide variety of offerings wherever inexpensive space was available—churches, lofts, warehouses, large basements.

An important development in American theatre is that counterparts to off-off-Broadway have been established in other major cities across the United States—Washington, Atlanta, Chicago, Minneapolis, Los Angeles, San Francisco, Seattle—where small theatre groups perform as alternatives to large organizations. It is in these smaller theatres, in New York and across the country, that most experimental and new works are performed.

In addition, all across the country there are cabaret and dinner theatres in which the atmosphere of a nightclub or restaurant is combined with that of a theatre. In these informal settings, guests eat and drink before watching a performance.

Young People's and Children's Theatre

A branch of theatre that has earned an important place in the overall picture is children's theatre, sometimes called *theatre for youth.* These theatres include a wide spectrum from the most sophisticated professional organizations to semiprofessionals to improvisational groups to undertakings that are predominately amateur or educational. The aim in all cases, however, is to provide a theatrical experience for young people. In some cases it is to offer school-age children an opportunity to see first-class productions of plays dealing with people and subjects in which they might be personally interested. In other cases, the emphasis is on dramatizing the lives of significant figures in history—Abraham Lincoln, Martin Luther King, Jr., Eleanor Roosevelt—or giving dramatic life to literary classics such as *Tom Sawyer* or *Huckleberry Finn.*

A number of young people's or children's theatre organizations across North America have a long history and feature first-class theatre spaces and production facilities. Moreover, the caliber of those responsible for their productions—performers, designers, directors, etc.—is excellent and the equal of any professional regional or not-for-profit theatre. Among those in this category are the Children's Theatre Company of Minneapolis, the Children's Theatre of Charlotte, the Orange County Children's Theater, the Nashville Children's Theatre, and TheatreworksUSA in New York City.

College and University Theatre

In the last few decades, *college* and *university theatre* departments have also become increasingly important, not only in teaching theatre arts but also in presenting plays. In some localities, college productions are virtually the only form of theatre offered. In other areas, they are a significant supplement to professional theatre.

The theatre facilities in many colleges are excellent. Most large colleges and universities have two or three theatre spaces—a full-size theatre, a medium-size theatre, and a smaller space for experimental drama—as well as extensive scene shops, costume rooms, dressing rooms, and rehearsal halls. Productions are usually scheduled throughout the school year.

The quality and complexity of these productions vary. In some places, productions are extremely elaborate, with full-scale scenery, costumes, lighting, and sound. Colleges vary, too, in the level of professionalism in acting. Many colleges use only performers from the undergraduate theatre program. If a college has a master's degree program, it will use both graduate and undergraduate performers. Colleges or universities may also bring in outside professionals to perform along with students. Most college and university theatres offer a variety of plays, including classics and experimental plays rarely done by professional theatres.

COLLEGE AND UNIVERSITY THEATRE
A vital segment of theatre in the United States is the many productions mounted by theatre departments in colleges and universities, which often achieve a high degree of professionalism. They also provide excellent training for theatre practitioners, as well as affording audiences first-rate productions. Seen here are (left to right) Danny Pancratz, Nathan Grant, and T. J. Nichols in a production of Molière's *The Miser* at Western Illinois University, directed by Professor Jeannie M. Woods. (Photo courtesy of WIU Visual Production Center/Larry Dean, photographer)

PLAYING YOUR PART: EXPERIENCING THEATRE

1. Imagine that you were required to attend a production of a play by Shakespeare. List the information about the playwright and period you would be able to bring to your appreciation of the production. List what you are worried you would not know as you prepared to attend the presentation.

2. Search the Internet for a website of a regional theatre closest to your community. What types of plays are they doing? Would you be interested in attending the whole season or just one or two productions? Why? What does that tell us about the types of plays you like?

3. Tour the theatre(s) and backstage areas of your university theatre. What surprised you about these spaces?

4. Read a review online by a *New York Times* or *Chicago Tribune* theatre critic. Which of the critical criteria discussed in this chapter does he or she address? How did the critic help you decide whether you might want to see the production?

Community and Amateur Theatre

In addition to the many forms of professional theatre, and to college and university theatre, another area in which theatre activity thrives is community and amateur theatre. In hundreds of locations throughout the United States and Canada, and in many parts of the world, one finds semiprofessional or nonprofessional theatres serving local communities. In some cases, those involved—actors, directors, designers, crew members—have had professional training and experience but have chosen not to pursue a full-time career, for a number of reasons. Along with the part-time professionals, community theatres often include amateurs who also love the theatre. Many of these theatres approach their productions—the selection of plays, rehearsals, the building of scenery, advertising, and ticket sales—in much the same way as their professional counterparts and in many cases, the level of work is surprisingly good. In many parts of the country, community and amateur theatres afford the only live theatre available to audiences.

THE CRITIC, THE REVIEWER, AND THE BLOGGER

Most of us who go to the theatre or the movies, or who watch a television show, are amateur critics. When we say about a performance, "It started off great, but it fizzled," or "The star was terrific, just like someone in real life," or "The woman was OK, but the man overacted," or "The acting was good, but the story was too downbeat for me," we are making a critical judgment. The difference between a critic/reviewer and those of us in the audience is that the former presumably is better informed about the event and has developed a set of critical standards by which to judge it.

The Critic/Reviewer

A *critic*, loosely defined, is someone who observes theatre and then analyzes and comments on it. Ideally, the critic serves as a knowledgeable and highly sensitive audience member. Audiences can learn from critics not only because critics impart information and judgments but also because a critic shares with an audience the point of view of the spectator. Unlike those who create theatre—writers, performers, designers—critics sit out front and watch a performance just as other members of the audience do. Critics generally write serious articles that appear in newspapers, magazines, and books.

A familiar type of critic is the reviewer. A *reviewer,* who usually works for a newspaper, a magazine, or a television station, reports on what has occurred at the theatre. He or she will tell briefly what a theatre event is about, explaining that it is a musical, a comedy, or a serious play, and perhaps describing its plot. The reviewer might also offer an opinion about whether or not the event is worth seeing. The reviewer is usually restricted by time, space, or both.

Today, in addition to critics and reviewers, whose opinions appear in print or on television, we have a new source of theatre criticism: blogs, YouTube, and popular websites like Theatremania.com. Many of these sites have their own theatre reviewers; other sites may have amateur critics who send in their unsolicited opinions. In addition, opinions about theatre productions are frequently found on social media such as Facebook and Twitter. At times these assessments of a production can be helpful and informative, but a word of caution is in order here. A number of these self-appointed reviewers may have little or no background in theatre criticism, or, in fact, in theatre itself. They enjoy being part of the wider world of theatre criticism, but they may not have the credentials to do so. In other words, these amateur critics may not have the preparation for criticism described in the pages that follow.

Preparation for Criticism

In order to make criticism more meaningful to audiences, ideally the critic/reviewer or blogger should have a thorough theatre background. This would consist of a full knowledge of theatre history, as well as other aspects of theatre, such as acting, directing, and design. The critic/reviewer must be familiar with plays written in various styles and modes and should know the body of work of individual writers. Also, the critic ought to be able to relate what is happening in theatre to what is happening in the other arts and, beyond that, to events in society generally.

In addition, the person commenting on theatre should understand the production elements discussed later in this book—directing, acting, and design. The critic/reviewer must know what a director does and what constitutes good and bad direction. He or she should also understand acting and should be able to judge whether a performer has the skills and the talent to be convincing in a role and whether the role has been interpreted appropriately. In addition, the critic should be familiar with the principles and practices of design—scenery, costumes, and lighting. He or she ought to have some idea of what is called for in each area and be able to judge whether the design elements measure up in a given production.

Fact and Opinion in Criticism

In reading the commentary of the critic/reviewer or the blogger, it is important to distinguish between *fact* and *opinion.* The opinions they express should be carefully weighed. On the other hand, the facts or insights they provide can be extremely helpful. In addition to our professors and instructors, a critic/reviewer or a blogger can often make us aware of information we might not otherwise have known—for example, by explaining

Certain plays, both past and present, can prove difficult for an audience to understand fully, especially when first seen. Included in this group are avant-garde or experimental plays. A good example of the latter is *Fefu and Her Friends* by Maria Irene Fornés, which focuses on eight women. During the course of the action, the audience is divided into four groups and taken to four separate locations to see different scenes. Without the proper orientation, this unusual arrangement might at first prove confusing. Shown here are Julianna Margulies as Emma and Joyce Lynn O'Connor as Fefu in a production at the Yale Repertory Theatre.
(© Gerry Goodstein/Yale Repertory Theatre)

a point that was confusing to the audience or noting how a particular scene in a play relates to an earlier scene. They might also offer background material about the playwright, the subject matter of the play, or the style of the production. Such information can broaden our understanding and appreciation of a production we are about to see. The more we know about what a playwright is attempting to do and why a playwright arranges scenes in a certain way, the better we will be able to judge the value of a theatre event we attend.

A good example would be an explanation by a critic of the intentions and techniques of the playwright Maria Irene Fornés in her play *Fefu and Her Friends.* The first act takes place in the living room of Fefu's New England home. The audience sits in one location watching the action in the living room. The second act, however, is presented in four different locations, spaces in the theatre such as backstage, offstage, in the lobby, or in a rehearsal hall. One represents a lawn outside the house, a second a bedroom, a third the study, and the fourth the kitchen. The characters in the play split up and perform separate scenes in each of the four locations. The scenes are supposed to be occurring all at the same time. The audience is divided into four groups as well and members move from one location to the next; the scenes in the separate locations are repeated four times so that each group of audience members can see them. For the third act of the play, the audience reassembles in the main auditorium to watch a scene again in the living room, onstage.

Among other things, Fornés uses the second act to break out of the usual theatre setting. She also wants to show the fragmentation of life as well as its simultaneity. She wants the audience to get a sense of life overlapping and continuing in different places in addition to those on which we usually focus. If the construction of the play, as well as Fornés's purpose and techniques, have been explained to us prior to our seeing the play, then we, as audience members, will be better prepared to understand the experience when we attend a performance.

Critical Criteria

It has often been said that in commenting on a theatre production, a critic/reviewer should ask three questions to guide her or him in arriving at a judgment. These same criteria will aid the rest of us, ordinary theatergoers, as well, to be better informed in expressing our own feelings about a production we have seen.

What Is Being Attempted?   The first question is: *What is the play, and the production, attempting to do?* This question must be raised both about the script and about the production. A critic/reviewer should make clear what the playwright is trying to accomplish. Is the play a tragedy meant to raise significant questions and stir deep emotions? Is it a light comedy intended to entertain and provide escape? Is it a political drama arguing for a point of view?

Have the Intentions Been Achieved?   A second question is: *How well have the intentions of the playwright been carried out?* If a theatre piece originates with an acting ensemble, or with a director, the question is, *How well have the intentions of the original creator been realized?* A theatre company may be producing an acknowledged masterpiece such as *Hamlet* or *Macbeth*, in which case the question becomes how well the play has been acted, directed, and designed. Have the performers brought Shakespeare's characters to life convincingly and excitingly? Or has the director—perhaps by striving to be too original or by updating the play and putting the characters into modern dress—distorted Shakespeare's intentions beyond recognition?

In the case of a new script, one must also ask how well the playwright has realized his or her own intentions. If the play is intended to probe deeply into family relationships—between parents and children, or husbands and wives—how convincingly and how insightfully has the dramatist accomplished this? If the intention is to entertain, to make the audience laugh, the question to be asked is: Just how funny is the play? Did it succeed in providing entertainment? Was it clever, witty, and full of amusing situations, or did it fall flat?

Was the Attempt Worthwhile?   A third question to ask when judging a production falls more into the realm of personal taste and evaluation: *Was the play or production worth doing in the first place?* Many critics think that anything that succeeds at giving pleasure and providing entertainment is as worthwhile in its own way as anything else, perhaps a more serious undertaking. Others, however, do not agree. Theatergoers such as yourself must make up their own minds.

If audience members are aware of these three criteria, they not only can note whether critics—in print, on television, or online—address these questions, but also can ask the questions for themselves.

THE DRAMATURG OR LITERARY MANAGER

Sometimes when we enter the theatre, we see in the theatre program an article or note written by theatre's dramaturg. The term **dramaturg** comes from a German word for "dramatic adviser." In Europe, the practice of having a dramaturg, or *literary manager,* attached to a theatre goes back well over a century. In the United States, the role of the dramaturg is relatively new; in recent years, however, many regional professional groups and other not-for-profit theatres have engaged full-time dramaturges. Among the duties frequently undertaken by dramaturges are discovering and reading promising new plays, working with playwrights on the development of new scripts, identifying significant plays from the past that may have been overlooked, conducting research on previous productions of classic plays, preparing reports on the history of plays, researching criticism and interpretations of plays from the past, and writing articles for the programs that are distributed when plays are produced.

Just as a good critic/reviewer can be helpful to audience members, so, too, can a perceptive dramaturg. He or she is usually the person who prepares educational material for students and teachers who attend performances. And if there is a discussion with audiences and members of the artistic team before or after a performance, the dramaturg often leads such a discussion.

> **Dramaturg** Also, literary manager. On the staff of a theatre, a person who consults with and advises authors and directors, writes program notes and edits scripts.

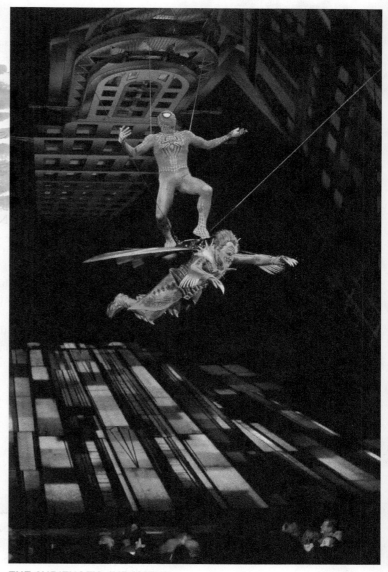

THE AUDIENCE'S RELATION TO CRITICISM

As suggested earlier, when we, as audience members, combine awareness of criticism with the theatre event itself, the experience can be greatly enhanced: background information and critical appraisals are added to our own firsthand reactions. There are cautionary notes, however, of which we should be aware.

The Audience's Independent Judgment

Quite often critic/reviewers state unequivocally that a certain play is extremely well written or badly written, beautifully performed or atrociously performed, and so on. Because these so-called authorities often speak so confidently and because their opinions

THE AUDIENCE'S JUDGMENT
Critics and reviewers can be enormously helpful to theatre audiences in providing background material, critical criteria, and other information. In the end, though, audiences should make up their own minds. A good example is the Broadway musical *Spider-Man: Turn Off the Dark,* which opened to negative reviews from critics, but has been a commercial success with audiences. (© Sara Krulwich/The New York Times/Redux)

PLAYING YOUR PART: THINKING ABOUT THEATRE

1. Think of a contemporary play or musical you have seen in which the characters and the story remind you of something you are familiar with in your own life. How did the knowledge of the real event help you to appreciate and understand what you saw on stage?

2. Imagine two friends viewing the same theatre production. One friend is captivated, feeling that what he or she saw was genuine and moving, a deeply affecting experience. The other friend was not moved and felt that the performance was artificial and inauthentic. Why do you think the same performance can elicit two such different reactions?

3. Make a list of all the places near your hometown or near your college where live theatre is presented. Have you ever attended a performance at one of these theatres? Describe the kind of physical theatre it is. Describe the experience; what was it like?

appear in print or on the Internet, their words have the ring of authority. But as theatergoers, we should reserve our own judgment and should certainly not be intimidated by this.

In certain large cities—New York, Chicago, Los Angeles, London, Paris—where a number of critics and reviewers in various media comment on each production, there is a wide range of opinion. It is not unusual for some critic/reviewers to find a certain play admirable, while others find the same play quite inferior, and still others find a mixture of good and bad. This implies that there is no absolute authority among such people, and that we should make up our own minds. If a critic/reviewer, for example, dislikes a certain play because he or she finds it too sentimental and you happen to like that kind of sentiment, you should not be dissuaded from your own preferences. Attending the theatre is a unique, individual experience—it is *your* experience—and you must trust and be guided by your own judgment.

SUMMARY

1. Each individual attending a theatre event brings to it a personal background of experience that becomes a vital ingredient in his or her response.

2. Theatre—like other arts—is closely linked to the society in which it is produced; it mirrors and reflects the attitudes, philosophy, and basic assumptions of its time.

3. Spectators attending a play written in their own day bring to it an awareness of their society's values and beliefs, and this background information forms an important part of the overall experience.

4. A play from the past can be better understood if the spectator is aware of the culture from which it came.

5. For any play that presents difficulties in language, style, or meaning, familiarity with the work itself can add immeasurably to a spectator's understanding and appreciation of a performance.

6. With an unfamiliar work, it is also helpful to learn about the playwright and his or her approach to theatre.

7. Expectations about the nature of the theatre experience affect our reaction to it. The various experiences in theatre today in the United States include Broadway and touring theatre; resident professional theatre; alternative theatre; young people's and children's theatre; college and university theatre; community and amateur theatre; and multiethnic, multicultural, global, and gender theatre.

8. Most people who attend theatre events are amateur critics, making judgments and drawing conclusions about what they see.

9. The professional critic has several tasks: to understand exactly what is being presented, including the intentions of the playwright and the director; to analyze the play, the acting, and the direction, as well as other elements such as scenery and lighting; to evaluate the presentation—was this worth doing? Does it serve a purpose?

10. People commenting on theatre can be divided into *reviewers,* who report briefly on a theatre event in newspapers, in magazines, or on television, and *critics,* who write longer articles analyzing in depth a performance or the work of a playwright.

11. The dramaturg or literary manager is a position that originated in Europe and is now found in many theatres in the United States, particularly not-for-profit theatres. The dramaturg analyzes scripts, advises directors, and works with playwrights on new dramas.

12. Audience members must realize that critics, too, have their limitations and prejudices and that ultimately each individual spectator must arrive at his or her own judgment regarding a theatre event.

Theatre Spaces: The Audience Views the Stage

When we attend the theatre, our experience begins in advance. Sometimes we read or hear reports of the play; we anticipate seeing a particular actress or actor; we buy tickets and make plans with friends to attend; and before the performance, we gather outside the theatre auditorium with other members of the audience.

CREATING THE ENVIRONMENT

When we arrive inside a theatre building for a performance, we immediately take in the environment in which the event will occur. When we move from the lobby into the theatre itself, the atmosphere inside has a great deal to do with our mood in approaching a performance, not only creating expectations about the event but conditioning the experience once it gets under way. As spectators, we have one feeling if we come into a formal setting, such as a picture-frame stage surrounded by carved gilt figures, with crystal chandeliers and red plush seats in the auditorium. We have quite a different feeling if we come into an old warehouse converted into a theatre, with bare brick walls, and a stage in the middle of the floor surrounded by folding chairs.

For many years people took the physical arrangement of theatres for granted. This was particularly true in the period when all houses were facsimiles of the Broadway theatre, with its proscenium, or picture-frame, stage. In the past half century, however, not only have people been exposed to other types of theatres; they have also become more aware of the importance of environment. Many experimental groups have deliberately made awareness of the environment a part of the experience.

An avant-garde production of Euripides's *The Bacchae*, called *Dionysus in 69*, by the Performance Group in New York, introduced the audience to the performance in a controlled manner. Spectators were not allowed into the theatre when they arrived but

◄ STAGE SPACES: AN OUTDOOR THRUST STAGE

The Allen Pavilion at the Oregon Shakespeare Festival is a 1,200-seat theatre with an Elizabethan thrust stage. With the audience on three sides, this is one of the oldest and most popular configurations for a theatre performance space. The production shown here is Shakespeare's Love's Labour's Lost, *directed by Kenneth Albers. (© T Charles Erickson)* were made to line up on the street outside. The procedure is outlined by Victoria Strang in a book describing the production.

> The audience begins to assemble at around 7:45 P.M. They line up on Wooster Street below Greenwich Village. Sometimes the line goes up the block almost to the corner of Broome. On rainy nights, or during the coldest parts of the winter, the audience waits upstairs over the theater. The theater is a large space, some 50 by 40 and 20 feet high. At 8:15 the performance begins for the audience when the stage manager, Vickie May Strang, makes the following announcement. Inside the performers begin warming up their voices and bodies at 7:45.
>
> Vickie: Ladies and gentlemen! May I have your attention, please. We are going to start letting you in now. You will be admitted to the theater one at a time, and if you're with someone you may be split up. But you can find each other again once you're inside. Take your time to explore the environment. It's a very interesting space, and there are all different kinds of places you can sit. We recommend going up high on the towers and platforms, or down underneath them. The password is "Go high or take cover." There is no smoking inside and no cameras. Thank you.[1]

In an interview included in the book, Strang gave her own view of this procedure.

> We let the public in one at a time. People on the queue outside the theater ask me why. I explain that this is a rite of initiation, a chance for each person to confront the environment alone, without comparing notes with friends. People are skeptical. Some few are angry. Many think it's a put-on. I must confess to a perverse pleasure in teasing people on a line. Many will come up and ask anxiously, "Has it already begun?" I say, "It begins before we let anybody in, but it begins when everybody is in, and really it begins when you go in." True.[2]

The feeling we have about the atmosphere of a theatre building as we enter it has always been an important element in the experience. In the past, spectators may not have been conscious of it, but they were affected by it nevertheless. Today, with the many varieties of theatre experience available to us, the first thing we should become aware of is the environment in which an event takes place: whether it is large or small, indoors or outdoors, formal or informal, familiar or unfamiliar.

At times scenic designers are able to alter the architecture of a theatre space to create a new arrangement or configuration. If the auditorium space is too large for a specific production, balconies might be blocked off, or the rear of the orchestra might be closed in some manner. Also, the decor can be altered: bright colors, banners, and bright lighting could create a festive atmosphere in a space that is ordinarily formal and subdued. The first things for us, as audience members, to note are general characteristics: Is the space formal or informal? Is it large or small? Next is the question of the configuration of stage and audience seating.

THEATRE SPACES

A consideration of environment leads directly to an examination of the various forms and styles of theatre buildings, including the arrangements of audience seating. Throughout theatre history, there have been five basic stage arrangements, each with its own advantages and disadvantages, each suited to certain types of plays and certain types of productions, and each providing the audience with a somewhat different experience. The five are (1) the *proscenium,* or picture-frame, stage; (2) the *arena,* or circle, stage; (3) the *thrust* stage with three-quarters seating;[3] (4) *created* and *found* stage spaces; and (5) all-purpose or *"black box"* theatre spaces, out of which a version of any one of the other four can be created.

Proscenium ("pro-SEEN-ee-um") Arch or frame surrounding the stage opening in a box or picture stage.

Arena Stage entirely surrounded by the audience; also known as *circle theatre* or *theatre-in-the-round.*

Thrust stage Stage space that thrusts into the audience space; a stage surrounded on three sides by audience seating.

Black box A theatre space that is open, flexible, and adaptable, usually without fixed seating. The stage-audience configuration can be rearranged to suit the individual requirements of a given production, making it both economical and particularly well suited to experimental work.

Fourth wall Convention, in a proscenium-arch theatre, that the audience is looking into a room through an invisible fourth wall.

Proscenium or Picture-Frame Stage: History and Characteristics

Perhaps the most familiar type of stage is the proscenium (pro-SEEN-ee-um), or picture-frame, stage. Broadway-style theatres, which for many years were models for theatres throughout the country, have proscenium stages.

The term *proscenium* comes from *proscenium arch*, the frame that separates the stage from the auditorium and that was first introduced in Italy during the Renaissance. Today this frame is not an arch but a rectangle. As the term *picture-frame stage* suggests, it resembles a large frame through which the audience looks at the stage. Another term for this type of stage is **fourth wall,** from the idea of the proscenium opening as a transparent glass wall through which the audience looks at the other three walls of a room.

Because the action takes place largely behind the proscenium opening, or frame, the seats in the auditorium all face in the same direction, toward the stage, just as seats in a movie theatre face the screen. The auditorium itself—the **house,** or **front of the house,** as it is called—is slanted downward from the back to the stage. (In theatre usage, the slant of an auditorium or stage floor is called a **rake**.) The stage is raised several feet above the auditorium floor, to aid visibility. There is usually a balcony (sometimes two balconies) protruding about halfway over the main floor. The main floor, incidentally, is called (in American usage) the **orchestra.** (In ancient Greek theatre, the orchestra was the circular acting area at the base of the hillside amphitheatre, but in modern usage it is the main floor of the theatre, where the audience sits.) In certain theatres, as well as concert halls and opera houses that have the proscenium arrangement, there are horseshoe-shaped tiers, or **boxes,** which ring the auditorium for several floors above the orchestra.

The popularity of the proscenium stage on Broadway and throughout the United States in the nineteenth century and the early twentieth century was partly due to its wide acceptance throughout Europe. Beginning in the late seventeenth century, the proscenium theatre was adopted in every European country. For the next two centuries in Europe both the mechanics of stage machinery and the artistry of scene painting improved steadily allowing designers to create extraordinary stage pictures.

An Italian, Giacomo Torelli (1608–1678), developed methods of moving scenery on and off stage felicitously, and throughout the eighteenth century, members of one family, the Bibiena family, dominated the art of scene painting. The Bibiena sets usually consisted of vast halls, palaces, or gardens with towering columns and arches that framed spacious corridors or hallways, which disappeared into an endless series of vistas as far as the eye could see. At times during this period, audiences, as well as scene designers and technicians, became so carried away with spectacle that the visual aspects were emphasized to the exclusion of everything else, including the script and the acting.

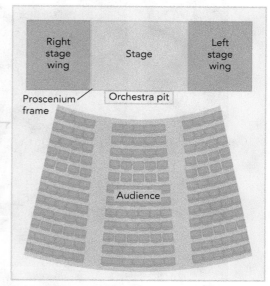

PROSCENIUM THEATRE
The audience faces in one direction, toward an enclosed stage encased by a picture-frame opening. Scene changes and performers' entrances and exits are made behind the proscenium opening, out of sight of the audience.

Front of the house
Portion of a theatre reserved for the audience; sometimes called simply the *house*.

Rake (1) To position scenery on a slant or at an angle other than parallel or perpendicular to the curtain line. (2) An upward slope of the stage floor away from the audience.

Orchestra (1) In American usage, ground-floor seating in an auditorium. (2) Circular playing space in ancient Greek theatres.

Box Small private compartment for a group of spectators built into the walls of a traditional proscenium-arch theatre.

THE PROSCENIUM THEATRE

The traditional proscenium theatre resembles a movie theatre in terms of audience seating: all the seats face in one direction, toward the stage. The frame of the stage is like a picture frame, and behind the frame are all the elements of the visual production such as scenery, painted drops, pieces that move across the stage, platforms, steps, perhaps the interior of a room or several rooms. The theatre shown here, the Bolton Theatre at the Cleveland Play House, is an excellent example of a proscenium theatre. It was redesigned by the architect Philip Johnson and renovated in 1983. (Photo by Paul Tepley, Courtesy of Cleveland Play House)

A MODERN PROSCENIUM-STAGE THEATRE

In this cutaway drawing we see the audience seating at the left, all facing in the one direction, toward the stage. Behind the orchestra pit in the center is the apron on the stage; and then the proscenium frame, behind which are the flats and other scenic elements. Overhead, scenery can be raised into the fly loft above the stage area.

A BIBIENA SET FOR A FORMAL PROSCENIUM THEATRE
The standard theatre throughout Europe and the United States from the eighteenth century to the early twentieth century was a formal proscenium space. The audience sat in a downstairs orchestra, in balconies, and in side boxes facing an ornate picture-frame stage. Impressive scenery and other visual effects were created and changed behind the curtain that covers the proscenium opening. In the eighteenth century, the Bibiena family from Italy created scene designs on a grand scale for such theatres throughout Europe. They painted backdrops with vistas that seemed to disappear into the far distance. This scene is by Giuseppe di Bibiena (1696–1757). (© Victoria and Albert Museum, London)

Although there have been many changes in theatre production, and today we have a wide variety of production approaches, we are still attracted to ingenious displays of visual effects in proscenium theatres. This is especially true of large musicals such as *The Phantom of the Opera*, *The Lion King*, *Wicked*, and *Cinderella*. Because the machinery and the workings of scene changes can be concealed behind a proscenium opening, this type of stage offers a perfect arrangement for spectacle.

There are other advantages to the proscenium stage. Realistic scenery—a living room, an office, a kitchen—looks good behind a proscenium frame; the scene designer can create the illusion of a genuine, complete room more easily with a proscenium stage than with any other. Also, the strong central focus provided by the frame rivets the attention of the audience. There are times, too, when we want the detachment, the distancing, that a proscenium provides.

THE PROSCENIUM THEATRE: IDEAL FOR SPECTACLE
For large-scale musicals the proscenium theatre is ideal. The scenery and other elements can be hidden above, behind, and around the stage, and then moved into the main stage area, as if by magic. In addition, the scale of the scenic effects can be extensive and sometimes electrifying. The scene shown here is from Rodgers & Hammerstein's *Cinderella,* directed by Mark Brokaw; choreography by Josh Rhodes; sets by Anna Louizos; costumes by William Ivey Long; lighting by Kenneth Posner. (© Sara Krulwich/The New York Times/Redux)

There are disadvantages as well, however. As we have seen, the proscenium stage creates a temptation to get carried away with visual pyrotechnics. In addition, a proscenium stage tends to be remote and formal. Some of us, as spectators, prefer the intimacy and informality—the experience of being close to the action—found in the arena and thrust theatres.

Arena Stage: History and Characteristics

To some of us, proscenium theatres, decorated in gold and red plush, look more like temples of art than theatres. We prefer a more informal, intimate theatre environment. A movement in this direction began in the United States just after

World War II, when a number of theatre practitioners decided to break away from the formality of proscenium theatres. This was part of an overall desire to bring many aspects of theatre closer to everyday life: acting styles, the subject matter of plays, the manner of presentation, and the shape of the theatre space. One form this reaction took was the *arena stage*—a return to one of the most ancient stage arrangements.

From as far back as we have records, we know that tribal ceremonies and rituals, in all parts of the world, have been held in some form of circle space. For example, many scholars believe that the ancient Greek theatre evolved from an arena form. In an arena theatre (also called *circle theatre* or *theatre-in-the-round*) there is a playing space in the center of a square or circle, with seats for spectators all around it. The arrangement is similar to that in sports arenas featuring boxing or basketball. The stage may be a raised area a few feet off the main floor, with seats rising from the floor level; or it may be on the floor itself, with seats raised on levels around it. When seating is close to the stage, there is usually some kind of demarcation indicating the boundaries of the playing area.

One advantage of the arena theatre is that it offers more intimacy than the ordinary proscenium. With the performers in the center, even in a larger theatre, we can be closer to them. If the same number of people attends an arena event and a proscenium event, at least half of those at the arena will be nearer the action: someone who would have been in the twelfth row in a proscenium theatre will be in the sixth row in an arena theatre. Besides, with this proximity to the stage, the arena theatre has another advantage: there is no frame or barrier to separate the performers from us.

Beyond these considerations, in the arena arrangement there is an unconscious communion, basic to human behavior, which comes when people form a circle—from the embrace of two of us to a circle for children's games to a larger gathering where we form an enclosure around a fire or an altar. It is no coincidence that virtually all of the earliest forms of theatre were "in the round."

A practical advantage of the arena theatre is economy. All you need for this kind of theatre is a large room: you designate a playing space, arrange rows of seats around the sides, and hang lights on pipes above, and you have a theatre. Elaborate scenery is impossible because it would block the view of large parts of the audience. A few pieces of furniture, with perhaps a lamp or sign hung from the ceiling, are all you need to indicate where a scene takes place. Many low-budget groups have found that they can build a workable and even attractive theatre-in-the-round when a proscenium theatre would be out of the question. These two factors—intimacy and economy—no doubt explain why arena theatre is one of the oldest stage forms, as well as one still very much in use today.

In spite of its long history, however, and its resurgence in recent years, the arena stage has often been eclipsed by other forms. One reason is that its design, while allowing for intimacy, also dictates a certain austerity. As we noted before, it is impossible to have elaborate scenery because that would block the view of many spectators. Also, the performers must make all their entrances and exits along aisles that run through the audience, and they can sometimes be seen before and after they are supposed to appear onstage. The arena's lack of adaptability in this respect may explain why some of the circle theatres that opened twenty or thirty years ago

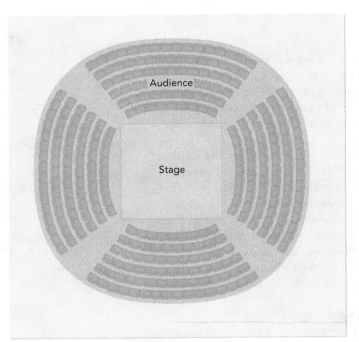

PLAN OF AN ARENA STAGE
The audience sits on four sides or in a circle surrounding the stage. Entrances and exits are made through the aisles or through tunnels underneath the aisles. A feeling of intimacy is achieved because the audience is close to the action and encloses it.

Stage House   Stage floor and the space around it to the side walls, as well as the space above it up to the grid.

have since closed. A number survive, however, and continue to do well. One of the best-known is the Arena Stage in Washington, D.C. In addition, throughout this country there are a number of *tent theatres* in arena form where musical revivals and concerts are given.

Thrust Stage: History and Characteristics

Falling between the proscenium and the arena is a third type of theatre: the *thrust stage* with three-quarters seating. In one form or another, this U-shape arrangement has been the most widely used of all stage spaces. In the basic arrangement for this type of theatre, we sit on three sides, or in a semi-circle, enclosing a stage, which protrudes into the center. At the back of the playing area is some form of **stage house** providing for the entrances and exits of the performers as well as for scene changes. The thrust stage combines some of the best features of the other two stage types: the sense of intimacy and the "wraparound" feeling of the arena, and the focused stage placed against a single background found in the proscenium.

The thrust stage was developed by the classical Greeks for their tragedies and comedies. They adapted the circle used for tribal rituals and other ceremonies—

THE STAGE AND SEATING IN AN ARENA THEATRE
The arena theatre attempts to capture the immediacy of primitive theatre. It uses the barest essentials of stage scenery but the full resources of contemporary stage lighting.

ARENA STAGE
With an arena stage, also referred to as a circle stage or theatre-in-the-round, the audience surrounds the stage area on all sides. In addition to aisles for audience members to enter, there are passages that the performers use to enter and leave the stage. One effect of the arena stage is to create a close rapport between actors and audience. Seen here is the newly renovated Fichandler Stage at the Arena Stage in Washington, D.C. (Photo by Nic Lehoux courtesy of Bing Thom Architects.)

the circle called the *orchestra*—by locating it at the base of a curving hillside. The slope of the hill formed a natural amphitheatre for the spectators. At the rear of the orchestra circle, opposite the hillside, was placed a stage house, which had formal doors through which characters made their entrances and exits and served as a background for the action. The stage house also provided a place for the actors to change their costumes. The largest Greek theatres seated 15,000 or more spectators. While they were originally wooden structures in the classical Greek era, their design was duplicated in stone structures all over Greece in the following two centuries. Remnants of these stone theatres remain today throughout that part of the world, in such places as Epidaurus, Priene, Ephesus, Delphi, and Corinth, to name a few.

The Romans, who took the Greek form and built it as a complete freestanding structure, had a theatre that was not strictly a thrust stage but a forerunner of the proscenium. Instead of using the natural amphitheatre of a hillside, they constructed a stone building, joining the stage house to the seating area and making the orchestra a semicircle. In front of the stage house, decorated with arches and statues, they erected a long platform stage where most of the action occurred.

Another example of the thrust stage is found in the medieval period, when short religious plays began to be presented in churches and cathedrals in England and parts of continental Europe. Around 1200 CE, performances of these religious plays were

AN ORIGINAL THRUST STAGE: THE GREEK AMPHITHEATRE
An original prototype of the thrust stage was the amphitheatre in ancient Greece. Shown here is the theatre at Epidauros, Greece. The seating surrounds the playing area on three sides. Acting took place on the raised platform at the back, but also in the circular area that is thrust into the audience. Among many other remarkable traits of these theatres are the incredible view of the mountains in the distance and the amazing acoustics of the theatre. A person in the back, top row can hear an actor speaking without any artificial amplification. (© Jose Fuste Raga/Corbis)

Platform stage Elevated stage with no proscenium, sometimes called a *trestle stage*.

moved outdoors. One popular arrangement for these outdoor performances was the ***platform stage.*** A simple platform was set on trestles (it was sometimes called a *trestle stage*), with a curtain at the back, which the performers used for entrances and costume changes. The area underneath the stage was closed off and provided, among other things, a space from which devils and other characters could appear, sometimes in a

THRUST STAGE WITH THREE-QUARTERS SEATING
The stage is surrounded on three sides by the audience. Sometimes seating is a semicircle. Entrances and exits are made from the sides and backstage. Spectators surround the action, but scene changes and other stage effects are still possible.

THE CLASSIC
SPANISH STAGE
A variation on the thrust
stage used in Elizabethan
England is the Spanish
corral. A version of this
stage, uncovered by
accident in 1953, is shown
here in Almagro, Spain,
where a theatre festival is
held each year. Not strictly
speaking a thrust stage, it
has all the other
components of a
Renaissance outdoor
theatre, with the platform
stage and audience seating
in boxes or a balcony
around three sides.
(Courtesy Festival d'Almagro)

cloud of smoke. In some places the platform was on wheels (a **_wagon stage_**) and was moved from place to place through a town. The audience stood on three sides of the platform, making it an improvised thrust stage. This type of stage was widely used from the thirteenth to the fifteenth centuries in England and various parts of Europe.

The next step following the wagon stage was a thrust stage that appeared in England in the sixteenth century, just before Shakespeare began writing for the theatre. A platform stage would be set up at one end of the open courtyard of an inn. The inns of this period were three or four stories high, and the rooms facing the inner courtyard served as boxes from which spectators could watch the performance. On the ground level, spectators stood on three sides of the stage. The fourth side of the courtyard, behind the platform, served as the stage house. An interesting coincidence is that an almost identical theatre took shape in Spain at the same time. The inns in Spain were called **_corrales,_** and this name was given to the theatres that developed there.

The formal English theatres of Shakespeare's day, such as the Globe and the Fortune, were similar to the inn theatres: the audience stood in an open area around a platform stage, and three levels of spectators sat in closed galleries at the back and sides. A roof covered part of the stage; at the back of the stage, some form of raised area served for balcony scenes (as in *Romeo and Juliet*). At the rear of the stage, also, scenes could be concealed and then "discovered." On each side at the rear was a door used for entrances and exits.

These theatres were fascinating combinations of diverse elements: they were both indoors and outdoors; some spectators stood while others sat; and the audience was composed of almost all levels of society. The physical environment must have been stimulating: performers standing at the front of the thrust stage were in the center of a hemisphere of spectators, on three sides around them as well as above and below. These theatres held 2,000 to 3,000 spectators, but no one in the audience was more than 60 feet or so from

Wagon stage   Low
platform mounted on
wheels or casters by means
of which scenery is moved
on- and offstage.

Corral   Theatre building of
the Spanish golden age,
usually located in the
courtyard of a series of
adjoining buildings.

AN ELIZABETHAN PLAYHOUSE
This drawing shows the kind of stage on which the plays of Shakespeare and his contemporaries were first presented. A platform stage juts into an open courtyard, with spectators standing on three sides. Three levels of enclosed seats rise above the courtyard. There are doors at the rear of the stage for entrances and exits and an upper level for balcony scenes.

the stage, and most people were much closer. Being in the midst of so many people, enclosed on all sides but with the open sky above, must have instilled a feeling of great communion among audiences and performers. Something of the same feeling can be recaptured when one visits the recently reconstructed Globe Theatre in London.

Shortly after Shakespeare's day, in the latter part of the seventeenth century, there were two significant theatrical developments in England, in Spain, and throughout Europe: (1) the theatre moved almost completely indoors; and (2) the stage began a slow but steady retreat behind the proscenium opening, partly because performances were indoors, but more because the style of theatres changed. For more than two centuries the thrust stage was in eclipse, not to reappear until about 1900, when a few theatres in England began using a version of the thrust stage to produce Shakespeare. The return of the thrust stage resulted from a growing realization that Elizabethan plays could be done best on a stage similar to the one for which they had been written.

THE STAGE AND SEATING AREA OF A THRUST-STAGE THEATRE
This cutaway drawing of a thrust stage shows how the playing area juts into the audience, which surrounds the stage on three sides. This configuration affords intimacy, but at the back (shown here at the right) is an area that furnishes a natural backdrop for the action.

In the United States and Canada, though, it was not until the mid-twentieth century that the thrust stage came to the fore again. Since then a number of fine theatres of this type have been built, including the Guthrie in Minneapolis; the Shakespeare Theater in Stratford, Ontario; the Mark Taper Forum in Los Angeles; and the Long Wharf in New Haven.

We should also note that the basic stage of traditional Chinese and Japanese drama (including no theatre in Japan) is a form of thrust stage: a raised, open platform stage frequently covered by a roof, with the audience sitting on two or three sides around the platform. Entrances and exits are made from doors or ramps at the rear of the stage.

The obvious advantages of the thrust stage—the intimacy of three-quarters seating and the close audience-performer relationship, together with the fact that so many of the world's great dramatic works were written for it—give it a significant place alongside the other major forms.

Created and Found Spaces

After World War II a number of avant-garde theatre artists, such as the Polish director Jerzy Grotowski (1933–1999), undertook to reform theatre at every level. Since the various elements of theatre are inextricably bound together, their search for a more

PLAYING YOUR PART: EXPERIENCING THEATRE

1. Rearrange your classroom seating into proscenium, arena, and thrust configurations. Read a speech aloud from a play or a paragraph from a novel to the class in each of these configurations. How is your presentation affected by the arrangement of the space?

2. Visit a gym or sports arena on your campus. What is the configuration of the space? How does it relate to a theatre environment? What type of popular entertainment might be staged there?

3. Find an outdoor space on your campus that might be used for theatre. What type of presentation would you stage there? Why?

A MODERN THRUST STAGE

The thrust stage, with a stage area extending into audience seating that surrounds it on three sides, is one of the oldest arrangements, having been used by the Greeks and by the Elizabethans in the time of Shakespeare. It has been revived successfully in the modern period and is widely used in Europe and the United States. A good example is the recently renovated Mark Taper Forum in Los Angeles. (© Craig Schwartz/Center Theatre Group, Ahmanson Theatre)

basic kind of theatre included a close look at the physical arrangement of the playing area and its relationship to the audience.

The Performance Group, which led spectators one at a time into the production of *Dionysus in 69* (as described earlier in this chapter), is typical in this regard. It presented its productions in a large garage converted into an open theatre space. At various places in the garage, scaffolding and ledges were built for audience seating. The Performance

SITE-SPECIFIC THEATRE CREATED AND FOUND SPACE Shown here are two examples of site-specific theatre. In the first, a production loosely based on *Macbeth*, entitled *Sleep No More* by the British group Punchdrunk, was presented in three abandoned warehouses in New York City through which the audience was led to see various segments, some of which involved movement, some of which were like tableaus. In the scene here, the Macbeth character (Nicholas Bruder) is seen in a bathtub, with the Lady Macbeth character (Sophie Bortolussi) outside the tub. (© Sara Krulwich/The New York Times/Redux) The second example shows the Polish theatre company Biuro Podrozy in a production of *Macbeth*, using its trademark stilts on a street, at the Edinburgh Fringe Festival in Edinburgh, Scotland. (© Jeff J Mitchell/Getty Images)

Group, like other modern avant-garde companies, owed a great debt to a Frenchman, Antonin Artaud (1896–1948), one of the first theatre people to examine in depth the questions raised by the avant-garde. An actor and director who wrote a series of articles and essays about theatre, Artaud was brilliant but inconsistent (he spent several periods of his life in mental institutions). Many of Artaud's ideas, however, were to prove prophetic: notions he put forward in the 1920s and 1930s, considered impossible or impractical at the time, have since become common practice among experimental theatre groups. Among his proposals was one on the physical theatre:

> We abolish the stage and auditorium and replace them by a single site, without partition or barrier of any kind, which will become the theater of the action. A direct communication will be reestablished between the spectator and the spectacle, between the actor and the spectator, from the fact that the spectator, placed in the middle of the action, is engulfed and physically affected by it. This envelopment results, in part, from the very configuration of the room itself. Thus, abandoning the architecture of present-day theaters, we shall take some hangar or barn which we shall have reconstructed according to processes which have culminated in the architecture of certain churches or holy places, and of certain temples in Tibet.[4]

Some of Artaud's ideas were put into practice when the movement to explore new concepts became widespread. In the generation after Artaud, Jerzy Grotowski included the physical arrangements of stage space in his experiments. Not only Grotowski but others in the avant-garde movement developed theatre space in a variety of ways.

Nontheatre Buildings   Artaud mentioned a barn or hangar for performances. In recent years virtually all kinds of structures have been used: lofts, warehouses, fire stations, basements, churches, breweries, and gymnasiums. This practice should not be confused with the conversion of unusual spaces to full-scale theatres, which has numerous precedents in the past; historically, indoor tennis courts, palace ballrooms, and monastery dining halls have been converted into theatres. We are, instead, describing here the use of nontheatre structures as they are, with their original architectural elements intact, and carving out special areas for acting and viewing—as with the garage used by the Performance Group. In our contemporary theatre, site-specific companies are theatre groups that create productions for specific nontheatre locations. For example, the English company Punchdrunk staged *Sleep No More,* an adaptation of Shakespeare's *Macbeth,* in three abandoned warehouses in Manhattan with the audiences moving through various spaces created in them.

Adapted Spaces   One frequent practice was using or creating a space to fit a play, rather than (as is normally the case) making the play fit the space. Grotowski, in particular, pursued the notion of finding a different, appropriate configuration for each production. In Grotowski's production of the Doctor Faustus story, for example, the theatre was filled with two long tables at which spectators sat as if they were guests at a banquet hosted by Faustus. The action took place at the heads of the tables and even on the tabletops. For his production of *The Constant Prince,* a fence was built around the playing area, and the audience sat behind the fence, looking over it like spectators at a bullfight. In recent decades there have been similar attempts to deal with theatre spaces in many parts of Europe and the United States.

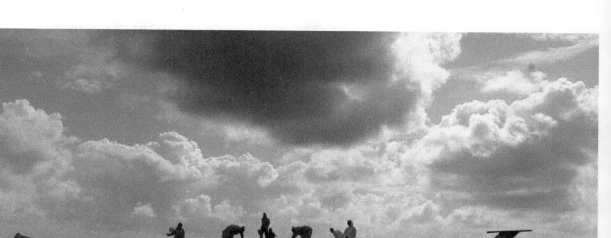

AN ISLAND FOR SITE-SPECIFIC THEATRE
In the Netherlands there is a festival, known as the Oerol Festival, in which for ten days in June an entire island, Terschelling, is used by a variety of theatre companies to present their pieces. Groups set up in all kinds of places on the island—taverns, barns, tents, and garages, and on beaches—to offer their productions. Shown here on a beach is a production entitled *Salted,* written and directed by Judith de Rijke and produced by Tryater of Holland, which brought together young artists from various regions to celebrate the linguistic diversity of Europe. (© Sake Elzinga)

Street Theatre   One development—which was actually a return to practices in medieval Europe—is theatre held outdoors in nontraditional settings. A good example is *street theatre.* Generally, street theatre is of three types: (1) plays from the standard repertoire presented in the streets; (2) *neighborhood theatre,* in which an original play deals with problems and aspirations of a specific population of a city, such as Puerto Ricans, African Americans, or Italians; and (3) *guerrilla theatre,* aggressive, politically oriented theatre produced by an activist group in the streets in an attempt to persuade us to become more politically involved, such as street presentations during the Occupy Wall Street movement in 2012. Whatever the form, the important point for our purposes is that these productions take place not in theatre buildings but in places like parks, hospitals, jails, and bus stations.

In these productions, theatre is brought to those of us who might not otherwise see it. Also, audiences in such unusual settings are challenged to rethink what theatre is all about. On the other hand, there are inherent disadvantages to impromptu productions in the streets or other "found spaces": the audience must be caught on the run, and there is rarely time for more than a sketch or vignette. Nor are there facilities for presenting a fully developed work—but often that is not the purpose of these undertakings in the first place.

Multifocus Environments   An approach that sometimes accompanies these unusual arrangements is *multifocus theatre.* In simple terms, this means not only that there is more than one playing area, such as the four corners of the room (as

Artaud suggested in one article), but also that something is going on in several of them simultaneously. This is somewhat like a three-ring circus, where we see an activity in each ring and must either concentrate on one or divide our attention among two or three.

There are several theories behind the idea of multifocus theatre. One is that a multifocus event is more like everyday life; if you stand on a street corner, there is activity all around you—in the four directions of the streets, in the buildings above—not just in one spot. You select which area you will observe, or perhaps you watch several areas at one time. The argument is that in theatre, you should have the same choice. In multifocus productions no single space or activity is supposed to be more important than any other. We either take in several impressions at once and synthesize them in our own mind or select one item as most arresting and concentrate on that. There is no

THE MULTIPURPOSE OR "BLACK BOX" THEATRE
A popular type of modern theatre is the multipurpose space, sometimes called a "black box." It consists of an open space with perhaps a pipe grid on the ceiling from which lighting and sound instruments can be suspended. A stage platform can be positioned at any place in the space, and movable chairs for spectators can be placed around the playing area. The diagrams suggest some of the possibilities of stage arrangements in a multipurpose theatre.

DYNAMICS OF DRAMA

Popular Performance Spaces

Many spaces used for live popular entertainments are reminiscent of theatre environments. Arenas used for sports, circuses, and rock concerts are configured much like theatrical spaces discussed in this chapter. Madison Square Garden in New York, Soldier Field in Chicago, the Rose Bowl in Pasadena, California, and university sports arenas are all large spaces that primarily house sporting events but are also used for rock concerts and other popular spectacles. Madison Square Garden, for example, has housed circuses, elaborate rock concerts, and music award ceremonies. This means that an arena like the Garden is often equipped with the most innovative technology for lighting, stage, and sound effects.

Spectacular performance spaces for magicians, circuses, concerts, and stage extravaganzas are found in all of the major hotels in Las Vegas. There is live entertainment also presented in fairgrounds and amusement parks across our country.

These spaces for popular performances are most often configured in the round, with spectators surrounding the events. Some are configured three-quarters round. The reason is to maximize the number of audience members as well as to create an electrifying interactive entertainment. With these configurations, we, as spectators, are also able to watch and possibly influence each other's reactions.

Such popular performance spaces are usually extremely large, much larger than environments created exclusively for theatre. For example, the Rose Bowl accommodates over 90,000 fans for football games. Even a comparatively small collegiate athletic facility, Western Hall on the Western Illinois University campus, can accommodate approximately 5,000 spectators.

The relationship between spaces for popular entertainments and theatrical environments is complex. Throughout theatre history, the same spaces were used for popular arts and for theatrical performances. Modern theatre artists have experimented with staging dramatic performances within spaces created for concerts and circuses.

For that matter, the performance qualities of sports, the circus, and rock concerts underscore their shared heritage with the theatrical arts. It is not surprising, then, that their spaces are also similar and often multipurpose.

such thing as the "best seat in the house"; all seats are equally good, because the activity in all parts of the theatre is equally important. Sometimes multifocus theatre is joined with *multimedia theatre*—presentations that offer some combination of acting, films, video, dance, music, slides, and light show.

All-Purpose Theatre Spaces: The Black Box

Because of the interest in a variety of spaces in modern theatre production, and the requirements of many different kinds of productions, a number of theatre complexes, including many college theatre departments, have built spaces that can be adapted to an almost infinite variety of configurations. Seats, lights, platforms, levels—every aspect of such a theatre is flexible and movable.

PLAYING YOUR PART: THINKING ABOUT THEATRE

1. As discussed in this chapter, there are four major types of stage spaces: proscenium, arena, thrust, and found space. What do you think are the advantages and disadvantages of each? On which type of stage space would you prefer to watch a performance?

2. Using information from this chapter, explain which type of stage space you would feel is best suited for the following productions: a large-scale musical, an intimate personal drama, a Shakespearean drama, and a play of political protest.

3. The size of theatre spaces can range from fewer than 100 spectators to more than 3,000. What do you consider an ideal-sized theatre for the following types of productions: a musical, a Shakespearean play, a modern family drama? Suggest the ideal number of audience seats for each and the shape and size of the ideal stage space for each.

In this kind of space the designers can create a proscenium, a thrust, an arena, or some combination of these, but the designers can also create corner stages, island stages, and multifocus arrangements with playing areas in several parts of the studio. This space is sometimes referred to as a *black box* because it is often an empty rectangular space into which various audience seating and stage arrangements can be introduced.

SPECIAL REQUIREMENTS OF THEATRE ENVIRONMENTS

Simply assigning a theatre to a category does not adequately describe the environment; we must also take into account a number of other variables. Two theatres may be of the same type and still be quite different in size, atmosphere, and setting. The experience in a small off-off-Broadway-type thrust theatre will be far different from that in a thrust theatre several times larger, such as the Guthrie in Minneapolis. Also, one theatre may be indoors and another of the same type outdoors.

There are other factors that architects, producers, and designers must take into account, one of which is the human scale. No matter what the configuration, the performer is the basic scale by which everything is measured in theatre. Theatre architects as well as scenic and lighting designers must always keep this in mind, and we should be aware of it as well. When the theatre environment and the stage space violate this human scale in some way, problems are created for performers and us.

There is also the question of appropriateness. By *appropriateness* we mean the relationship of a stage space to a play or production. A large-scale musical requires a full stage—usually a proscenium stage—and a large auditorium from which we can get the full effect of the spectacle. However, an intimate, small cast family drama with its intense personal confrontations might require a small playing area so that we are close enough to the action to make a connection with the characters onstage.

Rather than being limited to one type of building and one type of stage, we are fortunate today in having a full range of environments in which to experience theatre. Taken all in all, whether single-focus or multifocus, indoors or outdoors, the recent innovations in theatre milieus have added new alternatives, rich in possibilities, to the traditional settings for theatrical productions. They have also called attention to the importance of environment in our total theatre experience.

SUMMARY

1. The atmosphere and environment of the theatre space play a large part in setting the tone of an event.

2. Experimental theatre groups in recent years have deliberately made spectators aware of the environment.

3. Throughout theatre history there have been five basic stage and auditorium arrangements: proscenium, arena, thrust, created or found space, and all-purpose or "black box" spaces.

4. The proscenium theatre features a picture-frame stage, in which the audience faces directly toward the stage and looks through the proscenium opening at the "picture." The proscenium stage aids illusion: placing a room of a house behind the proscenium, for example, allows the scene designer to create an extremely realistic set. This type of stage also allows elaborate scene shifts and visual displays because it generally has a large backstage area and a fly loft. It also creates a distancing effect, which works to the advantage of certain types of drama. At the same time, however, the proscenium frame sets up a barrier between the performers and the audience.

5. The arena or circle stage places the playing area in the center with the audience seated in a circle or square around it. This offers an economical way to produce theatre and an opportunity for great intimacy between performers and spectators, but it cannot offer full visual displays in terms of scenery and scene changes.

6. The thrust stage with three-quarters seating is a platform stage with seating on three sides. Entrances and exits are made at the rear, and there is an opportunity for a certain amount of scenery. This form combines some of the scenic features of the proscenium theatre with the intimacy of the arena stage.

7. Created or found space takes several forms: use of nontheatre buildings, adaptation of a given space to fit individual productions, use of outdoor settings, street theatre, multifocus environments, and all-purpose spaces.

8. The theatre space referred to as a *black box* is an open, adaptable space that can be configured into a variety of stage-audience arrangements, providing for maximum flexibility and economy.

9. Size and location (indoors or outdoors, etc.), along with the shape and character of a theatre building, affect the environment.

The Performers and the Director

2

The Performers and the Director

THE PERFORMERS TAKE THE STAGE

Actors and actresses are at the heart of theatre. They embody the characters as well as projecting the story and language of the play. Seen here is the cast in a scene from the comedy, *Charley's Aunt*, by Brandon Thomas, directed by John Miller-Stephany at the Guthrie Theater.
(© T Charles Erickson)

66

4 Acting

5 The Director and
the Producer

Part Two

The Performers and the Director

Performers, by their presence, set theatre apart from films, television, and the visual arts; they serve as the direct, immediate contact that we, as members of the audience, have with theatre. More than that, performers embody the heart and soul of theatre. The words of a script, the characters created by a dramatist, and the scenery and costumes come to life only when an actor or actress steps onto a stage.

Acting, however, is not confined to theatre. Of course, there is acting on film and television. But there are also many forms of "acting" in our daily lives. Most of us might be surprised to learn that acting is almost as old as the human race. From the earliest days of civilization, people have mimicked other people and have told stories, imitating the voices and gestures of the characters in those stories. There have also

been rituals and ceremonies in which the celebrants wore costumes and performed assigned roles—one example is the person officiating in a religious service.

Another familiar type of "acting" in daily life is imitation. A good example is the attempt by individuals to copy the lifestyle of a hero—a singer, a film actor, or some other well-known personality. The imitator adopts the same

Religious celebrations, such as the Jewish bar mitzvah—shown here at the Western Wall in Jerusalem—have many things in common with theatre. (© Richard T. Nowitz/Corbis)

Virtually all types of ceremonies and performance worldwide—ancient and modern, religious and secular—have theatrical elements. Here, in Mali, west Africa, teetering on stilts high above a crowd of villagers, masked Dogon dancers imitate a long-legged waterbird. (© Charles & Josette Lenars/Corbis)

wardrobe, the same stance, the same physical movements, and the same hairstyle as the hero or heroine. Another form of imitation is mimicry. Someone who tells a story or recounts an event copies the voices and gestures of the persons being described. A second type of "acting" prevalent in our daily lives is role playing. Much has been written about role playing in recent years, and a currently popular term is *role model,* referring to people whose lives, or "roles," serve as models or guides for others.

On the less admirable side, how often have we had a behind-the-scenes revelation of the behavior of a politician, a movie star, or a corporate executive just before the person is to appear at a press conference? Sometimes the person is scowling, peppering his or her language with profanity and invective, speaking

sharply to assistants. Then, suddenly, when the person moves before the television cameras, he or she breaks into a smile and takes on the persona of someone who is affable, pleasant, and charming. In a public appearance, the person is playing a "role." Looked at from a different perspective, in the age of the Internet, of Facebook, Twitter, and YouTube, a certain kind of acting in everyday life has become commonplace. As George Vecsey, a columnist for the *New York Times,* has written, "In the YouTube era, everybody under a certain age is a performer."

We have been speaking of "acting" in everyday life. When we turn

to acting for the stage, we will observe that for all the similarities, there are significant, even crucial, differences between imitation or role playing in daily life and the acting that takes place onstage. For one thing, everyone concerned—audiences as well as those onstage—will recognize that it is a performance. It is a conscious act that requires not only talent but a tremendous amount of training and discipline. In Part Two, we will look at the art and craft of theatrical performance. We will also look at the role of a person who works most closely with actors: the director.

Imitation and role playing are two types of acting in which everyone participates, even the very young.

(© Art Montes De Oca/Getty Images)

PERFORMING IN EVERYDAY LIFE
Many activities not usually thought of as theatre are theatrical in nature. Here, drum major Bill Pierpont, in costume, leads a Memorial Day parade at Shelton, Connecticut. (© Peter Hvizdak/The Image Works)

70

4

Acting

At the heart of the theatre experience is the partnership between actors and the audience. We in the audience observe the performers on stage: their gestures, their movements. And we listen to their words. Actors, in turn, are acutely aware of us in the audience: our presence, our reactions and responses. Previously we have focused on the role of the audience at a performance; in this chapter we examine the art and craft of acting for the stage. Before we turn to the stage actor, however, we should take note of another type of performance in which we are all participants: acting in everyday life.

ACTING IN EVERYDAY LIFE

Two examples of acting in daily life are imitation and role playing. The first of these, *imitation,* is found on all levels of society and at all ages. Children, for example, are among the best imitators in the world, and we are often amused by a child who imitates a parent or some other grown-up: a four-year-old girl, for instance, who puts on a long dress, makeup, and high heels. As we grow older, imitation continues to be a part of our experience: in every class in school, from elementary school through college, there is usually one person—a clever mimic—who imitates the teacher or the principal with great humor, and sometimes with cruelty.

The second type of acting in everyday life we mentioned is *role playing,* which can generally be divided into two categories: social and personal.

Imitation   To simulate or copy behavior observed in real life.

Social Roles

Social roles are general roles recognized by society: father, mother, child, police officer, store clerk, teacher, student, business executive, physician, and so on. Every culture expects certain types of behavior from people who are assigned specific social roles, sometimes resulting in stereotyping or oppressing those individuals. For many years in western culture, for example, the roles of women as secretaries, teachers, or housewives

Role playing   In everyday life, the acting out of a particular role by copying the expected social behavior of that position.

◀ **STAGE ACTING**

To play a character convincingly, an actor must develop both outer techniques and inner emotional resources. This is true whether performing in a classical play or a modern, realistic play. Shown here in a production at the ART in Boston is Cherry Jones as Amanda Wingfield, the possessive mother in The Glass Menagerie *by Tennessee Williams. In her performance, Jones must convey not only the feelings and emotions of her character, but also the movements, gestures, and vocal qualities of this older Southern lady living in the past. Celia Keenan-Bolger plays the painfully shy daughter, Laura. (© Michael J. Lutch)*

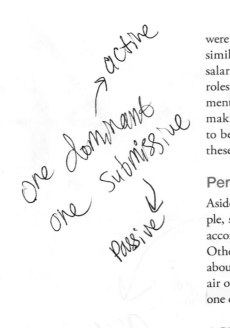

were considered subordinate to the roles of men. Even today when women hold positions similar to those of men in business and the professions, they frequently receive a lower salary for the same job. The women's movement challenged the notion of subservient roles for women. So entrenched was the idea, however, that it took an entire movement to call it into question. (One aspect of this movement was *consciousness raising:* making people aware of social attitudes toward women.) Before changes could begin to be made in the subordinate roles women played, everyone had to understand that these *were* roles and were clearly unacceptable.

Personal Roles

Aside from social roles, we develop personal roles with our family and friends. For example, some people become braggarts, boasting of their (sometimes imaginary) feats and accomplishments and embellishing the truth to appear more impressive than they are. Others become martyrs, constantly sacrificing for others and letting the world know about it. Still others are conspirators, people who pull their friends aside to establish an air of secrecy whenever they talk. Frequently, two people fall into complementary roles: one dominant and the other submissive, one active and the other passive.

ACTING IN LIFE VERSUS ACTING ON STAGE

Some of the differences between stage acting and acting in daily life are obvious. For one thing, actors and actresses onstage are always being observed. In real life there may be observers, but their presence is not essential to an event. Bystanders on a street corner where an accident has occurred form a kind of audience, but their presence is incidental and unrelated to the accident itself. Onstage, however, the performer is always on display and often in the spotlight.

Acting onstage, too, requires a performer to play roles he or she does not play in life. A scene between a father and his son arguing about money, or between a young husband and wife discussing whether or not to have children, is one thing when it is actually occurring in our lives, but something quite different onstage. Generally, the roles we play in life are genuine. A father who accepts his responsibilities toward his children does not just play a father; he *is* a father. A woman who writes novels does not just play a novelist; she *is* one.

In real life, a lawyer knows the law; but onstage, an actor playing the role of a lawyer may not know the difference between jurisprudence and habeas corpus, and probably has never been inside a law school. Playing widely divergent parts or parts outside their personal experience requires actors and actresses to stretch their imagination and ability. For example, a young actress at one time or another might be called on to play parts as dissimilar as the fiery, independent heroine in Sophocles's *Antigone;* the vulnerable, love-struck heroine in Shakespeare's *Romeo and Juliet;* and the neurotic, obsessed heroine in Strindberg's *Miss Julie.* Beyond playing different roles at different times, performers are even called on at times to *double,* that is, perform several parts in one play.

Another significant difference between acting for the stage and "acting" in life is that dramatic characters are not real people. Any stage character—Joan of Arc, Antigone, Oedipus, Hamlet, Willy Loman—is a symbol or an image of a person. Stage characters are fictions created by dramatists and performers to represent people. They remind us of people—in many cases they seem to *be* these people, but they are not. The task of

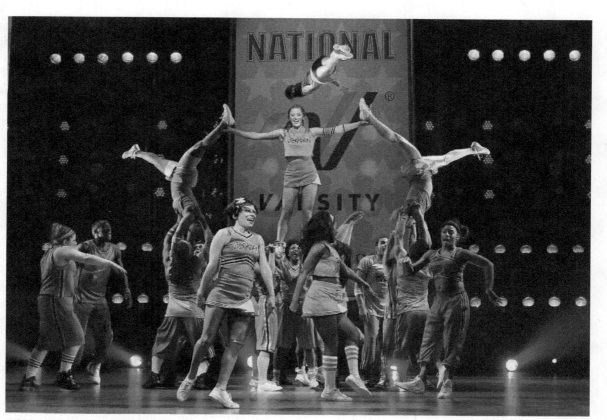

REAL-LIFE ROLES SEEN ONSTAGE
Roles onstage are often similar to roles people are called on to play in real life. Cheerleaders at athletic events are a good example. Here we see a scene from *Bring It On: The Musical,* about rival high school cheerleading squads. (© Sara Krulwich/The New York Times/Redux)

the performer in attempting to make the characters onstage *appear* to be real requires not only talent but training and discipline as well.

THREE CHALLENGES OF ACTING

Throughout theatre history, three main challenges have faced an actor or actress:

1. To make characters believable—inner truth.
2. Physical acting—the use of the voice and body.
3. Synthesis and integration—combining inner and outer skills.

   To understand the first two aspects of acting, we will examine them separately. We begin with making characters believable and then turn to the craft of acting—specific physical and vocal techniques required in performance.

Making Characters Believable

One major aspect of the craft of acting is credibility: the ability to make those of us in the audience believe in the characters that appear onstage, to make their characters convincing.

The Development of Realistic Acting

Realism Broadly, an attempt to present onstage people and events corresponding to those in everyday life.

The Development of Realistic Acting   From the mid-seventeenth century on, serious attempts were made to define the craft or technique of credible, natural acting. Such an approach became more important than ever at the end of the nineteenth century, when drama began to depict characters and situations close to everyday life. Three playwrights—Henrik Ibsen of Norway, August Strindberg of Sweden, and Anton Chekhov of Russia—perfected a type of drama that came to be known as *realism*. This drama was called realistic because it closely resembled what people could identify with and verify from their own experience. In performing plays by these dramatists, not only the spirit of the individual dramatic characters but also the details of their behavior had to conform to what people saw of life around them.

The Stanislavski System: A Technique for Realistic Acting   Before the realistic drama of the late 1800s, individual actresses and actors, through their own talent and genius, had achieved believability onstage, but no one had developed a system whereby it could be taught to others and passed on to future generations. The person who eventually did this most successfully was the Russian actor and director Konstantin Stanislavski. A cofounder of the Moscow Art Theater in Russia and the director of Anton Chekhov's most important plays, Stanislavski was also an actor. By closely observing the work of great performers of his day, and by drawing on his own acting experience, Stanislavski identified and described what these gifted performers did naturally and intuitively. From his observations he compiled and then codified a series of principles and techniques.

We might assume that believable acting is simply a matter of being natural; but Stanislavski discovered first of all that acting realistically onstage is extremely artificial and difficult. He wrote:

> All of our acts, even the simplest, which are so familiar to us in everyday life, become strained when we appear behind the footlights before a public of a thousand people. That is why it is necessary to correct ourselves and learn again how to walk, sit, or lie down. It is essential to reeducate ourselves to look and see, on the stage, to listen and to hear.[1]

To achieve this "reeducation," Stanislavski said, "the actor must first of all believe in everything that takes place onstage, and most of all, he must believe what he himself is doing. And one can only believe in the truth." To give substance to his ideas, Stanislavski developed a series of exercises and techniques for the performer, among them the following.

Relaxation.   When he observed the great actors and actresses of his day, Stanislavski noticed how fluid and lifelike their movements were. They seemed to be in a state of complete freedom and relaxation, letting the behavior of the character come through effortlessly. He concluded that unwanted tension has to be eliminated and that the performer must at all times attain a state of physical and vocal relaxation.

Concentration and observation.   Stanislavski also discovered that gifted performers always appeared fully concentrated on some object, person, or event while onstage. Stanislavski referred to the extent or range of concentration as a *circle of attention*. This circle of attention can be compared to a circle of light on a darkened stage. The performer should begin with the idea that it is a small, tight circle including only himself or herself and perhaps one other person or one piece of furniture. When the performer has established a strong circle of attention, he or she can enlarge the circle outward to include the entire stage area. In this way performers will stop worrying about the audience and lose their self-consciousness.

TECHNIQUES OF ACTING: THE IMPORTANCE OF SPECIFICS
Konstantin Stanislavski believed that performers should concentrate on specifics. In *The Glass Menagerie*, the playwright Tennessee Williams has provided the character Laura with a collection of glass animals with which she is preoccupied. Shown here are Celia Keenan-Bolger as Laura and Brian J. Smith as the Gentleman Caller, in a production at the A.R.T. (© Michael J. Lutch)

Importance of specifics.   One of Stanislavski's techniques was an emphasis on concrete details. A performer should never try to act in general, he said, and should never try to convey a feeling such as fear or love in some vague, amorphous way. In life, Stanislavski said, we express emotions in terms of specifics: an anxious woman twists a handkerchief, an angry boy throws a rock at a trash can, a nervous businessman jangles his keys. Performers must find similar concrete activities. Stanislavski points out how Shakespeare has Lady Macbeth in her sleepwalking scene—at the height of her guilt and emotional upheaval—try to rub blood off her hands.

The performer must also conceive of the situation in which a character exists—what Stanislavski referred to as the *given circumstances*—in terms of specifics. In what kind of space does an event take place: formal, informal, public, domestic? How does it feel? What is the temperature? The lighting? What has gone on just before? What is expected in the moments ahead? Again, these questions must be answered in concrete terms.

Inner truth.   An innovative aspect of Stanislavski's work has to do with inner truth, which deals with the internal or subjective world of characters—that is, their thoughts and emotions. The early phases of Stanislavski's research took place while he was also directing the major dramas of Anton Chekhov. Plays like *The Sea Gull* and *The Cherry Orchard* have less to do with external action or what the characters say than with what the characters are feeling and thinking but often do not verbalize. It becomes apparent that Stanislavski's approach would be very beneficial in realizing the inner life of such characters. Stanislavski had several ideas about how to achieve a sense of inner truth, one being the ***magic if.*** *If* is a word that can transform our thoughts; through it we can imagine ourselves in virtually any situation. "*If* I suddenly became wealthy . . ." "*If* I were vacationing on a Caribbean island . . ." "*If* I had great talent . . ." "*If* that person who insulted me comes near me again . . ." The word *if* becomes a powerful lever for the mind; it can lift us out of ourselves and give us a sense of absolute certainty about imaginary circumstances.

Magic if   Stanislavski's acting exercise, which requires the performer to ask, "How would I react *if* I were in this character's position?"

IN FOCUS: HISTORICAL PERSPECTIVES

Demands of Classical Acting

Before the twentieth century, the challenges facing performers were dictated by the very specific demands of the type of theatre in which performers appeared. Both classic Greek theatre and traditional Asian theatre stressed formal movement and stylized gestures similar to classical ballet. The chorus in Greek drama both sang and danced its odes, and Asian theatre has always had a significant component of singing and dancing. In addition, Greek performers wore masks and Asian performers often wore richly textured makeup.

In Western theatre, from the time of the Renaissance through the nineteenth century, actions onstage were not intended to replicate the movements or gestures of everyday life. For example, performers would often speak not to the character they were addressing but directly to the audience. In England during the eighteenth and nineteenth centuries, acting alternated between exaggerated and more natural styles. Throughout this period, every generation or so an actor or actress would emerge who was praised for performing in a less grandiose, more down-to-earth way. But exaggerated or not, performance before the twentieth century was more formal and stylized than the acting we are accustomed to today, especially in films and on television.

In Western theatre, from the fifth century BCE in Greece to the middle of the nineteenth century, vocal demands on actors and actresses were greater than they are today. The language of plays was most often poetry; and poetry—with its demanding rhythms, sustained phrases, and exacting meters—required intensive training in order for the performer to speak the lines intelligently and distinctly. There were problems of projection, too. A Greek amphitheatre was an acoustical marvel, but it seated as many as 15,000 spectators in the open air, and throwing the voice to every part of the theatre was no small task.

In Elizabethan England, Christopher Marlowe, a contemporary of Shakespeare, wrote superb blank verse that made severe demands on performers' vocal abilities. One example is found in Marlowe's *The Tragical History of D. Faustus*. Here is a speech by Faustus to Helen of Troy, who has been called back from the dead to be with him:

> O' thou art fairer than the evening's air
> Clad in the beauty of a thousand stars;
> Brighter art thou than flaming Jupiter
> When he appear'd to hapless Semele;
> More lovely than the monarch of the sky
> In wanton Arethusa's azured arms;
> And none but thou shalt be my paramour!

These seven lines of verse are a single sentence and, spoken properly, will be delivered as one overall unit, with the meaning carried from one line to the next. How many of us could manage that? A fine classical actor can speak the entire passage as a whole, giving it the necessary resonance and inflection as well. Beyond that, he can stand onstage for two or three hours delivering such lines.

No one would expect an actress or actor today to perform a classical play in the manner in which it was originally presented; such a performance would no doubt seem ludicrous. Besides, we do not know exactly how classical acting looked or sounded. At the same time, it should be clear that any performer today who is appearing in a play from the past must develop a special set of skills and be able to respond successfully to a number of challenges. Not only should an actor have the necessary psychological and emotional tools—a Hamlet, for instance, who must express a wide range of emotions as well as contradictory impulses, or an Ophelia who must play a "mad scene" in which she has lost her mind—but the same actor must also master the necessary physical and vocal techniques. Physically, an actor playing Hamlet would have to move with confidence as well as with the precision of a dancer. He would also be required to climb steps and levels with ease, and since he must engage in sword fighting, he must have mastered fencing techniques.

The Social Status of the Performer

On the subject of historical acting styles, we should also note that through the centuries there has been a wide fluctuation in the social and political position of performers. First, it is important to be aware that in several key periods of theatre history, women were prohibited from performing at all. Two prime examples are the theatre of ancient Greece—the era of the playwrights Aeschylus, Sophocles, and Euripides—and the Elizabethan age, during which Shakespeare and his contemporaries wrote. In both periods women could not even appear onstage. In Roman theatre, women were allowed to perform, but only in a lower form of theatre known as *mime*. In Europe, during the Renaissance, acting became more professional, but the social position of actors was still problematic. Women began to appear with acting troupes in Italy and Spain; but in Spain it was required that any actress in a company be a relative (wife, mother, sister) of one of the leaders of the troupe.

The next point to be noted is that frequently in the history of acting, performers were regarded as quite low on the

M.rs SIDDONS as LADY MACBETH.

L. Macb.—hark!—I laid their daggers ready.

ACTING IN THE PAST

Acting requirements in the past were often different from those of today. Forceful, sometimes exaggerated movements and a powerful voice were two essentials for successful performers. Actors were expected to declaim their lines and strike impressive poses, while wearing elaborate costumes. Two examples from the late eighteenth century and early nineteenth century are shown here. The first is an actress in the costume for a character in *Athalie* by Jean Racine; the second is a famous English performer, Sarah Siddons, portraying Lady Macbeth. (Historical Picture Archive/Corbis; Private Collection/Bridgeman Art Library)

social scale. An early exception was the classical period in Greece. Because theatre presentations were part of a religious festival, actors were treated with dignity. Through most of theatre history, however, this was not the case. An example of the problems faced by actors is the fate of the Frenchman Molière. Though he was one of the most renowned actors and playwrights of his day, France at that time had laws preventing actors from receiving a Christian burial, and thus Molière was buried secretly at night. When women began to appear on the English stage in the Restoration period, after 1660, they were regarded by some as on a par with courtesans or prostitutes. Other people, however, accepted them into high society, and one actress, Nell Gwynn, was a mistress of the king. During the eighteenth

and nineteenth centuries there were a number of famous and celebrated actors and actresses on the European continent, in England, and in the United States. In England, when the actor Henry Irving was knighted in 1895, it was felt that actors had finally arrived socially.

In Asian theatre, performers for many centuries were primarily men, though a curious phenomenon occurred at the beginning of kabuki in Japan. Kabuki began in the early seventeenth century with all-women troupes. Social disruptions arose, however, because of feuds over the sexual services of the women, and in 1629 the shogun forbade performances of women's kabuki. From that point on, kabuki was all-male, as were nō theatre and puppet theatre, bunraku.

Action onstage: What? Why? How?   Another important principle of Stanislavski's system is that all action onstage must have a purpose. This means that the performer's attention must always be focused on a series of physical actions (also called *psychophysical actions*), linked together by the circumstances of the play. Stanislavski determined these actions by asking three essential questions: What? Why? How? An action is performed, such as opening a letter (the *what*). The letter is opened because someone has said that it contains extremely damaging information about the character (the *why*). The letter is opened anxiously, fearfully (the *how*), because of the calamitous effect it might have on the character.

Through line of a role.   According to Stanislavski, in order to develop continuity in a part, the actor or actress should find the *superobjective* of a character. What is it, above all else, that the character wants during the course of the play? What is the character's driving force? If a goal can be established toward which the character strives, it will give the performer an overall objective. From this objective can be developed a *through line* that can be grasped, as a skier on a ski lift grabs a towline and is carried to the top. Another term for through line is *spine.* To help develop the through line, Stanislavski urged performers to divide scenes into units (sometimes called *beats*). In each unit there is an objective, and the intermediate objectives running through a play lead ultimately to the overall objective.

Ensemble playing   Acting that stresses the total artistic unity of a group performance rather than individual performances.

Ensemble playing.   Except in one-person shows, performers do not act alone; they interact with other people. Stanislavski was aware that many performers tend to "stop acting," or lose their concentration, when they are not the main characters in a scene or when someone else is talking. This tendency destroys the through line and causes the performer to move into and out of a role. That, in turn, weakens ***ensemble playing***— the playing together of all the performers.

Stanislavski and Psychophysical Action   Stanislavski began to develop his technique in the early twentieth century, and at first he emphasized the inner aspects of training: for example, various ways of getting in touch with the performer's unconscious. Beginning around 1917, however, he began to look more and more at purposeful action, or what he called *psychophysical action.* A student at one of his

ENSEMBLE PLAYING
Good actors are aware of the importance of ensemble playing. Performers coordinate their work by listening carefully to each other, sensing each other's actions and moods, and responding alertly. Ensemble playing is especially important in plays where interaction between characters is crucial. Anton Chekhov's plays call for an emphasis on ensemble acting. One example, seen here, is *The Cherry Orchard* directed by Howard Davies, with Zoe Wanamaker (second from left) as Ranyevskaya, in a London production. (© Geraint Lewis)

lectures that year took note of the change: "Whereas action previously had been taught as the expression of a previously established 'emotional state,' it is now action itself which predominates and is the key to the psychological."[2] Rather than seeing emotions as leading to action, Stanislavski came to believe that it was the other way around: purposeful action undertaken to fulfill a character's goals was the most direct route to the emotions.

Modern Approaches to Realistic Acting

In the second half of the twentieth century, there were three broad approaches to actors' training in the United States. Two of these derived from the methods of Stanislavski. In the 1930s and 1940s a number of performers and directors in the United States became greatly interested in the ideas of Stanislavski. One of these, Lee Strasberg, a founder of the Actors Studio in New York City, focused on the inner aspects of Stanislavskian theory. Strasberg emphasized a technique called ***emotional recall***, a tool intended to help performers achieve a sense of emotional truth onstage. By recalling sensory impressions of an experience in the past (such as what a room looked like, and the temperature and any prevalent odors in the room), emotions associated with that experience are aroused and can be used as the basis of feelings called for in a role in a play.

Emotional recall Stanislavski's exercise, which helps the performer to present realistic emotions. The performer feels a character's emotion by thinking of the conditions surrounding an event in his or her own life that led to a similar emotion.

Though the teachings of Strasberg and his followers were successful with certain performers, other acting teachers, such as Stella Adler (1902–1992), Sanford Meisner (1905–1997), and Uta Hagen (1919–2004), felt that Strasberg emphasized the inner aspects of acting to the exclusion of everything else. Following the lead of Stanislavski in his later approach with psychophysical action, they balanced the emphasis on inner resources with the inclusion of given circumstances and purposeful action.

Three examples of current approaches to training actors are represented by Uta Hagen, Robert Cohen (1938–), and Robert Benedetti (1939–). Hagen, in her book *Respect for Acting,* places a large emphasis on emotional recall and memory in general. She provides a number of exercises that enable the students to pull from past experiences in their own lives as a means of reaching the emotions required within the context of any given role. Hagen's idea is not to allow the student to become overwhelmed by past emotion, but to use it as a springboard into the action of the play.

In *Acting One,* Cohen encourages students to use text as an instrument of action. In an exercise that he calls the "Content-less Scene," he has students memorize the same text. He then asks them to perform the scene but changes the given circumstances of the scene each time. The outcome is the obvious realization that the words are not nearly as important as the meaning behind them. And, clearly, without solid given circumstances, actors are simply saying lines instead of using those lines to further the action of the play.

Finally, Benedetti in *The Actor at Work* focuses on the actor's body and how performers can use it to help shape character. Using a variety of movement exercises, Benedetti encourages students to explore elements of rhythm, time, weight, intensity, and space through improvisational work. These exercises allow the students to start with the "outside" (physical) aspects of a character's definition. Once the physical form is found, they can then use it to define the character's inner life (emotion).

The important thing for students of acting is to explore different methods of and approaches to acting, such as those outlined above, and to decide which techniques and types of training—or which combination of these—work best for them. Ultimately each individual actor must develop his or her own methodology.

photo essay

John Douglas Thompson as the lead in Eugene O'Neill's *The Emperor Jones,* Irish Repertory Theatre, 2009.

In theatre, performers are often called on to play a wide range of diverse parts. Frequently, too, actors portray people unlike themselves. Many performers welcome this challenge. An American actor who has demonstrated tremendous versatility is John Douglas Thompson, shown here in five contrasting roles.

John Douglas Thompson as *Richard III* in a production at Shakespeare & Company, Lenox, MA.

(© Liz Lauren, Courtesy Goodman Theatre)

Kate Arrington, John Douglas Thompson, Salvatore Inzerillo in Eugene O'Neill's *The Iceman Cometh* at the Goodman Theatre.

John Douglas Thompson as Macbeth, directed by Arin Arbus at the Theater for a New Audience.

(© Sara Krulwich/The New York Times/Redux)

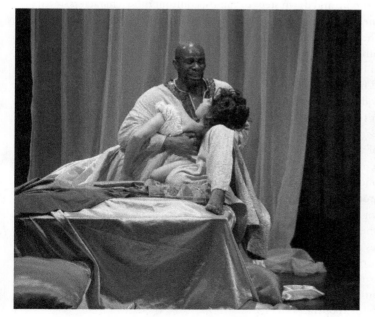

John Douglas Thompson as Othello, Merritt Janson as Desdemona, directed by Tony Simotes, Shakespeare & Company, 2008.

(© Kevin Sprague/Studio Two)

THE CRAFT OF ACTING: PHYSICAL DEMANDS
Among the many skills involved in becoming a performer are various vocal and physical skills: speaking clearly and distinctly, "projecting" the voice into the auditorium, moving gracefully, and meeting a variety of physical challenges, including sword fights, such as the one shown here. The scene is from a production of Tony Kushner's adaptation of Pierre Corneille's *The Illusion,* at A Noise Within Theatre in Pasadena, CA.
(© Craig Schwartz)

Physical Acting: Voice and Body

We have been looking at training that helps actors make stage characters truthful and believable. We turn now to a second aspect of actor training: the instruments of the performer, specifically the voice and the body.

Physical elements have always been important in the art of acting. Traditional theatre makes strong demands on the performer's body. In Shakespeare, for instance, performers must frequently run up and down steps or ramps, confront other characters in sword fights, and enact prolonged death scenes. Anyone who has seen an impressive sword fight onstage senses how difficult it must be. A duel, in which the combatants strike quickly at one another—clashing swords continually without hitting each other—resembles a ballet in its precision and grace, and it entails a great deal of physical exertion. Adept physical movement is also required in modern realistic acting. For example, an activity in a modern play analogous to a sword fight would be a headlong fall down a flight of stairs or two people engaged in a knife fight, like the one in Arthur Miller's *A View from the Bridge.*

As to the importance of voice training, because of microphones and sound amplifications, today we have increasingly lost our appreciation of the power of the human voice. But in the past, public speakers from Cicero to Abraham Lincoln stirred men and women with their oratory; and throughout its history, the stage has provided a natural platform for stirring speeches. Beginning with the Greeks and continuing through the Elizabethans, the French and Spanish theatres of the seventeenth century, and other European theatres at the close of the nineteenth century, playwrights wrote magnificent lines that performers, having honed their vocal skills to a fine point, delivered with zest. Any performer today who intends to act in a revival of a traditional play must learn to speak and project stage verse, which requires much the same kind of vocal power and breath control as opera.

PERFORMING IN CLASSICS TODAY
Contemporary performers in classic plays must have vocal training to be able to speak and project poetry properly; they must have the physical training necessary to engage in sword fights and other activities; and they must be familiar with the historical eras of the playwrights and of the texts they are to perform. Here we see Stephen Fry as Malvolio and Mark Rylance as Olivia in Shakespeare's *Twelfth Night,* in a Shakespeare's Globe production with an all male cast directed by Tim Carroll. (© Geraint Lewis)

In order to develop projection and balance it with credibility, a performer must train and rehearse extensively. For example, an actor or actress might use breathing exercises, controlling the breath from the diaphragm rather than the throat so that vocal reproduction will have power and can be sustained. Many of these exercises are similar to those used by singers. Also, head, neck, and shoulder exercises can be used to relax the muscles in those areas, thus freeing the throat for ease of projection. In the nearby chart we see a group of elementary vocal and body exercises. It must be stressed that these are basic exercises that represent only the earliest beginnings of a true regimen of exercises for the voice and body.

The Actor's Instrument: Voice and Body

Throughout the twentieth century, at the same time that many acting teachers were focusing on the inner life of the actor, another group of teachers and theoreticians were turning to a different aspect, they physical side of performing. This includes the freeing and development of the voice and body and combining these with improvisation to create maximum flexibility, relaxation, and imagination in the actor's instrument—his or her voice and body.

There were a number of key figures who contributed to this movement. For example, in the second and third decades of the twentieth century, the Russian director Vsevolod Meyerhold (1874–1942) developed a program called *biomechanics* that emphasized physical exercises and full control of the body, in the manner of circus performers such as acrobats and trapeze artists. In France in the 1920s, Jacques Copeau (1878–1949) incorporated such disciplines as mime, masks, Italian commedia dell'arte, and Asian acting into his system of training. Beginning in mid-century and continuing for the next fifty years, a Frenchman, Jacques Lecoq (1921–1999), ran an influential school in Paris dedicated to explaining and exploring the physical side of performance. In addition to emphasizing the elements on which Copeau concentrated, Lecoq also incorporated a clown figure in his work.

DYNAMICS OF DRAMA

Warm-Up Exercises for Body and Voice

To give an indication of the types of exercises performers must undertake during their years of training—and during their careers as professionals—it is interesting to look at some samples of warm-up exercises. The exercises here are designed to relax the body and the voice. The following are typical warm-up exercises for *body* movement:

1. Lie on your back; beginning with the feet, tense and relax each part of the body—knees, thighs, abdomen, chest, neck—moving up to the face. Note the difference in the relaxation of various muscles and of the body generally after the exercise is completed.
2. Stand with feet parallel, approximately as far apart as the width of the shoulders. Lift one foot off the ground and loosen all the joints in the foot, ankle, and knee. Repeat with the other foot off the ground. Put the feet down and move to the hip, spine, arms, neck, etc., loosening all joints.
3. Stand with feet parallel. Allow all tension to drain out of the body through the feet. In the process, bend the knees, straighten the pelvis, and release the lower back.
4. Begin walking in a circle; walk on the outside of the feet, then on the inside, then on the toes, and then on the heels. Notice what this does to the rest of the body. Try changing other parts of the body in a similar fashion and observe the effect on feelings and reactions.
5. Imagine the body filled with either helium or lead. Notice the effect of each of these sensations, both while standing in place and while walking. Do the same with one body part at a time—each arm, each leg, the head, etc.

The following *vocal* exercises free the throat and vocal cords:

1. Standing, begin a lazy, unhurried stretch. Reach with your arms to the ceiling, meanwhile lengthening and widening the whole of your back. Yawn as you take in a deep breath and hum on an exhalation. Release your torso so that it rests down toward your legs. Yawn on another deep breath and hum on an exhalation. On an inhalation, roll up the spine until you are standing with your arms at your sides. Look at something on the ceiling and then at something on the floor; then let your head return to a balance point, so that the neck and shoulder muscles are relaxed.
2. Put your hands on your ribs, take a deep breath, and hum a short tune. Repeat several times. Hum an *m* or *n* up and down the scale. Drop your arms; lift the shoulders an inch and drop them, releasing all tension.
3. Take a deep breath and with the palm of your hand push gently down on your stomach as you exhale. Do this several times. Exhale on sighs and then on vowels.
4. Standing, yawn with your throat and mouth open and be aware of vibrations in the front of your mouth, just behind your front teeth, as you vocalize on the vowels *ee, ei,* and *o.* Take these up and down the scales. Sing a simple song and then say it, and see if you have just as much vibration in your mouth when you are speaking as when you are singing.
5. Using a light, quick tempo, shift to a tongue twister (such as *Peter Piper picked a peck of pickled peppers*). Feel a lively touch of the tongue on the gum ridge on the *t*'s and *d*'s, and a bounce of the back of the tongue on the *k*'s and *g*'s. Feel the bouncing action on the lips on the *p*'s and *b*'s.

Source: Provided by Professor John Sipes of University of Tennesse–Knoxville and Emeritus Professor Barbara F. Acker of Arizona State University.

THE FORMAL GESTURES OF ASIAN THEATRE
In most Asian theatre, acting requires careful, precise, formal gestures. The first example here is a scene from *The Monkey King,* a piece from Beijing (or Peking) opera in China (top). The second example is the Hindu Chief Dance in a performance of kathakali in India (bottom). Note the poses, the physical requirements, and the dexterity that are required, as well as the elaborate costumes, heavy makeup, and striking headpieces. (*Monkey King,* © Dean Conger/Corbis; Hindu Chief Dance, © Charles and Josette Lenars/Corbis)

Along with European influences, there has also been a strong global presence in the new approaches to actor training. A good example is Asian theatre. Stylization and symbolism characterize the acting of the classical theatres of India, China, and Japan. To achieve the absolute control, the concentration, and the mastery of the body and nerves necessary to carry out the stylized movements, performers in the

ACTING TRAINING FROM OTHER DISCIPLINES
Actors' training today often involves exercises and other activities from related disciplines such as circus routines, juggling, acrobatics, and Asian martial arts. A good example is tai chi, a refined form of martial arts from China, here being practiced in a park. (© Inge King)

various classical Asian theatres train for years under the supervision of master teachers. Every movement of these performers is prescribed and carefully controlled, combining elements of formal ballet, pantomime, and sign language. Each gesture tells a story and means something quite specific—contributing to a true symbolism of physical movement.

One Asian discipline, not from theatre but from martial arts, which modern acting teachers have found helpful is tai chi chuan, commonly called *tai chi*. Unlike some martial arts, tai chi is not aggressive: it is a graceful, gentle exercise regimen performed widely by men, women, and children in China. It has spread to other countries, where it is sometimes practiced in conjunction with meditation or body awareness. The movements of tai chi are stylized and often seem to be carried out in slow motion. Among other things, tai chi requires concentration and control, both valuable qualities for a performer. The Japanese director, Tadashi Suzuki (1939–), developed a training technique, again taken from ancient Japanese practices, emphasizing the connection between the feet and the ground underneath. Consciousness of this connection is accomplished by exercises involving "stomping."

An approach to training that originated in the United States and has gained acceptance and wider use in our contemporary theatre is known as *viewpoints theory*. Based on ideas from the avant-garde choreographer Merce Cunningham (1919–2009) and the experimental director Jerzy Grotowski (1933–1999), it combines elements of dance and stage movement with concepts of time and space. The director Anne Bogart (1951–), one of its chief proponents, feels that viewpoints theory provides a new vocabulary for certain elements that have always been significant in performance: spatial relationships onstage, movement, and the notion of time, among others.

In the United States in the twenty-first century the emphasis on physical movement—training in the use of the voice and the body—has become more pronounced and widespread than ever. In the words of author David Bridel in an article in *American Theatre* magazine:

> Body awareness and alignment, mask work, clowning and circus skills, physical characterization, spatial relationships, ensemble work, improvisation, games, mime . . . so many forms of movement training exist today, and so many specialists work in these related fields, that the opportunity to connect the craft of acting with the movement of the body has never been richer.[3]

Today, no one approach, no one master, no one technique appears to have become universally recognized as the single authority in the field. Rather, teachers, coaches, and directors draw on a wide variety of sources, including those mentioned above as well as others, to develop their individual approaches to training the voice

TRAINING FOR MUSICAL THEATRE
Along with the classics and various types of theatre from other nations, the American musical, with its physical and vocal demands, requires extensive training. A prime example is the exuberant dancing by the men in the Broadway musical *Newsies,* choreographed by Christopher Gattelli, directed by Jeff Calhoun, with music by Alan Menken, lyrics by Jack Feldman. (© Sara Krulwich/ The New York Times/Redux)

and body. The field also goes by various names: body movement, physical theatre, and a term favored by many, *physical acting.*

As a way of integrating and unifying various approaches to body and voice training, many acting teachers emphasize a process called *centering.* This is a way of pulling everything together and allowing the performer to eliminate any blocks that impede either the body or the voice. *Centering* involves locating the place—roughly in the middle of the torso—where all the lines of force in the body come together. When performers are able to "center" themselves, they achieve a balance, a freedom, and a flexibility they could rarely find otherwise.

All this should make it clear that to master the many techniques required to play a variety of roles and to be at ease onstage—moving and speaking with authority, purpose, and conviction—performers must undergo arduous training and be genuinely dedicated to their profession.

Training for Special Forms of Theatre

Certain types of theatre and theatre events require special discipline or training. For example, musical theatre obviously requires talent in singing and dancing. Coordination is also important in musical theatre: the members of a chorus must

PLAYING YOUR PART: EXPERIENCING THEATRE

1. Read a speech from Shakespeare aloud in class or to yourself. Why would this speech be difficult for an actor? What are some of the challenges an actor would face in bringing this speech to life?

2. Remember a situation recently that made you happy. Re-create the circumstances in your mind. Where were you? Whom were you with? Can you once again feel the emotions you felt during that situation? Is this similar to an acting exercise developed by Stanislavski?

3. Make a fist. Now make it tighter and tighter. Does it change how you are feeling emotionally? Does this help you understand how an actor might approach developing an emotional moment in a play physically?

4. Analyze why you felt a recent film performance was successful. Describe how the main performer brought his or her character to life.

5. Attend a rehearsal at your university or community theatre. Then attend the final performance. What changes were made between the rehearsal and the performance by one of the actors in the production? Explain how the change affected the performance.

frequently sing and dance in unison. Pantomime is another demanding category of performance: without words or props, a performer must indicate everything by physical suggestion, convincingly lifting an imaginary box or walking against an imaginary wind.

Various forms of modern avant-garde and experimental theatre also require special techniques. A good example is Samuel Beckett's *Happy Days,* in which an actress is buried onstage in a mound of earth up to her waist in the first act, and up to her neck in the second. She must carry on her performance through the entire play while virtually immobile. In some types of avant-garde theatre, the performers become acrobats, make human pyramids, or are used like pieces of furniture. In the theatres of Robert Wilson, Mabou Mines, and similar groups, the elements of story, character, and text are minimized or even eliminated. The stress, rather than being on a narrative or on exploring recognizable characters, is on the visual and ritualistic aspects of theatre, like a series of tableaux or a moving collage.

Stage movement in this approach to theatre is often closely related to dance; thus the performers must have the same discipline, training, and control as dancers. In Wilson's work, performers are frequently called on either to move constantly or to remain perfectly still. In *A Letter to Queen Victoria,* two performers turn continuously in circles like dervishes for long periods of time—perhaps thirty or forty minutes. In other works by Wilson, performers must remain frozen like statues.

Synthesis and Integration

The demands made on performers by experimental and avant-garde theatres are only the most recent example of the rigorous, intensive training that acting generally requires. The goal of all this training—both internal and external—is to create for the performer an instrument that is flexible, resourceful, and disciplined. Above all, the actor must bring together the inner approach to acting, the work on truthfulness

THE SPECIAL DEMANDS OF ACTING

At times performing makes exceedingly strong demands, requiring performers to convey a range and depth of emotions, or to transform themselves in terms of age, mood, and the like. A good example is Samuel Beckett's *Happy Days,* in which the actress playing Winnie—in this case, Fiona Shaw—must perform while buried in a mound of sand up to her waist, and later up to her neck. This production was directed by Deborah Warner at the National Theatre in London in 2006. (© Robbie Jack/Corbis)

UNIQUE ACTING DEMANDS OF AVANT-GARDE THEATRE

Avant-garde theatre often requires special training and techniques—acrobatics, tumbling, mime, and special control of voice and body. Here we see an actor spinning while suspended upside down in Robert Wilson's production of *Quartett,* Heiner Müller's adaptation of Choderlos de Laclos's 18th-century novel *Les Liaisons Dangereuses.* (© Richard Termine)

and believability, with the physical aspects discussed above. He or she must combine inner and outer into one indivisible whole. What is important to remember is that whatever the starting point, the end result must be a synthesis of these two aspects. The inner emotions and feelings and the outer physical and vocal characteristics become one.

IN FOCUS: GLOBAL CONNECTIONS

Puppetry around the World

Puppetry in its various forms (puppets, marionettes, shadow puppets) has a long and honorable history. Remarkably, it emerged independently in widely separated parts of the world: in Indonesia, in Japan, in sections of Europe, and among Native Americans in the far northwest of what is now the United States.

In whatever form, the puppet figure is the image, reflection, and embodiment of a theatrical character and, therefore, a replacement for the actor. Puppets can run the gamut of emotions. They can be evil, demonic figures; they can be eerie, otherworldly creatures; they can be wildly comic, as in Punch and Judy shows when they biff one another across the head and knock one another down; they can be intensely human, as in the suffering characters in Japanese bunraku. In short, when puppets are onstage, audiences usually experience these silent, nonhuman characters as real people.

It should be noted as well that while puppet or marionette characters are often either comic or tragic figures, they are also frequently employed as advocates for a political point of view. The Bread and Puppet Theatre of San Francisco, founded by Peter Schuman (1934–), features larger-than-life, exaggerated figures made of papier-mâché. This theatre began with protests against the Vietnam War but has continued, often with the figures proceding down city streets, in protests against all wars, including the Iraq War.

Puppet characters are created and manipulated in various ways. In Indonesia and other parts of Southeast Asia, two kinds of puppets were developed. One kind is rod puppets, so called because the movements of these puppets are controlled by rods attached to the head and limbs and operated by one or more persons, from either above or below. (Though they are most often associated with Southeast Asia, rod puppets, nearly life-size, were developed as well on the island of Sicily in the Mediterranean.) The other type of puppet popular in Southeast Asia—in Java and Bali as well as Indonesia—is the shadow puppet. In this case, silhouette figures, often made of leather, are highlighted on a screen that is lit from behind.

Marionettes are puppets controlled by strings attached to the head, arms, and legs, and operated from above. A unique type of puppet is the *bunraku* puppet from Japan, which will be discussed in more detail later. Originating in the late seventeenth century, it was firmly established by the eighteenth century and has continued to this day. In the early eighteenth century, one of the most famous playwrights of all time, Chikamatsu Monzaemon, wrote masterful plays for *bunraku* theatre. In the case of *bunraku* figures, which today are roughly two-thirds life-size, one man operates the feet, another operates the left hand, and a third controls the face, head, and right hand.

Probably the puppet figures most familiar to Western audiences are hand puppets, operated by a person who has one or two hands inside the puppet itself. Among the immediately recognizable hand puppets are the Muppets, featuring such popular and enduring characters as Kermit the Frog and Miss Piggy. Another example of hand puppets onstage appeared in the successful Broadway production *Avenue Q*. Remarkable recent examples of puppetry were the horses and other animals created for the play *War Horse*. Puppetry remains, and will continue to remain, a vital art form in its own right, and an important adjunct to live theatre.

Quanzhou Marionette Theater, from China. (James Estrin/The New York Times/Redux)

Only then will the character be forcefully and convincingly portrayed. This process is termed *integration*. When a performer is approaching a role in a play, the first task is to read and analyze the script. The actress or actor must discover the *superobjective* of the character she or he is playing and put together not only the *spine* of the role but the many smaller moments, each with its own objective and given circumstances. The next challenge is to begin specific work on the role. In taking this step, some performers begin with the *outer* aspects of the character—with a walk, a posture, or a peculiar vocal delivery. They get a sense of how the character looks in terms of makeup and other characteristics, such as a mustache or hairstyle. They consider the clothes the character wears and any idiosyncrasies of speech or movement, such as a limp or a swagger. Only then will they move on to the inner aspects of the character: how the character feels; how the character reacts to people and events; what disturbs the character's emotional equilibrium; what fears, hopes, and dreams the character has.

Other performers, by contrast, begin with the *internal* aspects: with the feelings and emotions of the character. These performers delve deeply into the psyche of the character to try to understand and duplicate what the character feels inside. Only after doing this will they go on to develop the outer characteristics. Still other performers work on both aspects—inner and outer—simultaneously. Finally, we must realize that although a competent, well-trained performer may become a successful actress or actor, another ingredient is required in order to electrify an audience as truly memorable stage artists do. This results from intangibles—qualities that cannot be taught in acting schools—that distinguish an acceptable, accomplished actor or actress from one who ignites the stage. *Presence, charisma, personality, star quality:* these are among the terms used to describe a performer who communicates directly and kinetically with the audience. Whatever term one uses, the electricity and excitement of theatre are enhanced immeasurably by performers who possess this indefinable attribute.

JUDGING PERFORMANCES

As observers, we study the techniques and problems of acting so that we will be able to understand and judge the performances we see. If a performer is unconvincing in a part, we know that he or she has not mastered a technique for truthful acting. We recognize that a performer who moves awkwardly or cannot be heard clearly has not been properly trained in body movement or vocal projection. We learn to notice how well performers play together: whether they listen to one another and respond appropriately. We also observe how well performers establish and maintain contact with the audience.

Before leaving the subject of the performer, we should note that actors and actresses have always held a fascination for audiences. In some cases this is because they portray larger-than-life characters; it can also result from the exceptional talent they bring to their performances. Also, of course, some performers have personal charisma or appeal. Theatre audiences have often responded to stars onstage in the same way that people tend to respond to a rock star or a film star. There is something in these personalities that audiences find immensely attractive or intriguing. Moreover, the personal lives of actors are often of great interest to the public, and some people find it difficult to separate a stage character from the offstage woman or man.

PLAYING YOUR PART: THINKING ABOUT THEATRE

1. What is the most convincing performance you've seen, where you felt the actor on stage was really the person being portrayed? What was it about the performance that made it believable? In contrast, what was the least convincing and effective performance you have seen? Explain why this was so.

2. In Shakespearean and other classic plays, the actors often speak in verse. In what way are the various vocal techniques described in this chapter important to actors in preparing to play a role in this kind of play and in the performance itself?

3. Identify a scene in a play in which two, three, or four actors are locked in conflict. What can individual actors do to hold the attention of the audience and make their actions and feelings convincing? How do you think these actors can best prepare for conflict scenes?

4. Read either *Miss Julie* or *A Doll's House,* both of which are available online. What kinds of background information would the actors in these plays need to know? What are the physical attributes actors would need to create for some of the key characters? Choose one scene and one character and discuss what is motivating the character. How might you employ some of Stanislavski's concepts in order to bring the character to life?

NOTE: *A Doll's House* is also available in *Anthology of Living Theatre,* Third Edition, by Edwin Wilson and Alvin Goldfarb.

SUMMARY

1. All human beings engage in certain forms of acting; imitation and role playing are excellent examples of acting in everyday life.

2. Acting onstage differs from acting in everyday life, for several reasons—including the fact that a stage actor or actress is always being observed by an audience, and the fact that acting for the stage involves playing roles with which the performer may have no direct experience in life.

3. Historically, stage performances have required exceptional physical and vocal skills: the ability to move with agility and grace and to engage in such actions as sword fights and death scenes; the ability to deal with poetic devices (meter, imagery, alliteration, etc.); the skill to project the voice to the farthest reaches of the theatre space.

4. Acting is a difficult, demanding profession. Despite its glamour, it calls for arduous training and preparation. Looking at what is called for in a role like Hamlet gives some idea of the challenges involved.

5. From the end of the nineteenth century to the present day, many plays have been written in a very realistic, lifelike style. The characters in these plays resemble ordinary people in their dialogue, behavior, etc. Presenting them requires that performers make the characters they portray believable and convincing.

6. A Russian director, Konstantin Stanislavski, developed a system or method of acting to enable performers to believe in the "truth" of what they say and do. His suggestions included applying techniques of relaxation and concentration; dealing with specific objects and feelings (a handkerchief, a glass of water, etc.); using the power of fantasy or imagination (the "magic if") to achieve a sense of inner truth in a role; using psychophysical action; developing a *spine,* or *through line,* which runs through a role from the beginning to the end of a play; and playing together as an ensemble.

7. In the later stages of his work on actor training, Stanislavski moved from an emphasis on internal elements to more external ones—to what he called *psychological action*. Rather than emotion leading to action, he suggested that action leads to emotion.

8. Exercises and tasks have been developed to train performers. These include numerous physical and vocal exercises and techniques taken from other disciplines such as tai chi and the circus. "Centering" is often emphasized as a part of body and voice training.

9. Avant-garde theatre and some other theatres make additional demands on the performer with regard to voice and body training. The voice is sometimes used to emit odd sounds—screams, grunts, and the like. The body must perform feats of acrobatics and gymnastics.

10. The end result must be a synthesis or integration of the inner and outer aspects of acting.

11. Audience members should familiarize themselves with the problems and techniques of acting in order to judge performances properly.

94

The Director and the Producer

When we see a theatre performance, our most immediate connection is with the actresses and actors onstage. We begin to identify with the characters they play and absorb the situations in which they find themselves. Behind the performances, however, is the work of another creative person—the *director.* He or she, with the support of the stage manager, rehearses the performers and coordinates their work with that of others, such as the designers, to make certain the event is performed appropriately, intelligently, and excitingly. In this chapter, we will look at the role of the director, and also at the role of the producer or manager—the person who is responsible for the management and business aspects of theatre.

director In American usage, the person responsible for the overall unity of a production and for coordinating the work of contributing artists. The American director is the equivalent of the British producer and the French *metteur-en-scène.* ("meh-TURR ahn SENN").

THE THEATRE DIRECTOR

The director is the person who works most closely with performers in the theatre, guiding them in shaping their performances. When a new play is being presented, the director also works closely with the playwright. The director is responsible, as well, for coordinating other aspects of the production, such as the work of the scene, costume, lighting, and sound designers. The stage manager communicates the breadth of the director's conceptual vision daily with every production area to clarify ongoing production and rehearsal choices.

For many of us, as audience members, the director's work on a production is one of the least obvious components. Other elements, such as performers, scenery, and costumes, are onstage and immediately visible to us, and the words of the playwright are heard throughout the performance. But we are often not aware that the way performers speak and move, the way the scenery looks, and the way the lights change colors and intensity often originate with the director. After the playwright, the director is usually the first person to become involved in the creative process of a production, and the choices made by the director at every step along the way have a great deal to do

◀ **THE DIRECTOR SHAPES A PRODUCTION**

The director of a production works closely with the cast and the designers (scenic, costumes, lighting, sound). The director gives shape to the arc of the play or musical, and determines its style, its pace, and the way the actors create their characters and interact with one another. If the production is a new play or musical, the director also collaborates with the playwright and the lyricist and composer. Shown here is choreographer-director Bill T. Jones in a rehearsal demonstrating to actor Sahr Ngaujah how he should move in a scene from the musical Fela! *in which Ngaujah plays the title role. (© Richard Termine)* with determining whether the ultimate experience will be satisfactory for us, the members of the audience.

While the playwright incorporates a point of view toward the material dramatized in a script—it may be, for example, a tragedy, a melodrama, or a comedy—it is crucial for the director to understand this point of view and translate it into terms relevant to the production. The director must then make both the playwright's and his or her point of view clear to the performers, designers, and other artists and technicians involved. Although they work together, these artists and technicians must of necessity work on segments of the production rather than the entire enterprise. During rehearsals, for instance, the performers are much too busy working on their own roles and their interactions with each other to worry much about scenery. To take another example, a performer who appears only in the first act of a three-act play has no control over what happens in the second and third acts. The one person who does have an overall perspective is the director. The person who aids in communicating this perspective to everyone involved on a continuing basis is the production stage manager, the only other member of the production team to experience the entire rehearsal process with the director.

Directors get their training in a variety of ways. Many of them begin as actors and actresses and find that they have a talent for working with other people and for coordinating the work of designers as well as performers. Others train in the many academic institutions that have specific programs for directors. These include large universities with theatre as part of a liberal arts focus as well as special conservatories and institutes.

THE TRADITIONAL DIRECTOR

In this chapter we will look at three approaches to directing: traditional, auteur, and postmodern. We begin with the traditional approach, which might also be called a text-based method. The starting point, or the foundation, of the traditional director's work is the script. It might be a well-known play by Shakespeare, Ibsen, or Strindberg, or a more recent work, such as one by Lorraine Hansberry, August Wilson, or Sarah Ruhl. The play might also be a new script by a very young or emerging playwright.

The Director and the Script

For the most part, we experience theatre as a unified event. But, as pointed out before, theatre is a complex art involving not one or two elements but many simultaneously: script, performance, costumes, scenery, lighting, and point of view. These diverse elements—a mixture of the tangible and intangible—must be brought together into an organic whole, and that is the responsibility of the director.

Choosing a Script   Frequently, the director chooses the script to be produced. Generally it is a play to which the director is attracted or for which he or she feels a special affinity. If the director does not actually choose the script but is asked to direct it by a playwright or a producer, he or she must still understand and appreciate the material. The director's attraction to the script and basic understanding of it are important in launching a production. Once the script is chosen, the actual work on the production begins.

If the play is new and has never been tested in production, the director may see problems in the script, which must be corrected before rehearsals begin. The director will have a series of meetings with the playwright to iron out the difficulties ahead of time. The director may feel, for example, that the leading character is not clearly defined, or that a clash of personalities between two characters never reaches a climax. If the playwright agrees with the director's assessment, he or she will revise the manuscript. Generally there is considerable give-and-take between the director and the playwright in these preliminary sessions, as well as during the rehearsal period. The stage manager must maintain well-organized rehearsal documentation of possible script revisions for the playwright and director to discuss outside rehearsals. Ideally, there should be a spirit of cooperation, compromise, and mutual respect in this relationship.

Once the script is selected, the director begins analyzing it and preparing a production. There is no one way a director should go about this: individual directors adopt their own personal approach. One method of undertaking this task was suggested by the work of the Russian director Konstantin Stanislavski. In this case, an initial step is to determine the *spine* of the play.

The "Spine" of the Play   The spine of the drama, also referred to as the *main action,* is determined by the goal, or the primary objective, of the characters in the play, both collectively and individually. There is nothing magical about the spine: it is a working hypothesis that gives directors a foundation and a through-line on which to base their analysis and their work with the actors.

Finding a spine for a play allows the director to understand the action and provides a nerve center from which to develop it. Different directors may find different spines for the same play. With *Hamlet,* for instance, several spines are possible: much will depend on the period in which the play is produced and on the point of view of the individual director. One spine could be simple revenge; another could be Hamlet's attempt to resolve his inner conflicts; still another could be Hamlet's attempt to locate and expose the duplicity and corruption he senses in Denmark. Such varied interpretations are to be expected and are acceptable as long as the spine chosen remains true to the spirit and action of the play.

The Style of the Production   Once a spine has been found, a second task for a director is to find the *style* in which the play is to be presented. The concept of style in a theatrical production is difficult to explain. It means the *way* a play is presented. When we speak of a "casual style" of clothing, we mean that the clothing is loose and informal; when we speak of a "1960s" style, we mean that it has the look and feel of clothing worn in the 1960s. In theatre, one way to consider style is in terms of realism and nonrealism, or as noted elsewhere, sometimes referred to as departures from realism. These two types can also be further subdivided.

For example, there are several types of realism. At one extreme is **naturalism,** a kind of superrealism. The term *naturalism* was originated by several nineteenth-century French writers who wanted a theatre that would show human beings—often in wretched circumstances—as products of heredity and environment. In addition to this special use, the term *naturalism* refers more broadly to attempts to put onstage as exact a copy of life as possible, down to the smallest detail. In a naturalistic stage set of a kitchen, for instance, a performer can actually cook a meal on the stove, the toaster makes toast, the faucet produces water, and the light in the refrigerator goes on when the door opens. Characters speak and act as if they had been caught unobserved by a sound camera. In this sense, naturalism is supposed to resemble a documentary film.

Naturalism   Attempts to put on stage exact copies of everyday life; sometimes also called "slice of life."

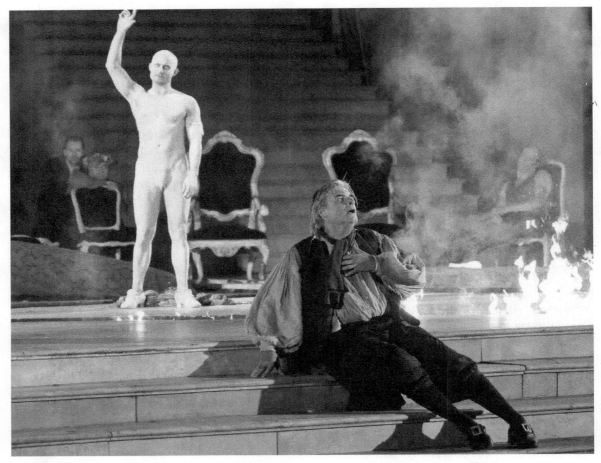

ALLEGORY

The medieval morality play *Everyman* is an excellent example of an allegory, with the title character representing all humankind. In an allegory, characters personify ideas or other-worldly characters in order to illustrate an intellectual or moral lesson. In this scene from a revival of a version of *Everyman* by Hugo von Hoffmannsthal, we see (left to right) Clemens Schick in the role of Death Peter Simonischek as Everyman, and Sven-Eric Bechtolf as the Devil. The director was Christian Stueckl for a presentation at the Salzburg Festival in Austria in 2008. (© Kerstin Joensson/AP Images)

Naturalism is sometimes called *slice-of-life* drama, suggesting that a section has been taken from life and transferred to the stage.

At the other extreme of realism is *heightened realism,* sometimes referred to as *selective realism.* Here the characters and their activities are intended to resemble life, but a certain license is allowed. The scenery, for example, might be skeletal—that is, incomplete and in outline—although the words and actions of the characters are realistic. Or perhaps a character is allowed a modern version of a soliloquy in an otherwise realistic play. All art calls for selectivity, and heightened realism recognizes the necessity for the artist to make choices and to inject creativity into the process. *Realism* itself occupies the middle ground between naturalism and heightened, or selective, realism; but when it is used as a broad umbrella term, it includes the extremes at each end.

Nonrealism, or departures from realism, can also be divided into types, which might include such forms as fantasy, poetic drama, musical theatre, absurdist theatre, and symbolism. Examples of two well-known types of nonrealism are *allegory* and *expressionism.*

Allegory is the representation of an abstract theme or subject through symbolic characters, actions, or other elements of a production, such as scenery. Good examples are the medieval morality plays, in which characters personify ideas in order to teach an intellectual or moral lesson. In *Everyman,* performers play parts with names such as Good Deeds, Fellowship, and Worldly Goods. In less direct forms of allegory, a relatively realistic story serves as a parable or lesson. *The Crucible* by Arthur Miller is about the witch hunts in Salem, Massachusetts, in the late seventeenth century; but it can also be regarded as dealing with specific investigations into communism by the United States Congress in the early 1950s that Miller and others considered modern "witch hunts."

Expressionism was at its height in art, literature, and theatre during the first quarter of the twentieth century, but traces of it are still found today, and contemporary plays using its techniques are called *expressionistic.* In simple terms, expressionism gives outward expression to inner feelings. In Elmer Rice's *The Adding Machine,* when the main character, Mr. Zero, is fired from his job, his feelings are conveyed by having the room spin around in a circle amid a cacophony of shrill sounds, such as loud sirens and whistles.

Deciding on a directorial style for a production involves giving a signature and an imprint to the entire production: the look of the scenery and lights, and the way performers speak and handle their costumes and props. It also involves the rhythm and pace at which the play moves, a subject that is taken up below. When a director arrives at a style for a production, two things are essential: (1) the style should be appropriate for the play, and (2) it should be consistent throughout every aspect of the production.

The Directorial Concept One way for the director to embody the spine in a production and to implement style is to develop a *directorial concept.* Such a concept derives from a controlling idea, vision, or point of view that the director feels is appropriate to the play. The concept should also create a unified theatrical experience for those of us in the audience.

Concept and period. To indicate what is involved for the director in developing a concept, let us begin with period and location. Take, for instance, Shakespeare's play *The Tempest.* It is set on a faraway, remote island, and an air of mystery is present throughout the play. One director might take a traditional approach and present it as she or he believes it was performed in Shakespeare's day, with appropriate costumes and scenery. Another director might wish to set it in modern times on a secluded island in the Caribbean, with scenery and costumes reflecting a decidedly modern, Latin feeling, including calypso and other native music. A third director might take a *Star Wars* approach, placing the action at some future period on a small planet in outer space. In this case, performers arrive and depart by intergalactic rocket ships and wear futuristic space outfits. This kind of transposition has been carried out frequently with Greek plays, Elizabethan plays, seventeenth-century French plays, and other dramatic classics.

Concept and central image. Another way to implement a directorial concept is to find a *central,* or *controlling, image* or *metaphor* for a theatrical production. An example would be a production of *Hamlet* that envisioned the play in terms of a vast net or spiderweb in which Hamlet is caught. The motif of a net or spiderweb could be carried out on several levels: in the design of the stage set, in the ways the performers relate to one another, and in a host of details relating to the central image. There might be a

Allegory Symbolic representation of abstract themes through characters, action, and other concrete elements of a play.

Expressionism The attempt in drama to depict the subjective state of a character or group of characters through shush nonrealistic techniques as distortion, striking images, and poetic language.

IN FOCUS: HISTORICAL PERSPECTIVES

The Evolution of the Director

It is sometimes argued that the theatre director did not exist before 1874, when a German nobleman, George II (1826–1914), duke of Saxe-Meiningen, began to supervise every element of the productions in his theatre—rehearsals, scenic elements, and other aspects, which he coordinated into an integrated whole. It is true that Saxe-Meiningen was one of the first people to emerge as a separate, indispensable member of the theatrical team. Although the title may have been new, however, the *function* of the director had always been present in one way or another, usually in the person of a playwright or an actor.

We know, for example, that the Greek playwright Aeschylus directed his own plays and that the chorus in a Greek play would rehearse under the supervision of a leader for many weeks before a performance. At various times in theatre history, the leading performer or playwright of a company served as a director, though without the title. The French dramatist Molière, for instance, not only was the playwright and the chief actor of his company but also functioned as the director. In Molière's short play *The Impromptu of Versailles* he made clear his definite ideas about the way actors and actresses should perform—no doubt the same advice he offered to performers in his company when rehearsing other plays.

When Hamlet gives instructions and advice to the players who perform the play-within-the-play in *Hamlet,* he is functioning as a director. In England after the time of Shakespeare—from the seventeenth century through the nineteenth—there was a long line of *actor-managers* who gave strong leadership to individual theatre companies and performed many of the functions of a director, although they were still not given that title. Among the most famous were Thomas Betterton (1635–1710), David Garrick (1717–1779), Charles Kemble (1775–1854), William Charles Macready (1793–1873), and Henry Irving (1838–1905).

Toward the end of the nineteenth century the term *director* came into common usage and the clearly defined role of the director was fully recognized. Perhaps significantly, the emergence of the director as a separate creative figure coincided with important changes that began to take place in society during the nineteenth century. First, there was a breakdown in established social, religious, and political concepts, resulting in part from the influence of Freud, Darwin, and Marx. Second, there was a marked increase in communication. With the advent of the telegraph, the telephone, photography, motion pictures, and—later—television, various cultures that had remained remote from or unknown to one another were suddenly made aware of each other.

The effect of these changes was to alter the monolithic, ordered view of the world that individual societies had maintained for over 2,000 years prior to that time. By the early twentieth century, societies and nations had become heterogeneous and interconnected. Previously, consistency of style in theatre had been easier to achieve. Within a given society, writers, performers, and spectators were on common ground. For example, the comedies of the English playwrights William Wycherley (1640–1716) and William Congreve (1670–1729), written at the end of the seventeenth century, were aimed at a specific audience—the elite upper class, which relished gossip, clever remarks, and well-turned phrases.

The code of social behavior in this case was well understood by performers and audiences alike, and questions of style in a production hardly arose, because a common approach to style was already present in the fabric of society. The way a man took a pinch of snuff or a lady flung open her fan was so clearly delineated in daily behavior that performers had only to refine and perfect these actions for the stage. Today, however, due to diversity, multiculturalism, and globalization, achieving a unity of style is much more difficult and the director's task, therefore, is that much more important.

huge rope net hanging over the entire stage, for instance, and certain characters could play string games with their fingers. In short, the metaphor of Hamlet's being caught in a net would be emphasized and reinforced on every level.

Concept and purpose.   The directorial concept should serve the play. The best concept is one that remains true to the spirit and meaning of the script. A director who can

THE DIRECTORIAL CONCEPT

At times, directors create an overall image or metaphor in presenting their interpretation of a play. This can serve both to illuminate the text and to give the production unity and cohesion. The South African actor John Kani inspired the Royal Shakespeare Company director Gregory Doran to set Shakespeare's *Julius Caesar* in modern-day Africa with an all-black cast. Kani had referred to the play as "Shakespeare's Africa play" and Nelson Mandela had annotated a copy he read while imprisoned at Robben Island. In this scene we see Cyril Nri (left) as Cassius, and Jeffery Kissoon as Julius Caesar in the RSC production staged in Moscow as part of the Chekhov International Theatre Festival. (© Sharifulin Valey/ITAR-TASS Photo/Corbis)

translate that spirit and meaning into stage terms in an inspired way will create an exciting theatre experience; however, a director who is too intent on displaying his or her own originality may distort or violate the integrity of the script. For instance, a director might decide to make *Macbeth* into a cowboy play, with Duncan as a sheriff and Macbeth as a deputy who wants to kill the sheriff in order to take the job himself. In this version, Lady Macbeth would be the deputy's wife, whom he had met in a saloon. *Macbeth* could be done this way, but it might also come across as simply a gimmick—a means of calling attention to the director rather than to the script.

In most instances the best directorial concept is a straightforward one deriving from the play itself, not a scheme superimposed from outside.

The Director and the Dramaturg

A person who can be of great assistance to the director is the dramaturg, or literary manager, whom we mentioned earlier. The duties of the dramaturg are discovering promising new plays, working with playwrights on developing their scripts, identifying significant plays from the past that may have been overlooked, preparing material for teachers whose students will be attending performances, and writing articles for the

IN FOCUS: GLOBAL CONNECTIONS

Peter Brook: International Director

The English director Peter Brook (b. 1925) presented some of the most memorable productions of the late twentieth century, a number of which drew extensively from the theatrical traditions and source materials of many countries. His major productions include Peter Weiss's *Marat / Sade* (1964), Shakespeare's *A Midsummer Night's Dream* (1970), and his own adaptation of an Indian epic, *The Mahabharata* (1985). His best-known writings include *The Empty Space* (1968), *The Shifting Point* (1987), and *The Open Door* (1993).

As a means of escaping commercial theatre and allowing himself to address the universality of the theatrical experience, Brook founded the International Center for Theatre Research in Paris in 1970. This company was formed of actors from a variety of countries including Algeria, Japan, England, France, America, Spain, and Portugal, with directors from Armenia, England, and Romania and a designer from Switzerland. There was much sharing of ideas and techniques, with the Japanese actor teaching daily classes in nō, for example. Brook's vision was for the actors to learn from each other and to approach a kind of universal theatrical language. A production entitled *Orghast* (1971) first allowed the company to present its experimentation with language. The text was written by Ted Hughes in an invented language influenced heavily by Latin and ancient Greek, and was performed in Iran.

In 1989, Brook's continued interest in identifying a universality of language in theatre was manifest in his production of *The Mahabharata*. The source text for this play was the Indian epic of the same name, which is more than 90,000 verses long, concerns wars between the Pandavas and the Kauravas, and addresses a great number of philosophical questions. Brook's production of this epic text originally took place at the Avignon Festival in France and took a full nine hours to perform. The source text was Indian, the director English, the theatre company French, and the composer Japanese, and the actors were from all over the globe. This production, which toured widely, clearly drew from a large number of different cultures.

Peter Brook in Paris, 1927. (© Julio Donoso/Sygma/Corbis)

Although Brook has been criticized for exploiting some of his source material (such as *The Mahabharata*, which he greatly simplified), his work has shown a creative and continued interest in drawing from many different theatrical traditions. Unlike other directors who have "borrowed" certain aspects of other theatrical traditions, Brook has sought to use them to identify a common language or universality understood by them all.

Prepared by Naomi Stubbs, CUNY Graduate Center.

programs that are distributed at performances. Of particular importance to directors is the work of dramaturges in conducting research on previous productions of classic plays, as well as researching past criticism and interpretations of these plays. It is easy to see how the work of the dramaturg can be invaluable in assisting the director to arrive at decisions regarding style, approach, and concept.

THE AUTEUR DIRECTOR AND THE POSTMODERN DIRECTOR

In addition to the traditional director, there are two other types of stage directors: the auteur director and the postmodern director. There are a number of similarities between these two, but we will look at them one at a time, beginning with the auteur director.

The Auteur Director

Auteur is a French word meaning "author." Just after World War II, French critics began using this term to describe certain film directors, who, they said, were really the authors of the films they made. In these films the point of view and the implementation of that point of view came almost entirely from the director, not from a writer. The term has since been applied to a type of stage director as well. We are not speaking here of directors who alter the time or place in which the action occurs but retain the original script—the playwright's words and the sequence of scenes. We are speaking rather of directors who make more drastic alterations or transformations in the material, taking responsibility for shaping *every* element in the production, including the script.

Interestingly, one of the first and most important auteur directors began his work with a traditional director, Stanislavski, and then went out on his own: the Russian director Vsevolod Meyerhold (1874–1940), who developed a type of theatre in which he controlled all the elements. The script was only one of many aspects that Meyerhold used for his own purposes. He would rewrite or eliminate text in order to present his own vision of the material. Performers, too, were subject to his overall ideas. Often they were called on to perform like circus acrobats or robots. The finished product was

DYNAMICS OF DRAMA

MODERN VERSUS POSTMODERN PRODUCTION AESTHETICS

Modern	Postmodern
Organic unity	Interdisciplinary
Single view	No single view can predominate
Single viewer approach	Multiperspective, multifocus
Shared values of audience	Multicultural
Metaphorical or representational	Presentational
Linear	Nonlinear, simultaneous
Closeness	Distance
Time is singularly staged	Multiple time frames are presented simultaneously
Space is unified	Space is fragmented and can be simultaneously conceived

(Prepared by Tom Mikotowicz)

frequently exciting and almost always innovative, but it reflected Meyerhold's point of view, strongly imposed on all the elements, not the viewpoint of a writer or anyone else.

Following in Meyerhold's footsteps, many avant-garde directors of the mid-twentieth century, such as Jerzy Grotowski (1933–1999), Richard Foreman, and Robert Wilson, can also be classified as auteur directors. Each in his own way demanded that the text serve his purposes, not the other way around. In some cases, such as many of Wilson's pieces, the text is only fragmentary and is one of the least important elements. In the former Soviet Union and Eastern Europe, before the political changes of the early 1990s, certain directors, who had not been allowed to deal with material that questioned the government hierarchy, drastically reworked established texts in order to make a political comment. These directors, too, imposed their own vision, rather than that of the playwright, on the material.

Another recent auteur director is Ivo van Hove (b. 1958), a Flemish director who enjoys reinventing the classics. In his *Streetcar Named Desire,* Blanche DuBois performs a good part of the play naked in a bathtub; and his version of *The Misanthrope* by Molière, which he transfers to the present day, features cell phones, laptops, BlackBerrys, and digital cameras. Two highly regarded contemporary American auteur directors are Julie Taymor (b. 1952) and Mary Zimmerman (b. 1960).

The Postmodern Director

There is a great deal of overlap between the auteur director and the postmodern director. What is postmodernism? Probably the best way to answer the question is historically. The modern period in drama began in the late nineteenth century with plays like those of Ibsen and Strindberg that broke long-held taboos. The subject matter of their plays included explicit sexual content, social diseases, the subjugation of women, and the hypocrisy of religious figures. The twentieth century, therefore, was the period of *modern drama.*

At mid-century, however, there were people who felt that as advanced as theatre had become, it remained bound by the strictures of the text. In their minds this state of affairs did not properly reflect the chaos, the confusion, and the alienation of the world around us. Two groups especially advanced these ideas: the theoreticians who propounded the doctrine of postmodernism; and a series of stage directors who embodied postmodernism in their work with a radical, rebellious, free-form approach to theatre production.

What are the hallmarks of postmodern production? One, which began with Meyerhold and continued with Grotowski in his "poor theatre," was a taking apart of the text, often called *deconstruction,* in which portions of a text may be altered, deleted, taken out of context, or reassembled.

A second hallmark is the abandonment of a narrative or linear structure in a theatre piece. In a later chapter we will explain how Robert Wilson (b. 1941) and Richard Foreman (b. 1937) in his Ontological Hysteric Theatre both replace traditional structure with the use of segments, tableaux, and other nonsequential devices. A third hallmark is unfamiliar, cross-gender, multicultural casting. Lee Breuer (b. 1937) in a Mabou Mines production of *King Lear* recast the title role as a female ranch owner in the southern United States who has difficulty leaving her inheritance to her three "good ole boy" sons. *The Emperor Jones,* a play by Eugene O'Neill (1888–1953), is about the ruler of a Caribbean island who is gradually stripped of his powers. When the Wooster Group produced this play, an actress, Kate Valk, played the ruler, appearing in blackface.

In addition to those discussed above, other postmodern directors include Anne Bogart (b. 1951) and her SITI organization and Elizabeth LeCompte (b. 1944) with the Wooster Group.

THE DIRECTOR AND THE PRODUCTION: THE PHYSICAL PRODUCTION

While developing his or her approach to the play, the director is also working with the designers on the physical production. At the outset—once the director's concept is established—the director confers with the costume, scene, lighting, and sound designers to give visual shape and substance to the concept. It is the responsibility of designers to provide images and impressions that will carry out the style and ideas of the production. (See the chapters on all of the design elements.)

ANNE BOGART: POSTMODERN DIRECTOR
Anne Bogart is a postmodern, auteur director who creates her own theatre pieces, controlling every aspect of a production and making it her own. *The Trojan Women* by Euripides takes place in Troy the day after the Trojan Horse episode when the women await their terrible fate at the hands of conquering Greeks. Bogart's contemporary version, adapted by Jocelyn Clarke, explores the struggle to move forward in the face or overwhelming, tragic loss. The scene here is from the Bogart production performed outdoors at the Getty Villa, with (l-r:) Akiko Aizawa (Kassandra), Ellen Lauren (Hecuba), Makela Spielman (Andromache). (© Craig Schwartz)

During the preproduction and rehearsal period, the director meets with the designers to make certain that their work is on schedule and keeping pace with the rehearsals. Obviously, the preparation of these elements must begin long before the actual performance, just as rehearsals must, so that everything will be ready on time for the performance itself. Any number of problems can arise with the physical elements of a production. For example, the appropriate props may not be available, a costume may not fit a performer, or scene changes may be too slow. Early planning will allow time to solve these problems.

THE DIRECTOR'S WORK WITH THE PERFORMERS

Casting

Now we come to the director's work with the performers. Along with choosing and developing a script and settling questions of concept, style, and the physical production, the director also casts the play. In theatre, *casting* means fitting performers into roles; the term *casting* is derived from the phrase "casting a mold." Generally speaking, directors attempt to put performers into the roles for which their personalities and physical characteristics are best suited. A young actress will play Juliet in *Romeo and Juliet,* a middle-aged or elderly actor with a deep voice will play *King Lear,* and so on. When a performer closely resembles in real life the character to be enacted, this is known as *typecasting.* There are times, however, when a director will deliberately put someone in a role who does not appear to be right for the part. This is frequently done for comic or satiric purposes and is called *casting against type.* For example, a sinister-looking actor might be called on to play an angelic part.

In the modern American theatre, performers frequently *audition* for parts in a play, and the director casts from those performers who audition. In an audition, actors and actresses read scenes from a play or perform portions of the script to give the director an indication of how they talk and move, and how they would interpret a part. From this the director determines whether or not a performer is right for a given role.

Historically, casting was rarely done by audition, because theatrical companies were more permanent. In Shakespeare's time, and in Molière's, as well as in Asian theatre, certain people in a theatrical troupe always played certain parts: one person would play heroic roles while another always played clowns. Today each production begins with a fresh cast. "Today, however, stars are still often cast without auditions."

From our standpoint as members of the audience, it is important to be aware of casting and the difference it can make to the effectiveness of a production. Perhaps an actor or actress is just right for the part he or she is playing. On the other hand, sometimes the wrong performer is chosen for a part: the voice may not be right, or the gestures or facial expressions may be stilted or inappropriate for the character. One way to test the appropriateness of casting is to imagine a different kind of actor or actress in a part while watching a performance.

Rehearsals

Once a play is cast, the director supervises all the rehearsals. He or she listens to and watches the performers as they go through their lines and begin to move about the stage. Different directors work in different ways during the early phases of rehearsal. Some directors *block* a play in advance, giving precise instructions to the performers. The term **blocking** means deciding when and where performers move and position themselves on the stage. Other directors let the actors and actresses find their own movements, their own vocal interpretations, and their own relationships. And of course, there are directors who do a bit of both.

Also, some directors want the actors to become thoroughly familiar with the script while they remain seated. Others wish to get the play "on its feet" as soon as possible, meaning that the actors are moving about the rehearsal hall early in the process. Regardless of the director's approach to staging, the production stage manager keeps detailed notes of all the actors' movements and actions to help maintain consistency during rehearsals.

At the beginning of the rehearsal process the director often has the cast sit around a table, while reading through the script and discussing individual scenes as well as the play in general. After this, the director may break down the script into segments or scenes, which will be rehearsed separately. Some scenes will involve only a few people; others, as in a Shakespearean play, may be crowd scenes. At a certain point, the actors will be expected to be "off book," meaning that they have memorized their lines. Gradually, scenes are put together, and an entire act is played without stopping. After that, individual scenes are refined, and then there is a run-through, when the play is performed straight through without stopping.

Throughout the rehearsal period, the director must make certain that the actors and actresses are realizing the intention of the playwright—that they are making sense of the script and bringing out its meaning. Also, the director must ensure that the performers are working well together—that they are listening to one another and beginning to play as an ensemble. The director must be aware of performers' needs, knowing when to encourage them and when to challenge or criticize them. The director must understand their personal problems and help them overcome such obstacles as insecurity about a role or fear of failure.

Blocking Pattern and arrangement of performers' movements onstage with respect to each other and to the stage space, usually set by the director.

The Director as the Audience's Eye

One could say that there are two people in theatre who stand in for us, the audience, serving as surrogate or substitute spectators. One, the critic or reviewer (discussed earlier), does his or her work after the event; the other, the director, does his or her work before it. In preparing a theatrical production, the director acts as the eye of the audience. During rehearsals, only the director sees the production from our point of view. For this reason, the director must help the performers to show the audience—us—exactly what they intend to show. If one performer hides another at an important moment, if a crucial gesture is not visible, if an actor makes an awkward movement, if an actress cannot be heard when she delivers an emotional speech, the director points it out.

Also, the director underscores the meaning of specific scenes through *visual composition* and *stage pictures,* that is, through the physical arrangement of performers onstage. The spatial relationships of performers convey information about characters. For example, important characters are frequently placed on a level above other

USING STAGE AREAS PROPERLY
One responsibility of the director is to make appropriate use of stage areas to create clarity, balance, and the proper emphasis in the visual picture on stage. The scene here is from Chekhov's *The Cherry Orchard*, in a production at the Huntington Theatre. Note how the director Nicholas Martin has arranged the performers so that Kate Burton as Madame Ranevskaya in light grey costume, the leading figure in the play, stands out in front of the other actors who surround her expertly positioned. (© T Charles Erickson)

characters—on a platform, say, or a flight of stairs. Another spatial device is to place an important character alone in one area of the stage while grouping other characters in another area. This causes our eye to give special attention to the character standing alone. Also, if two characters are opposed to each other, they should be placed in positions of physical confrontation onstage. Visual composition is more crucial in a play with a large cast, such as a Shakespearean production, than in a play with only two or three characters.

Certain areas onstage can assume special significance. A fireplace, with its implication of warmth, can become an area to which a character returns for comfort and reassurance. A door opening onto a garden can serve as a place where characters go when they want to renew their spirits or relieve a hemmed-in feeling. By guiding performers to make the best use of stage space, the director helps them communicate important visual images to us—images consistent with the overall meaning of the play.

It is important to note, too, that directors must adjust their notions of blocking and visual composition to different types of stages, discussed in our chapter on stage spaces: the arena stage, the thrust stage, and the proscenium stage. Each of these calls for different approaches to the performers' movements and to the audience's sight lines.

Movement, Pace, and Rhythm

The director gives shape and structure to a play in two ways: in *space,* as was just described, and in *time*. Since a production occurs through time, it is important for the director to see that the *movement, pace,* and *rhythm* of the play are appropriate. If a play moves too quickly, if we miss words and do not understand what is going on, that is usually the director's fault. The director must determine whether there is too little or too much time between speeches and whether a performer moves across the stage too slowly or too quickly. The director must also attempt to control the pace and rhythm within a scene and the rhythm between scenes.

One of the most common faults of directors is not establishing a clear rhythm in a production. At a performance we are often impatient to see what is coming next, and the director must see to it that the movement from moment to moment and scene to scene has enough thrust and drive to maintain our interest. Variety is also important. If a play moves ahead at only one pace, whether slow or fast, we will become fatigued simply by the monotony of that pace. Rhythm within scenes and between scenes works on us subliminally, but its effects are very real. It enters our psyche as we watch a performance and thus contributes to our overall response.

It must be borne in mind as well that although pace, rhythm, and overall effect are initially the responsibility of the director, ultimately they become the performers' responsibility. Once a performance begins, the actors and actresses are onstage and the director is not. In cinema, pace and rhythm can be determined in the editing room; in theatre, by contrast, they are in the hands of the performers. Then, too, the audience's reaction will vary from night to night, and that will also alter pace and rhythm. The director must therefore instill in the performers such a strong sense of inner rhythm that they develop an internal clock that tells them the pace at which they should play.

Technical Rehearsal

Just before public performances begin, a *technical rehearsal* is held. The performers are onstage in their costumes with the scenery and lighting for the first time, and there is a *run-through* of the show from beginning to end, with all the props and scene changes. The stagehands move scenery, the crew handles props, and the lighting technicians control the dimming and raising of lights. The backstage crew must coordinate its work with that of the performers.

Let us say that one scene ends in a garden, and the next scene opens in a library. When the performers leave the garden set, the lighting fades, the scenery and furniture are removed. Then, the scenery for the library must be brought onstage and the books and other props put in place. Next, the performers for the new scene in the library take their places as the lighting comes up. Extensive rehearsals are required to ensure that all these changes occur smoothly. Any mishap on the part of the stage, lighting, or prop crew, or the performers would affect the illusion and destroy the aesthetic effect of the scene change.

Dress Rehearsal

Just after the technical rehearsal, but before the first preview or tryout with an audience, the director will hold a **dress rehearsal.** The purpose of the dress rehearsal is to put all the elements together: the full involvement of the performers as well as the technical components. The dress rehearsal is performed as if an audience were present, with no stops or interruptions and with full lights, scenery, costumes, and sound.

Dress rehearsal   The first full performances of a production before performances for the public.

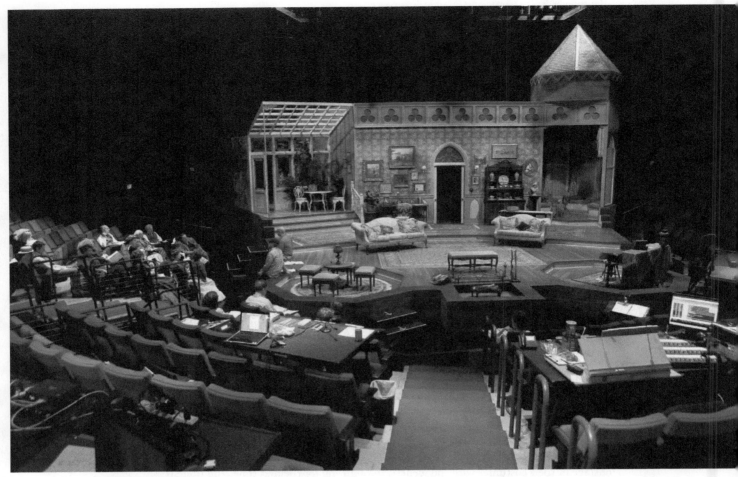

TECHNICAL REHEARSAL

Before performances begin, a technical rehearsal is held. All the technical aspects—scenery, lighting, sound, costumes, props—are employed in the same sequence and manner as in performance. This is in order to see that everything is in proper working order and is coordinated. Shown here is a rehearsal at the Guthrie Theater in Minneapolis for a production of *When We Are Married*, directed by John Miller-Stephany. Note the tables on which computers are being used by sound, light, and scenic designers to check out the running order and the coordination of all the elements. The set was designed by Frank Hallinan. (© T Charles Erickson)

Sometimes a few people are invited—friends of the director or cast members—to provide a token audience.

One function of the dress rehearsal is to give everyone concerned—cast, crew, and director—a sense of what the performance will be like. The dress rehearsal also allows for any last-minute changes before the first performance in front of a full audience.

Previews

Once the technical rehearsals and the dress rehearsal are completed and any problems are solved, the next step is a performance in front of an audience. We have stressed from the beginning the importance of performer-audience interaction and the fact that no play is complete until it is actually enacted for an audience. It is crucial, therefore, for a production to be tried out before a group of spectators. What has gone

PLAYING YOUR PART: EXPERIENCING THEATRE

1. Have you ever had to pick someone for a team or for a job? How did you go about making your choice? Is that similar to casting in the theatre? Why? Why not?

2. Have one of your classmates read a short speech from a play. Ask her or him to change the pace or rhythm of delivery. What terms or phrases did you use to make this request? Were your directions understood? How did the change in pace or rhythm affect the delivery of the speech and its impact on those listening?

3. Observe how one of your instructors interacts with the class through his or her movement. How does this movement affect the way in which the class material is delivered? Does your observation of this provide you any insight into the importance of stage blocking?

4. Ask if you can attend a technical rehearsal or dress rehearsal at your university theatre. What insights did you gain from attending those rehearsals?

before, in terms of rehearsals and other elements, must now meet the test of combining harmoniously in front of an audience.

For this purpose there is most often (but not always) a period of *previews*—also called *tryouts*—when the director and the performers discover which parts of the play are successful and which are not. Frequently, for example, the director and performers find that one part of the play is moving too slowly; they know this because the audience members become restless and begin to cough or stir. Sometimes, in a comedy, there is a great deal of laughter where little was expected, and the performers and the director must adjust to this. In this preview period the audiences become genuine collaborators in shaping the play. After several performances in front of an audience, the director and the performers get the "feel" of the audience and know whether or not the play is ready.

Previews Tryout performances of a production before an audience, preceding the official "opening" performance.

Throughout the final stages of preparing the production, the stage manager continues to give detailed notes to all actors to ensure consistency in dialogue and movement. Once the play has opened and the director is no longer present at every performance, it is the stage manager's responsibility to maintain the consistency of the director's vision. In commercial theatre it is important to realize that stage managers and actors are members of the same union, Actors' Equity Association (AEA).

For an idea of the director's full range of responsibilities, see the chart on page 112.

THE DIRECTOR'S POWER AND RESPONSIBILITY

Any artistic event must have a unity not encountered in real life. We expect the parts to be brought together so that the total effect will enlighten us, move us, or amuse us. In theatre, the director—who has a voice in so many areas of a production—is in a unique position to bring this about. This power, however, is a double-edged sword. If a director gets too carried away with one idea, for example, or lets the scene designer create scenery that overpowers the performers, the experience for the audience will be unsatisfactory or incomplete. If, on the other hand, the director has a strong point of view—one that is appropriate for the theatre piece and illuminates the script—and if all the parts fit and are consistent with one another, the experience will be meaningful and exciting, and at times even unforgettable.

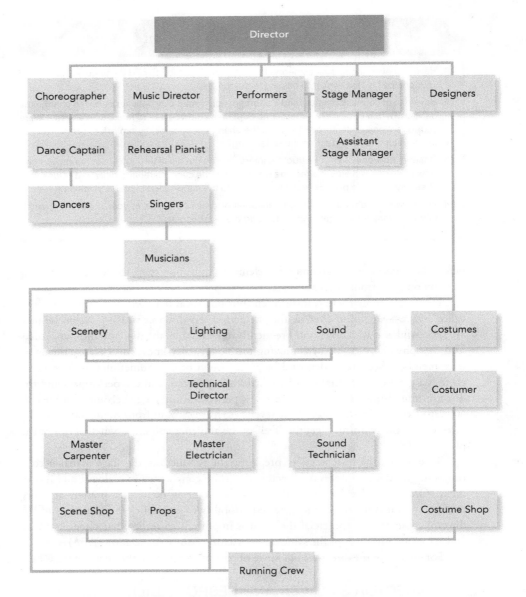

DUTIES OF A DIRECTOR IN A THEATRE PRODUCTION

Once a director has decided on a script (and has worked with the playwright, if it is a new play), he or she must organize the entire artistic side of the production. This chart indicates the many people that the director must work with and the many elements that must be coordinated.

The Audience's View

While watching a production or experiencing a performance, we do not have time to pause and analyze every aspect of the production, from the acting and the script to the visual and aural elements. There is even less time, perhaps, to analyze the work of the director. But the topics covered in this chapter should give us, as audience members, some idea of what might or might not be the responsibility of the director: when the director might be at fault for a failure, or, on the other side, when he or she should be given credit for the successful unfolding of a theatrical event.

THE PRODUCER OR MANAGING DIRECTOR

As spectators, we naturally focus on the event onstage rather than on what happens behind the scenes. But no production would ever be performed for the public without a business component. Here, too, the coordination of elements is crucial, and the person chiefly responsible, known as the ***producer*** in the commercial theatre, or ***managing director*** in the noncommercial theatre, is the behind-the-scenes counterpart of the director.

The Commercial Producer

In a commercial theatre venture, the producer has many responsibilities. (See the nearby chart.) In general, the producer oversees the entire business and publicity side of the production and has the following duties:

1. Raising money to finance the production.
2. Securing rights to the script.

Producer In American usage, the person responsible for the business side of a production, including raising the necessary money. (In British usage, a producer for many years was the equivalent of an American director.)

Managing director In nonprofit theatre organizations, the individual who controls resources and expenditures.

(handwritten margin note: -Producer in Commercial theatre, -Managing Director in non commercial theatre)

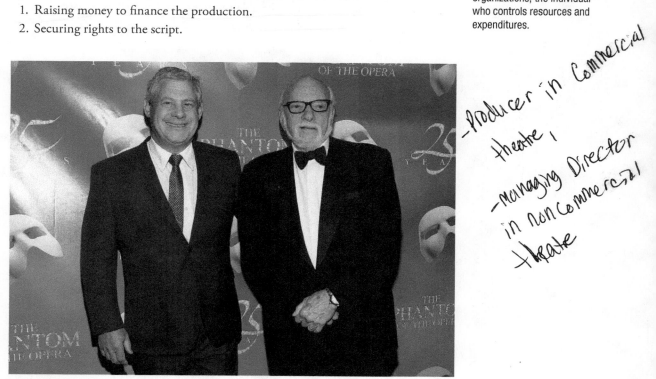

THE PRODUCER

The person who puts a production together is the producer or, in the case of a nonprofit company, the artistic director. He or she selects the play or musical to be presented, and then decides who will carry out each function: direction, design, and all other components. The producer must also see that all elements are properly coordinated. In a commercial production, the producer must in addition raise the necessary funds and determine a number of other factors such as advertising, marketing, and ticket prices. Shown here are two of the most important producers of the 20th century: Cameron Mackintosh and Harold Prince. The occasion was the 25th Anniversary of the Broadway musical *The Phantom Of The Opera*, produced by Mackintosh, in January 2013. Following his successful career as a major producer Prince became a director of musicals, including *Phantom*.
(© John Lamparski/WireImage/Getty Images)

3. Dealing with the agents for the playwright, director, and performers.

4. Hiring the director, performers, designers, and stage crews.

5. Dealing with theatrical unions.

6. Renting the theatre space.

7. Supervising the work of those running the theatre: in the box office, auditorium, and business office.

8. Supervising the advertising.

9. Overseeing the budget and the week-to-week financial management of the production.

It is clear that the responsibilities of the commercial producer range far and wide. They require business acumen, organizational ability, aesthetic judgment, marketing know-how, and an ability to work with people. The producer in commercial theatre must have the artistic sensibility to choose the right script and hire the right director, but at the same time must be able to raise capital as well as oversee all financial and business operations in a production.

RESPONSIBILITIES OF THE COMMERCIAL THEATRE PRODUCER
When a commercial theatre production is mounted, the person responsible for organizing the full range of nonartistic activities is the producer. This chart shows the producer at the top and indicates the people the producer must deal with and the numerous elements he or she must coordinate.

Noncommercial Theatres

In a nonprofit theatre the person with many of the same responsibilities as the producer is called the *executive director,* or *managing director.*

Administrative Organization of a Nonprofit Theatre　Most nonprofit theatres—including theatres in smaller urban centers as well as the large noncommercial theatres in major cities like New York, Chicago, and Los Angeles—are organized with a board of directors, an artistic director, and an executive or managing director. The board is responsible for selecting both the artistic and the managing director. The board is also responsible for overseeing the financial affairs of the theatre, for fundraising, for long-range planning, and the like. To carry out some of these tasks, the board frequently delegates authority to an executive committee.

The artistic director is responsible for all creative and artistic activities. He or she selects the plays that will constitute the season and chooses directors, designers, and other creative personnel. Frequently, the artistic director also directs one or more plays during the season.

Responsibilities of a Noncommercial Managing Director　The managing director in a noncommercial theatre is, in many respects, the counterpart of a producer in commercial theatre. In both a commercial production and the running of a nonprofit theatre organization, the tasks of the person in charge of administration are many and complex.

The managing director is responsible for the maintenance of the theatre building, including the dressing rooms, the scene and costume shops, the public facilities, and the lobby. The managing director is also responsible for the budget, making certain that the production stays within established limits. The budget includes salaries for the director, designers, performers, and stage crews, as well as expenditures for scenery, costumes, and music. Again, an artistic element enters the picture. Some artistic decisions—such as whether a costume needs to be replaced or scenery needs to be altered—affect costs. The managing director must find additional sources of money or must determine that a change is important enough artistically to justify taking funds away from another item in the budget. In other words, she or he must work very closely with the director and the designers in balancing artistic and financial needs.

The managing director, often with additional staff members, is also responsible for publicity. The audience members would never get to the theatre if they did not know when and where a play was being presented. The managing director must work with staff to advertise the production and decide whether the advertisements should be placed in daily newspapers, on radio, on television, in student newspapers, in magazines, or elsewhere.

A host of other responsibilities come under the supervision of the managing director and his or her staff: tickets must be ordered, the box office must be maintained, and plans must be made ahead of time for how tickets are to be sold. Securing ushers, printing programs, and maintaining the auditorium—usually called the *front of the house*—are also the responsibility of the managing director's staff.

Once again, plans must be made well in advance. In many theatre organizations, an entire season—the plays that will be produced, the personnel who will be in charge, and the supplies that will be required—is planned a year ahead of time. It should be

Front of the house
Portion of a theatre reserved for the audience; sometimes called simply the *house.*

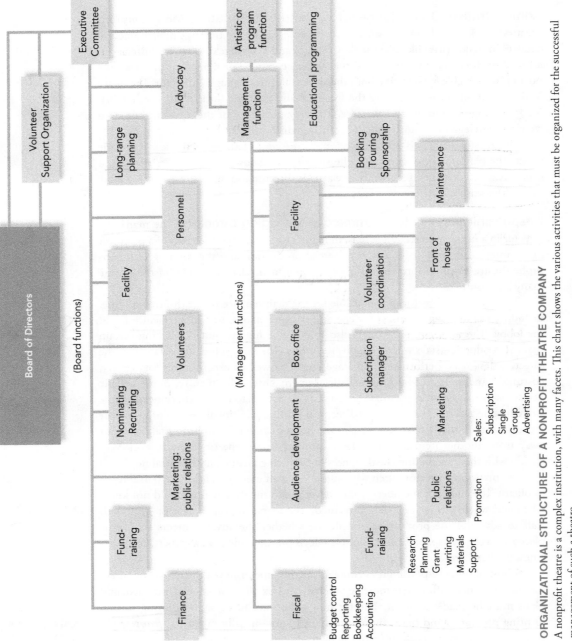

ORGANIZATIONAL STRUCTURE OF A NONPROFIT THEATRE COMPANY

A nonprofit theatre is a complex institution, with many facets. This chart shows the various activities that must be organized for the successful management of such a theatre.

PLAYING YOUR PART: THINKING ABOUT THEATRE

1. Imagine that while you are watching a production, one performer is overacting badly, to the point that he or she is quite unbelievable. Another performer is listless and has no energy. In each case, to what extent do you think this is the director's fault, and to what extent the performer's failure?

2. If you get bored or impatient when watching a performance, what do you think the director could have done in preparing the production to prevent this from happening?

3. Is it fair to say, as some critics do, that when everything "clicks" in a production—that is, when the acting, the scenery and lighting, and the pace of the action all seem to be beautifully coordinated—the director's hand is "invisible"?

4. If you have read a play this semester (or sometime in the past), what do you think the spine of that play is? What would your directorial concept be if you were directing a production of that play?

clear that coordination and cooperation are as important in this area as they are for the production onstage. (For the organization of a nonprofit theatre company, see the chart on page 116.)

COMPLETING THE PICTURE: PLAYWRIGHT, DIRECTOR, AND PRODUCER

A theatre presentation can be compared to a mosaic consisting of many brightly colored pieces of stone that fit together to form a complete picture. The playwright puts the words and ideas together; the performers bring them to life; the designers provide the visual and aural environment; the director integrates the artistic elements; the producer or managing director coordinates the business side of a production. The separate pieces in the mosaic must become parts of an artistic whole, providing us with a complete theatre experience.

SUMMARY

1. The term *director* did not come into general use until the end of the nineteenth century. Certain functions of the director, however—organizing the production, instilling discipline in the performers, and setting a tone for the production—have been carried out since the beginning of theatre by someone in authority.

2. The director's duties became more crucial in the twentieth century. Because of the fragmentation of society and the many styles and cultures that now exist side by side, it is necessary for someone to impose a point of view and a single vision on individual productions.

3. The director has many responsibilities: working with the playwright if the script is a new work; evolving a concept or approach to the script; developing the visual side of the production with the designers; holding auditions and casting roles; working with the performers to develop their individual roles in rehearsals; ensuring that stage action communicates the meaning of the play; establishing appropriate pace and rhythm in the

movement of the scenes; establishing the dynamics of the production as a whole; and supervising the technical and preview rehearsals.

4. *Auteur* directors demand that a text serve their own purposes, rather than shaping their purposes to serve the text. *Postmodern* directors often "deconstruct" a text or rearrange elements to create a theatre piece.

5. Because the director has such wide-ranging power and responsibilities, he or she can distort a production and create an imbalance of elements or an inappropriate emphasis. The director is responsible for a sense of proportion and order in the production.

6. The producer or manager of a production is responsible for the business aspects: maintaining the theatre, arranging publicity, handling finances, as well as managing the ticket sales, budgets, and ushers.

Setting the Stage: The Playwright and the Play

3

The Playwright and the Play

CREATING THE PLAY: THE PLAYWRIGHT

Historically, the subject, the tone, the structure, and the point of view of a dramatic script are the creation of the playwright. Interestingly, the most popular playwright of the 20th and 21st centuries in the U.S. is the master playwright of Elizabethan England, William Shakespeare. Shown here is a scene from Shakespeare's *Taming of the Shrew* directed by Toby Frow in a production at the Globe Theatre in London. (© Geraint Lewis)

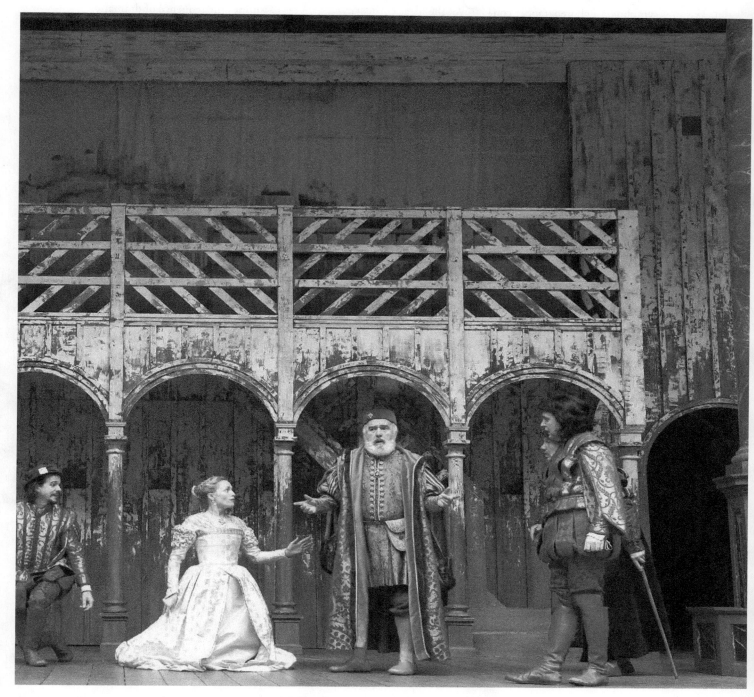

Part Three

The Playwright and the Play

It begins with an impulse, a story, an event, an inspiration: a composer has an idea for a song or a symphony, a choreographer conceives of a ballet, a playwright has a story for a drama or a musical, an architect conceives of a building. Following that beginning, the person who envisions the artwork sets about putting the idea into a form that will be recognizable to those with whom he or she will be collaborating. What emerges is the musical score, the script, the blueprint that others can bring alive as an orchestral concert, a theatrical production, an imaginative piece of architecture. The finished script,

musical score, or blueprint establishes guidelines that point everyone toward the ultimate realization of the idea.

A theatre production is a collaboration, not only between the audience and the performers but among a whole range of people who work together to make it happen: performers, directors, designers, technicians. All these are essential, but like any enterprise, a theatre production must begin somewhere, and in most cases that starting point is the script. For more than 2,000 years, in both the west and Asia, the script of a play has been created by

the dramatist or playwright, the person who chooses the story to be told, selects the characters, determines the sequence of dramatic episodes, and composes the dialogue for the characters to speak. Like theatre, other forms of art also involve collaboration. For instance, in architecture a team of engineers, designers, and contractors will work to create the finished structure. It is the vision of the architect, however, that drives the project.

In recent years, architects have used computer diagrams to render their plans, allowing the architect to create and be involved in many

Choreographer Christopher Wheeldon (right) rehearsing *Carousel (A Dance)* with dancers Kathryn Morgan and Andrew Veyette of the New York City Ballet. (© Paul Kolnik)

An often-repeated story is akin to a drama, with words, characters, and a plot. Here we see a storyteller repeating a folk legend to a group of Native American children on the Barona Indian Reservation. (© Bob Rowan/Corbis)

variations of his or her original idea. In the end, however, one plan is decided on—the equivalent of the blueprint, the script, the score, the scenario. During the past 100 years, theatre artists other than the playwright have sometimes assumed the work of creating a script. One is the auteur director, who not only conceives and originates the work but also directs and controls what happens onstage. Others creating scenarios—outlines for performances that are sometimes developed through improvisation—include ensemble theatre groups and performance artists.

It is important to understand, however, that these alternative approaches have not eliminated the playwright; rather, these other artists have taken the place of the playwright and become "dramatists." The creation of a blueprint, a scenario, or script remains an essential element of creating a theatrical event.

Anyone who creates a theatre piece faces the same challenge: how to turn nontheatrical material into a viable work for the stage. At what point in the story does the dramatic action begin? Who are the characters; what actions are they given; what words do they speak? How are interest and excitement developed and maintained? How is suspense created and increased? Will the work be serious or comic, funny or sad? In the process of answering these questions, a script emerges—a script that is both the embodiment of a vision and a blueprint for a production. Through the centuries, certain principles and strategies have emerged as most effective in creating a dramatic work. In Part Three we look at these principles and strategies, as well as the point of view that is adopted by the creator and that makes the work tragic, comic, or other dramatic type.

An architect conceives and designs a building in the way that a composer or dramatist creates a composition or a drama. The acclamed architect Frank Gehry is shown here with his models for the new business school at the University of Technology in Sydney, Australia. (© Renee Nowytarger/Newspix/Getty Images)

A composer creates a musical score.

(© PhotoLink/Getty Images)

124

Creating the World of the Play

Beginning in ancient times, in virtually every culture, there have been storytellers: a person who recounted recount tales to people gathered around a fire, describing heroic figures, daring deeds, frightening encounters, and humorous episodes. These chroniclers told stories of adventure, ghost stories, tall tales, horror stories, legends and histories, and fantastic fables.

In the theatre many people work together to present a story—actors and directors, designers and technicians—but it all begins with the theatre's storyteller: the playwright. Consciously or unconsciously the playwright makes a number of decisions that will determine exactly what kind of event audiences will see on stage. Among those decisions are what story will be told, the time and place of the story, the characters who will take part, the tone and emphasis of the story (will it be serious and tragic, or comic and humorous?), the way the story is told (the structure of the drama), and how it unfolds and ends. In the next chapter after this one we will focus on decisions concerning the structure of the play and the characters who are featured. In the chapter after that we will turn to the question of whether the play is funny or sad, comic or tragic.

Before those decisions, however, there are other choices the playwright makes. For example, the playwright or dramatist determines what subject matter to present and which characters to include. Will the work be based on history—for example, an episode or incident from the American Civil War, from World War II, from the Vietnamese War, or from the war in Iraq or Afghanistan? Perhaps the play will be based on biography—on the life of Eleanor Roosevelt or Martin Luther King, Jr. Perhaps it will be an exploration of the creator's own life—facing the problems of growing up or facing

◀ **THE PLAYWRIGHT CREATES THE TEMPLATE**

In undertaking to write a script, the playwright makes a number of decisions. His or her intention may be to entertain; to raise timeless questions, as is often the case in tragedy; or to make a political or social comment. In any case, the person or persons who create a theatre script set the tone, the agenda, and the approach to be followed by director, actors, designers, and others. Samuel Beckett in Waiting for Gogot *wrote a play, usually placed in the category of the Theatre of the Absurd, in which two characters, adrift in time, are forced to repeat the same pattern day after day waiting for Godot, a figure they believe will be their savior, but Godot never comes. Shown here as two men are Alan Mandell (Estragon) and Barry McGovern (Vladimir) in a production directed by Michael Arabian at the Mark Taper Forum, 2012.*
(© Craig Schwartz)

FOCUS AND EMPHASIS
A playwright can choose to emphasize a particular character trait in one play and its opposite in another. Henrik Ibsen in his *Brand,* presents the leading character as a stark, uncompromising figure who will sacrifice everything—family, friends, love—for his principles. The leading character in Ibsen's *Peer Gynt,* however, is always compromising, always running away. Here we see actor Barret O' Brien in the role of Peer Gynt in production at the Yale School of Drama directed by Mike Donahue. (© T Charles Erickson)

a personal crisis as an adult. Still another possibility would be an imaginary story, either resembling everyday life or based on a fantasy or a nightmare.

Along with the subject to be dramatized, there is also the question of whom and what to focus on. For example, a playwright can emphasize a particular character trait in one play and its opposite in another. This is what Henrik Ibsen often did. In his *Brand,* the leading character is a stark, uncompromising figure who will sacrifice everything—family, friends, love—for his principles. In contrast, the leading character in Ibsen's *Peer Gynt* is just the opposite: always compromising, always running away. In creating a theatre piece there is great leeway in making a number of such decisions.

The playwright must also determine the order of events in a play. A good example is the way the myth of Electra was treated by three prominent tragic dramatists in Greece in the fifth century BCE. The story concerns Electra's revenge on her mother, Clytemnestra, and her stepfather, Aegisthus, for having murdered her natural father, Agamemnon. In carrying out her revenge, Electra enlists the help of Orestes, her brother, who has just returned from exile. In the versions by Aeschylus and Euripides, the stepfather is murdered first, and the mother, Clytemnestra, is murdered last. This puts emphasis on the terror of murdering one's own mother.

Sophocles, however, saw the story differently. He wanted to emphasize the idea that Electra and her brother were acting honorably and to play down the mother's murder. And so he reversed the order of the murders: he had the mother killed first; then he built up to the righteous murder of the stepfather as the final deed. The change made by Sophocles indicates the latitude writers, directors, and performance artists have in altering events to suit their artistic purposes. Still another choice open to a dramatist is what degree of seriousness to convey, or what point of view to take toward the subject of the drama: will it be comic or tragic, sympathetic or satiric, cynical or celebratory?

THE SUBJECT AND VERB OF DRAMA: PEOPLE AND ACTION

Before turning to the specifics of creating a dramatic work, we should note an important point about the nature of drama. The subject of theatre is always people—their hopes, their joys, their foibles, their fears. In other words, if we were to construct a

CONFLICT: THE CRUCIBLE OF DRAMA Theatre requires conflict: between people; among family members; between opposing nations, ideologies, or political agendas. Here we see Amy Morton, left, and Tracy Letts, as a fiercely battling married couple, in Edward Albee's *Who's Afraid of Virginia Woolf?* in the Steppenwolf Theater Company's revival directed by Pam MacKinnon on Broadway. (© Sara Krulwich/ The New York Times/Redux)

"grammar of theatre," the *subject* would be people: that is, dramatic characters. In grammar, every subject needs a verb; so, in the grammar of theatre, dramatic characters need some form of action that defines them.

The terms *to act* and *to perform* are used in theatre to denote the impersonation of a character by an actor or an actress, but these words also mean "to do something," or "to be active." The word *drama* derives from a Greek root, the verb *dran,* meaning "to do" or "to act." At its heart, theatre involves action. One way to provide action is to create a test or challenge for the characters. The American dramatist Arthur Miller named one of his plays *The Crucible.* Literally, a *crucible* is a vessel in which metal is tested by being exposed to extreme heat. Figuratively, a crucible has come to stand for any severe test of human worth and endurance—a trial by fire. In a sense, every play provides a crucible: a test devised by the playwright to show how the characters behave under conditions of stress. Through this test, the meaning of the play is brought out.

STRUCTURAL CONVENTIONS: THE RULES OF THE GAME

Despite the options open to a dramatist with regard to the focus of the drama and the characters involved, there is one thing every dramatist is compelled to do if the work is to succeed as a theatre piece, and that is to transform the raw material of the drama into a viable work for the stage. In order to make certain that the events onstage will be dynamic and that the characters will face a meaningful test, conventions or "ground rules" have evolved for dramatic structure. A good analogy would be the rules in games such as card games, board games, video games, and sports. In each case, rules are developed to ensure a lively contest.

Consider, for example, how theatre can be compared to sports. Theatre is more varied and complex than most sports events, and theatrical rules are not so clearly defined or so consciously imposed as rules in sports. Nevertheless, there are similarities that highlight the ways a play makes its impact.

Limited Space

Most sports have a limited playing area. In some cases this consists of a confined space: a boxing ring, a basketball court, a baseball field. The playing area is clearly defined, and invariably there is some kind of "out of bounds."

Theatre, of course, is usually limited to a stage; but there is also a limit within the play itself. The action of a play is generally confined to a "world" of its own—that is, to a fictional universe that contains all the characters and events of the play—and none of the characters or actions moves outside the orbit of that world. Sometimes the world of a play is restricted to a single room.

In his play *No Exit,* Jean-Paul Sartre (1905–1980), a French existentialist, confines three characters to one room, from which, as the title suggests, there is no escape. The room is supposed to be hell, and the three characters—a man, Garcin, and two women, Estelle and Inez—are confined there forever. Estelle loves Garcin, Garcin loves Inez, and Inez (a lesbian) loves Estelle. Each one, in short, loves the one who will not reciprocate, and by being confined to a room, they undergo permanent torture. There are numerous modern plays in which the action takes place in a single room, a good example being *'Night, Mother* by Marsha Norman (b. 1947), about a mother and daughter in crisis, which takes place in their rural home.

Limited Time

Sports events put some limit on the duration of action. In football and basketball, there is a definite time limit. In golf, there is a given number of holes; in tennis, there is a limited number of sets. Theoretically, some sports, such as baseball, are open-ended and could go on forever; but spectators tend to become impatient with this arrangement. Tennis, for instance, was originally open-ended but now has a "sudden

LIMITED SPACE
In his play *No Exit,* Jean-Paul Sartre presents three characters involved in an impossible love triangle confined to one room, from which, as the title suggests, there is no escape. Karen MacDonald as Estelle, Will Lebow as Garcin, and Paula Plum as Inez are shown in this scene, directed by Jerry Mouawad at the A. R. T. in Boston. (© T Charles Erickson)

death" or tiebreaker play-off when a set reaches six-all. A time limit or score limit ensures that the spectators can see a complete event, with a clear winner and loser and no loose ends. The time limit in theatre can be looked at in two ways: first, as the length of time it takes a performance to be completed; second, as the time limit placed on the characters within the framework of the play itself.

Most theatrical performances last from one to three hours. In the drama festivals of ancient Greece, plays were presented for several days in a row. On a single day there might be a trilogy of three connecting plays followed by a short comic play. Still, even if we count a Greek trilogy as one play, it lasted only the better part of a day.

More important than the actual playing time of a performance is the time limit or deadline *within* the play. This means the time that is supposed to elapse during the events of the play, the time covered by those events—a few hours, a few days, or longer. Frequently, we find in a play a fixed period within which the characters must complete an action. For instance, at the end of the second act of Ibsen's *A Doll's House,* the heroine, Nora, is trying desperately to persuade her husband to put off until the following evening the opening of a letter that she fears will establish her as a forger and will threaten their marriage. When he agrees, Nora says to herself, "Thirty-one hours to live."

Strongly Opposed Forces

Most sports, like many other types of games, involve two opposed teams or individuals. This ensures clear lines of force: the old guard versus the young upstarts, the home team versus the visitors. The musical *West Side Story* (based on Shakespeare's *Romeo and Juliet*) features two opposed gangs, not unlike opposing teams in sports. In the simplest dramatic situations, one character directly opposes another. The man and woman, Julie and Jean, in Strindberg's *Miss Julie* are a perfect example of characters bound to clash. Julie, an aristocrat, is the daughter of the owner of an estate. She has had an unhappy engagement and is deeply suspicious of men, but at the same time sexually attracted to

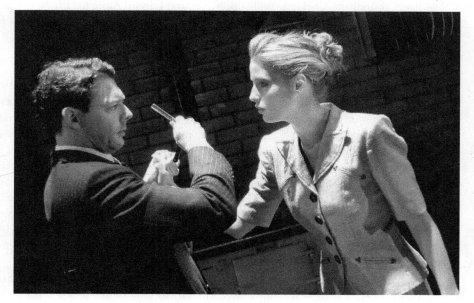

STRONGLY OPPOSED FORCES
Traditional plot structure calls for strongly opposing forces: the antagonist opposes the protagonist; one group opposes another. Here we see Richard Coyle as Jean, squaring off with Kelly Reilly as Julie in *After Miss Julie,* Patrick Marber's adaptation of Strindberg's *Miss Julie,* directed by Michael Grandage in a Donmar Warehouse production in London. (© Geraint Lewis)

them. Jean is a servant, an aggressive man who dreams of escaping his life of servitude and owning a hotel. These two characters experience strong forces of repulsion and attraction and are drawn together on a midsummer eve in a climactic encounter.

One device frequently used by dramatists to create friction or tension between forces is restricting the characters to the members of one family. Relatives have built-in rivalries and affinities: parents versus children, sisters versus brothers. Being members of the same family, they have no avenue of escape. Mythology, on which so much drama is based, abounds in familial relationships.

Shakespeare frequently set members of one family against one another: Hamlet opposes his mother; Lear opposes his daughters; Othello kills his wife, Desdemona. In modern drama, virtually every writer of note has dealt with close family situations: Ibsen, Strindberg, Chekhov, Williams, Miller, and Edward Albee (b. 1928), to mention a few. The American dramatist Eugene O'Neill wrote what many consider his finest play, *Long Day's Journey into Night,* about the four members of his own family.

A Balance of Forces

In most sports, there are rules designed to ensure that the contest will be as equal as possible without coming to a draw. We all want our team to win, but we would rather see a close, exciting contest than a runaway. And so rules are set up, with handicaps or other devices to equalize the forces. In basketball or football, for instance, as soon as one team scores, the other team gets the ball so that it will have an opportunity to even the score. In theatre, a hard-fought and relatively equal contest is implicit in what has been said about opposing forces.

Even in the somewhat muted, low-key plays of Anton Chekhov, there is a balance of forces among various groups. In *The Cherry Orchard,* the owners of the orchard are set against the man who will acquire it; in *The Three Sisters,* the sisters are opposed in the possession of their home by their acquisitive sister-in-law.

Incentive and Motivation

In sports, as in other kinds of games, a prize is offered to guarantee that the participants will give their best in an intense contest. In professional sports it is money; in

IN FOCUS: GLOBAL CONNECTIONS

The Asian Influence on the Playwrights Brecht and Wilder

During the past 100 years, many European and U.S. playwrights have been influenced by the structures, styles, and subject matter of traditional theatres of other continents. Two mid–twentieth-century dramatists from the West who were strongly influenced by Asian theatre were the German playwright Bertolt Brecht (1889–1956) and the American playwright Thornton Wilder (1897–1975). Brecht, for example, drew from Asian legends, and used techniques and styles borrowed from Chinese, Japanese, and Indian theatre. Chinese theatre and literature were to prove particularly important for his *Good Woman of Setzuan* (1938–1949), which was set in China; and *The Caucasian Chalk Circle* (1944–1945), based on a Chinese play, *The Story of the Chalk Circle*.

Bertolt Brecht. (© Hulton-Deutsch Collection/Corbis)

Thomson Wilder. (© Bettmann/Corbis)

Both Brecht and Wilder had seen Beijing opera and adopted certain features of this dramatic style into their own work. Beijing opera (also called *jingju* and Peking opera) blends song, dance, martial arts, theatre, acrobatics, and dance and uses much symbolism. Beijing opera takes place on an almost bare stage (often with just a table and a few chairs onstage throughout) and uses simple props brought on by stage attendants, and symbolic movements by the actors. For example, an actor walking in a circle around the stage indicates a long journey; a banner with a fish design indicates water, although rolled up on a tray, the same banner would represent a fish. Brecht used such symbolic props and actions to achieve his alienation or distancing effect, which prevented the audience from identifying emotionally with the drama. In 1935, Brecht saw a performance by the Beijing opera star Mei Lanfang (1894–1961) in Moscow, and the following year he wrote his essay "Alienation Effects in Chinese Acting," which noted aspects of Beijing opera conducive to the distancing effect he desired.

Similarly, Wilder had been exposed to Chinese theatre first at an early age, when his father's work took him to Hong Kong and Shanghai; and then as an adult, when he saw Mei Lanfang perform in New York in 1930. Aspects of Beijing opera that Wilder adopted can best be seen in his Pulitzer Prize–winning *Our Town* (1938). In this play, Wilder uses an almost bare stage with just two tables and six chairs positioned by the stage manager (who also acts as a narrator), and other locales are suggested by very simple alterations; in the third act, for example, the cemetery is suggested by just ten or twelve people sitting in chairs. Both playwrights illustrate the increasing prevalence of Asian influences in twentieth-century playwriting.

Prepared by Naomi Stubbs, CUNY Graduate Center.

amateur sports, a trophy, such as a cup. In addition, there is the glory of winning, as well as the accolades of television and the press and the plaudits of family and friends. In the same way, good drama never lacks incentive or motivation for its characters: Macbeth wants desperately to be king in *Macbeth*, and Blanche DuBois must find protection and preserve her dignity in *A Streetcar Named Desire*.

CREATING STRUCTURE

Applying the principles and conventions outlined above, the dramatist sets about developing a dramatic structure for the theatre piece. Every work of art has some kind of structure, or framework. It may be loosely connected or tightly knit; the important thing is that the framework exists. In theatre, structure usually takes the form of a *plot,* which is the arrangement of events or the selection and order of scenes in a play. Plot, in turn, is generally based on a *story.*

Plot As distinct from story, patterned arrangements of events and characters in a drama, with incidents selected and arranged for maximum dramatic impact.

Plot versus Story

Stories—narrative accounts of what people do—are as old as the human race, and they form the substance of daily conversation, of newspapers and television, of novels and films. But every medium presents a story in a different form. In theatre, the story must be presented in a limited period of time by living actors and actresses on a stage, and this requires selectivity.

It is important for us to recognize that the plot of a play differs from a story. A story is a full account of an event, or series of events, usually told in chronological order. Plot is a selection and arrangement of scenes taken from a story for presentation onstage. It is what actually happens onstage, not what is talked about. The story of Abraham Lincoln, for example, begins with his birth in a log cabin and continues to the day he was shot at Ford's Theater in Washington. To create a play about Lincoln, a playwright would have to make choices. Would the dramatist include scenes in Springfield, Illinois, where Lincoln worked as a lawyer and held his famous debates with Stephen Douglas? Or would everything take place in Washington after Lincoln became president? Would there be scenes with Lincoln's wife, Mary Todd, or would the other characters be only government and military officials? The plot of a play about Abraham Lincoln and Mary Todd would have scenes and characters related primarily to their lives. The plot of a play about the Lincoln-Douglas debates would consist mostly of scenes relating to the debates.

Even when a play is based on a fictional story invented by the playwright, the plot must be more restricted and structured than the story itself: characters and scenes must still be selected and the sequence determined.

The Opening Scene

The first scene of a drama starts the action and sets the tone and style for everything that follows. It tells us whether we are going to see a serious or a comic play and whether the play will deal with fantasy or with affairs of everyday life. The opening scene is a clue or signal about what lies ahead. It also sets the wheels of action in motion, giving the characters a shove and hurtling them toward their destination.

The playwright poses an initial problem for the characters, establishing an imbalance of forces or a disturbance in their equilibrium that compels them to respond. Generally, this imbalance has occurred just before the play begins, or it develops immediately after the play opens. In *Antigone,* for example, two brothers have killed each other just before the opening of the play. In *Hamlet,* "something is rotten in the state of Denmark," and early in the play the ghost of Hamlet's father tells Hamlet to seek revenge. At the beginning of *Romeo and Juliet,* the Capulets and the Montagues are at one another's throats in a street fight.

THE OPENING SCENE
The first scene of a play is crucial, usually setting the location; establishing mood and tone; and introducing characters, themes, and action. A famous opening scene is that in Shakespeare's *Romeo and Juliet,* in which the Capulet and Montague families confront each other in a street fight. Shown here is the opening scene in a production directed by Dominic Dromgoogle at Shakespeare's Globe, with Ukweli Roach as Tybalt and Philip Cumbus as Mercutio in the foreground. (© Geraint Lewis)

Obstacles and Complications

Having met the initial challenge of the play, the characters then move through a series of steps—alternating between achievement and defeat, between hope and despair. The moment they seem to accomplish one goal, certain factors or events cut across the play to upset the balance and start the characters on another path. In theatre these may be *obstacles,* which are impediments put in a character's way; or they may be *complications—* outside forces or new twists in the plot introduced at an opportune moment.

Shakespeare's *Hamlet* provides numerous examples of obstacles and complications. Hamlet stages a "play within the play" in order to confirm that his uncle Claudius has killed his father. Claudius reacts to the play in a manner that makes his guilt obvious. But when Hamlet first tries to kill Claudius, he discovers him at prayer. An obstacle has been thrown into Hamlet's path: if Claudius dies while praying, he may go to heaven rather than to hell. Since Hamlet does not want Claudius to go to heaven, he does not kill him.

Later, Hamlet is in his mother's bedroom when he hears a noise behind a curtain. Surely Claudius is lurking there, but when Hamlet thrusts his sword through the curtain, he finds that he has killed Polonius, the father of Ophelia, the young lady he is close to. This provides Claudius with an excuse to send Hamlet to England with Rosencrantz and Guildenstern, who carry with them a letter instructing the king of England to murder Hamlet. Hamlet escapes that trap and returns to Denmark. Now, at last, it seems that he can carry out his revenge. But on his return, he discovers that Ophelia has killed herself while he was away, and her brother, Laertes, is seeking revenge on him. This complicates the situation once again, as Hamlet is prevented from meeting Claudius head-on because he must also deal with Laertes. In the end Hamlet does carry out his mission, but only after many interruptions.

Crisis and Climax

As a result of conflicts, obstacles, and complications in a play, the characters become involved in a series of *crises.* A play usually builds from one crisis to another. The first crisis will be

Obstacles That which delays or prevents the achieving of a goal by a character. An obstacle creates complication and conflict.

Complications Introduction, in a play, of a new force, which creates a new balance of power and entails a delay in reaching the climax.

Crises A point in a play when events and opposing forces are at a crucial moment, and when the course of further action will be determined. There may be a series of crises leading to the definitive climax.

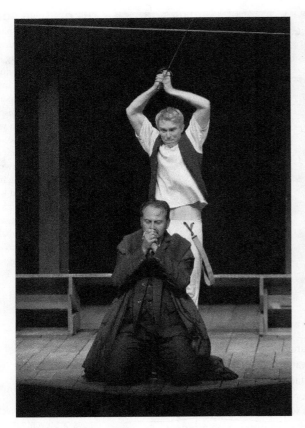

PLOT COMPLICATIONS IN *HAMLET*

In conventional plot structure, the action is prolonged and tension is increased by a series of problems confronting the characters. The twists and turns in the plot of Shakespeare's *Hamlet* are an example. Shown here is Michael Benz as Hamlet, preparing to kill King Claudius (Dickon Tyrrell), who he thinks has murdered his father. But Hamlet hesitates because he does not want to send Claudius to heaven, as he fears might happen if he kills Claudius at prayer. This scene is from a production at The Broad Stage in Santa Monica, California. (© Noel Vasquez/ WireImage/Getty Images)

Climax   The high point in the development of a dramatic plot. The scene toward the end of a drama in which all the forces reach their highest pitch and the fate of all the characters is determined.

resolved only to have the action lead to a subsequent crisis. The final and most significant crisis is referred to as the ***climax.*** In the climax the issues of the play are resolved, either happily or, in the case of tragedies, unhappily, often with the death of the hero or heroine.

It should be noted that a series of crises leading to a climax in a drama applies most readily to traditional plays—that is, works created before the modern period. During the past 100 years, a number of variations of classic plot structure have appeared in which the notion of a climax has been either eliminated or minimized. These approaches to structure will be looked at in detail in Chapter 8.

POINT OF VIEW

In addition to structure and character portrayal, the person or persons creating a dramatic work must determine the point of view represented in the work: will it be tragic or comic, humorous or sad, or perhaps a mixture of the two? People and events can always be interpreted in widely different ways. How we perceive them depends on our point of view. There is a familiar story of two people looking at a bottle that is partly full of wine. The optimist will say that the bottle is half-full, the pessimist that it is half-empty.

Anyone familiar with the presentation of evidence in a courtroom—in a trial involving an automobile accident, for instance—knows that different witnesses, each of whom may be honest and straightforward, will describe the same incident differently. One will say that she saw a minivan go through a stoplight and hit a blue car; another will say that he remembers clearly that the blue car pulled out before the light had changed and blocked the path of the van. The same variation in viewpoint affects our assessment of politicians and other public figures. To some people, a certain politician will be a dedicated, sincere public servant, interested only in what is best for the nation. But to others, the same politician will be a hypocrite and a charlatan.

Point of view is particularly important in the arts. Under ordinary circumstances, those who attempt to influence our point of view, such as advertisers and politicians, frequently disguise their motives. They use subtle, indirect techniques to convince us that they are not trying to impose their views on us, though people who understand the process know that this is exactly what an advertiser or a politician is trying to do. In the arts, on the other hand, the imposition of a point of view is direct and deliberate. The artist makes it clear that he or she is looking at the world from a highly personal and perhaps unusual angle, possibly even turning the world upside down.

DYNAMICS OF DRAMA

Structure in Feminist Plays

As a result of the women's movement of the 1970s, some feminist theatre critics examined Aristotle's *Poetics* and suggested that his concept of the ideally structured tragedy, which had been the template for western drama for centuries, reflected the West's dominant male culture. Radical feminist theorists, for instance, saw the plot complications, crisis, and denouement in tragedy as a duplication of the male sexual experience of foreplay, arousal, and climax. Other feminist critics viewed traditional linear, cause-and-effect plot development as a reflection of the step-by-step approach that men have traditionally used to empower their lives and control society. The leading figures, or subjects, of these plays, according to feminist critics, were invariably male.

To counter this Aristotelian tradition, feminist theatre critics and practitioners aimed to create what Professor Sue-Ellen Case, in her groundbreaking book *Feminism and Theatre* (1988), called a "new poetics." The idea was to explore a "women's form" of drama, and also to construct new, feminist ways of analyzing and responding to theatrical texts and performance.

Among the pioneers was the French feminist and playwright Hélène Cixous (b. 1937), who, in her famous essay "The Laugh of the Medusa," called for women to create a new language that would be suggestive and ambiguous. Other feminists called for a dramatic form that stressed "contiguity," a form, writes Case, which is "fragmentary rather than whole" and "interrupted rather than complete." This form is often cyclical and without the single climax. It is frequently open-ended and offers woman as subject. One example is *Fefu and Her Friends*, written and directed in 1977 by the Cuban-born American dramatist Maria Irene Fornés (b. 1930). Instead of a plot, there is a cyclical, physical action; and in place of logical cause and effect, Fornés writes each scene as though it were a new event. There is no hero; the subject of the play is a group of educated women sharing thoughts and ideas.

Not all women have embraced the new poetics. But increasingly, feminists have experimented with dramatic form and theatrical styles, to confront, expose, and rewrite what they see as centuries of male cultural domination.

Prepared by Alexis Greene.

In films, for example, we have become familiar with the various points of view, angles of vision, and perspectives that the camera selects for us. In a close-up, we do not see an entire room or even an entire person—we see one small detail: hands on a computer keyboard or a finger on the trigger of a gun. In a medium shot we see more—a couple embracing, perhaps—but still only part of the scene. In an exterior scene we might have a panorama of the Grand Canyon or a military parade. The camera also predetermines the angle from which we see the action. In a scene emphasizing the strength of a figure, the camera might look up from below to show a person looming from the top of a flight of stairs. In another scene we might look down on the action. In still other instances the camera might be tilted so that a scene looks off balance; a scene might be shot out of focus so that it is hazy or blurred, or it might be filmed through a special filter.

Similarly, the viewpoint of the theatre artist tells us how to interpret the words and actions of the characters we see onstage; it provides a key to understanding the entire experience.

THE INDIVIDUAL POINT OF VIEW
In addition to the social and cultural climate, the individual artist's outlook also determines whether a work will be serious or comic. Even two people writing in the same country at the same time will view the world differently. In seventeenth-century France, Racine wrote mostly tragedies, such as *Phèdre*. Shown above (left) is a London production at the National Theatre featuring Helen Mirren in the title role with Dominic Cooper as Hippolytus, directed by Nicholas Hytner. (© Geraint Lewis) However, in the same period Racine's countryman and contemporary, Molière, wrote comedies like *The Bungler*, with Michael A. Newcomer as Lelie (the title character) and JD. Cullum as his servant Mascarille shown here from a production at A Noise Within in Pasadena, California, directed by Julia Rodriguez-Elliott. (© Graig Schwartz)

The Dramatist's Point of View

"There is nothing either good or bad, but thinking makes it so," Shakespeare wrote in *Hamlet*. To this could be added a parallel statement: "There is nothing either funny or sad, but thinking makes it so." One's point of view determines whether one takes a subject seriously or laughs at it, whether it is an object of pity or of ridicule. Horace Walpole (1717–1797), an English author, wrote: "This world is a comedy to those that think, a tragedy to those that feel." Walpole's epigram underlines the fact that people see the world differently.

It is difficult to say just why some people look at the world and weep while others look at it and laugh, but there is no question that they do. In theatre, point of view begins when a dramatist, a director, or a performance artist takes a strong personal view of a subject, deciding that it is grave, heroic, or humorous. As in other art forms,

PLAYING YOUR PART: EXPERIENCING THEATRE

1. If you were to write a play about your life, what would you choose as your opening scene? What would some of your complications be? Would there be a climactic moment?

2. If you were to write a play about a family you know (your own or another), what point of view would you take? Why? Are there strongly opposed forces or balanced forces in this family?

3. If you were told you were going to have to attend a play that lasted over four hours, what would your reaction be? Why? What are your traditional expectations about the space and time of a play?

4. After watching a popular film, describe how the opening scene aids in setting the action. Describe one or two of the complications in the film. Can you discuss the film's point of view?

opportunities for selectivity are greater than in everyday life; hence a point of view can be adopted in drama consciously and deliberately. In the case of a play, point of view is incorporated by the playwright into the script itself, with characters being given words to speak and actions to perform that convey a certain attitude. In a serious work the writer will choose language and actions suggesting sobriety and sincerity. Take the lines spoken by Shakespeare's Othello:

> Oh, now for ever
> Farewell the tranquil mind! Farewell content!
> Farewell the plumed troop and the big wars
> that make ambition virtue!

These words express unmistakably Othello's profound sense of loss.

Another writer might take what is ordinarily a serious subject and treat it humorously. A good example is Arthur Kopit (b. 1937), who gave a comic twist to a dead body in his play *Oh, Dad. Poor Dad. Mama's Hung You in the Closet, and I'm Feelin' So Sad.* The title itself, with its mocking tone and its unusual length, makes it clear from the beginning that Kopit wants us to laugh at his subject. Once the playwright's intentions are known, the director and the performers transmit them to the audience.

Society's Point of View

In discussing point of view, we cannot overlook the role that society plays in the viewpoint adopted by an artist such as a playwright. As discussed in Chapter 2, there is a close relationship between theatre and society. This relationship manifests itself particularly in the point of view artists adopt toward their subject matter.

Tragedy, for example, generally occurs in periods when society as a whole assumes a certain attitude toward people and toward the universe. Two periods conducive to the creation of tragedy were the golden age of Greece in the fifth century BCE and the Renaissance in Europe during the fourteenth, fifteenth, and sixteenth centuries CE. Both periods incorporated two ideas essential to tragic drama: on the one hand, a concept of human beings as capable of extraordinary accomplishments; and on the other, the notion that the world is potentially cruel and unjust. A closer look at these two periods will demonstrate how they reflect these two viewpoints.

A CLIMATE FOR TRAGEDY

The worldview of a society is one factor that determines whether it will embrace and encourage tragedy. Some cultures, such as Athens in the fifth century BCE and Elizabethan England, were particularly conducive to the creation of tragic drama. Sophocles' *Electra* is a good example. Shown here are Dallas Milholland as Electra (left) and Kristin Katsu as Chrysothemis (right) in a production at Western Illinois University directed by Brennin Weiswerda. (© Photo courtesy of WIU Visual Production Center/Caiflin Salmon, Photographer)

In both the fifth century BCE in Greece and the Renaissance in continental Europe and England, human beings were exalted above everything else. The gods and nature were given a much less prominent place in the scheme of things. The men and women of those periods considered the horizons of human achievement unlimited. In the fifth century BCE, Greece was enjoying its golden age in commerce, politics, science, and art; nothing seemed impossible in the way of architecture, mathematics, trade, or philosophy. The same was true in Europe and England during the centuries of the Renaissance. Columbus had reached the new world in 1492, and the possibilities for trade and exploration appeared infinite. Science and the arts were on the threshold of a new day as well.

In sculpture during the two periods, the human figure was glorified as it rarely had been before or has been since, and the celebration of the individual was apparent in all the arts as well, including drama. The Greek dramatist Sophocles exclaimed:

> Numberless are the world's wonders, but none
> More wonderful than man.

And in the Renaissance, Shakespeare has Hamlet say:

> What a piece of work is man! How noble in reason! How infinite in faculty! In form, in moving, how express and admirable! In action how like an angel! In apprehension how like a god!

The credo of both ages was expressed by Protagoras, a Greek philosopher of the fifth century BCE:

PLAYING YOUR PART: THINKING ABOUT THEATRE

PLAYING YOUR PART: THINKING ABOUT THEATRE

1. Think of a play you have read or seen where the main character encounters one impediment or roadblock after another. Describe the various obstacles that must be overcome before the end of the play.

2. Think of a play or musical you have seen or read where two major characters are in conflict with one another. Describe the two characters and explain the source of their conflict. How does it play out?

3. Think of a situation some people saw as very serious, but another person viewed as humorous. Explain what you believe led different people to see it so differently. What was your own feeling—was the incident funny or sad?

Man is the measure of all things.

But there is another side to the tragic coin. Along with this optimistic, humanistic view, there was a faculty for admitting, unflinchingly, that life can be—and frequently is—cruel, unjust, and even meaningless. Shakespeare put it this way in *King Lear:*

> As flies to wanton boys, are we to the gods;
> They kill us for their sport.

In *Macbeth,* he expressed it in these words:

> Out, out brief candle!
> Life's but a walking shadow, a poor player
> That struts and frets his hour upon the stage
> And then is heard no more; it is a tale
> Told by an idiot, full of sound and fury,
> Signifying nothing.

These periods of history—the Greek golden age and the Renaissance—were expansive enough to encompass both strains: the greatness of human beings on the one hand, and the cruelty of life on the other.

To clarify the distinction between the tragic point of view and other points of view, we need only examine periods in history when one or both of the attitudes forming the tragic viewpoint were absent or were expressed quite differently. In continental Europe and Great Britain, the eighteenth century was known as the *age of enlightenment,* and the nineteenth century as the *century of progress.* Enlightenment and progress: together they express the philosophy that men and women can analyze any problem—poverty, violence, disease, injustice—and, by applying their intelligence, solve it. An age of unbounded optimism in which no problem is thought insurmountable, and a sense of moral justice runs strong, is not one in which tragic drama can easily emerge.

Before we examine tragedy, comedy, and other dramatic forms in detail we will look first at dramatic structure and dramatic characters—the way a playwright moves the action from scene to scene to develop a plot and creates individual stage characters.

SUMMARY

1. Drama is written and produced for different purposes: to move us, to involve us, to amuse us, to entertain us, to inform us, to shock us, to raise our awareness, to inspire us. The dramatist must determine which of these purposes the work being created will serve.

2. The action of a play frequently consists of a test, or crucible, for the characters, in which their true nature is defined. This test involves some form of conflict.

3. Dramatic conventions, ensuring a strong plot and continuation of tension, are analogous to rules in sports. In both sports and theatre there are limited spaces or playing areas, time limits imposed on the action, strongly opposing forces, evenly matched contestants, and prizes or goals for the participants.

4. A play generally begins with an imbalance of forces or a loss of equilibrium by one of the characters; this propels the characters to action.

5. As a play progresses, the characters encounter a series of obstacles and complications in attempting to fulfill their objectives or realize their goals. These encounters produce the tension and conflict of drama.

6. Generally, every work of art, including theatre, has some kind of structure. In theatre, structure usually takes the form of a plot.

7. A dramatic plot is not the same as a story. A story is a complete account of an episode or a sequence of events, but a plot is what we see onstage. In a plot the events have been selected from a story and arranged in a certain sequence.

8. Point of view is the way we look at things: the perspective, or angle of vision, from which we view people, places, and events.

9. In the arts, the establishment of a point of view is direct and deliberate; it is an integral part of a performance or work of art, giving the audience a clue about how to interpret and understand what is being seen and heard.

10. Whether a theatre piece is serious, comic, or some combination of the two depends on the point of view of the artists who create it.

11. The viewpoint of society also affects the outlook of individual artists in terms of whether they create tragedy, comedy, or other genres.

142

7

Dramatic Structure and Dramatic Characters

DRAMATIC STRUCTURE

Throughout theatre history, we find basic dramatic forms reappearing. In western civilization, a form adopted in Greece in the fifth century BCE emerges, somewhat altered, in France in the seventeenth century. The same form shows up once more in Norway in the late nineteenth century, and is repeated throughout the twentieth century. This form can be referred to as *climactic*. Another, contrasting form, best illustrated by the plays of Shakespeare, can be called *episodic*. Through most of the history of western theatre, one or the other of these two forms—or some combination of the two—has predominated.

In addition, there are other forms. An approach in which dramatic episodes are strung together without any apparent connection has emerged in a new guise in recent times. Structure based on a ritual or pattern is both old and new. And musical theatre has a structure of its own. The characteristics of the basic types will be clearer when we look at each separately, beginning with climactic form. We then turn to the episodic structure, and then take up additional forms.

Characteristics of Climactic Structure.

The Plot Begins Late in the Story   The first hallmark of climactic drama is that the plot begins quite late in the story. Ibsen's *Ghosts,* written in 1881, is a clear example. Before *Ghosts* begins, a number of events have already occurred: Mrs. Alving has married a dissolute man who fathers an illegitimate child by another woman and contracts a venereal disease. When she discovers her husband's infidelity early in their marriage, Mrs. Alving visits the family minister, Pastor Manders, telling him she wishes to end the marriage. Although Manders is attracted to her and realizes that she has been wronged, for religious reasons, he sends her back to her husband with whom

◀ **EPISODIC DRAMATIC STRUCTURE**

In different periods and different countries, various approaches to dramatic structure have been followed. Climactic structure was created by the Greeks and adopted by many cultures in the years after that. Another structure is episodic, found in the plays of Shakespeare and his contemporaries as well as modern playwrights such as Bertolt Brecht. Here we see a scene from Shakespeare's Richard III *with Mark Rylance in the title role and Samuel Barnett as Queen Elizabeth in a production directed by Tim Carroll at Shakespeare's Globe Theatre in London. (© Geraint Lewis)*

CHARACTERISTICS OF CLIMACTIC DRAMA
A climactic play usually has a minimum number of characters, covers a short space of time, and takes place in a limited space—often one room. A good example is Ibsen's *Hedda Gabler,* with Roxanna Hope in the title role in the Hartford Stage Company production directed by Jennifer Tarver. (© T Charles Erickson)

Climax   The highpoint in the development of a dramatic plot.

Exposition   Information necessary for an understanding of the story but not covered by the action onstage; events or knowledge from the past, or occurring outside the play, which must be introduced so that the audience can understand the characters or plot.

she stays out of a sense of duty. She does, however, send her son, Oswald, away to escape his father's influence. When her husband dies, Mrs. Alving builds an orphanage in his honor to camouflage his true character. At this point—as is typical with climactic plot structure—the play itself has still not begun. It begins later, when the son returns home and the facts of the past are unearthed, precipitating the crisis.

In climactic structure the play begins when all the roads of the past converge at a crucial intersection in the present, at the *climax,* a situation that has two important consequences. First, it is frequently necessary to explain what has happened earlier by having one or more characters report the information to others. The technical term for this background information is *exposition.* A second consequence of the plot beginning late is that the time span covered within a climactic play is usually brief—in many cases a matter of a few hours, and at the most a few days. Some playwrights, attempting to push events as near the climax as possible, have stage time (the time we imagine is passing when we are watching a play) coincide with real time (that is, clock time). An example is Tennessee Williams's *Cat on a Hot Tin Roof:* the events depicted in the story last the same time as the play itself—a little over two hours.

Scenes, Locales, and Characters Are Limited   Climactic drama typically has a limited number of long segments, or acts. In Greek plays there are generally five episodes separated by choral interludes. The French neoclassicists invariably used five acts. For much of the nineteenth and twentieth centuries, three acts were standard. Today, the norm is two acts, though the long one-act play performed without intermission is also frequently presented.

Limiting the scenes in a play usually entails restricting the locale as well, sometimes to one room or one house. Along with restriction of locale, there is a restriction of characters. Greek drama generally has four or five principal characters. Many modern plays have no more than a similar number of main characters.

Construction Is Tight

Because it is carefully constructed, a climactic play fits together tightly, with no loose ends. It is like a chain linked in a cause-and-effect relationship. As in a detective story, event A leads to event B; B leads to C, causing D; D leads in turn to E; and so on. Just as the time frame and the restricted space afford no exit, so the chain of events is locked in. Once the action begins, there is no stopping it. Because climactic dramas are so carefully and tightly constructed, they are frequently referred to as **well-made plays.** In this form the aim is always to make events so inevitable that there is no escape—at least not until the very last moment, when a ***deus ex machina*** may intervene to untangle the knot. (*Deus ex machina* means "god from the machine," referring to the apparatus in Greek theatre when gods were brought down from the top of the stage house at the end of a play to resolve the action. The term has since become used to describe any outside intervention at the end of a play to bring the play to a close.)

Clearly, the method of climactic drama is compression. All the elements— characters, locale, events—are severely restricted. As if by centripetal motion, everything is forced to the center, in a tighter and tighter nucleus, making the ultimate eruption that much more explosive.

Characteristics of Episodic Structure

When we turn to episodic structure, we see a sharp contrast to climactic structure. Episodic drama begins relatively early in the story and does not compress the action but expands it. The forces in episodic drama are centrifugal, moving out to embrace additional elements. Also, unlike climactic drama, episodic plays do not necessarily follow a close cause-and-effect development.

People, Places, and Events Proliferate

In a typical episodic play the action begins relatively early in the story and covers an extensive period of time—sometimes many years. It also ranges over a number of locations. In one play we can go anywhere: to a small antechamber, a large banquet hall, the open countryside, a mountaintop.

Short scenes (some only half a page or so in print) alternate with longer ones. Two examples of episodic dramas are Shakespeare's *Antony and Cleopatra,* which has thirty-four characters and forty-plus scenes; and the Spanish playwright Lope de Vega's *The Sheep Well,* which has twenty-six characters and seventeen scenes.

There May Be a Parallel Plot or Subplot

In place of compression, episodic drama offers other techniques. One is the *parallel plot,* or **subplot.** In *King Lear,* by Shakespeare, Lear has three daughters, two evil and one good. The two evil daughters

Well-made plays Type of play popular in the nineteenth century and early twentieth century that combines apparent plausibility of incident and surface realism with a tightly constructed, highly causal, and contrived plot.

Deus ex machina ("DEH-oos eks MAH-kih-nah") Literally, "god from a machine," a resolution device in classic Greek drama; hence, intervention of supernatural forces—usually at the last moment—to save the action from its logical conclusion. In modern drama, an arbitrary and coincidental solution.

Subplot Sometimes referred to as parallel plot, a secondary plot that reinforces or runs parallel to the major plot in an episodic play.

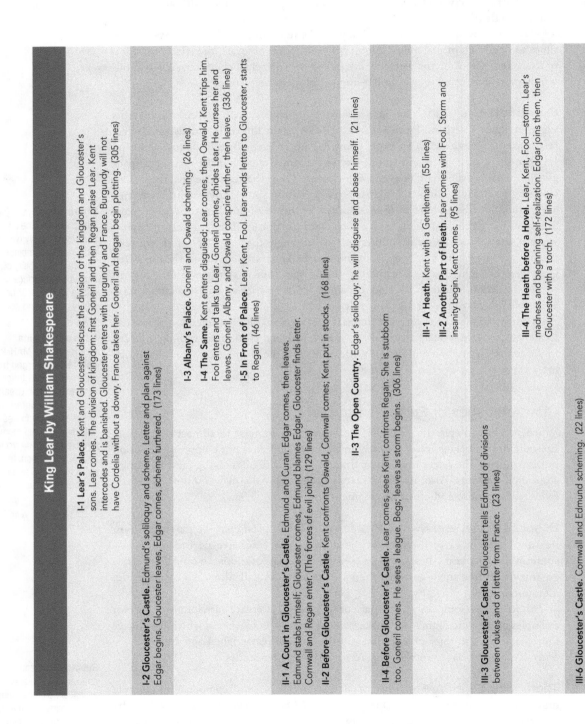

King Lear by William Shakespeare

I-1 Lear's Palace. Kent and Gloucester discuss the division of the kingdom and Gloucester's sons. Lear comes. The division of kingdom: first Goneril and then Regan praise Lear. Kent intercedes and is banished. Gloucester enters with Burgundy and France. Burgundy will not have Cordelia without a dowry. France takes her. Goneril and Regan begin plotting. (305 lines)

I-2 Gloucester's Castle. Edmund's soliloquy and scheme. Letter and plan against Edgar begins. Gloucester leaves, Edgar comes, scheme furthered. (173 lines)

I-3 Albany's Palace. Goneril and Oswald scheming. (26 lines)

I-4 The Same. Kent enters disguised; Lear comes, then Oswald, Kent trips him. Fool enters and talks to Lear. Goneril comes, chides Lear. He curses her and leaves. Goneril, Albany, and Oswald conspire further, then leave. (336 lines)

I-5 In Front of Palace. Lear, Kent, Fool. Lear sends letters to Gloucester, starts to Regan. (46 lines)

II-1 A Court in Gloucester's Castle. Edmund and Curan. Edgar comes, then leaves. Edmund stabs himself; Gloucester comes, Edmund blames Edgar, Gloucester finds letter. Cornwall and Regan enter. (The forces of evil join.) (129 lines)

II-2 Before Gloucester's Castle. Kent confronts Oswald, Cornwall comes; Kent put in stocks. (168 lines)

II-3 The Open Country. Edgar's soliloquy: he will disguise and abase himself. (21 lines)

II-4 Before Gloucester's Castle. Lear comes, sees Kent; confronts Regan. She is stubborn too. Goneril comes. He sees a league. Begs; leaves as storm begins. (306 lines)

III-1 A Heath. Kent with a Gentleman. (55 lines)

III-2 Another Part of Heath. Lear comes with Fool. Storm and insanity begin. Kent comes. (95 lines)

III-3 Gloucester's Castle. Gloucester tells Edmund of divisions between dukes and of letter from France. (23 lines)

III-4 The Heath before a Hovel. Lear, Kent, Fool—storm. Lear's madness and beginning self-realization. Edgar joins them, then Gloucester with a torch. (172 lines)

III-6 Gloucester's Castle. Cornwall and Edmund scheming. (22 lines)

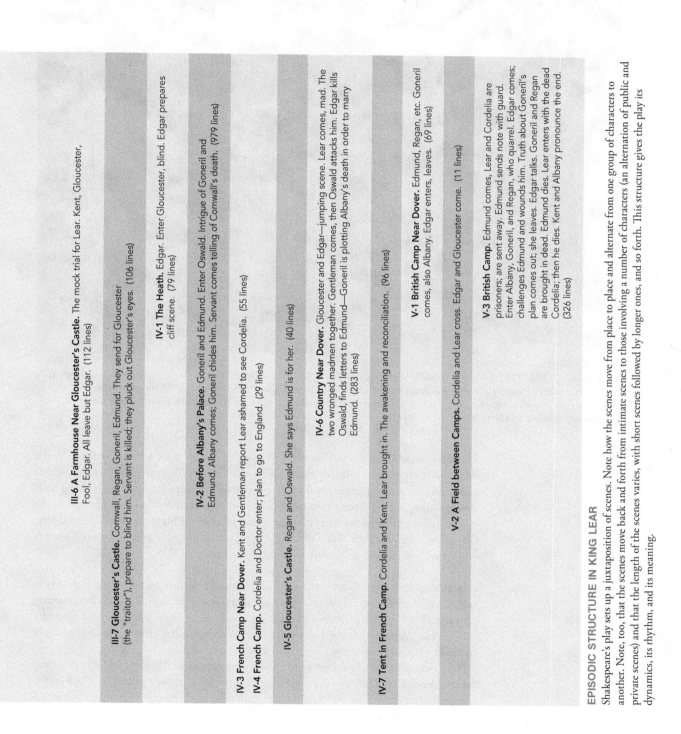

III-6 A Farmhouse Near Gloucester's Castle. The mock trial for Lear. Kent, Gloucester, Fool, Edgar. All leave but Edgar. (112 lines)

III-7 Gloucester's Castle. Cornwall, Regan, Goneril, Edmund. They send for Gloucester (the "traitor"), prepare to blind him. Servant is killed; they pluck out Gloucester's eyes. (106 lines)

IV-1 The Heath. Edgar. Enter Gloucester, blind. Edgar prepares cliff scene. (79 lines)

IV-2 Before Albany's Palace. Goneril and Edmund. Enter Oswald. Intrigue of Goneril and Edmund. Albany comes; Goneril chides him. Servant comes telling of Cornwall's death. (979 lines)

IV-3 French Camp Near Dover. Kent and Gentleman report Lear ashamed to see Cordelia. (55 lines)

IV-4 French Camp. Cordelia and Doctor enter; plan to go to England. (29 lines)

IV-5 Gloucester's Castle. Regan and Oswald. She says Edmund is for her. (40 lines)

IV-6 Country Near Dover. Gloucester and Edgar—jumping scene. Lear comes, mad. The two wronged madmen together. Gentleman comes, then Oswald attacks him. Edgar kills Oswald, finds letters to Edmund—Goneril is plotting Albany's death in order to marry Edmund. (283 lines)

IV-7 Tent in French Camp. Cordelia and Kent. Lear brought in. The awakening and reconciliation. (96 lines)

V-1 British Camp Near Dover. Edmund, Regan, etc. Goneril comes, also Albany. Edgar enters, leaves. (69 lines)

V-2 A Field between Camps. Cordelia and Lear cross. Edgar and Gloucester come. (11 lines)

V-3 British Camp. Edmund comes, Lear and Cordelia are prisoners; are sent away. Edmund sends note with guard. Enter Albany, Goneril, and Regan, who quarrel. Edgar comes; challenges Edmund and wounds him. Truth about Goneril's plan comes out; she leaves. Edgar talks. Goneril and Regan are brought in dead. Edmund dies. Lear enters with the dead Cordelia; then he dies. Kent and Albany pronounce the end. (326 lines)

EPISODIC STRUCTURE IN KING LEAR

Shakespeare's play sets up a juxtaposition of scenes. Note how the scenes move from place to place and alternate from one group of characters to another. Note, too, that the scenes move back and forth from intimate scenes to those involving a number of characters (an alternation of public and private scenes) and that the length of the scenes varies, with short scenes followed by longer ones, and so forth. This structure gives the play its dynamics, its rhythm, and its meaning.

EPISODIC STRUCTURE: MANY CHARACTERS, PLACES, AND EVENTS
A good example of the typically wide-ranging episodic structure is *Julius Caesar* by William Shakespeare. Shown here are Dan Kremer in the title role, with Kryztov Lindquist as the Soothsayer and the cast of the Shakespeare Theatre Company in its production, directed by David Muse. (© Carol Rosegg)

have convinced their father that they are good and that their sister is wicked. In the subplot—a counterpart of this main plot—the Earl of Gloucester has two sons, one loyal and one disloyal, and the disloyal son has deceived his father into thinking he is the loyal one. Both old men have misunderstood their children's true worth, and in the end both are punished for their mistakes: Lear is bereft of his kingdom and his sanity; Gloucester loses his eyes. The Gloucester plot, with complications and developments of its own, is a parallel and reinforcement of the Lear plot.

Juxtaposition and Contrast Occur   Another technique of episodic drama is *juxtaposition* or *contrast*. Rather than moving in linear fashion, the action alternates between elements. Short scenes alternate with longer scenes, public scenes alternate with private scenes, we move from one group to an opposing group, and comic scenes alternate with serious scenes.

An example of this last alternation comes in Shakespeare's *Macbeth*. Just after Macbeth has murdered King Duncan, there is a knock on the door of the castle. This is one of the most serious moments of the play, but the man who goes to open the door is a comical character, a drunken porter, whose speech is a humorous interlude in the grim business of the play. In other words, comedy alternates with tragedy.

DYNAMICS OF DRAMA

Comparing Climactic and Episodic Forms

Climactic

1. Plot begins late in the story, toward the very end or climax.
2. Covers a short space of time, perhaps a few hours or at most a few days.
3. Contains a few solid, extended scenes, such as three acts with each act comprising one long scene.
4. Occurs in a restricted locale, such as one room or one house.
5. Number of characters is severely limited—usually no more than six or eight.
6. Plot is linear and moves in a single line with few subplots or counterplots.
7. Line of action proceeds in a cause-and-effect chain.
8. The characters and events are closely linked in a sequence of logical, almost inevitable development.

Episodic

1. Plot begins relatively early in the story and moves through a series of episodes.
2. Covers a longer period of time: weeks, months, and sometimes many years.
3. Has many short, fragmented scenes; sometimes an alternation of short and long scenes.
4. May range over an entire city or even several countries.
5. Has a profusion of characters, sometimes several dozen.
6. Is frequently marked by several threads of action, such as two parallel plots, or scenes of comic relief in a serious play.
7. Scenes are juxtaposed to one another. An event may result from several causes; or it may have no apparent cause, but arises in a network or web of circumstances.

The table outlines the chief characteristics of climactic and episodic forms and illustrates the differences between them. It is clear that the climactic and episodic forms differ from each other in their fundamental approaches. One emphasizes constriction and compression on all fronts; the other takes a far broader view and aims at a cumulative effect, piling up people, places, and events.

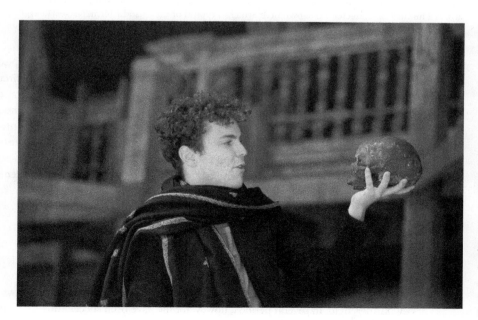

COMIC SCENES ALTERNATE WITH SERIOUS SCENES
One device possible in episodic drama is the juxtaposition and alternation of serious and comic scenes. Shakespeare often incorporates this technique in his plays. In the grave-digging scene in *Hamlet,* comedy interrupts very serious scenes involving the death of Ophelia and other tragic events. Shown here is Joshua McGuire as Hamlet with the skull of Yorick, in Shakeapeare's Globe production, directed by Dominic Dromgoole. (© Geraint Lewis)

COMBINING CLIMACTIC AND EPISODIC STRUCTURES
Though we often separate the episodic and climactic structures, there have been a number of times when the two forms are combined, joining together characteristics from each. Good examples are plays from the English Restoration and, 200 years later, the plays of the Russian dramatist Anton Chekhov. Shown here is a scene from a Restoration comedy, William Congreve's *The Way of the World*, directed by Michael Kahn at the Shakespeare Theatre Company. The play has some of the economy of climactic drama but features a number of characters, as shown here, which is typical of the episodic form. (© Carol Rosegg)

The Overall Effect Is Cumulative   With regard to cause and effect in episodic drama, the impression created is of events piling up: a tsunami, a tidal wave of circumstances and emotions sweeping over the characters. Rarely does one letter, one telephone call, or one piece of information determine the fate of a character. Time and again, Hamlet has proof that Claudius has killed his father; however, what eventually leads him to kill Claudius is not a single piece of hard evidence but a rush of events. In modern theatre both climactic form and episodic form have been adopted, sometimes by the same playwright. This is characteristic of the diversity of our age. Ibsen, for example, wrote a number of "well-made" or climactic plays—*Ghosts, A Doll's House,* and others—but also several episodic plays, such as *Brand* and *Peer Gynt.*

Combinations of Climactic and Episodic Form

There is no requirement that a play be exclusively episodic or exclusively climactic. It is true that during certain periods one form or the other has been predominant. Also, it is not easy to mix the two forms, because—as we have seen—each has its own laws and its own inner logic. In several periods, however, they have been successfully integrated.

A group of plays that combine elements of the climactic and episodic forms are the comedies of the Restoration period in England (from 1660, when the English monarchy was restored, to 1700). These comedies usually had a large cast, a subplot as well as a main plot, and several changes of scene. They did not, however, cover extended periods of time or move rapidly from place to place as the plays of Shakespeare did.

The climactic and episodic forms have frequently been combined successfully in the modern period. The Russian playwright Chekhov, who generally wrote about one principal action and set his plays in one household, usually has more characters than is customary in climactic drama. For instance, there are fifteen in *The Cherry Orchard.* Frequently, too, Chekhov's plays cover a period of several months or years.

Rituals as Dramatic Structure

Like acting, ritual is a part of everyday life of which we are generally unaware. Basically, ***ritual*** is a repetition or reenactment of a proceeding or transaction that has acquired special meaning. It may be a simple ritual like singing the national anthem before a sports contest, or a deeply religious ritual such as the Roman Catholic mass or the Jewish *kaddish,* a prayer for the dead. All of us develop rituals in our personal or family life: a certain meal we eat with the family once a week, for example, or a routine we go through every time we take an examination in school. Occasions like Thanksgiving, Christmas, and Ramadan become family rituals, with the same order of events each year, the same menu, and perhaps even the same conversation. Rituals give us continuity, security, and comfort. Often, as in the case of primitive tribes, people assume that if they perform a ritual faithfully, they will be blessed or their wishes will be granted. Conversely, they assume that failure to follow a ritual to the letter will lead to punishment.

In theatre, ritual is an activity where the old and new come together. Traditional plays are full of rituals: coronations, weddings, funerals, and other ceremonies. And in modern theatre, ritual has been discovered and given new life. Certain avant-garde theatre groups, for example, have made a conscious attempt to develop new rituals or revive old ones. Ritual has structure. Actions are repeated in a set fashion; these actions have a beginning, a middle, and an end; and there is a natural progression of events.

RITUAL IN MODERN THEATRE
Many avant-garde playwrights and groups use ceremonies and rituals. *The Blacks,* a highly theatrical piece by the French playwright Jean Genet, is part ritual, part minstrel show, part court trial. It takes place in an imaginary Africa. As a part of the various ceremonies and other actions, Genet uses masks, such as the ones shown here. (© Dennis Stock/Magnum Photos)

Ritual Ceremonial event, often religious, which takes place in a prescribed sequence.

Patterns as Dramatic Structure

Related to ritual is a pattern of events. In Samuel Beckett's *Waiting for Godot,* the characters have no personal history, and the play does not build to a climax in the ordinary way. But if Beckett has sacrificed traditional plot structure, he has replaced it with a repeated sequence of events containing its own order and logic. The play has two acts, and in each act a series of incidents is duplicated. Each act opens with the two chief characters coming together on a lonely crossroads after having been separated. Then, in both acts, a similar sequence of events occurs: they greet each other; they despair of Godot's ever coming; they attempt to entertain themselves. Two other men, Pozzo and Lucky, appear and, following a long scene, disappear. The first two men are left alone once more. The two acts continue to follow the same sequence: a small boy comes to tell the men that Godot will not come that day, the boy leaves, and the men remain together for another night. There are important differences between the two acts, but the identical sequence of events in each act achieves a pattern, which takes on a ritualistic quality.

Serial Structure

Another kind of structure is a series of acts or episodes—individual theatre events—offered as a single presentation. In this case, individual segments are strung together like beads on a necklace. Sometimes a central theme or common thread holds the various parts together. Sometimes there is little or no connection between the parts.

The musical *revue* is a case in point. In a revue, short scenes, vignettes, skits, dance numbers, songs, and possibly even vaudeville routines are presented on a single program. There may be an overall theme, such as political satire or the celebration of a past event or period. Sometimes a master of ceremonies provides continuity between the various segments. Also, in today's theatre we frequently see a program of short plays. Sometimes there will be a bill of one-act plays by the same author; at other times there will be two or three plays by different authors. On some occasions an attempt is made to relate the separate plays to a central theme; but sometimes the plays are chosen simply to complete an evening's entertainment.

Structure in Experimental and Avant-Garde Theatre

Special Structures   In the second half of the twentieth century, a number of theatre groups in Europe and the United States experimented with forms such as ritual. These included the Polish Laboratory Theater, headed by Jerzy Grotowski, and the Living Theater, the Open Theater, the Performance Group, Mabou Mines, and the Wooster Group in the United States. These groups had two things in mind. On one hand, they felt that the theatre of the past was no longer relevant to the problems of the present and that new forms had to be found to match the unique challenges and aspirations of the modern world. On the other hand, they wanted to look back beyond the traditions of the past 2,500 years to the beginning of theatre, to scrape off the layers of formality and convention that have accumulated through the centuries and rediscover the roots of theatre.

From the experiments of this radical theatre movement, several significant departures from traditional theatre practice were developed. Among them were the following: (1) emphasis on *nonverbal theatre,* that is, theatre in which gestures, body movements,

SEGMENTS AND TABLEAUX IN AVANT-GARDE THEATRE
The works of many modern experimental theatre directors consist of separate segments, almost like pictorial tableaux. The emphasis is on the visual aspect, and also on images, sounds, music, and dancelike movement. An example of segments and tableaux can be seen in this scene from Robert Wilson's interpretation of the Brecht-Weill *Threepenny Opera,* a Berliner Ensemble production, with Stefan Kurt (center) as Macheath (Mack the Knife). (© David Baltzer/Zenit/Laif/Redux)

and sounds without words are stressed rather than logical or intelligible language; (2) reliance on improvisation or a scenario developed by performers and a director to tell the story, rather than a written text; (3) interest in ritual and ceremony; and (4) stress on the importance of the physical environment of theatre, including the spatial relationship of the performers to the audience. The theatre groups that developed these ideas were referred to as *avant-garde,* a French term that literally means "advance guard in a military formation." The term has come to mean an intellectual or artistic movement in any age that breaks with tradition and therefore seems ahead of its time.

Segments and Tableaux as Structure   The experimental pieces of the directors Robert Wilson (noted in Chapters 4 and 5) and Richard Foreman (b. 1937), like other types of avant-garde theatre, often stress nonverbal elements. At times they include *non sequitur* as well. In spite of this, their work does have structure. Often the various elements are united by a theme, or at least by a pronounced point of view on the part of the director. Also, the material is organized into units analogous to the frames of film and television, or to the still-life tableaux of painting or the moving tableaux of dance. (In theatre, a *tableau*—plural, *tableaux*—is a static scene onstage featuring performers in costume.) Robert Wilson, in productions such as *A Letter to Queen Victoria, Einstein on the Beach,* and *CiVil WarS: A Tree Is Best Measured When It Is Down,* begins a segment with a visual picture—like a large painting, but three-dimensional. The performers move from this static image into the activities of the segment. When one segment has concluded, another picture or tableau will be formed to initiate the next segment. Frequently directors like Foreman and Wilson will use rapid movements—as in silent films—or slow-motion movements. At times several activities will occur simultaneously. All of these, however, relate both to an image and to a tableau or frame.

For many years Foreman, under the banner of his Ontological-Hysteric Theatre, presented new work almost annually. In 2013 he directed a piece that many considered a retrospective of his career entitled *Old-Fashioned Prostitutes (A True Romance).*

Structure in Musical Theatre

In musical theatre, structure often involves alternation and juxtaposition. Musical numbers alternate with spoken scenes; solos and duets alternate with choral numbers; singing alternates with dance numbers; and sometimes comic songs and scenes alternate with serious ones. An example of structural principles in musicals is found in *My Fair Lady,*

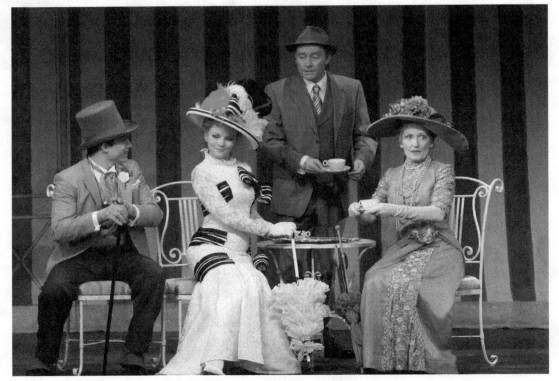

MY FAIR LADY: A MUSICAL WITH A CLEAR DRAMATIC STRUCTURE
Musicals, like other forms of theatre, require a definite form and structure. In *My Fair Lady* by Lerner and Loewe (which was based on Shaw's play *Pygmalion*), scenes of dialogue alternate with musical and dance numbers; solos alternate with duets and choral numbers. Here we see (left to right:) David Bryant Johnson as Freddy Eynsford-Hill, Jennifer Hope Wills as Eliza, Jamie Jackson as Henry Higgins and Melinda Tanner as Higgins's mother in a production at the Gateway Playhouse in Bellport, NY.
(© Jeff Bellante, The Gateway, Performing Arts Center of Suffolk County)

with book and lyrics by Alan Jay Lerner and music by Frederick Loewe. The story is based on George Bernard Shaw's play *Pygmalion*.

My Fair Lady concerns a speech teacher, Henry Higgins, who claims that the English judge people by how they speak. He bets his friend Colonel Pickering that he can take an ordinary cockney flower girl, Eliza Doolittle, and by teaching her correct diction, pass her off as a duchess. The comic subplot of *My Fair Lady* deals with Eliza's father, Alfred P. Doolittle, a ne'er-do-well who doesn't want to achieve middle-class respectability, because if he does he will have to marry the woman he lives with.

The first song in the show is sung by Higgins—"Why Can't the English Learn to Speak?" The next song shifts to Eliza and her dreams of luxury as she sings "Wouldn't It Be Lovely?" The action now shifts to the subplot, and Alfred Doolittle is joined by two buddies to sing of how he hopes to avoid working, "With a Little Bit of Luck." We then move back to a scene with Higgins, who is pushing Eliza very hard to learn to speak properly. After a song by Higgins, "I'm an Ordinary Man," Eliza vows revenge on him in her next song: "Just You Wait."

The musical proceeds in this manner, moving from one character to another, from a solo to a trio to a dance routine to an ensemble. There is variety in these numbers— some are serious; some are comic; some explain the characters' feelings; some describe a situation. It is on such alternation that structure in musical theatre is based. Always, too, it must be remembered, spoken scenes are interspersed with musical numbers, and ballet or modern dance routines with other numbers.

DRAMATIC CHARACTERS

Along with structures, the playwright creates dramatic characters. These can range from fully rounded human beings to so-called ***stock characters*** who are two-dimensional.

Stock characters Two dimensional, stereotypical characters.

Extraordinary Characters

In most important dramatic works of the past, the heroes and heroines are extraordinary in some way. They are larger than life. Historically, major characters have been kings, queens, bishops, members of the nobility, or other figures clearly marked as holding a special place in society. In drama, as in life, a queen is accorded respect because of her authority, power, and grandeur; a high military official is respected because of the position he holds. Dramatists go one step farther, however, in depicting extraordinary characters. In addition to filling prestigious roles, dramatic characters generally represent men and women at their best or worst—at some extreme of human behavior. Lady Macbeth is not only a noblewoman; she is one of the most ambitious women ever depicted onstage. In virtually every instance, with extraordinary characters, we see men and women at the outer limits of human capability and endurance.

Comic characters can also be extremes. The chief character in *Volpone* by Ben Jonson (1572–1637) is an avaricious miser who gets people to present him with expensive gifts because they think he will remember them in his will. Characters may also be extraordinary because of their exceptional personalities or achievements. A good example is Joan of Arc, the heroine of George Bernard Shaw's *Saint Joan,* a simple peasant girl who rises to become commander of an army that triumphs in the name of the king of France.

photo essay

Extraordinary Characters

In dramas of the past, the leading characters are often people who are exceptional in some way. Shown here is a gallery of exceptional characters from a range of dramas.

(© Sara Krulwich/The New York Times/Redux)

Mary, Queen of Scots, and Queen Elizabeth I of England, rivals in real life, made for admirable dramatic characters—women of strong virtues and telling weaknesses. The photo above Janet McTeer portrays Mary, flanked by Michael Countryman (Sir Amias Paulet) and Maria Tucci (Hanna Kennedy) in Friedrich Schiller's *Mary Stuart*, directed by Phyllida Lloyd on Broadway.
(© Sara Krulwich/The New York Times/Redux)

At right, Frances Barber as Cleopatra, the powerful, alluring queen of Egypt with whom Antony fell in love in Shakespeare's *Antony and Cleopatra*, in a production at Shakespeare's Globe in London.

(© Geraint Lewis)

At the left Anne-Marie Duff as the exceptional historical figure Joan of Arc in George Bernard Shaw's *Saint Joan*, directed by Marianne Elliott at the National Theatre, London.

(© Kevin Cummins/National Theatre)

To the right Greek actor Grigoris Valtinos as the quintessentially extraordinary figure of Oedipus in the Greek National Theater's *Oedipus Rex* by Sophocles presented in Rome's Colosseum.

(© Pier Paolo Cito/AP Images)

THE TRAGIC FIGURE: AN EXCEPTIONAL CHARACTER
A good example of an extraordinary figure in tragedy is
Tamburlaine, a larger-than-life character who through terror and
cunning conquered much of the known world in central Asia and
was the hero of two plays by Christopher Marlowe in the late
1580s. Shown here are Avery Brooks and the cast of the
Shakespeare Theatre Company's *Tamburlaine,* adapted and directed
by Michael Kahn. (© Carol Rosegg)

Some characters are mixtures, combining
extreme virtue and extreme vice. Faustus, treated by
Christopher Marlowe in *The Tragical History of Doctor
Faustus* and by Johann Wolfgang von Goethe in
Faust, is a great scholar but becomes so bored with his
existence and so ambitious that he makes a compact
with the devil, forfeiting his soul in return for unlimited power. Cleopatra, an exceedingly vain, selfish
woman, also has "immortal longings." Queen Elizabeth I of England and Mary Queen of Scots, rivals in
real life, have made admirable dramatic characters—
women of strong virtues and telling weaknesses.

In sum, larger-than-life characters become the
heroes and heroines of drama not only because of
their station in life but also because they possess
traits common to us all—ambition, generosity,
malevolence, fear, and achievement—in such great
abundance.

In the eighteenth century, ordinary people began
taking over from royalty and the nobility as the heroes
and heroines of drama—a reflection of what was
occurring in the real world. But despite this move
away from royalty and the nobility, the leading figures
of drama continued in many cases to be exceptional
men and women at their best and worst.

Representative or Quintessential Characters

When characters from everyday life replaced
kings and queens as the leading figures in drama,
a new type of character emerged alongside the
extraordinary character. Characters of this new
type are in many respects typical or ordinary, but
they are significant because they embody an entire
group. Rather than being notable as "worst,"
"best," or some other extreme, they are important
as *representative* or *quintessential* characters. A
good example of such a character is Nora Helmer,
the heroine of Henrik Ibsen's *A Doll's House.* A traditional wife and mother, she has
secretly forged a signature to get money for her husband when he was very ill and
needed medical attention. All her life, first by her father, then by her husband, she has
been treated like a doll or a plaything, not as a mature, responsible woman.

In the last act of the play, Nora rebels against this attitude; she makes a declaration of
independence to her husband, slams the door on him, and walks out. It has been said that
Nora's slamming of the door marks the beginning not only of modern drama but of the
emancipation of modern women. Certainly Nora's defiance—her demand to be treated as

QUINTESSENTIAL CHARACTERS
Certain key characters in drama, especially in modern drama, are not extraordinary or exceptional in the same way as royalty or military leaders, but become important because they embody qualities of an entire group of people. Included in this description would be the lead characters in Arthur Miller's *Death of a Salesman*. Shown here are Elizabeth Franz as Linda Loman and Brian Dennehy as Willy in the Goodman Theatre production directed by Robert Falls. (© HO, Eric Y. Exit/AP Images)

an equal—has made her typical of all housewives who refuse to be regarded as pets. In one sense, Nora is an ordinary wife and mother, but she is unusual in the way she sums up an entire group of women. *A Doll's House* was written in 1879; but today, well over a century later, Nora is still a symbol of modern women, and the play is revived year after year.

In *Who's Afraid of Virginia Woolf?* by Edward Albee, the main characters are a husband and a wife who are in many ways quite commonplace. He is a somewhat ineffectual college professor; she is the daughter of the college president. They argue and attack each other almost to the point of exhaustion. Another unhappily married couple? Yes. But again, they are quintessential. To Albee, they represent an American type: a bitter, alienated couple, bored with themselves and each other. To underline this point, he names them Martha and George—the same first names as Martha and George Washington, America's "first couple." Another example is Willy Loman, in Arthur Miller's *Death of a Salesman,* who sums up all salesmen, traveling in their territories on a "smile and a shoeshine." Willy has lived by a false dream: the idea that if he puts up a good front and is "well liked," he will be successful and rich.

Still another example is Troy Maxon in *Fences* by August Wilson. Maxon epitomizes the proud, headstrong man who in order to survive in a world of oppression and prejudice has developed firmness and resolution, which serve him well but take their toll on his wife and son. Nora Helmer, Martha and George, Willy Loman, and Troy

examples of representative characters

PLAYING YOUR PART: EXPERIENCING THEATRE

1. If you were to dramatize your life, how might you use a climactic structure? Describe the moments you would dramatize.

2. How might you use an episodic structure to structure a play about your life? What events would you dramatize?

3. Have you seen a movie or television show that uses stock characters? Describe the characters? Have you seen a film that employs quintessential characters? Describe.

4. Describe a family ritual. What are the elements of the ritual?

5. Are there any films or television shows that present nonhuman characters? Describe.

Maxon: all are examples of characters who stand apart from the crowd, not by standing above it but by summing up in their personalities the essence of a certain type of person.

Stock Characters

The characters we have been describing, whether extraordinary or representative, are generally fully rounded figures. Many characters in drama, however, are not three-dimensional; rather, they exemplify one particular characteristic to the exclusion of virtually everything else. Frequently they are known by their station in life, their sex, and their occupation along with some tendency of personality: the clever servant, for instance, or the absentminded

STOCK CHARACTERS OF COMMEDIA DELL'ARTE
Italian Renaissance comedy developed stereotyped characters who were always the same: each of them was famous for a certain trait—greed, boastfulness, gullibility, or the tike—and was always easily identifiable by his or her costume. Here we see Tommaso Minniti as Dr. Lombardi, Stefano Guizzi as Brighella, and Giorgio Bongiovanni as Pantalone in *Arlecchino: Servant of Two Masters,* by Carlo Goldoni in a production by the Piccolo Teatro di Milano. (© Diego Ciminaghi/Piccolo Teatro di Milano-Teatro d'Europa)

professor. They are referred to as *stock* characters, and they appear particularly in comedy and melodrama, though they can be found in all kinds of drama and also today in films and television shows.

Some of the most famous examples of stock characters are found in ***commedia dell'arte.*** This is a form of popular comedy that flourished in Italy during the sixteenth and seventeenth centuries. In *commedia dell'arte*, there was no script but rather a scenario that gave an outline of a story. The performers improvised or invented words and actions to fill out the play. The stock characters of commedia were either straightforward or exaggerated and were divided into servants and members of the ruling class. In every character, however, one particular feature or trait was stressed.

Whenever such a character appeared, he or she would have the same propensities and would wear the same costume. The bragging soldier, called *Capitano,* always boasted of his courage in a series of fictitious military victories. *Pantalone,* an elderly merchant, spoke in clichés and chased girls; and a pompous lawyer called *Dottore* spoke in Latin phrases and attempted to impress others with his learning. Among servants, *Harlequin* was the most popular; displaying both cunning and stupidity, he was at the heart of most plot complications. These are but a few of a full range of commedia characters, each with his or her own peculiarities. As for examples of stock characters in melodrama, we are all familiar with such figures as the innocent young heroine, "pure as the driven snow"; and the villain, lurking in the shadows, twirling his moustache. In today's television, the familiar figures on weekly situation comedies are examples of stock or stereotypical characters.

Commedia dell'arte Form of comic theatre, originating in Italy in the sixteenth century, in which dialogue was improvised around a sceario involving a set of stock characters, each with a traditional costume, name, and often mask.

CHARACTERS WITH A DOMINANT TRAIT
Many comic plays feature characters with one predominant trait—greed, ambition, self-importance, and so forth. The extremes of the character are one of the elements that create the comic effect. The French playwright Molière often named his plays for such characters. Shown here are Nancy Robinette as Toinette and René Auberjonois as Argan in the Shakespeare Theatre Company's production of Molière's *The Imaginary Invalid,* directed by Keith Baxter. (© Carol Rosegg)

THE NARRATOR OR CHORUS
A role in drama in which a performer or group steps out of character to address the audience directly is a narrator or a chorus. In Thornton Wilder's *Our Town,* the character of the Stage Manager is the narrator of the piece, and he also plays small roles such as the preacher who marries the young couple. Here, Paul Newman played the role in a production at the Westport Country Playhouse. (© Sara Krulwich/The New York Times/Redux)

Closely related to stock characters are characters with a *dominant trait,* that is, a single excess or "humor." The French playwright Molière and the English dramatist Ben Jonson wrote a number of comedies in which the chief character's excesses—avarice, self-importance, greed, pride, pomposity—lead to wildly humorous results. To further point up the one-sided nature of these characters, Jonson often named his characters for their single trait: his play *The Alchemist,* for example, includes characters with names like Subtle, Face, Dapper, Surly, Wholesome, and Dame Pliant.

Minor Characters

Stock characters or characters with a dominant trait are not to be confused with *minor characters.* Minor characters are those—in all types of plays—who play a small part in the overall action. Generally they appear briefly and serve chiefly to further the story or to support more important characters. Typical examples of minor characters are servants and soldiers; but even figures such as generals, bishops, judges, dukes, and duchesses are considered minor if they play only a small role in the action. Since we see so little of these characters, the dramatist can usually show only one facet of their personalities; but this is a different case from that of a main character who is deliberately portrayed as one-sided.

A Narrator or Chorus

A special type of character is a narrator or the members of a chorus. Generally, a *narrator* speaks directly to the audience. He or she may or may not assume a dramatic persona as the other characters do. In Tennessee Williams's *The Glass Menagerie* and Thornton Wilder's *Our Town,* for instance, a performer appears both as a narrator and as one or more characters in the play. The chorus in ancient Greek drama, in song and dance, commented on the action of the main plot and reacted to events in the story. Use of a chorus or narrator creates a *dialectic* or *counterpoint* between a party outside the play and characters in the central action. (*Counterpoint* is a term from music denoting a second melody that accompanies or moves in contrast to the main melody.)

The dramatist Bertolt Brecht used a narrator, and sometimes singers, in a pointed way: to startle the audience by making a sudden shift from the main story to the presentation of a moral or political argument. In *The Caucasian Chalk Circle,* for instance,

THE CHORUS: A TIME-HONORED DEVICE
The Greeks were the first to use a chorus. It extended the range and sweep of their plays, which otherwise adhered closely to the climactic form. Here we see the chorus in the London production of *Bacchai* by Euripides, directed by Peter Hall at the National Theatre.
(© Donald Cooper/PhotoSTAGE)

Grusha—an innocent, peace-loving peasant woman—steps out of character at one point to sing a song extolling the virtues of a general who loves war. Grusha, in other words, momentarily becomes a sort of chorus when she is asked to sing a song with a point of view opposite to her own. This wrenching of characters and attitudes is deliberate on Brecht's part: it is meant to make us think seriously about some issue, such as war and the ravages of war.

Nonhuman Characters

In Greece in the fifth century BCE, and in many earlier cultures, performers portrayed birds and animals, and this practice has continued to the present. Aristophanes, the Greek comic dramatist, used a chorus of actors to play the title parts in his plays *The Birds* and *The Frogs.* In the modern period, Eugene Ionesco has men turn into animals in *Rhinoceros;* and the French playwright Edmond Rostand wrote a poetic fable called *Chantecler,* about a rooster.

Occasionally performers are called on to play other nonhuman roles. Karel Čapek (1890–1938) wrote a play, *R.U.R.,* in which people enact robots. (The initials in the title stand for "Rossum's Universal Robots," and it is from this play that the word *robot* derives.) In the medieval morality play *Everyman,* characters represent ideas or concepts, such as Fellowship, Good Deeds, Worldly Possessions, and Beauty.

NONHUMAN CHARACTERS
Sometimes characters are nonhuman, although they usually have human characteristics. This tradition goes back at least as far as the comedies of the Greek writer Aristophanes in the fifth century BCE in Greece. Frequently they are animals of some sort. Shown here is a scene from Aristophanes' *The Birds* at the national Theatre, London. Franky Mwangi (right) portrays Sparrow and Josette Bushell-Mingo is Hoopoe. (© Pete Jones/ArenaPal/Topham/The Image Works)

Dramatic characters in the guise of animals or robots are the exception rather than the rule, and when they do appear, it is usually their human qualities that are emphasized.

The Audience and Character Types

Classifying characters in categories is neither artificial nor arbitrary. Different types of characters are part of the fabric of various dramatic forms, and being aware of them is a helpful tool in appreciating and understanding those forms. It should also be remembered that not every character fits neatly into a single category, and that various character types are not necessarily mutually exclusive. For example, an extraordinary or quintessential character might also be a character with a dominant trait. At the same time, knowledge of the character types we have been studying can greatly help audiences understand how characters function in a drama and enhance their experience when seeing a performance.

When a playwright in ancient Greece or Elizabethan England wrote a tragedy, he did not think of the central figure in his drama as an extraordinary character. In nineteenth century France, when a dramatist composed a bedroom farce, he was not consciously employing stock characters. And when a twentieth century playwright wrote a serious drama, he or she did not focus on developing quintessential figures as the play's chief characters. Dramatists create characters, not labels. In the same way, we as audience members attending a performance should not be preoccupied with assigning characters onstage to a specific category. During a theatre event we should let the action onstage unfold, taking it in as a whole, and observing particular elements only when they appear evident or are especially striking. Focusing on character types should be undertaken in studying a play before seeing it, or in analyzing it afterward.

Juxtaposition of Characters

We turn now from single characters to the way characters interact with and relate to one another. Often in the creation of a dramatic work, characters are combined in important, significant ways to bring out certain qualities.

Protagonist Principal character in a play, the one whom the drama is about.

Antagonist Opponent of the protagonist in a drama.

Protagonist and Antagonist   From Greek theatre we have the terms *protagonist* and *antagonist.* The *protagonist* in a play is the main character—Othello, for instance—and the *antagonist* is the main character's chief opponent. In *Othello,* the antagonist is Iago. It is through the contest between these two characters that their individual qualities are developed.

Contrasting Characters   Another way characters are contrasted is by setting them side by side rather than in opposition. Sophocles created two exceptionally strong-willed, independent female characters—Antigone and Electra—each one the title character in a play. Both are young women intent on defying an older person and willing to risk death to fight for a principle. But unlike other dramatists who had told the same story, Sophocles gave each of them a sister with a sharply contrasting personality. To Antigone he gave Ismene, a docile, compliant sister who argues that Antigone should obey the law and give in to authority. To Electra he gave Chrisothemis, a meek, frightened creature who protests that as women they are powerless to act. Sophocles strengthened and clarified Antigone and Electra by providing them with contrasting characters to set off their own determination and courage.

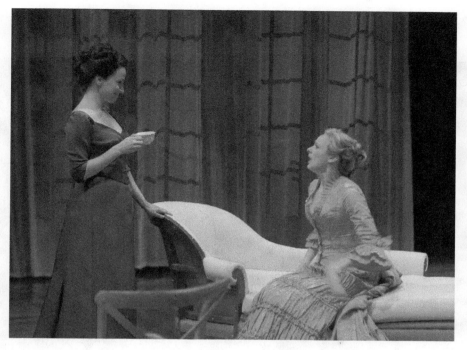

CONTRASTING CHARACTERS
Playwrights often set two characters beside each other, or against each other, so that they stand in sharp contrast. In Henrik Ibsen's *Hedda Gabler,* the frustrated, volatile, reckless Hedda is juxtaposed with her friend Mrs. Elvsted, a calmer, wiser, quieter person. In this scene Roxanna Hope as Hedda is on the left and Sara Topham as Mrs. Elvsted is on the right, under the direction of Jennifer Tarver at the Hartford Stage Company. (© T Charles Erickson)

Orchestration of Characters

Anton Chekhov, the Russian dramatist, is said to have "orchestrated" his characters. The reference is to a musical composition in which the theme is played first by one section of the orchestra, such as the violins, and then by another, such as the brasses or woodwinds. Not only is the theme taken up by various sections, but it can be played in different ways as well—first in a major key, for instance, and then in a minor key. Beyond that, there is the way the various segments of the orchestra—strings, brass, woodwinds, percussion—are blended together, how they play with one another or in counterpoint to one another. In a similar fashion, Chekhov created his characters, giving each a distinctive voice. But his real genius was in the way he blended his characters, creating differences, similarities, subtle shadings, and contrasts.

In each of his plays, Chekhov drew a series of characters with a common problem, and each character represented some aspect of the central theme. In *Uncle Vanya,* for example, Chekhov's theme of disillusionment and frustration with life is reflected by virtually every character in the play, each of whom longs for a love that cannot be fulfilled. The title character, Vanya, who has been working on an estate to help support a pompous professor, falls in love with the professor's young wife, who does not return his love. A neighbor, Dr. Astrov, who has grown dissatisfied with his life, also loves the professor's wife, but nothing can come of it. Vanya's niece, a plain woman who works hard for little reward, is in love with Dr. Astrov, who does not return her love. And so it goes; practically everyone embodies the theme of unrequited love. But all this is done subtly and carefully brought out through gradations and shadings of meaning, which are interwoven like threads in a tapestry.

Chekhov was a master at orchestrating his characters, but he was not the only dramatist to use the technique. In one way or another, most dramatists try to arrange their characters so as to produce a cumulative effect. It is not what one character does or says but what all the characters do together that creates the effect.

ORCHESTRATION OF CHARACTERS

Characters in a play serve as contrasts, counterparts, or foils to each other; sometimes one group of characters is set in opposition to another, sometimes they complement one another. In every case, the playwright should make the relationships among characters serve the aims of the drama. Anton Chekhov was a master at combining and contrasting characters, sometimes a great many characters in one play. A good example is his work *The Three Sisters*, shown here with Heather Wood, in white, as Irina Prozorov in a new version of the play by Sarah Ruhl, directed by Les Waters at the Yale Repertory Theatre. (© Joan Marcus)

PLAYING YOUR PART: THINKING ABOUT THEATRE

1. During the last performance you attended, did the action take place in one locale (one room, for instance) or, instead, in three or four locations? Did the action move frequently, returning at times to a former location? What effect did these elements of place or location have on your experience of the play?

2. Look at the cast of characters in a Shakespearean play you have seen or read. Place each character in a category: major character; minor character; or a character in between—that is, a character with a clear personality but not a large role. Which characters are in opposition to one another? Which characters in the play dominate in the struggle? Is there a reversal of their fortunes?

3. While you are watching a modern play or drama involving a small group of characters locked in a struggle for dominance or control, how does the action usually play out? Is first one person in the ascendency and then another? What do shifts of power and control have to do with revealing the personalities of the characters? What do these changes have to do with the meaning of the play?

SUMMARY

1. There are several basic types of dramatic structure. *Climactic* form was adopted by the ancient Greeks and has been used frequently ever since. Its characteristics are a plot beginning quite late in the story, a limited number of characters, a limited number of locations and scenes, little or no extraneous material, and tight construction, including a cause-and-effect chain of events.

2. *Episodic* form involves a plot covering an extended span of time, numerous locations, a large cast of characters, diverse events (including mixtures of comic and serious episodes), and parallel plots or subplots. Shakespeare's plays are good examples of episodic form.

3. The climactic and episodic forms can be combined, as they have been in the Restoration period and in the modern period, in the works of Anton Chekhov and others.

4. Ritual or pattern is often used as the basis of dramatic structure. Words, gestures, and events are repeated; they have a symbolic meaning acquired both through repetition and through the significance invested in them from the past.

5. Theatre events are sometimes strung together to make a program. Examples are a group of unrelated one-act plays and a group of skits and songs in a revue. In this case, structure is within the individual units themselves; among the units the only structure might be the unfolding of the separate elements; or there can be a common theme uniting them.

6. Avant-garde theatre sometimes arranges events in a random way to suggest the random or haphazard manner in which life unfolds in everyday situations.

7. Experimental groups in the modern period have often used radical forms, including non-verbal and improvisational structures.

8. Segments and tableaux have also been used as structure.

9. Structurally, musical theatre consists of different elements put together in a sequence, in which solo musical numbers alternate with group numbers and dances and these musical elements alternate with dramatic scenes.

10. Dramatic characters symbolize people and fall into several categories. Frequently the chief characters of theatre are extraordinary characters: men and women at the outer limits of human behavior. Also, these characters often hold important positions: king, queen, general, admiral, duchess.

11. In modern serious theatre we frequently find typical or ordinary characters—complete, fully rounded portraits of people—who embody a whole group or type. An example is Willy Loman, the salesman in *Death of a Salesman*.

12. Some characters are stereotypes. Stock characters, for instance, are predictable, clearly defined types. Other characters have one dominant trait, which overshadows all other features.

13. A special type of character in drama of many periods is a narrator or the members of a chorus.

14. Occasionally performers are asked to play nonhuman parts—animals, birds, etc.—but these parts generally have a strong human flavor.

15. Characters are placed together by the playwright in certain combinations to obtain maximum effectiveness. A protagonist may be opposed by an antagonist; minor characters support major characters; and individual characters are orchestrated into a whole.

Theatrical Genres

When we attend a theatre performance, within the first fifteen minutes or so, we sense a tone and a mood that are being communicated. We become aware that those presenting the play—the playwright, the actors, the director—are signaling to the audience that they have adopted a definite point of view and attitude toward what is to follow. For example, in the opening scene of Shakespeare's *Hamlet,* the ghost of Hamlet's father appears to men on guard at the castle. It is an ominous, eerie scene that tells us this will be a serious play, perhaps even a tragedy. On the other hand, at the beginning of Shakespeare's *A Midsummer Night's Dream,* Theseus, the Duke of Athens, says: "Stir up the Athenian youth to merriment, awake the pert and nimble spirit of mirth," a clear sign that this will be a comedy.

TYPES OF DRAMA

In Greece in the fifth century BCE, where Western theatre began, the actors wore masks covering their faces when they performed. The Greeks took the idea of the mask to create symbols of the two kinds of plays presented at their dramatic festivals—the mask of tragedy and the mask of comedy—symbols that are still used today. Similarly, in Japan in the fourteenth century CE, a theatre called nō had become established as the serious form of drama. Alongside nō, however, was a comical, farcical type of drama called Kyogen.

In other words, wherever theatre has appeared, there has been a tendency to divide it into categories or types, often referred to by the French term *genre* (JAHN-ruh). In addition to tragedy and comedy, additional genres have developed: farce, melodrama, tragicomedy, and a number of others.

This tendency to divide dramatic works into categories is not confined to theatre. We find it widespread, not only in the arts, but in many aspects of life. Not only those who create theatre adopt different points of view toward events and toward life in general; all of us do. Depending on our perspective, we can see the same subject as funny or sad, take it seriously or laugh at it, make it an object of pity or of ridicule. Just why we look at events from different points of view is difficult to say, but there is no question that we do. The English author Horace Walpole (1717–1797) wrote: "This world is a comedy to those that think, a tragedy to those that feel."

◀ **DRAMATIC GENRE: COMEDY**

Drama is often divided into categories or types, referred to as genres. The Greeks separated tragedy and comedy. To those two genres have been added farce and tragicomedy and others. Shown here are Jerry Kernion (Dromio) and Bruce Turk (Antipholus) in Shakespeare's A Comedy of Errors, *directed by Michael Michetti, at A Noise Within Theatre. (© Craig Schwartz)*

Genre A French word meaning type or category. In theatre, genre denotes the category into which a play falls: for example, tragedy, comedy, or tragicomedy.

In theatre, this question of viewpoint—looking at people or events from a particular perspective—becomes crucial. Viewpoint is not taken for granted, as it is in everyday life; rather, it is a conscious act on the part of whoever creates the text. To take an example, in most cases death is considered a somber matter; but in his play *Arsenic and Old Lace* (1941), the dramatist Joseph Kesselring (1902–1967) makes it clear that in his play we are to regard death as comic. Kesselring presents two elderly women who kill no fewer than 12 old men by serving them arsenic in glasses of wine. But because the dramatist removes from the play any feeling that the deaths are to be taken seriously, he engenders in the audience the notion that it is all in fun.

Before examining genre, we should note that often a play does not fit neatly into a single category. Those who create a text do not write categories or types of plays; they write individual, unique works—and preoccupation with genre may distract us from the individuality of a play or a production. Still, if we keep these reservations in mind, we will find that it is helpful to understand the traditional genres into which Western dramatic literature has fallen.

TRAGEDY

Serious drama takes a thoughtful, sober attitude toward its subject matter. It puts the spectators in a frame of mind to think about what they are seeing and to become involved with the characters onstage: to love what these characters love, fear what they fear, and suffer what they suffer. The best-known form of serious drama, to which we turn first, is *tragedy*. Other forms of serious theatre are *heroic drama, domestic drama,* and *melodrama*.

Tragedy asks very basic questions about human existence. Why are people sometimes cruel to one another? Why is the world unjust? Why are men and women called on to endure suffering? What are the limits of human suffering and endurance? In the midst of cruelty and despair, what are the possibilities of human achievement? To what heights of courage, strength, generosity, and integrity can human beings rise? Tragedy assumes that the universe is indifferent to human concerns and often cruel and malevolent. Sometimes the innocent appear to suffer while the evil prosper. In the face of this, some humans are capable of despicable deeds, but others can confront and overcome adversity, attaining a nobility that places them "a little lower than the angels." We can divide tragedy into two basic kinds: traditional and modern. *Traditional tragedy* includes works from several significant periods of the past. *Modern tragedy* generally includes plays from the late nineteenth century to the present day.

Tragedy Dramatic form involving serious actions of universal significance and with important moral and philosophical implications, usually with an unhappy ending.

Traditional Tragedy

Three noteworthy periods of history in which tragic drama was produced are Greece in the fifth century BCE, England in the late sixteenth century and early seventeenth century, and France in the seventeenth century. Tragedies from these three ages have in common the following characteristics, which help define traditional tragedy.

Tragic Heroes and Heroines   Generally, the hero or heroine of a tragedy is an extraordinary person: a king, a queen, a general, a nobleman or noblewoman—in other words, a person of stature. In Greek drama, Antigone, Electra, Oedipus, Agamemnon, Creon, and Orestes are members of royal families. In the plays of Shakespeare, Hamlet, Claudius, Gertrude, Lear, and Cordelia are also royal; Julius Caesar, Macbeth, and Othello are generals; and others—Ophelia, Romeo, and Juliet—are members of the nobility.

Tragic Circumstances   The central figures of the play are caught in a series of tragic circumstances: Oedipus, without realizing it, murders his father and marries his mother; Antigone must choose between death and dishonoring her dead brother; Phaedra falls hopelessly and fatally in love with her stepson, Hippolytus; Othello is completely duped by Iago; and Lear is cast out by the daughters to whom he has given his kingdom. In traditional tragedy, the universe seems determined to trap the hero or heroine in a fateful web.

Tragic Irretrievability   The situation becomes irretrievable: there is no turning back. The tragic figures are in a situation from which there is no honorable avenue of escape; they must go forward to meet their fate.

Acceptance of Responsibility   The hero or heroine accepts responsibility for his or her actions and also shows willingness to suffer and an immense capacity for suffering. Oedipus puts out his own eyes; Antigone faces death with equanimity; Othello kills himself. King Lear suffers immensely, living through personal humiliation, a raging storm on a heath, temporary insanity, and the death of his daughter, and finally confronts his own death. A statement by Edgar in *King Lear* applies to all tragic figures: "Men must endure their going hence even as their coming hither."

Tragic Verse   The language of traditional tragedy is verse. Because it deals with lofty and profound ideas—with men and women at the outer limits of their lives—tragedy soars to the heights and descends to the depths of human experience; and many feel that such thoughts and emotions can best be expressed in poetry. Look at Cleopatra's lament on the death of Mark Antony. Her sense of admiration for Antony, and her desolation, could never be conveyed so tellingly in less poetic terms:

> Oh, wither'd is the garland of war,
> The soldier's pole is fall'n! Young boys and girls
> Are level now with men. The odds is gone,
> And there is nothing left remarkable
> Beneath the visiting moon.

These words have even more effect when heard in the theatre spoken by an eloquent actress.

The Effect of Tragedy   When the elements of traditional tragedy are combined, they appear to produce two contradictory reactions simultaneously. One is pessimism: the heroes or heroines are "damned if they do and damned if they don't," and the world is a cruel,

MAJOR CHARACTERS CAUGHT IN A TRAGIC WEB

In traditional tragedy the fall of a hero or heroine has a special significance because of the combination of his or her personality and position. An example of a tragic heroine is the Duchess of Malfi in the play of the same name by John Webster. Despite her title and station in life, the duchess is taunted and destroyed by her evil brothers when she marries someone of a lower social rank. Seen here are Eve Best in the title role and Harry Lloyd as Ferdinand, one of the brothers, in a U.K. production. (© Nigel Norrington/ArenaPAL) uncompromising place, a world of despair. And yet, in even the bleakest tragedy—whether *Hamlet, Medea, Macbeth,* or *King Lear*—there is affirmation. One source of this positive feeling is found in the drama itself. Sophocles, Euripides, Shakespeare, and the French dramatist Jean Racine, although telling us that the world is in chaos and utterly lost, at the same time affirmed just the opposite by creating brilliant, carefully shaped works of art.

There is another positive element, which has to do with the tragic heroes and heroines themselves. They meet their fate with such dignity and such determination that they defy the gods. They say: "Come and get me; throw your worst at me. Whatever happens, I will not surrender my individuality or my dignity." In Aeschylus's play *Prometheus, Bound* the title character—who is one of the earliest tragic heroes—says: "On me the tempest falls. It does not make me tremble." In defeat, the men and women of tragedy triumph.

As for the deeper meanings of individual tragedies, there is a vast literature on the subject, and each play has to be looked at and experienced in detail to obtain the full measure of its meaning. Certain tragedies seem to hold so much meaning, to contain so much—in substance and in echoes and reverberations—that one can spend a lifetime studying them.

Modern Tragedy

Tragedies of the modern period—that is, beginning in the late nineteenth century—do not have queens or kings as central figures, and they are written in prose rather than poetry. For these as well as more philosophical reasons, purists argue that modern tragedies are not true tragedies.

In answer to this, it should be pointed out that today we have few kings or queens—either in mythology or, except in certain places like Great Britain, in real life. At the same time, we may ask: do we not have characters today who can stand as symbolic figures for important segments of society? Many would answer that we still do. In attempting to create modern tragedy, the question is not whether we view the human condition in the same way as the French did in the seventeenth century or the Greeks

A MODERN TRAGIC FAMILY

In Federico García Lorca's play *The House of Bernarda Alba,* a widow who has grown to hate and distrust men keeps her daughters confined as virtual prisoners in their own home, preventing them from going out. In this production, directed by Elizabeth Huddle at the Madison Repertory Theatre, we see four of the daughters, with the mother in the center. Left to right, the performers are Jamie England, Monica Lyons, Elisabeth Adwin, Margaret Ingraham, and Diane Robinson. (© Zane Williams/Madison Repertory Theatre) did in the fifth century BCE—those two societies did not view life in the same way either—but whether our age allows for a tragic view on its own terms.

The answer seems to be yes. Compared with either the eighteenth or the nineteenth century—ages of enlightenment, progress, and unbounded optimism—our age has its own tragic vision. Modern tragic dramatists probe the same depths and ask the same questions as their predecessors: Why do men and women suffer? Why do violence and injustice exist? And perhaps most fundamental of all: What is the meaning of our lives?

On this basis, many commentators would argue that writers like Ibsen, Strindberg, García Lorca, O'Neill, Williams, and Miller can lay claim to writing legitimate modern tragedy. The ultimate test of a play is not whether it meets someone's definition of tragedy but what effect it produces in the theatre and how successful it is in standing up to continued scrutiny. Eugene O'Neill's *Long Day's Journey into Night* takes as bleak a look at the human condition, with, at the same time, as compassionate a view of human striving and dignity as it seems possible to take in our day.

HEROIC DRAMA

The term **heroic drama** is not used as commonly as *tragedy* or *comedy*, but there is a wide range of plays for which *heroic drama* seems an appropriate description. I use the term specifically to indicate serious drama of any period that incorporates heroic or noble figures and other features of traditional tragedy—dialogue in verse, extreme situations, and the like—but differs from tragedy in having a happy ending, or in assuming a basically optimistic worldview even when the ending is sad.

Several Greek plays ordinarily classified as tragedies are actually closer to heroic drama. In Sophocles's *Electra,* for instance, Electra suffers grievously, but at the end of the play she and her brother Orestes triumph. Another example is *The Cid,* written by Pierre Corneille (1606–1684) in France. It has a hero who leads his men to victory in battle but who is not killed; in the end, he wins a duel against his rival. In the late seventeenth century in England, a form of drama also called *heroic drama,* or sometimes *heroic tragedy,* was precisely the type about which we are speaking: a serious play with a happy ending for the hero or heroine.

Many Asian plays—from India, China, and Japan—though resisting the usual classifications and including a great deal of dance and music, bear a close resemblance to heroic drama. Frequently, for example, a hero goes through a series of dangerous adventures, emerging victorious at the end. The vast majority of Asian dramas end happily.

A second type of heroic drama involves the death of the hero or heroine, but the overall effect is not considered tragic. Several of the plays of Johann Wolfgang von Goethe (1749–1832) follow this pattern. (Many of Goethe's plays, along with those of his contemporaries in the late eighteenth century and early nineteenth century, form a subdivision of heroic drama referred to as *romantic drama*. **Romanticism,** a literary movement that took hold in Germany at the time and spread to France and throughout much of Europe, celebrated the spirit of hope, personal freedom, and natural instincts.)

A number of plays in the modern period fall into the category of heroic drama. *Saint Joan,* by George Bernard Shaw, is a good example: although Joan is burned at the stake, her death is actually a form of triumph. As if that were not enough, Shaw provides an epilogue in which Joan appears alive again.

In the history of theatre, the plays we are discussing as *heroic drama* occupy a large and important niche, cutting across Asia and western civilization and across periods from the Greek golden age to the present.

Heroic drama   Serious but basically optimistic drama written in verse or elevated prose, with noble or heroic characters in extreme situations or unusual adventures.

Romanticism   Nineteenth century dramatic movement that imitated the episodic structure of Shakespeare, and thematically focused on the gulf between human being's spiritual aspirations and physical limitations.

photo essay

Modern Domestic Drama

(© Geraint Lewis)

Serious drama in America came of age in the mid-twentieth century, with plays by Eugene O'Neill, Tennessee Williams, Arthur Miller, and Lillian Hellman, among others. Though all four experimented with nonrealistic dramatic devices, much of their strongest work was realistic domestic drama. Included here are examples, in photographs from recent productions.

At left *Long Day's Journey Into Night* by Eugene O'Neill, directed by Anthony Page; David Suchet as James Tyrone, Kyle Soller as Edmund Tyrone, Laurie Metcalf as Mary Cavan Tyrone, Trevor White as James Tyrone Jr., London, 2012.

At right Natasha Lowe as Blanche, Matt Hawkins as Stanley and Stacy Stoltz as Stella in Tennessee Williams' *A Streetcar Named Desire,* Writers Theatre, 2010

(© Courtesy Writers Theatre, 2010. Photo by Michael Brosilow)

At left Lee Aaron Rosen as Chris Keller, Michael Tisdale as George Deever, and Diane Davis as Ann Deever in *All My Sons,* by Arthur Miller, directed by David Esbjornson at the Huntington Theatre Company.

(© T Charles Erickson)

To the right Seth Numrich, left, and Danny Burstein in a recent Broadway revival of *Golden Boy* by Clifford Odets, directed by Bartlett Sher.

(© Sara Krulwich/The New York Times/Redux)

BOURGEOIS OR DOMESTIC DRAMA

Bourgeois or domestic drama Drama dealing with problems—particularly family problems—of middle-and lower-class characters. There are serious and comic domestic dramas.

With the changes in society that resulted from the rise of the middle class and the shift from kings and queens to more democratic governments, we move from classic tragedy to modern tragedy. In the same way, during the past 150 years heroic drama has largely been replaced by **bourgeois** or **domestic drama.** *Bourgeois* refers to people of the middle or lower middle class rather than the aristocracy, and *domestic* means that the plays often deal with problems of the family or the home rather than great affairs of state. In the Greek, Roman, and Renaissance periods, ordinary people served as main characters only in comedies; they rarely appeared as heroes or heroines of serious plays. Beginning in the eighteenth century, however, as society changed, there was a call for serious drama about men and women with whom members of the audience could identify and who were like themselves.

In England in 1731, George Lillo (1693–1739) wrote *The London Merchant,* a story of a merchant's apprentice who is led astray by a prostitute and betrays his good-hearted employer. This play, like others that came after it, dealt with recognizable people from the daily life of Britain, and audiences welcomed it.

From these beginnings, bourgeois or domestic drama developed through the balance of the eighteenth century and the whole of the nineteenth, until it achieved a

DOMESTIC DRAMA OF EVERYDAY LIFE
Domestic drama concerns itself with family problems: parents and children, husbands and wives, growing up, growing old. The characters in it are recognizable people, and it has long been a mainstay of modern drama. Shown here are Luka Kain as Travis, left, with Lynda Gravátt as Lena, and Susan Kelechi Watson as Ruth in a recent production of *A Raisin in the Sun* by Lorraine Hansberry, directed by Phylicia Rashad at the Westport Country Playhouse. (© T Charles Erickson)

place of prominence in the works of Ibsen, Strindberg, and Chekhov. In the mid-twentieth century, three major American playwrights of domestic drama emerged: Eugene O'Neill, Arthur Miller, and Tennessee Williams. O'Neill, in such plays as *The Iceman Cometh* and *Long Day's Journey into Night* probed the depth of his characters' anguish as successfully as any dramatist of modern times. Miller, in *The Crucible* and *Death of a Salesman,* combined the tragic lives of its characters with political and moral investigations. Williams, the most lyrical of the three, in *The Glass Menagerie* and *A Streetcar Named Desire*, explored the limits of human sorrow and endurance.

These three were followed in the decades to come by other important American playwrights such as Lorraine Hansberry, Edward Albee, August Wilson, and Paula Vogel. Problems with society, struggles within a family, dashed hopes, and renewed determination are typical characteristics of domestic drama. When sufficiently penetrating or profound, domestic drama achieves the level of modern tragedy.

In one form or another, bourgeois or domestic drama has become the predominant form of serious drama throughout Europe and the United States during the past hundred years.

MELODRAMA

During the eighteenth and nineteenth centuries, one of the most popular forms of theatre was **melodrama.** The word, which comes from Greek, means "music drama" or "song drama." Its modern form was introduced by the French in the late eighteenth century and applied to plays that had background music of the kind we hear in movies: ominous chords underscoring a scene of suspense and lyrical music underscoring a love scene.

Among the effects for which melodrama generally strives is fright or horror. It has been said that melodrama speaks to the paranoia in all of us: the fear that someone is pursuing us or that disaster is about to overtake us. How often do we have a sense that others are ganging up on us or a premonition that we have a deadly disease?

Melodrama brings these fears to life; we see people stalked or terrorized, or innocent victims tortured. Murder mysteries and detective stories are almost invariably melodramas because they stress suspense, danger, and close brushes with disaster. This type of melodrama usually ends in one of two ways: either the victims are maimed or murdered (in which case our worst paranoid fears are confirmed); or, after a series of dangerous episodes, they are rescued (in which case the play is like a bad dream from which we awaken to realize that we are safe in bed and everything is all right).

Probably the easiest way to understand melodrama is to look at film and television examples. Among the kinds of popular melodramas we are familiar with are *westerns, science fiction films, horror films, superhero films* and *detective* or *spy films.* All of these emphasize heroes and villains, other stock characters such as sidekicks and love interests, as well as spectacular events and effects. But the key to the melodramatic form, on stage, and in film and television, is that good is almost always victorious over evil.

Still another form of melodrama argues a political or moral issue. Melodrama invariably shows us the good guys against the bad guys. Therefore, a playwright who wants to make a strong political case will often write a melodrama in which the good characters represent his or her point of view.

A list of significant melodramas would range over most of theatre history and would include writers from Euripides through Shakespeare and his contemporaries to

Melodrama Dramatic from made popular in the nineteenth century that emphasized action and spectacular effects and also used music to underscore the action; it had stock characters, usually with clearly defined villains and heroes.

SUSPENSION OF NATURAL LAWS IN COMEDY
Frequently in various kinds of comedy, particularly in farce, our natural reaction to events is reordered to achieve a comic effect, and the audience accepts this. An excellent example is the play *Arsenic and Old Lace* by Jospeh Kesselring, in which two elderly women, who appear to be helpless and harmless, actually murder a number of old men by giving them elderberry wine laced with poison. Because we have accepted the comic premise of the play, however, we do not condemn their acts, but rather become amused. Shown here (left to right) are Nathaniel Fuller (Mr. Witherspoon) Sally Wingert (Martha Brewster) and Kristine Nielsen (Abby Brewster) in a production at the Guthrie Theater directed by Joe Dowling. (© Michal Daniel)

dramatists throughout Europe and the Americas in the modern period. Other types of serious drama, tragic and nontragic, frequently have strong melodramatic elements as well.

Aside from those taking a basically serious point of view, there are two other fundamental approaches to dramatic material. One is *comedy*, with its many forms and variations; the other is a mixture of the serious and the comic, called *tragicomedy*.

COMEDY

Comedy   In general, a play that is light in tone, is concerned with issues that point out the excesses and folly of human behavior, has a happy ending, and is designed to amuse.

People who create **comedy** are not necessarily more frivolous or less concerned with important matters than people who create serious works; they may be extremely serious in their own way. Writers of comedy like Aristophanes, Molière, and George Bernard Shaw cared passionately about human affairs and the problems of men and women. But those with a comic view look at the world differently: with a smile or a deep laugh or an arched eyebrow. Writers like these perceive the follies and excesses of human behavior and develop a keen sense of the ridiculous, with the result that they show us things that make us laugh.

It should also be noted that there are many kinds of laughter. They range all the way from mild amusement at a witty saying or a humorous situation to a belly laugh at some wild physical comedy to cruel, derisive laughter. Theatre, which reflects life and society, encompasses comedies that display a similar range, from light comedies to outrageous farces.

Characteristics of Comedy

If we cannot fully explain comedy, we can at least understand some of the principles that make it possible.

Suspension of Natural Laws   One characteristic of most comedy is a temporary suspension of the natural laws of probability, cause and effect, and logic. Actions do not have the consequences they do in real life. In comedy, when a haughty man walking down the street steps on a child's skateboard and goes sprawling on the sidewalk, we do not fear for his safety or wonder if he has any bruises. The focus in comedy is on the man's being tripped up and getting his comeuppance.

In burlesque, a comic character can be hit on the backside with a fierce thwack, and we laugh, because we know that it does not hurt anything but his or her pride. At one point in stage history a special stick consisting of two thin slats of wood held closely together was developed to make the sound of hitting someone even more fearsome. The stick was known as a *slapstick,* a name that came to describe all kinds of raucous, knockabout comedy.

Prime examples of the suspension of natural laws in comedy are found in film and television cartoons. In animated cartoons, characters are hurled through the air like missiles, are shot full of holes, and are flattened on the sidewalk when they fall from buildings. But they always get up, with little more than a shake of the head. In the audience, there are no thoughts of real injury, of cuts or bruises, because the cause-and-effect chain of everyday life is not operating.

Under these conditions, murder itself can be viewed as comic. In *Arsenic and Old Lace,* by Joseph Kesselring (1902–1967), two sweet elderly women—sisters—thinking they are being helpful, put lonely old men "out of their misery" by giving them arsenic in elderberry wine. The two sisters let their brother, who thinks he is Teddy Roosevelt, bury the bodies in the cellar, where he is digging his own version of the Panama Canal. All together, these innocent-seeming sisters murder twelve men before their scheme is uncovered. But we do not really think of it as murder, and we have none of the feelings one usually has for victims. The idea of suffering and harm has been suspended, and we are free to enjoy the irony and incongruity of the situation.

The Comic Premise   The suspension of natural laws in comedy makes possible the development of a *comic premise.* The comic premise is an idea or concept that turns the accepted notion of things upside down and makes this upended notion the basis of a play. The premise can provide thematic and structural unity and can serve as a springboard for comic dialogue, comic characters, and comic situations.

Aristophanes, the Greek satiric dramatist, was a master at developing a comic premise. In *The Clouds,* Aristophanes pictures Socrates as a man who can think only when perched in a basket suspended in midair. In *The Birds,* two ordinary men persuade a chorus of birds to build a city between heaven and earth. The birds comply, calling the place Cloudcuckoo Land, and the two men sprout wings to join them. In another play, *Lysistrata,* Aristophanes has the women of Greece agree to go on a sex strike to end a war: they will not make love to their husbands until the husbands stop fighting and sign a peace treaty with their opponents.

Techniques of Comedy

The suspension of natural laws and the establishment of a comic premise in comedy involve exaggeration and incongruity, and the contradictions that result from these show up in three areas—verbal humor, characterization, and comic situations.

Slapstick   Type of comedy, or comic business, that relies on ridiculous physical activity—often violent in nature—for its humor.

Comic premise   Idea or concept in a comedy that turns the accepted notion of things upside down.

VERBAL HUMOR

One key element of comedy is verbal wit. No one was more the master of wit than playwright Oscar Wilde, whose epigrams and clever word play are still quoted today. Shown here is a scene from his play *The Importance of Being Earnest* in a production at the Ahmanson Theatre in Los Angeles, directed by Peter Hall. It featured (left to right) Robert Petkoff as Algernon Moncrieff, Lynn Redgrave as Lady Bracknell and Charlotte Parry as Cecily Cardew. (© Craig Schwartz)

Verbal Humor Verbal humor can be anything from a pun to the most sophisticated discourse. A *pun*—usually considered the simplest form of wit—is a humorous use of words with the same sound but different meanings. A man who says he is going to start a bakery if he can "raise the dough" is making a pun.

Close to the pun is the *malaprop*—a word that sounds like the right word but actually means something quite different. The term comes from Mrs. Malaprop, a character in *The Rivals* by the English playwright Richard Brinsley Sheridan (1751–1816). Mrs. Malaprop wants to impress everyone with her education and erudition but ends up doing just the opposite because she constantly misuses long words. For example, she insists that her daughter is not "illegible" for marriage, meaning that her daughter is not "ineligible," and when asked to explain a situation she says that someone else will provide the "perpendiculars" when she means the "particulars."

A sophisticated form of verbal humor is the *epigram*. Oscar Wilde (1854–1900), a man devoted to verbal humor, often turned accepted values upside down in his epigrams. "I can resist anything except temptation," says one of his characters; and "A man cannot be too careful in the choice of his enemies," says another.

Comedy of Character In comedy of character the discrepancy or incongruity lies in the way characters see themselves or pretend to be, as opposed to the way they actually are. A good example is a person who pretends to be a doctor—using obscure medicines, hypodermic needles, and Latin jargon—but who is actually a fake. Such a person is the chief character in Molière's *The Doctor in Spite of Himself.* Another example of incongruity of character is Molière's *The Would-Be Gentleman,* in which the title character, Monsieur Jourdain, a man of wealth, but without taste or refinement, is determined to learn courtly behavior. He hires a fencing master, a dancing master, and a teacher of literature to teach him these skills, but in every case Jourdain is ridiculed.

Comedy of character is also a basic ingredient of Italian *commedia dell'arte* and all forms of comedy where stock characters, stereotypes, and characters with dominant traits are emphasized.

We can also find examples of comedies of characters today in film and on television. The popular TV show *The Big Bang Theory* focuses on quirky scientists and much of the comedy is created by their unusual exaggerated behaviors.

Plot Complications Still another way the contradictory or the ludicrous manifests itself in comedy is in plot complications, including coincidences and mistaken identity.

PLOT COMPLICATIONS: A HALLMARK OF FARCE
Frequently used devices of comedy include twists and turns in the plot, mistaken identity, unexpected developments, and ridiculous situations. Michael Frayn's comedy *Noises Off* contains an abundance of these elements. The production shown here was directed by Lindsay Posner in London. (© Geraint Lewis)

A time-honored comic plot is Shakespeare's *The Comedy of Errors,* based on *The Menaechmi,* a play of the late third century BCE by the Roman writer Titus Maccius Plautus (c. 254–184 BCE). *The Comedy of Errors* in turn was the basis of a successful American musical comedy *The Boys from Syracuse,* with songs by Richard Rodgers (1902–1979) and Lorenz Hart (1895–1943). In *The Comedy of Errors,* identical twins and their identical twin servants were separated when young. As the play opens, however, both masters and both servants—unknown to one another—are in one place. The confusion among the twin brothers and the twin servants leads to an endless series of comic encounters.

A classic scene of plot complication occurs in Sheridan's *The School for Scandal,* written in 1777. Joseph Surface, the main character in the play, is thought to be an upstanding man but is really a charlatan, whereas Charles, his brother, is mistakenly considered a reprobate. In a famous scene called the "screen scene," both Lady Teazle, a married woman visiting Surface, and her husband, Sir Peter Teazle, are hidden, one behind a screen, one in a closet. When the honest Charles suddenly appears he discovers both of them, exposing their deceptions at a single moment.

Forms of Comedy

Comedy takes various forms, depending on the dramatist's intent and on the comic techniques emphasized.

photo essay

Forms of Comedy

(© Craig Schwartz)

Comedy takes a number of forms, depending on whether the emphasis is on verbal wit, plot complications, or the characters' eccentricities. It can range all the way from intellectual comedy, to high comedy (dealing with the upper classes), to domestic comedy (similar to sit-coms on TV), to slapstick farce. Shown here is a variety of types of comedy.

Seen here at left Jason Dechert (Louis Dubedat) and Jules Willcox (Jennifer Dubedat) in *The Doctor's Dilemma*, a witty, intellectual satire by George Bernard Shaw, directed by Dámaso Rodriguez, at A Noise Within Theatre, Pasadena, California.

(© Donald Cooper/PhotoSTAGE)

Shown here at left is Owain Arthur as Francis Henshall in *One Man, Two Guvnors,* a farce by Richard Bean after Goldoni's "The Servant of Two Masters," in a production directed by Nicholas Hytner at the National Theatre, London.

Above we see Kristine Nielsen as Mrs. Hardcastle, Jeremy Webb as George Hastings, Rebecca, Brooksher, rear, as Constance Neville in a comedy of wit by Oliver Goldsmith, *She Stoops to Conquer,* which he called a "laughing comedy." The production was directed by Nicholas Martin at the McCarter Theatre. (© T Charles Erickson)

Shown here are David Shiner, left, and Bill Irwin performing in *Old Hats*, a slapstick comedy they created at the Pershing Square Signature Center, directed by Tina Landau.

(© Sara Krulwich/The New York Times/Redux)

One of the finest comic playwrights of all time was the French dramatist Molière. One of his most famous creations was the title character in his play *Tartuffe,* a man who dressed in clerical clothing and pretended to be extremely pious. He completely fooled a man named Orgon, who considered him religious when in reality he was after Orgon's money and his wife. Shown here is a scene with the wife, the husband, and Tartuffe, played by Rachel Botchan, T. J. Edwards, and Bradford Cover at the Pearl Theatre.

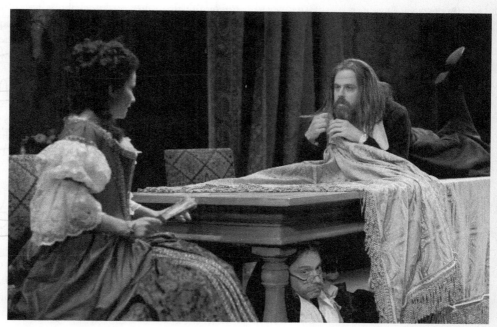

(© Gregory Costanzo)

PLAYING YOUR PART: EXPERIENCING THEATRE

1. What recent event in everyday life has been described as a "tragedy"? Would that event meet the traditional definition of tragedy? Does it have the elements of traditional tragedy?

2. Is there a contemporary figure whose life you believe could be dramatized as a "modern tragedy"? Describe.

3. Have you seen a film or television show that could be categorized as "domestic drama"? What are its characteristics that lead you to that categorization?

4. Have you seen a recent film that you would categorize as a "melodrama"? What are its characteristics that lead you to that categorization?

5. Have you seen films or television shows that could be categorized as farce, burlesque, satire, domestic comedy, comedy of manners, comedy of characters?

6. Can you describe any current events that might be dramatized as tragicomedy? Why?

Farce A subclass of comedy with emphasis on exaggerated plot complications and with few or not intellectual pretensions.

Farce Most plays discussed in the section on plot complications are *farces.* Farce thrives on exaggeration—not only plot complications but also broad physical humor and stereotyped characters. It has no intellectual pretensions but aims rather at entertainment and provoking laughter. In addition to excessive plot complications, its humor results from ridiculous situations as well as pratfalls and horseplay, not on the verbal wit found in more intellectual forms of comedy. Mock violence, rapid movement, and accelerating pace are hallmarks of farce. Marriage and sex are the objects of fun in *bedroom farce,* but farce can also poke fun at medicine, law, and business.

Burlesque A ludicrous, comic imitation of a dramatic form, play, piece of literature, or other popular entertainment.

Burlesque *Burlesque* also relies on knockabout physical humor, as well as gross exaggerations and, occasionally, vulgarity. Historically, burlesque was a ludicrous imitation of other forms of drama or of an individual play. In the United States, the term *burlesque* came to describe a type of variety show featuring low comedy skits and attractive women.

Satire Comic form, using irony and exaggeration, to attack and expose folly and vice.

Satire A form related to traditional burlesque, but with more intellectual and moral content, is *satire.* Satire uses wit, irony, and exaggeration to attack or expose evil and foolishness. Satire can attack specific figures; for example, the revue *Forbidden Broadway* makes fun of the more flamboyant or excessive stars in Broadway musicals. It can also be more inclusive, as in the case of Molière's *Tartuffe,* which ridicules religious hypocrisy generally.

Domestic Comedy The comic equivalent of domestic or bourgeois drama is *domestic comedy.* Usually dealing with family situations, it is found most frequently today in television situation comedies—often called *sitcoms*—which feature members of a family or residents of a neighborhood caught in a series of complicated but amusing situations. Television shows such as *Two and a Half Men, How I Met Your Mother,* and *Modern Family* are examples. This type of comedy was once a staple of theatre and can still be found onstage in plays by writers like Neil Simon (b. 1927).

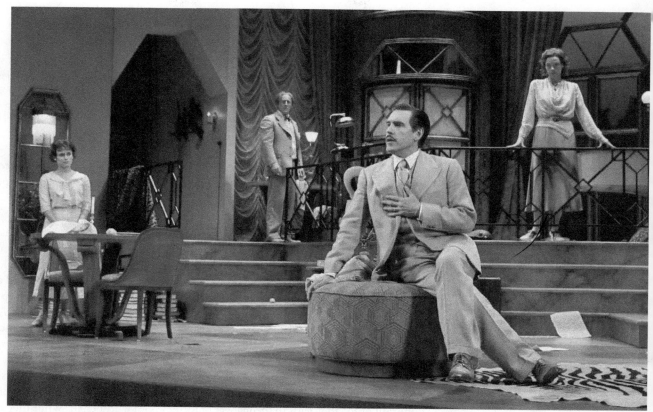

COMEDY OF MANNERS
Comedy of manners usually deals with the upper class in a given society. It stresses verbal humor, repartee, and irony. The precursors of modern comedy of manners were the Restoration comedies popular in London in the late seventeenth century. In the nineteenth century, Oscar Wilde was a master of comedy of manners, and in the twentieth century it was Noël Coward. One of Coward's best-known plays is *Private Lives,* about two upper-class couples whose marriages become comically entangled. Seen here in a production at the Guthrie Theater are Tracey Maloney (Sibyl), Kris L. Nelson (Victor), Stephen Pelinski (Elyot), and Veanne Cox (Amanda). (© Michal Daniel)

Comedy of Manners   *Comedy of manners* is concerned with pointing up the foibles and peculiarities of the upper classes. Against a cultivated, sophisticated background, it uses verbal wit to depict the cleverness and expose the social pretensions of its characters. Rather than horseplay, it stresses witty phrases. Pointed barbs are always at a premium in comedy of manners. In England a line of comedies of manners runs from William Wycherley, William Congreve, and Oliver Goldsmith (1730–1774) in the seventeenth and eighteenth centuries to Oscar Wilde in the nineteenth century and Noël Coward (1899–1973) in the twentieth.

Comedy of Ideas   Many of George Bernard Shaw's plays could be put under a special heading, *comedy of ideas,* because Shaw used comic techniques to debate intellectual propositions and to further his own moral and social point of view. Though witty and amusing, Shaw's plays frequently include provocative discussions of controversial social issues. *Mrs. Warren's Profession,* for example, about a woman who runs a house of prostitution, deals with hypocrisy in society and *Arms and the Man* is not only an amusing story of a pompous soldier but also a treatise on war and heroism.

Comedy of manners
Form of comic drama that became popular in the English Restoration, that is set within sophisticated society, while poking fun at its characters' social pretensions, usually through verbal wit.

Comedy of ideas   A comedy in which the humor is based on intellectual and verbal aspects of comedy rather than physical comedy or comedy of character. A drama whose emphasis is on the clash of ideas, as exemplified in the plays of George Bernard Shaw.

In all its forms, comedy remains a way of looking at the world in which basic values are asserted but natural laws are suspended in order to underline human follies and foolishness—sometimes with a rueful look, sometimes with a wry smile, and sometimes with an uproarious laugh.

TRAGICOMEDY

Tragicomedy During the Renaissance, a play having tragic themes and noble characters but a happy ending; today, a play in which serious and comic elements are integrated. Many plays of this type present a comic or ironic treatment of a serious theme.

In twentieth-century theatre a new genre came to the forefront—*tragicomedy.* In this section, we examine this form that has proved so important in the modern period.

What Is Tragicomedy?

In the past, comedy has usually been set in opposition to tragedy or serious drama: serious drama is sad, comedy is funny; serious drama makes people cry, comedy makes them laugh; serious drama arouses anger, comedy brings a smile. True, the comic view of life differs from the serious view, but the two are not always as clearly separated as this polarity suggests. Many comic dramatists are serious people; "I laugh to keep from crying" applies to many comic writers as well as to certain clowns and comedians. A great deal of serious drama contains comic elements. Shakespeare, for instance, included comic characters in several of his serious plays. The drunken porter in *Macbeth,* the gravedigger in *Hamlet,* and Falstaff in *Henry IV, Part 1* are examples.

In medieval plays, comic scenes are interpolated in the basically religious subject matter. One of the best-known of all medieval plays, *The Second Shepherds' Play,* concerns the visit of the shepherds to the manger of the newborn Christ child. While they stop in a field to spend the night, Mak, a comic character, steals a sheep and takes it to his house, where he and his wife pretend that it is their baby. When the shepherds discover what Mak has done, they toss him in a blanket, and after this horseplay the serious part of the story resumes.

The alternation of serious and comic elements is a practice of long standing, particularly in episodic plays; but *tragicomedy* does not refer to plays that shift from serious to comic and back again. It is a view in which one eye looks through a comic lens and the other through a serious lens; and the two points of view are so intermingled as to be one, like food that tastes sweet and sour at the same time. In addition to his basically serious plays and his basically comic plays, Shakespeare wrote others that seem to be a combination of tragedy and comedy, such as *Measure for Measure* and *All's Well That Ends Well.* Because they do not fit neatly into one category or the other, these plays have proved troublesome to critics—so troublesome that they have been officially dubbed *problem plays.*

The "problem," however, arises largely because of difficulty in accepting the tragicomic point of view, for these plays have many of the attributes of the fusion of the tragic and the comic. A sense of comedy pervades these plays, the idea that all will end well and that much of what happens is ludicrous or ridiculous; at the same time, the serious effects of a character's actions are not dismissed. Unlike true comedy, in which a fall on the sidewalk or a temporary danger has no serious consequences, these plays contain actions that appear quite serious. And so we have tragicomedy.

Modern Tragicomedy

In the modern period—during the past hundred years or so—tragicomedy has become the primary approach of many of the best playwrights. As suggested in Chapter 2, these

COMBINING TRAGEDY AND COMEDY

Tragicomedy has become more and more prominent in the modern period, and has taken its place alongside traditional tragedy, comedy, and other genres as a major form of our time. In several of Shakespeare's so-called problem plays, comic and serious elements are intermixed in the manner of contemporary tragicomedy. A good example is *All's Well That Ends Well*, which features a strange, almost bizarre, mixture of fairy-tale elements with cynical realism. Shown here is James Garnon as Parolles in a London production at Shakespeare's Globe Theatre, directed by John Dove. (© Geraint Lewis)

writers are not creating in a vacuum; they are part of the world in which they live, and ours is an age that has adopted a tragicomic viewpoint more extensively than most previous ages. As if to keynote this attitude and set the tone, the Danish philosopher Søren Kierkegaard (1813–1855) in 1842 wrote: "Existence itself, the act of existence, is a striving and is both pathetic and comic in the same degree." The plays of Anton Chekhov, written at the turn of the twentieth century, reflect the spirit described by Kierkegaard. Chekhov called two of his major plays *comedies;* but Stanislavski, who directed them, called them *tragedies*—an indication of the confusion arising from Chekhov's mixture of the serious and the comic.

An example of Chekhov's approach is a scene at the end of the third act of *Uncle Vanya* (1899). The lives of Vanya and his niece, Sonya, have been ruined by Sonya's father, a professor. At the moment where Sonya tells her father how cruel and thoughtless he is, Vanya comes in, waving a pistol in the air, and shoots twice at the professor, but misses both times. There is some doubt that Vanya honestly means to kill the professor and the scene itself is both tragic and comic: the two elements are inextricably joined together.

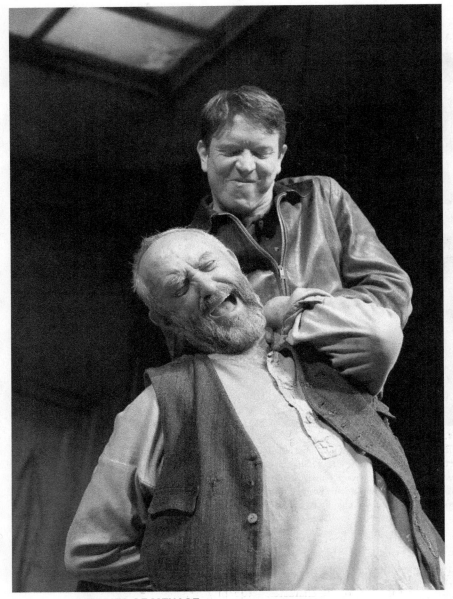

COMEDIES OF MENACE
Comedies range widely, from the pure entertainment of farce and light comedy to more substantive and probing comedies with a strong serious component. The playwright Harold Pinter calls many of his plays comedies of menace, meaning that they can provoke laughter but also have a deeper, more disturbing, sometimes frightening element. One of Pinter's best-known plays exemplifying this is *The Caretaker*. Shown here are Sam Spruell as Mick and Jonathan Pryce as Davies, directed by Christopher Morahan in a London production. (© Geraint Lewis)

Theatre of the absurd
Twentieth century plays expressing the dramatists' sense of absurdity and futility of human existence through the dramatic techniques they employ.

Theatre of the absurd (discussed below) is an example of modern tragicomedy. It probes deeply into human problems and casts a cold eye on the world, and yet it is also imbued with a comic spirit. The plays of Harold Pinter (1930–2008), a writer associated with theatre of the absurd, have been called *comedies of menace,* a phrase suggesting the idea of a theatre simultaneously terrifying and entertaining.

THEATRE OF THE ABSURD

After World War II, a new type of theatre emerged in Europe and the United States, which the critic Martin Esslin called **theatre of the absurd.** Although the dramatists whose work falls into this category do not write in identical styles and are not really a "school" of writers, they do have enough in common to be considered together. Esslin took the name for this form of theatre from a quotation in *The Myth of Sisyphus* by the French writer, dramatist, and philosopher Albert Camus (1913–1960). In *The Myth of Sisyphus,* Camus says that in the modern age there is a separation between "man and his life, the actor and his setting," and that this separation "constitutes the feeling of Absurdity."[1]

Plays falling into the category of absurdism convey humanity's sense of alienation and its loss of bearings in an illogical, unjust, and ridiculous world. Although serious, this viewpoint is generally depicted in plays with considerable humor; an ironic note runs through much of theatre of the absurd.

A prime example of theatre of the absurd is Beckett's *Waiting for Godot.* In this play Beckett has given us one of the most telling expressions of loneliness and futility ever written: two tramps on a barren plain waiting every day for a supreme being called "Godot," who they think will come but who never does. At the same time,

THEATRE OF THE ABSURD
Non sequitur, nonsensical language, existential characters, ridiculous situations—these are hallmarks of theatre of the absurd, which can also be viewed as a type of tragicomedy. One example is Eugene Ionesco's *Exit the King*. Shown here, left to right, are Lauren Ambrose (as Queen Marie), Geoffrey Rush (King Berenger), William Sadler (the Doctor, in the background), and Susan Sarandon (Queen Marguerite, the King's wife) in a 2009 Broadway production adapted and directed by Neil Armfield. (© Joan Marcus)

they themselves are comic. They wear baggy pants like burlesque comedians, and engage in any number of vaudeville routines. Also, the characters frequently say one thing and do just the opposite. One says to the other, "Well, shall we go?" and the other says, "Yes, let's go." But having said this, they don't move.

Absurdist plays suggest the idea of absurdity both in what they say—that is, their content—and in the way they say it, their form. Their structure, therefore, is a departure from dramatic structures of the past.

Absurdist Plots: Illogicality

Traditional plots in drama proceed in a logical way from a beginning through the development of the plot to a conclusion, an arrangement that suggests an ordered universe. In contrast, many absurdist plays not only proclaim absurdity but also embody it.

An example is *The Bald Soprano* by Eugène Ionesco. The very title of the play turns out to be nonsense; a bald soprano is mentioned once in the play, but with no explanation, and it is clear that the bald soprano has nothing whatever to do with the play as a whole. The absurdity of the piece is manifest the moment the curtain goes up. A typical English couple are sitting in a living room when the clock on the mantle strikes seventeen times; the wife's first words are, "There, it's nine o'clock."

Absurdist Language: Nonsense and Non Sequitur

Events and characters are frequently illogical in theatre of the absurd, and so too is language. *Non sequitur* is a Latin term meaning "it does not follow"; it implies that something does not follow from what has gone before, and it perfectly describes the method of theatre of the absurd. Sentences do not follow in sequence, and words do not mean what we expect them to mean.

An example of the irrationality or debasement of language is found in Beckett's *Waiting for Godot*. The character Lucky does not speak for most of his time onstage, but at the end of the first act he delivers a long speech consisting of incoherent religious and legalistic jargon. The opening lines offer a small sample.

> Given the existence as uttered forth in the public works of Puncher and Wattmann of a personal God quaquaquaqua with white beard quaquaquaqua outside time without extension who from the heights of divine apathia divine athambia divine aphasia loves us dearly with some exceptions for reasons unknown but time will tell. . . . [2]

Numerous examples of such language appear not only in Ionesco's and Beckett's plays but in plays written by many other absurdist writers.

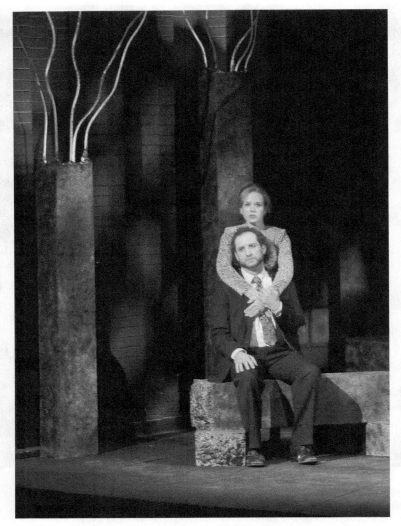

TRAGICOMEDY: FUNNY AND SAD AT THE SAME TIME
In *The Visit*, by Friedrich Dürrenmatt, serious and comic elements are intertwined. The chief character, the richest woman in the world, demands the death of the leading citizen of a small town because he wronged her when she was young. At the same time, the play also has comic, ironic elements. This scene is from a production at Western Illinois University, with Erin Roe, who also directed, and Joshua Murphy.
(© Photo courtesy of WIU Visual Production Center/Larry Dean, photographer)

Absurdist Characters: Existential Beings

A significant feature of absurdist plays is the handling of characters. Not only is there an element of the ridiculous in the characters' actions, but they frequently exemplify an *existential* point of view. In theatre, existentialism suggests that characters have no personal history and therefore no specific causes for their actions. The two main characters in *Waiting for Godot*, for example, are devoid of biography and personal motivation; we know nothing of their family life or their occupations. They meet every day at a crossroads to wait for Godot, but how long they have been coming there, or what they do when they are not there, remains a mystery.

PLAYING YOUR PART: THINKING ABOUT THEATRE

1. A play by Henrik Ibsen, Anton Chekhov, Tennessee Williams, Lorraine Hansberry, or August Wilson might be set in a time fifty years ago or 100 years ago. What do you think it is about these dramas that allow audience members in the twenty-first century to identify strongly with the characters and the situations in the play?

2. Which kind of play do you prefer: a classic tragedy, a serious contemporary drama, a knockabout farce, a comedy, a musical? Can you explain why you prefer one type over the others?

3. Do you favor a play with a strong story line, a tight plot, and unexpected twists and turns? Or do you prefer a looser play that reflects the randomness of everyday life? What do you think attracts you to these characteristics?

In addition to the plays of the absurdists, other modern plays also incorporate the tragicomic spirit. In *The Visit*, by Friedrich Dürrenmatt (1921–1990), a Swiss dramatist, a wealthy woman returns to her birthplace, a small, poverty-stricken village. She offers a huge sum of money to the village on the condition that the citizens murder a storekeeper who wronged her when she was young. The townspeople express horror at the idea, but at the same time they begin buying expensive items on credit—some from the man's own store. There is a comic quality to these scenes, but the conclusion is not funny, for the man is eventually murdered by his greedy neighbors.

In tragicomedy, a smile is frequently cynical, a chuckle may be tinged with a threat, and laughter is sometimes bitter. In the past, the attitude that produced these combinations was the exception rather than the rule. In our day, it seems far more prevalent, not to say relevant. As a result, tragicomedy has taken its place as a major form alongside the more traditional approaches.

SUMMARY

1. Tragedy attempts to ask very basic questions about human existence: Why do men and women suffer? Is there justice in the world? What are the limits of human endurance and achievement? Tragedy presupposes an indifferent and sometimes malevolent universe in which the innocent suffer and there is inexplicable cruelty. It also assumes that certain men and women will confront and defy fate, even if they are overcome in the process.

2. Tragedy can be classified as traditional or modern. In traditional tragedy the chief characters are persons of stature—kings, queens, and the nobility. The central figure is caught in a series of tragic circumstances, which are irretrievable. The hero or heroine is willing to fight and die for a cause. The language of the play is verse.

3. Modern tragedy involves ordinary people rather than the nobility, and it is generally written in prose rather than verse. In this modern form, the deeper meanings of tragedy are explored by nonverbal elements and by the cumulative or overall effect of events as well as by verbal means.

4. There are several kinds of nontragic serious plays, the most notable being heroic drama, bourgeois or domestic drama, and melodrama.

5. Heroic drama has many of the same elements as traditional tragedy—it frequently deals with highborn characters and is often in verse. In contrast to tragedy, however, it has a happy ending or an ending in which the death of the main character is considered a triumph, not a defeat.

6. Bourgeois or domestic drama deals with ordinary people, always seriously but not always tragically. It stresses the problems of the middle and lower classes and became a particularly prominent form in the twentieth century.

7. Melodrama features exaggerated characters and events arranged to create horror or suspense or to present a didactic argument for some political, moral, or social point of view.

8. Comedy takes a different approach from serious forms of drama. It sees the humor and incongruity in people and situations. Comic dramatists accept a social and moral order and suspend natural laws (a man falls flat on his face but does not really hurt himself).

9. Comedy is developed by means of several techniques. *Verbal humor* turns words upside down and creates puns, malapropisms, and inversions of meaning. *Comedy of character* creates men and women who take extreme positions, make fools of themselves, or contradict themselves. *Plot complications* create mistaken identity, coincidences, and people who turn up unexpectedly in the wrong house or the wrong bedroom. There are also physical aspects to comedy: slapstick and horseplay.

10. From these techniques, the dramatist fashions various kinds of comedy. For instance, depending on the degree of exaggeration, a comedy can be *farce* or *comedy of manners;* farce features strong physical humor, whereas comedy of manners relies more on verbal wit.

11. Another type of comedy is *domestic comedy,* which deals with ordinary people in familiar situations.

12. Depending on its intent, comedy can be designed to entertain, as with *farce* or *burlesque;* or to correct vices, in which case it becomes *satire.* Many of Shaw's plays represent *comedy of ideas.*

13. Serious and comic elements can be mixed in theatre. Many tragedies have comic relief—humorous scenes and characters interspersed in serious material.

14. Authentic tragicomedy fuses, or synthesizes, two elements—one serious, the other comic. We laugh and cry at the same time. Chekhov, Beckett, Dürrenmatt, and writers of theatre of the absurd use tragicomedy in their plays. Some commentators feel that this is the form most truly characteristic of our time.

The Designers

4

The Designers

THE VISION
OF THE DESIGNERS

The scenic, costume, lighting, and sound designers are essential members of any production. They give visual and aural life to the ideas of the playwright and director. They create an environment for the performers and a milieu in which the audience can place the play and enjoy the production. An example is the Cole Porter musical, *Anything Goes,* presented at Western Illinois University, under the direction of Carolyn Blackinton; musical direction: Matt Bean; scene design: Spencer Musser; lighting design: Will James Stacey; costume, make-up and hair design: Iiana Solomon; sound design: Zak Zubka. (© Photo courtesy of WIU Visual Production Center/Caitlin Salmon, photographer)

9 Scenery

10 Stage Costumes

11 Lighting and Sounds

Part Four

The Designers

Our experience of seeing a performance does not occur in a visual vacuum. We sit in the theatre watching what unfolds before us. Naturally, we focus most keenly on the performers who are speaking and moving about the stage. But the visual images of scenery, costumes, and lighting are always present. We also become aware of the elements of sound that are part of the production. The creation of these effects is the responsibility of designers.

As in other areas, there is a parallel between design elements in theatre and our experiences in everyday life. Every building or room we enter can be regarded as a form of stage set. Interior decorating, along with architectural design—the creation of a special atmosphere in a home or a public building—constitutes scene design in real life. A church decorated for a wedding is a form of stage set; so too is the posh lobby of a hotel, or an apartment interior with flowers, candlelight, and soft music. In every case the "designer"—the person who created the setting—has selected elements that signal something to us, thus making an impression.

Just as scenic design surrounds our daily lives, costumes are all around us. For instance, there are the outfits people wear in a holiday parade, at a masquerade ball, or in a pageant. Other obvious examples of the costumes we frequently see are in fashion magazines and runway shows. The dresses and other outfits created by top-name designers for haute couture shows are not what women would ordinarily wear; they are exotic, extreme, and offbeat.

In a less obvious way, costumes also play a significant role in daily life. We wear clothing not only for comfort, but also for the information we want to convey to others about ourselves. If we look around us, we are surrounded by costumes every day: the formal, subdued uniform of a police officer; the sparkling outfits of a marching band at a football game; a judge's long black robe; the cap and gown for graduation; the dresses worn by bridesmaids at a formal wedding. In this sense, everything we wear is a form of costume.

Stage lighting, quite simply, includes all forms of illumination on the stage. The lighting designer makes decisions in every area of lighting: the color of the lights, the mixture of colors, the number of lights, the intensity and brightness

The main reading room of the New York Public Library—a grand environment where researchers, scholars, and readers can do their work. (© Mark Lennihan/AP Images)

of the lights, the angles at which lights strike performers, and the length of time required for lights to come up or fade out.

As with costumes and scenery, we encounter lighting design in daily life: a dance club may use varying levels of light in addition to strobes or black lights to create a party atmosphere or to encourage people to dance.

A fourth type of designer in theatre is often referred to as the aural or sound designer. This is the person who arranges the sound components. Sound, of course, is all around us: the conversations in a meeting place; trains, trucks, and automobiles that pass by; music that blares from sound systems. In theatre, the sound designer is responsible for sound effects, recorded or digitized music, and

the placement and synchronization of microphones for the performers. Not only must he or she create all aural material not originating with the performers; the sound designer must also blend the sound from all sources.

In Part Four we examine the work of the scenery, costume, lighting, and sound designers, which includes the various skilled theatre technicians who assist designers in bringing their visions and sounds to life.

The austere plain black robes worn by judges indicate authority and formality. Seen here are the judges of the Texas Court of Criminal Appeals in Austin. (© Bob Child/AP Images)

High Fashion—a model walks the runway during a show at the Paris Womenswear Fashion Week for the Spring/Summer 2010 season. (© Karl Prouse/Catwalking/Getty Images)

Fireworks are part of colorful pyrotechnic displays on many occasions, such as these starbursts in Paris on Bastille Day, France's most important holiday, celebrated on July 14. (© Brand X Pictures/ PunchStock)

Scenery

9

When we attend a theatre production, we first encounter the environment—the look and size of the space. Is it large or small, formal or informal? Then, as the presentation begins, we become aware of the performers and the roles they are playing, as well as the story that begins to unfold.

But along with these elements, which initially strike us, there are other factors: the scenery, the costumes, the lighting, and the sound. In their own way, these are as crucial to the theatre experience as any other aspects.

THE AUDIENCE'S VIEW

As we begin to take in the visual elements of a performance, we should look for specifics. Is the scenery realistic, resembling a recognizable kitchen, bedroom, or office? Or is the scenery abstract: shapes, steps, levels, platforms on a relatively bare stage? Is it futuristic or dreamlike? What about the costumes? Are they like everyday clothes, or do they suggest some period: ancient Rome, the American Revolution, the Civil War, the 1920s? Are the costumes fanciful, like Halloween outfits, or do they resemble clothes from daily life: judges' robes, police uniforms, cheerleaders' outfits?

As for lighting, is it what we would expect in a normal setting, coming from sunlight outdoors, or lamps indoors? Or perhaps the lighting is abstract and arbitrary: beams of light cutting through the darkness, special lighting illuminating one part of the stage while the rest is dark. We must also take sound into account. Are there arbitrary sounds: a music track, specials effects such as sudden eruptions of synthetic noises? Or is the sound realistic: sirens for ambulances, thunder for a storm?

In all these areas, we should be conscious of the visual and aural signals that are being sent continuously. As for who prepares these signals, they are the designers and all the technicians and others who work with them.

◀ SCENE DESIGN PROVIDES THE VISUAL ENVIRONMENT

The set and costume designer Francis O'Connor has used a map of the world as the floor of the turntable set for the Huntington Theatre production of Two Men of Florence *by Richard N. Goodwin. The lighting designer, Ben Ormerod, has made use of candles and small lights to create a starry sky; sound design was by Matt McKenzie. The production was directed by Edward Hall. The actors are Jay O. Sanders as Galileo and Edward Herrmann as Pope Urban VIII. (© T Charles Erickson)*

THE SCENE DESIGNER
The set designer creates the scenic elements of a production. Once an approach to the play in terms of time period, atmosphere, and mood, has been determined, the designer, in sketches, models, and computer-generated materials, shows everyone concerned, from the director to technicians, exactly how the set will look. After the designer decides on the colors, materials, and style of the scenery he or she turns it over to those working with him in scene shops and elsewhere (projection preparation, etc.) to execute the final setting that appears on stage. Shown here is designer Derek McLane sitting on the edge of the stage in front of his setting for a revival of *The Heiress* which takes place in the early 20th century. (© Robert Wright/The New York Times/Redux)

THE SCENE DESIGNER

The scene designer creates the visual world in which a play unfolds. Together with the playwright and the director, the scene designer determines whether a scene is realistic or in the realm of fantasy. He or she decides on the colors, the shapes, the visual style that the spectators view and the actors inhabit. The set indicates the kind of world we are in—outdoors or indoors; an affluent environment or a humble one; a time period long ago, today, or in the future. When different locales are called for—in a play with an episodic structure, for instance—the scene designer must ensure that we move smoothly and quickly from one locale to another.

Designers and lead technicians in their respective areas must deal with practical as well as aesthetic considerations. A scene designer must know in which direction a door should open onstage and how high each tread should be on a flight of stairs. A lighting designer must know exactly how many feet above a performer's head a particular light should be placed and whether it requires a 500- or 750-watt lamp. A costume designer must know how much material it takes to make a certain kind of dress and how to "build" clothes so that performers can wear them with confidence and have freedom of movement. A sound designer must know about acoustics, be familiar with echoes, and understand electronic sound systems.

As in other elements of theatre, symbols play a large role in design. A single item onstage can suggest an entire room: a bookcase, for instance, suggests a professor's office or a library; a stained-glass window suspended in midair suggests a church or synagogue. A stage filled with a bright yellow-orange glow suggests a cheerful sunny day, whereas a single shaft of pale blue light suggests moonlight or an eerie graveyard at night. How designers deal with the aesthetic and practical requirements of the stage will be clearer when we examine the subject in detail: scene design in this chapter, costumes and lighting and sound in the following chapters.

A BRIEF HISTORY OF STAGE DESIGN

At the beginning of both western and Asian theatre there was little of what we now call scene design. The stage itself was the background for the action. In Greek theatre, for instance, the facade of the stage house usually represented a palace or some other imposing edifice. In medieval theatre, "mansions" were set up in town squares. These were small set pieces representing such things as Noah's ark, the whale that swallowed Jonah, and the manger in which Christ was born.

The Elizabethan and Spanish theatres of the Renaissance had bare stages in which the facade of the stage house functioned as the background for the action, just as it had in Greece. In Elizabethan England and Spain, set pieces as well as furniture such as thrones were used, but there was still no scenery as we know it. Actual scenery began to appear along with the proscenium theatres in Italy and later in France and England. These were the theatres (described in our chapter on Theatre Spaces) where designers such as the Bibiena family came to the forefront.

Since then, theatre has experienced a combination of improved stage machinery—the means by which scenery is shifted—and increasing realism in depicting scenes. This growing emphasis on mechanization, technology, and realism has been the basis of much modern stage scenery.

SCENIC DESIGN TODAY

We are accustomed to "stage settings" in everyday life; but as with other elements in theatre, there is an important difference between interior decoration in real life and set designs for the stage. For example, the stage designer must deal with scale: the relationship of the performer in the set to his or her surroundings. This must in turn correspond to the scale of settings we experience in the world outside the theatre. The scale in a stage set may be different from that of a living room or a courtroom in real life. Robert Edmond Jones, who is often considered the most outstanding American scene designer of the first half of the twentieth century, put it in these terms:

> A good scene should be, not a picture, but an image. Scene-designing is not what most people imagine it is—a branch of interior decorating. There is no more reason for a room on a stage to be a reproduction of an actual room than for an actor who plays the part of Napoleon to be Napoleon or for an actor who plays Death in the old morality play to be dead. Everything that is actual must undergo a strange metamorphosis, a kind of seachange, before it can become truth in the theater.[1]

A stage set does signal an atmosphere to us in the same way as a room in real life, but the scene designer must go a step farther. As has been pointed out many times, theatre is not life: it resembles life. It has, as Jones suggests, both an opportunity and an obligation to be more than mere reproduction.

SCENERY: AN ENVIRONMENT FOR A PLAY
Scenery provides the visual world in which a performance takes place. It indicates whether a play is realistic, expressionistic, or fantastic and where the action takes place: inside a home, at various locations, in some exterior setting; and also whether the story occurs in a past era or at the present time. For a production of Odets's *Golden Boy* scenic designer Michael Yeargan created a brick façade in the style of a 1930s building, against which he introduced such elements as an office, a training room, and a boxing ring. The atmospheric lighting was designed by Donald Holder. (© Sara Krulwich/The New York Times/Redux)

The special nature of scenery and other elements of scene design will be clearer when we examine the objectives and functions of scene design.

The Scene Designer's Objectives

In preparing scenery for a stage production, a scene designer has the following objectives:

1. Help set the tone and style of the production.
2. Establish the locale and period in which the play takes place.
3. Develop a design concept consistent with the director's concept.
4. Provide a central image or metaphor, where appropriate.
5. Ensure that scenery is coordinated with other production elements.
6. Solve practical design problems.

Establishing Tone and Style   A stage setting can help establish the mood, style, and meaning of a play. In the arts, style refers to the manner in which a work is done: how scenery looks, how a playwright uses language or exaggerates dramatic elements, how performers portray characters. (A realistic acting style, for example, resembles the way people behave in everyday life; in contrast, the lofty quality of traditional tragedy calls for formal, larger-than-life movements and gestures.)

A slapstick farce might call for a design style involving comic, exaggerated scenery, like a cartoon; and perhaps for outrageous colors, such as bright reds and oranges. Such

MOOD AND STYLE

The designers should establish the mood, tone, and style of a production; this is accomplished with architectural shapes, colors, fabrics, furniture, and other elements. For *The Blue Deep*, by Lucy Boyle at the Williamstown Theatre Festival, scenic designers Andrew Boyce and Takeshi Kata created a fresh garden set, with a partial in-ground swimming pool, blue skies and fair weather clouds everywhere, even painted on the sides of the house. At night the stars came out, the big dipper clearly visible over the doorway. The magic of this lighting was designed by Matthew Richards. Blythe Danner is on stage in a costume designed by Mimi O'Donnell. The production was directed by Bob Balaban. (© T Charles Erickson)

scenery would match the acting, which would also be exaggerated, with lots of physical comedy—people tripping over carpets, opening the wrong doors, and so forth. A satire would call for a comment in the design, like the twist in the lines of a caricature in a political cartoon. A serious play would call for less exaggerated or less comic scenery.

As an illustration of what is called for in scene design, let us consider two plays by the Spanish playwright Federico García Lorca. His *Blood Wedding* is the story of a young bride-to-be who runs away with a former lover on the day she is to be married. The two flee to a forest. In the forest, allegorical figures of the Moon and a Beggar Woman, who represents Death, seem to echo the fierce emotional struggle taking place within the characters who are torn between duty to their families and passion for each other. For this part of the play, the scenery and costumes must have the same sense of mystery, of the unreal, which rules the characters. The forest should not have real trees but should represent the thicket of emotions in which the man and woman are entangled; the costumes of the Moon and the Beggar Woman should not be realistic but should suggest the forces that endanger the lovers.

Another play by García Lorca, *The House of Bernarda Alba,* is a contrast in style: it has no fantasy or fantastic characters. This play concerns a woman and her five daughters. The mother has grown to hate and distrust men, and so she locks up her house, like a closed convent, preventing her daughters from going out. From a design point of

REALISTIC AND NONREALISTIC SCENERY

Generally, realism and nonrealism call for different design elements, underscoring the difference in style between these two types of theatre. Here (top), we see an extremely realistic set, designed by James Noone for a production of William Inge's *Bus Stop* at the Huntington Theatre, directed by Nicholas Martin. Lighting design: Philip Rosenberg; costume design: Miranda Hoffman. The bottom scene is a surrealistic landscape designed by the avant-garde director Robert Wilson for his rock opera *POEtry,* about Edgar Allan Poe. There is no attempt to portray reality; rather, there is a surrealistic presentation of images and ideas. (Top: © T Charles Erickson; bottom: © Hermann and Clärchen Baus) view, it is important to convey the closed-in, cloistered feeling of the house in which the daughters are held as virtual prisoners. The walls of the house and its furniture should all have solid reality, creating an atmosphere that will convey a sense of entrapment.

Scene design is especially important in indicating to us whether a play is realistic or departs from realism. *Realism* in theatre means that everything connected with a production conforms to our observation of the world around us. This includes the way characters speak and behave, the clothes they wear, the events that occur in the play, and the physical environment. Characters presented in a living room or a bar, for example, will look and act as we expect people in those settings to look and act.

On the other hand, **nonrealism,** or *departures from realism,* means all types of theatre that depart from observable reality. A musical in which characters sing and dance is nonrealistic because we do not ordinarily go around singing and dancing in public places. A play like Shakespeare's *Macbeth* is unrealistic because it has witches and ghosts—two types of creatures not encountered in our everyday existence. Also, the language of the play is poetry, and there are soliloquies in which characters speak thoughts out loud—again, these are elements that depart from the reality we see in our daily lives. Nonrealistic elements are, of course, highly theatrical and can increase our pleasure and excitement. Moreover, they often indicate a deeper reality than we see on the surface. Thus "departures from realism" does not imply that something is not genuine or not true; it simply means that something is a departure from what we see in the world around us.

The terms, then, are simply ways of categorizing aspects of theatre; and they are particularly important in scene design, because scenery can quickly signal to an audience which type of theatre we are viewing.

Realism Broadly, an attempt to present onstage people, places, and events corresponding to those in everyday life.

Establishing Locale and Period Whether realistic or not, a stage set should tell us where and when the play takes place. Is the locale a saloon? A bedroom? A courtroom? A palace? A forest? The set should also indicate the time period. A kitchen with old-fashioned utensils and no electric appliances sets the play in the past. An early radio and an icebox might tell us that the period is the 1920s. A spaceship or the landscape of a faraway planet would suggest that the play is set in the future.

In addition to indicating time and place, the setting can also tell us what kinds of characters a play is about. For example, the characters may be neat and formal or lazy and sloppy. They may be kings and queens or members of an ordinary suburban family. The scenery should suggest these things immediately.

Developing a Design Concept In order to convey information, the scene designer frequently develops a *design concept.* Such a concept should be arrived at in consultation with the director and should complement the directorial concept, as we discussed previously. The design concept is a unifying idea carried out visually. For García Lorca's *The House of Bernarda Alba,* for example, such a concept would be a claustrophobic setting that sets the tone for the entire play.

A strong design concept is particularly important when the time and place of a play have been shifted. Modern stage designs for Shakespeare's *A Midsummer Night's Dream* illustrate this point. In most productions, this play is performed in a palace and a forest, as suggested by the text. But the director Peter Brook, in his landmark production, wanted to give the play a clean, spare look so that the audience would see its contemporary implications. Accordingly, the scene designer, Sally Jacobs (1932–), fashioned a

SCENE DESIGN SETS THE TONE
Good scene design sets the tone and style of a production, letting the audience know where and when the action takes place and whether the play is a tragedy, a comedy, or some other type of drama. Also, it harmonizes with other elements of the production—script, acting, and direction—to create a unified whole. The scene designer Patrick Carl created this rural Russian setting for Chekhov's *The Three Sisters,* directed by Joe Dowling at the Guthrie Theater. The costumes are by Paul Tazewell. (© T Charles Erickson)

single set consisting of three bare white walls, rather like the walls of a gymnasium. This single set was used as the background for all the scenes in the play, giving visual unity to the production and also creating a modern, somewhat abstract atmosphere. As part of the action, trapezes were lowered onto the stage at various times, and in some scenes the performers actually played their parts suspended in midair.

A more recent example of a distinctive design concept was that of director Diane Paulus, scene designer Scott Pask, and other members of the design team to create on stage the world of a circus for a Broadway revival of the musical *Pippin* in 2013. To accomplish this, acrobats, high wire performers, jugglers and a host of other circus artists were incorporated into the production.

Providing a Central Image or Metaphor The design concept is closely related to the idea of a central image or metaphor. Stage design not only must be consistent with the play; it should have its own integrity. The elements of the design—lines, shapes, and colors—should add up to a complete visual universe for the play. Often, therefore, the designer tries to develop a central image or metaphor. In a production of Stephen Sondheim's *Sweeney Todd*, the designer, John Doyle, who was also the director, created a vast wooden cabinet in the center of the back wall. The subtitle of this musical is *The Demon Barber of Fleet Street*; and the cabinet, about twenty feet tall, had shelves for razors and all the tools of the barber trade as well as other bric-a-brac. A black coffin, which served other functions as well as its original purpose, stood at center stage

A CENTRAL DESIGN IMAGE
For a U.K. production of John Steinbeck's *The Grapes of Wrath*, the scene designer, Simon Higlett, selected an old jalopy as a central design image. The design conveys the futility of a deserted land, the Dust Bowl in the 1930s. In later scenes, trapdoors open to reveal a stream, and then a horrendous rainfall showers down, showing the extremes of weather faced by these wanderers. Through it all, however, an overstuffed jalopy is pushed around the stage by some of the actors, remaining a constant visual image and giving a sense of the characters' movements from place to place. The play was adapted by Frank Galati and directed by Jonathan Church. (© Geraint Lewis)

throughout. But it was the menacing presence of the towering cabinet that dominated the scene and served as a central design image for the entire production.

Coordinating Scenery with the Whole   Because scenic elements have such strong symbolic value and are so important to the overall effect of a production, the designer needs to provide scenery consistent with the playwright's intent and the director's concept. If the text and acting are highly stylized, the setting should be stylized too. If the text and acting are realistic, the setting should also be realistic, rather than, say, a fantastic or overpowering spectacle. As with other elements, the setting should contribute to the overall effect of a production.

Solving Practical Design Problems   Finally, the scene designer must deal with practical problems of design. Many of these involve physical elements of stage design, to which we'll now turn.

Elements of Scene Design

Five Elements of Scene Design   As the scene designer proceeds, he or she makes use of the following elements:

1. *Line*, the outline or silhouette of elements onstage; for example, predominantly curved lines versus sharply angular lines.
2. *Mass*, the overall bulk or weight of scenic elements; for example, a series of high, heavy platforms or fortress walls versus a bare stage or a stage with only a single tree on it.
3. *Composition*, the balance and arrangement of elements; the way elements are arranged; for example, mostly to one side of the stage, in a vertical or horizontal configuration, or equally distributed onstage.
4. *Texture*, the "feel" projected by surfaces and fabrics; for example, the slickness of chrome or glass versus the roughness of brick or burlap.
5. *Color*, the shadings and contrasts of color combinations.

The designer will use these elements to affect us, in conjunction with the action and other aspects of the production.

GROUND PLAN

To aid the director, performers, and stage technicians, the designer draws a ground plan, or blueprint of the stage, showing the exact locations of furniture, walls, windows, doors, and other scenic elements.

Physical Layout: The Playing Area   A playing area must, obviously, fit into a certain stage space and accommodate the performers. A designer cannot plan a gigantic stage setting for a theatre where the proscenium opening is only twenty feet wide and the stage is no more than fifteen feet deep. By the same token, to design a small room in the midst of a forty-foot stage opening might be ludicrous.

The designer must also take into account the physical layout of the stage space. If a performer must leave by a door on the right side of the stage and return a few moments later by a door on the left, the designer must obviously provide space for crossing behind the scenery. If performers need to change costumes quickly offstage, the scene designer must make certain that there is room offstage for changing. If there is to be a sword fight, the actors must have space in which to make their turns, to advance and retreat.

Any type of physical movement requires a certain amount of space, and the scene designer must allow for this in his or her ground plan.

A *ground plan* is a floor plan outlining the various levels on the stage and indicating the placement of all scenery, furniture, doors, windows, and so on. The designer, working in conjunction with the director, is chiefly responsible for ensuring a practical ground plan.

How doors open and close, where a sofa is placed, at what angle steps will lead to a second floor—all these are important. Performers must be able to execute stairs easily and to sit in such a way that the audience can readily see them, and they must have enough space to interact with each other naturally and convincingly. If a performer opens a door onstage and is immediately blocked from the view of the audience, this is obviously an error on the part of the scene designer.

To designate areas of the stage, scene designers, directors, performers, and technicians use terminology peculiar to theatre. *Stage right* and *stage left* mean the right side and the left side of the stage, respectively, as seen from the position of a performer facing the audience. (In other words, when we, as spectators, in the auditorium look at the stage, the area to their left is known as right stage and the area to their right as left stage.)

Ground plan   A blueprint or floor plan of the stage indicating the placement of scenery, furniture, doors and windows, and the various levels of the stage, as well as the walls of rooms, platforms, etc.

Stage right   Right side of the stage from the point of view of a performer facing the audience.

Stage left   Left side of the stage from the point of view of a performer facing the audience.

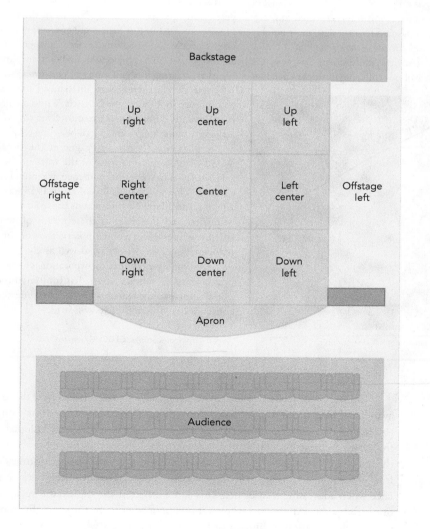

STAGE AREAS
Various parts of the stage are given specific designations. Near the audience is *downstage;* away from the audience is *upstage. Right* and *left* are from the performers' point of view, not the audience's. Everything out of sight of the audience is *offstage.* Using this scheme, everyone working in the theatre can carefully pinpoint stage areas.

IN FOCUS: GLOBAL CONNECTIONS

The Magic of the Designer Josef Svoboda

The Czech scene designer Josef Svoboda (1920–2002) developed a number of significant techniques in stage design, which have since been adopted and utilized by designers in countries around the world. Svoboda's work centered on his understanding of the kinetic stage and scenography. The term *kinetic stage* refers to his belief that the set should not function independently of the actors, but rather should develop and adapt as a performance progresses. *Scenography* was what he called his art, conveying the sense that he created a whole physical space, not just designs on paper intended for the back of the stage. His experiments with these ideas led to many significant concepts in modern stage design, most notably the *polyekran*, *diapolyekran*, and *laterna magika*.

Polyekran literally means multiscreen and was the practice, devised by Svoboda, of using multiple screens at multiple angles and heights. Although real people and objects were projected, the aim was to convince the spectators not that they were looking at the real object, but rather that they were looking at a projection, or a collage of projections. A later development of this technique was *diapolyekran*, which employed whole walls of small, square screens making up a composite image. The wall of screens could be used to present one unified image, cubist images, or a collage.

Laterna magika, the best-known of his innovations, used screens in conjunction with actors; the actors were part of the film, and the film was part of the action. The projections used in this form were not simply for decoration, or for communicating images independent of the action; rather, the projections and action functioned together, creating a new manner of performance.

These developments were introduced to the global community in 1958 at the Brussels World's Fair, where they instantly commanded attention from the wider theatrical community. Svoboda had been the chief designer at the National Theatre in Prague at the time of the World's Fair, and a showcase of the work of the theatre was displayed to the global audience, winning him three medals. What was seen as ingenious in 1958 was quickly adopted and adapted by numerous practitioners in many countries, and the effect of these means of design can still be witnessed in contemporary theatre, in performance art, and on Broadway, as well as at rock concerts and sporting events. This incorporation of screens and projections into onstage action has infiltrated the world of the theatre to the extent that it has become one of the conventional tools of theatre worldwide.

Josef Svoboda. (© Franco Origlia/Sygma/Corbis)

Prepared by Naomi Stubbs, CUNY Graduate Center.

Downstage Front of the stage, toward the audience.

Upstage At or toward the back of the stage, away from the front edge of the stage.

The stage area nearest to us, the audience, is known as *downstage;* the area farthest away from us is *upstage.* The designations downstage and upstage come from the eighteenth and nineteenth centuries, when the stage was raked—that is, it sloped downward from back to front. As a result of this downward slope, the performer farthest away from the audience was higher, or "up," and could be seen better. Also, performers downstage from—below—an upstage performer would be forced to turn their backs on the audience when addressing him or her. This is the origin of the expression "to upstage someone." Today the term is used whenever one performer grabs the spotlight from everyone else or calls attention to himself or herself by any means whatever. At first, however, it meant simply that one performer was in a better position than the others because he or she was standing farther back on the raked stage and hence was higher.

Materials and Devices of Scene Design
In creating a stage set, a designer begins with the stage floor. At times, trapdoors are set into the floor; through them, performers can enter or leave the stage. For some productions, tracks or slots are set into the stage floor, and set pieces or wagons are brought onstage in these tracks. A *wagon* is a low platform set on wheels. Wagon stages are brought onstage electronically or by stagehands hidden behind them. This type of scene change is frequently used in musical theatre. Another device used along the stage floor is a *treadmill*, which can carry performers, furniture, or props from one side of the stage to the other. Sometimes the stage floor includes a *turntable*—a circle, set into the floor, which is rotated mechanically or electronically to bring one set into view as another disappears.

Formerly, equipment such as turntables, wagons, and treadmills would be moved mechanically or by hand. In recent years, however, these operations have been computerized. Complicated scene changes can be controlled by computer so that they take place efficiently and simultaneously. Computers can also control the turning and shifting of scenic elements. In addition, safety features are built into the new computerized equipment. When performers are on a moving treadmill, for example, light beams or pressure-sensitive plates can detect a malfunction and shut the system down before anyone is hurt.

Instead of coming from the sides, scenery can be dropped from the *fly loft; to fly* is the term used when scenery is raised into the area above the stage, out of sight of the audience.

From floor level, ramps and platforms can be built to any height desired. To create walls or divisions of other kinds, for many years the most commonly used element was the *flat*, so named because it is a single flat unit, consisting of canvas stretched on a wood frame. The side of the flat facing the audience was painted to look like a solid wall, and flats used connected together were made to look like a complete room.

Wagon Low platform mounted on wheels or casters by means of which scenery is moved on and offstage.

Fly loft Space above the stage where scenery may be lifted out of sight by ropes and pulleys.

Flat A scenic unit consisting of canvas stretched on a wooden frame often used with similar units to create a set.

SPECIAL SCENIC EFFECTS: THE SCRIM
Scene designers use various materials and devices to achieve their effects. One popular scenic element is the scrim, which can be transparent when light comes from behind it and opaque when light comes from the front. It is especially effective for scenes of memory and fantasy. Shown here, in front of a scrim, is a character from a production at the Huntington Theatre entitled *36 Views*. The scenery was designed by Adam Stockhausen, the costumes by Teresea Snider-Stein, and the lighting by Chris Parry. (© T Charles Erickson)

SCENIC PROJECTIONS

An increasingly popular scenic resource is projections: rear-screen and front-screen projections, produced on an opaque surface or on a scrim. Projections allow rapid changes of locale, panoramic views, and abstract designs. Shown here are Rebecca Henderson at the piano (at right in the video image), with Candy Buckley, in *Autumn Sonata* by Ingmar Bergman, based on a literal translation by Wendy Weckwerth; directed by Robert Woodruff at the Yale Repertory Theatre. Mr. Woodruff uses video shot live and projected onto scrims to re-create some of the trademark shots in the movie. (© Joan Marcus)

Scrim Thin, open-weave fabric which is nearly transparent when lit from behind and opaque when lit from the front.

Today scene designers and shop technicians have turned increasingly to the *hard flat*, sometimes called a *movie* or *Hollywood flat*; it consists of a thin, solid material, called *lauan*, mounted on a wooden or hollow metal frame. A hard flat can be painted, and three-dimensional plastic moldings can be attached to it, creating cornices, chair rails, and other interesting features. Other vertical units are cutouts—small pieces made like flats or cut out of plywood. These too can be painted.

A special type of scenery is the **scrim**—a gauze or cloth screen. A scrim can be painted like a regular flat; however, the wide mesh of the cloth allows light to pass through. When light shines on a scrim from the front—that is, from our point of view in the audience—it is reflected off the painted surface, and the scrim appears to be a solid surface. When light comes from behind, the scrim becomes transparent and, as audience members, we can see performers and scenery behind it. Scrims are particularly effective in scenes where ghosts appear or when eerie effects are desired. Scrims are also useful in memory plays or plays with flashbacks: the audience sees the scene in the present in front of the scrim; then, as the lights in front fade and the lights behind come up, a scene with a cloudy, translucent quality appears through the gauzelike scrim, indicating a scene taking place in someone's memory or in the past.

Another scenic device is *screen projection*. A picture or drawing is projected on a screen either from in front—as in an ordinary movie theatre—or from behind. The advantage of projection from behind is that the performers will not be in the beam of light, and thus there will be no shadows or silhouettes. Obviously, projections offer many advantages: pictures can change with the rapidity of cinema, and vast scenes can be presented onstage in a way that would otherwise require tremendously elaborate scene painting. Two recent productions that used projections extensively and successfully in London and then on Broadway were the revival of the musical *Sunday in the Park with George* and *War Horse*.

In recent years, many avant-garde artists have also incorporated video screens and video projections into production design, frequently to draw stark parallels or contrasts between the live performance and something captured on video.

SPECIAL EFFECTS
An important element in many productions comes under the heading of special effects. These can run the gamut from swords that pierce bodies and the blood that flows from the wound to walls that collapse to smoke and fog, even explosions onstage. Here we see Fiona Shaw as the title character in Brecht's *Mother Courage and Her Children,* with smoke, fire, and explosions around her, in a production directed by Deborah Warner at the National Theatre, London. (© Robbie Jack/Corbis)

Special Effects Scrims and projections bring us to a consideration of special effects. These are effects of scenery, lighting, sound, and props that seem unusual or even miraculous. (The term *prop* comes from the word property; it refers to any object that will be used onstage but is not a permanent part of the scenery or costumes. Props are such things as smartphones, lamps, mirrors, computers, walking sticks, umbrellas, and fans.) Special effects include fog, ghosts, knives or swords that appear to stab victims, walls and windows that fall apart, and so forth. Today, films and television—because of their technical capabilities—have very realistic special effects, like burning buildings and exploding cars. Also, computers can create the world of dinosaurs, supernatural universes, or all forms of catastrophes. Special effects onstage, however, are almost as old as theatre itself. From the Greeks on, theatre has tried to create the illusion of the miraculous or extraordinary.

A modern version occurs in the long-running musical *The Phantom of the Opera,* when a huge chandelier falls from the top of the auditorium onto the stage. We will see, in a later discussion, that there are also many special effects using lighting and sound.

Prop Properties; objects that are used by performers onstage or are necessary to complete a set.

The Process of Scene Design: Steps in the Design Process

In meeting the objectives described above, how does the scene designer proceed? Although every designer has his or her own method, usually the same general pattern is followed.

The designer reads the script and develops ideas about scene designs and a design concept. He or she may even make a few rough sketches to illustrate thoughts about the designs. Meanwhile, the director also has ideas about the scenery. These ideas may vary considerably, depending on the director: they may be vague, or they may be an exact picture of what the scenery should look like.

Director and designer meet for a preliminary conference to exchange ideas about the design. During these discussions, they will develop and discuss questions of style, a visual concept for the production, and the needs of the performers.

Next, the designer develops preliminary sketches, called *thumbnail sketches*, and rough plans to provide a basis for further discussions about the scenic elements.

As the designer proceeds, he or she attempts to fill out the visual concept with sketches, drawings, models, and the like. Sometimes the designer will bring the director sketches showing several possible ideas, each emphasizing different elements to achieve different results.

Rendering A complete drawing of a set, usually in color.

When the director and the designer have decided on an idea and a rough design, the designer will make a more complete sketch, usually in color, called a *rendering*. If the director approves of the rendering, the designer will make a small-scale three-dimensional model that the director can use to help stage the show. There are two types of models. One shows only the location of the platform and walls, with perhaps some light detail drawn in; it is usually all white. The other is a complete, finished model: everything is duplicated as fully as possible, including color and perhaps moldings and texture.

STEPS IN THE SCENE DESIGN PROCESS

In designing a production, the scenic, costume, lighting, and sound designers look closely at the script and work cooperatively with the director and with one another. Scene designers often make sketches, computer-generated designs, and models in preparing for the scenic aspect of a production. Here we see three stages in the scene design for the musical *In the Heights,* which originated off-Broadway at the 37 Arts Theatre in New York and later moved to Broadway. The scene designer Anna Louizos carefully scouted out the Washington Heights neighborhood in Manhattan where the play takes place and made many rough pencil sketches, one of which is shown here at the top (© Anna Louizos). The second photo shows one of various set models she built (© Anna Louizos), and the bottom photo shows the completed set with actors onstage. (a: © Anna Louizos; b: © Anna Louizos; c: Sara Krulwich/The New York Times/Redux)

Computer-assisted design (CAD) Designs created by computer. All features of a set design, including ground plans, elevations, and walls, can be indicated by computer, and variations and alternations can be easily created and displayed.

Today, designers increasingly use computers and computer graphics to develop not only ground plans but also three-dimensional models of what a set will look like. Computerized design, known technically as *computer-assisted design (CAD)*, is very flexible: the designer can make instantaneous changes in what appears on the screen and can easily indicate to the director and others alternative plans and features of a stage set. Not only ground plans but also the three-dimensional look of a set can be instantaneously rearranged to let both director and designer see what various configurations would look like. In this way, the scene can be shown in three dimensions; it can also be looked at from various perspectives: from the right or left, from above, from the front.

THE SCENE DESIGNER'S COLLABORATORS AND THE PRODUCTION PROCESS

As with every element of theatre, there is a collaborative aspect to scene design: in addition to the director there are a number of other important people with whom the scene designer works. In fact, any scene design would be little more than a creative idea without the input of the following collaborators: technical directors, property designers, scenic charge artists, stage managers, design assistants, and skilled technicians working in every one of these areas, often with expanded new technologies. These scenic collaborators are essential at every level of production, from university theatre to regional professional theatre to Broadway.

Technical director Staff member responsible for scheduling, construction, and installation of all equipment; he or she is responsible for guaranteeing that designs are executed according to the designer's specifications.

A few definitions: the *technical director* is responsible for solving overall technical problems; he or she is in charge of scheduling, constructing and painting scenery, and in general making certain that all designs are executed as conceived by the scene designer. The *property designer* creates and executes all props; this work may include building special pieces of furniture, finding or devising magical equipment, and selecting items such as lamps and other accessories. *Scenic charge artists* are responsible for seeing that sets are built and painted according to the specifications of the scene designer. In the case of painting the set, the person in charge is referred to as the *paint charge artist.* As noted earlier in this chapter, projection design is becoming a more common feature of the scenic environment, also requiring additional skilled technicians to bring the world of the play to life.

Realizing the design typically begins with drafting (predominantly with CAD these days) all production ground plans, also known as floor plans, which are detailed layouts of each scenic location drafted within the context of a specific theatre space. Drawings that show all exact scenic details from the point of view of the audience are known as *designer/front elevations*. The drafting of the designer/front elevations is completed either by the scene designer or by various design assistants. These drawings are then used to construct accurate scenic models or perspective renderings that are useful visual tools for anyone involved in the production. Once they have been given final approval by the director, the floor plans are delivered to the stage manager, who will tape on the floor of the rehearsal spaces an accurate, full-scale version of all platforms, ramps, staircases, and entrances and exits to be used by the director and the actors in rehearsal.

The technical director uses the floor plans to determine where all the construction elements will go, as well as to determine backstage escapes for actors. The technical director then completes construction drawings for all those floor plan elements. The technical director also converts the complete set of designer/front elevations into a complete set of rear elevations or working drawings for construction purposes. Without this critical engineering and drafting step, the scenery could never be built accurately or safely. The technical director and scenic designer work together in much the same way an engineer will work with an architect in completing the blueprints to plan construction of a building.

The realm of scene design on Broadway is one of the last areas to begin the switch over to CAD drafting and design. Many of the designers who have been working for years on Broadway were already well along in their professional careers when CAD became common. Therefore they required their assistants to "draft by hand" as they themselves had done in the past. The use of CAD is now happening more rapidly as more recently trained designers and their associates and assistants are bringing advanced CAD skills with them to Broadway design studios and demonstrating the flexibility of CAD and the opportunity to make changes very quickly.

The visual world of many production designs is so complex that a property designer typically works as an essential collaborator with the scenic designer. The property area is also broken down into areas: (1) functional props used by actors, and (2) set dressing, which fills out the visual stage reality. Once the scene designer has approved all of the property designer's research, solutions, and drawings, those are also forwarded to the technical director to be worked into the construction schedule. It is also frequently the property designer who completes the mechanical special effects used in theatrical production. Owing to developments in computer and electronic technology, special effect solutions are frequently crafted by projection designers or electricians as well. Although not many productions utilize the level of scenic projection noted previously, projection technology solutions are finding their way into many production designs for special visual effects requiring the presence of yet another essential scenic collaborator.

The scene designer and his or her assistants also complete a full series of paint elevations that are delivered to the scenic charge artist who works with a group of scenic artists in completing the painting of the actual scenery. Paint charge and scenic artists require both talent and technique: for instance, to create the feeling of rare old wood in a library, or of bricks, or of a glossy, elegant surface in an expensive living room. In commercial theatre, construction drawings and paint elevations are sent to scenic houses separate from the theatre that specialize in both construction and painting. In regional theatres and university settings there are typically support spaces and support staff for scenic, property, painting, and costume construction on-site. In these settings the entire production team is typically present at all times, allowing for convenient tracking of the construction and painting process. In Broadway and other professional producing theatres without technical support spaces and staff, it is necessary for the designer or the assistant designers (or both) to visit the scenic houses and paint studios to check on progress and to assure consistency with the original design intent.

When the time comes for technical rehearsals, dress rehearsals, and the actual performances after the official opening, a production requires backstage leadership by the stage management team. The members of this team call all the cues for lights, sound, projections, scenic shifts, and actors' entrances. An entire crew of stagehands will work together to coordinate every change, no matter how small, in the visual world of the play. These changes may involve a fly crew for flown scenery, a shift crew for either

PLAYING YOUR PART: THINKING ABOUT THEATRE

1. What production that you have attended had the most elaborate scenery and special effects? What effect did these visual elements have on you? Were you captivated by the visual elements or did you think they were overdone?

2. What production that you have seen had the least amount of scenery and visual effects? Did you miss seeing an elaborate scene design or did you enjoy using your imagination to create the setting in your mind?

3. Have you seen a production that has many changes of setting? How efficiently and effectively were the scene changes carried out? What types of stage machinery was employed to create smooth transitions?

4. It is often argued that film and television can employ more realistic scenery and special effects than the theatre. Is there any way in which theatrical scenery and special effects compete with those in the media?

automated or manual shifting of entire settings, and a property crew for any preparation or movement of furniture and properties onstage or off. Meanwhile a crew of dressers, whose work will be covered in more detail in the next chapter, will work backstage with the actors helping them prepare for the upcoming scene. Once a production moves beyond opening night, it is controlled by the stage manager, who is also responsible for maintaining the director's artistic intent as well as maintaining consistency in cue placement and the visual world of the play.

Designing a Total Environment

Sometimes a designer goes beyond scenery and special effects to design an entire theatre space, rearranging the seating for spectators and determining the relationship of the stage area to the audience. For instance, in an open space such as a gymnasium or warehouse, a designer might build an entire theatre, including the seats or stands for the audience and the designated acting areas. In this case, the designer considers the size and shape of the space, the texture and nature of the building materials, the atmosphere of the space, and the needs of the play itself. This is also true of multifocus theatre.

Even in Broadway theatres some designers change the architecture of the theatre space in creating the world of the play. The Broadway scene designer Eugene Lee, designer of the musical *Wicked*, won two of his three Tony Awards doing just that for the original productions of *Candide* and *Sweeney Todd: The Demon Barber of Fleet Street*. When the rock musical *Bloody, Bloody Andrew Jackson* transferred to Broadway, the design for that production extended into the audience area.

A slight twist on the idea of creating a total environment was employed in the musical *Once*. The bar used as the set was also used during intermission to serve refreshments to audience members, thereby blurring the distinction between the auditorium and the playing space.

We have been examining the work of the scene designer. We turn next to someone whose work is closely related: the costume designer.

SUMMARY

1. We encounter forms of scene design in everyday life: in the carefully planned decor of a restaurant, in a hotel lobby, or in a decorated apartment.

2. Scene design for the stage differs from interior decorating in that it creates an environment and an atmosphere that are not filled until occupied by performers.

3. In addition to creating an environment, the scene designer has the following objectives: to set tone and style, distinguish realism from nonrealism, establish time and place, develop a design concept, provide a central design metaphor, coordinate scenery with other elements, and deal with practical considerations.

4. As in other aspects of theatre, in scene design there has been more and more crossover, and interaction, between theatre design and design for many types of popular entertainment.

5. In practical terms the scene designer must deal with the limits of the stage space and the offstage area. For example, ramps must not be inclined too steeply, and platforms must provide an adequate playing area for the performers. In short, the stage designer must know the practical considerations of stage usage and stage carpentry, as well as the materials available, in order to achieve desired effects. Close work with the technical director allows the scene designer to push the limits of construction in creating a unique visual world while maintaining a safe environment for performers.

6. In theatrical productions that stress visual elements over the play or the acting, the scene design must constantly engage and entrance the spectator.

7. Special effects are elements of scenery, lighting, costumes, props, or sound that appear highly unusual or miraculous. Technical expertise is required to develop them properly.

8. Elements of design include line, mass, composition, texture, color, rhythm, and movement.

9. The scene designer works closely with the director and other designers and creates a series of drawings (sketches and renderings) and models of what the final stage picture will look like.

10. In dealing with created or found space, the designer must plan the entire environment: the audience area as well as the stage area.

11. The technical director, with his or her staff, supervises the construction of scenery, special effects, and the like, in order to meet the designer's specifications.

12. A scenic charge artist and additional scenic artists must translate the look shown in models, renderings, and paint elevations into the full-scale version of the design.

13. Working with the technical director and the scenic charge artist are the property designer and the paint charge artist.

Stage Costumes

10

Costumes are the most personal aspect of the visual elements in theatre. When we attend a production, a performer and his or her costume are perceived as one; they merge into a single image onstage. At the same time, costumes have a value of their own, adding color, shape, texture, and symbolism to the overall effect. Other elements or accessories, such as makeup, hairstyles, masks, and personal items like bracelets and necklaces, are an important component of costumes.

Clothes have always indicated or signaled a number of things regarding the wearer, including the following:

- Position and status
- Sex
- Occupation
- Relative flamboyance or modesty
- Degree of independence or regimentation
- Whether one is dressed for work or leisure, for a routine event or a special occasion

As soon as we see what clothing people are wearing, we receive messages about them and form impressions of them. We instantaneously relate those messages and impressions to our past experience and our preconceptions, and we make judgments, including value judgments. Even if we have never before laid eyes on someone, we feel we know a great deal when we first see what he or she is wearing.

COSTUMES FOR THE STAGE

In theatre, clothes send us signals similar to those in everyday life, but as with the other elements of theatre, there are significant differences between the costumes of everyday life and theatrical costumes. Stage costumes communicate the same

◀ **STAGE COSTUMES: AESTHETIC, SYMBOLIC, AND SUITED TO THE CHARACTER**

In addition to being stylish and beautiful, costumes can convey a wealth of information to the audience. Here we see Eve Best in the title role in a London production of John Webster's The Duchess of Malfi. *Her attractive, aristocratic costume was designed by Soutra Gilmour, who also designed the sets. (© Nigel Norrington/ArenaPAL)* information as ordinary clothes with regard to sex, position, and occupation; but onstage this information is magnified because every element in theatre is a focus of attention. Also, costumes on a stage must meet other requirements not normally imposed in everyday life. These requirements will be clearer after we look at the objectives of costume design.

Objectives of Costume Design

Stage costumes should meet the following seven requirements:

1. Help establish the style of a production.
2. Indicate the historical period of a play and the locale in which it occurs.
3. Indicate the nature of individual characters or groups in a play—their stations in life, their occupations, their personalities.
4. Show relationships among characters—separating major characters from minor ones, contrasting one group with another.
5. Where appropriate, symbolically convey the significance of individual characters or the theme of the play.
6. Meet the needs of individual performers, making it possible for an actor or actress to move freely in a costume, perhaps to dance or engage in a sword fight, and (when required) to change quickly from one costume to another.
7. Be consistent with the production as a whole, especially other visual elements.

The Process of Costume Design

In order to achieve these objectives, the costume designer goes through a process similar to that of the scene designer. He or she reads the script, taking particular note of the characters: their age, gender, physical qualities, and special traits, as well as their roles in the play.

Early in the process, the costume designer also meets with the director and other designers to discuss the "look" that the show will have and how the various elements will be coordinated. The costume designer may make preliminary sketches to show the director and other designers. These may include not only suggestions about style (for example, historical, modern, futuristic) but also ideas for colors and fabrics. Once agreed upon, these designs will move from sketches to renderings of what the costumes will look like in their final form. Swatches of material may be attached to these designs, indicating the texture and color of the fabrics to be used.

As part of this process, the costume designer will meet with the members of the cast, measuring each performer and making certain that the costumes will be workable and appropriate for the individual actresses and actors.

The following sections discuss how the various objectives of costume design are realized by the designer in this process.

Setting Tone and Style   Along with scenery and lighting, costumes should inform us about the style of a play. For a production set in outer space, for instance, the costumes would be futuristic. For a Restoration comedy, the costumes would be quite elegant, with elaborate gowns for the women and lace at the men's collars and cuffs.

For a tragedy, the clothes would be formal and dignified—seeing them, we would know immediately that the play itself was serious.

Indicating Time and Place   Costumes indicate the period and location of a play: whether it is historical or modern, whether it is set in a foreign country or the United States, and so on. A play might take place in ancient Egypt, in seventeenth-century Spain, or in modern Africa. Costumes should tell us when and where the action occurs.

For most historical plays, the director and the costume designer have a range of choices, depending on the directorial concept. For a production of Shakespeare's *Julius Caesar,* for instance, the costumes could indicate the ancient Roman period when Caesar actually lived; in this case, the costumes would include Roman togas and soldiers' helmets. Or the costumes could be Elizabethan. We know that in Shakespeare's day costumes were heightened versions of the English clothes worn at the time, regardless of the period in which a play was set. As a third option, the designer could create costumes for an entirely different period, even our own day—with the men in business suits, modern military uniforms, and perhaps even tuxedos. Whatever the choice, the historical period should be clearly indicated by the costumes.

A Girl   *Dumas*

Benoit

Cyrano de Bergerac costume for Coquelin   *Eleonora Duse*   *Sarah Bernhardt*

COSTUME DESIGN: THE PROCESS
Costume designers often make preliminary sketches of costumes as they begin to design a production. Shown here are sketches for *The Ladies of the Camellias* by the costume designer Jess Goldstein for a production at the Yale Repertory Theatre. (© Jess Goldstein)

Identifying Status and Personality   Like clothing in everyday life, costumes can tell us whether people are from the aristocracy or the working class, whether they are blue-collar workers or professionals. But in theatre, these signals must be clear and unmistakable. For example, in real life a woman in a long white coat could be a doctor, a laboratory technician, or a hairdresser. A costume onstage must indicate the occupation exactly—by giving the doctor a stethoscope, for instance.

Costumes also tell us about the personalities of characters: a flamboyant person will be dressed in flashy colors; a shy, retiring person will wear subdued clothing.

Costumes also indicate age. This is particularly helpful when an older performer is playing a young person, or vice versa. A young person playing an older character, for instance, can wear padding or a beard.

Indicating Relationships among Characters   Characters in a play can be set apart by the way they are costumed. Major characters, for example, will be dressed differently from minor characters. Frequently, the costume designer will distinguish the major characters by dressing them in distinctive colors, in sharp contrast to the other characters. Consider, for instance, Shaw's *Saint Joan,* a play about Joan of Arc. Obviously, Joan should stand out from the soldiers surrounding her. Therefore, her

Stage Costumes Make a Strong Visual Statement

(© T Charles Erickson)

On these pages are five examples of striking costumes. Costume designers, using colors, fabric, intricate cuts and shapes of cloth, accessories, and other elements, create a special look for each production. The costumes must fit the actor and allow for easy movement, as well as be visually appealing. They must also be appropriate for the play, and communicate to the audience the period and the social status and the financial level of the characters wearing the costumes.

Seen at left are John Scherer (Hysterium) and Beth McVey (Domina) in vividly colorful costumes designed by Matthew Hemesath for *A Funny Thing Happened On The Way To The Forum*, at the Papermill Playhouse.

At right Jeffrey Bean as Cyrano de Bergerac in Brian Hooker's adaptation of Edmond Rostand's play *Cyrano de Bergerac*, with Elizabeth Heflin as Roxane. This Alley Theatre production was directed by Gregory Boyd with costume designs by Alejo Vietti.

(© Michal Daniel)

224

To the right For this African-themed production of Shakespeare's *The Tempest* directed by Janice Honeyman at the Royal Shakespeare Company in collaboration with the Baxter Theatre Centre of Cape Town, South Africa, Illka Louw designed the spectacular scenery and costumes worn by Antony Sher as Prospero and Atandwa Kani as Ariel.

Below Don Burroughs as Elyot Chase and Carol Linnea Johnson as Amanda Prynne in the Utah Shakespearean Festival's 2009 production of Noël Coward's *Private Lives*. Director, Joseph Hanreddy; costume designer, David Kay Mickelsen; scenic designer, Bill Forrester.

(© Geraint Lewis)

(© Utah Shakespearean Festival. Photo by Karl Hugh)

Deborah Hay (Celimene) sinks to the floor in exasperation in Chicago Shakespeare Theater's *The School for Lies*, adapted from Molière's *The Misanthrope*. Directed by CST Artistic Director Barbara Gaines, written by David Ives, with hilarious costumes designed by Susan E. Mickey. (© Liz Lauren)

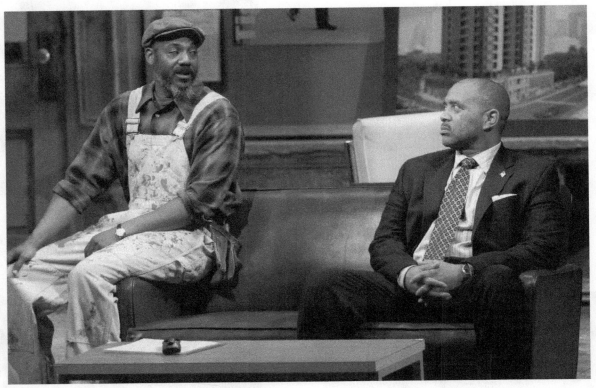

COSTUMES INDICATE SOCIAL RELATIONSHIPS
Along with their many other properties, costumes can signal the relationships and contrasts among characters in a production. Not only can costumes indicate the time period when a drama takes place, and the locale where it occurs, but they can and should indicate occupations and relative social positions. Who, for example, is a laborer or tradesman and who is a professional businessperson? In this scene from August Wilson's *Radio Golf* at the Goodman Theatre, we see John Earl Jelks as Sterling Johnson and Hassan El-Amin as Harmond Wilks in costumes designed by Susan Hilferty. The man on the right is a succcessful businessman; the man on the left is a laborer. (© Peter Wynne Thompson/Courtesy of the Goodman Theatre)

costume might be bright blue while their costumes are steel gray. In another play of Shaw's, *Caesar and Cleopatra,* Cleopatra should stand out from her servants and soldiers.

Costumes underline important divisions between groups. In *Romeo and Juliet,* the two feuding families, the Montagues and the Capulets, would be costumed in different colors. In a modern counterpart of *Romeo and Juliet,* the musical *West Side Story,* the two gangs of young men are dressed in contrasting colors: the Jets might be in various shades of pink, purple, and lavender; the Sharks in shades of green, yellow, and lemon.

Creating Symbolic and Nonhuman Characters   In many plays, special costumes are called for to denote abstract ideas or give shape to fantastic creatures. Here the costume designer must develop an outfit that conveys the appropriate imaginative and symbolic qualities. In *Macbeth,* for instance, how does one clothe the witches or the ghost of Banquo? For the musical *The Lion King,* the director Julie Taymor, who was also the costume designer, used puppets, masks, and other devices to create outfits for numerous animal characters, such as lions, tigers, giraffes, and elephants.

THE COSTUME DESIGNER MEETS PERFORMERS' NEEDS Many productions—especially musicals—call for rapid costume changes by performers. A good example is the musical *La Cage aux Folles,* in which some male performers dress as women (known as Les Cagelles). Here, Will Taylor is helped with a rapid costume change by the dresser Lizz Hirons (holding a flashlight in her mouth). (© Sara Krulwich/The New York Times/Redux)

Meeting Performers' Needs Virtually every aspect of theatre has practical as well as aesthetic requirements, and costume design is no exception. No matter how attractive or how symbolic, stage costumes must work for the performers. A long, flowing gown may look beautiful, but if it is too long and the actress wearing it trips every time she walks down a flight of steps, the designer has overlooked an important practical consideration. If actors are required to duel or engage in hand-to-hand combat, their costumes must stand up to this wear and tear, and their arms and legs must have freedom of movement. If performers are to dance, they must be able to turn, leap, and move freely.

Quick costume changes are also frequently called for in theatre. Tear-away seams and special fasteners are used so that one costume can be ripped off quickly and another put on. On Broadway and in national touring productions it is also necessary to make costumes for more than one actor for the same role, although this is not typically the case in shorter runs in regional or university theatre productions.

Unlike scenery, which stays in place until it is moved, a costume is always in motion, moving as the performer moves. This provides an opportunity for the designer to develop grace and rhythm in the way a costume looks as it moves across the stage, but with that goes the great responsibility of making the costume workable for the performer.

Each of these specific costuming needs points to the absolute importance of skilled *stitchers* (technicians who sew all the costumes) and *drapers* (technicians who pattern, pin, and drape the fabric to fit individual actors perfectly) in a costume shop.

Stitchers The technicians who sew all of the costumes for a production.

Drapers Technicians who pattern, pin, and drape the fabric to fit the actors in a production perfectly.

At times it is important for the costume designer to work closely with individual performers. Actresses and actors must know how to use the accessories and costumes provided for them. This is particularly true for historical costumes that re-create elements unique to that time period; such costumes often require the actor to work closely with the director and the costume designer and frequently with a movement specialist as well.

Maintaining Consistency   Finally, costumes must be consistent with the entire production—especially with the various other visual elements. A realistic production set in the home of everyday people calls for down-to-earth costumes. A highly stylized production requires costumes designed with flair and imagination.

The Costume Designer at Work

The Costume Designer's Responsibilities
As noted earlier, the person who puts all these ideas into effect is the costume designer. Every production requires someone who takes responsibility for the costumes. This is true whether the costumes are *pulled* or *built*.

Pull To choose a costume from an inventory owned by a theatre company or costume warehouse.

Pulling is a term used when costumes are rented and the designer goes to a costume house or storeroom and selects outfits that are appropriate for the production. The designer must already know about period, style, and the other matters discussed above. He or she must also have the measurements of all the performers for whom costumes are to be pulled. Seldom will pulled or rented costumes fit the actor perfectly, and it is the responsibility of stitchers, often with tailoring experience, to complete the necessary alterations.

Build To create a costume from scratch in a costume shop.

When costumes are *built,* they are created in a costume shop under the direction of the shop supervisor, who works closely with a costume designer in much the same way the technical director and scene designer work together. Before making a costume out of expensive fabrics, well-staffed costume shops will make *muslin mock-ups* of the costumes first, and those are then fitted to the actor. Next, the mock-ups are taken apart and used as patterns for the actual costume fabric. In these shops, costumes are built in two different ways. Some are drafted as flat patterns based on the performer's measurements, and some are draped. Draping involves pinning and tucking the fabric directly to a dress form of the proper size and marking the fabric while it is on the dress form, in preparation for stitching, detailed finish work, and closures.

The Costume Designer's Resources
Among the elements a costume designer works with are (as discussed below) (1) line, shape, and silhouette; (2) color; (3) fabric; and (as discussed later) (4) accessories.

Line   Of prime importance is the cut or line of the clothing. Do the lines of an outfit flow, or are they sharp and jagged? Does the clothing follow the lines of the body, or is there some element of exaggeration, such as shoulder pads for a man or a bustle at the back of a woman's dress? The outline or silhouette of a costume has always been significant. There is a strong visual contrast, for instance, between the line of an Egyptian woman's garment, flowing smoothly from shoulder to floor, and that of an empire gown of the early nineteenth century in Europe, which featured a horizontal line high above the waist, just below the breasts, with a line flowing from below the bosom to the feet. The silhouettes of these two styles would

(Sketches courtesy of William Ivey Long Studios)

One of the most active costume designers of recent times is William Ievy Long. Like many costume designers, he often sketches the costumes of the characters in the play, indicating the style of the clothes, the fabrics, the colors, and the silhouette. Long developed a collage board for all the characters in the "grand finale" of the musical *Hairspray*, not only sketching the costumes themselves but—below the sketches—adding swatches of fabric indicating colors and other qualities of the fabrics. Shown here are several of the costumes taken from the full cast of the finale, giving an indication of how the final costumes were developed.

At the right we see William Ivey Long with his costume sketches for *The Lost Colony*, the nation's longest running historical drama, presented annually on Roanoke Island, on the outer banks of North Carolina.

(The Virginian-Plot, Chris Curry/AP Images)

Chapter 10   *Stage Costumes*   229

stand in marked contrast to a woman's outfit in the United States during the early 1930s: a short outfit with a prominent belt or sash cutting horizontally across the hips.

Undergarments are an aspect of costume design often overlooked by audiences. For women's costumes, one example is the hoopskirt. In *The King and I,* a musical of 1951 that was revived on Broadway in 1996, Anna, an English schoolteacher in Siam, wears dresses with hoopskirts several feet in diameter, which were in fashion in England in the mid-nineteenth century, the time of the play.

Other undergarments include bustles, which exaggerate the lines in the rear; and corsets, which can greatly alter a woman's posture and appearance. For example, some corsets pull in the waist and cause the wearer to stand very straight. But in the first decade of the twentieth century, women in society often bent forward because they wore a curved corset that forced them to thrust their shoulders and upper body forward.

A costume designer will be aware of the importance of undergarments and will use them to create the appropriate silhouette and line. During the nineteenth century there were times when men also wore corsets to achieve the fashionable posture of the day.

Color   A second important resource for costume designers is color. Earlier, we saw that leading characters can be dressed in a color that contrasts with the colors worn by other characters, and that characters from one family can be dressed in colors different from those of a rival family. Color also suggests mood: bright, warm colors for a happy mood; dark, somber colors for a more serious mood.

Beyond these applications, however, color can indicate changes in character and changes in mood. Near the beginning of Eugene O'Neill's *Mourning Becomes Electra,* General Manon, who has recently returned from the Civil War, dies, and his wife and daughter wear dark mourning clothes. Lavinia, the daughter, knows that her mother was involved in her father's death, and she and her brother conspire to murder the mother. Once they have done so, Lavinia adopts characteristics of her mother, and as an important symbol of this transformation, she puts on brightly colored clothes of the same shades her mother had worn when she was young.

Fabric   Fabric is a third tool of the costume designer. In one sense, this is the costume designer's medium, for it is in fabric that silhouette and color are displayed. Just as important as those qualities are the texture and bulk of the fabric. What is its reflective quality? Does it have a sheen that reflects light? Or is it rough, so that it

COSTUMES WITH FLAIR AND PIZZAZZ
Costume designers for musicals, fantasies, and historical plays have the opportunity to create costumes that are highly decorative as well as eye-catching. Seen here are Joseph Marcell, Jeffrey Wright and Mos Def in *A Free Man of Color,* a play by John Guare set in early nineteenth-century New Orleans, about a wealthy African American who was free until the United States purchased Louisiana from the French, when he was no longer free. Directed by George C. Wolfe at Lincoln Center Theater; the colorful silk costumes were designed by Ann Hould-Ward. (© T Charles Erickson)

absorbs light? How does it drape on the wearer? Does it fall lightly to the floor and outline physical features, or does it hide them? Does it wrinkle naturally, or is it smooth? Ornamentation and trim can also be used. Fringe, lace, ruffles, feathers, beads—all these add to the attractiveness and individuality of a costume.

Beyond its inherent qualities, fabric has symbolic values. For example, burlap and other roughly textured cloths suggest people of the earth or of modest means. Silks and satins, on the other hand, suggest elegance and refinement—perhaps even royalty.

The connotations of fabrics may change with passing years. Two or three generations ago, blue denim was used only for work clothes, worn by laborers or by cowboys who rode horseback on a ranch. Today, denim is the fabric of choice in informal clothes for people of all incomes and all ages.

Using the combined resources of line, color, fabric, and trims, the costume designer arrives at individual outfits, which tell us a great deal about the characters who wear them and convey important visual signals about the style and meaning of the play as a whole.

The Costume Designer's Collaborators   Once again, it is important to recognize that a number of collaborators aid in the process of costume design. Remember that the costume shop supervisor is the lead costume technician, and there are other very specific job responsibilities in a typical costume shop. Often young professionals, beginning a career, will start as buyers for professional shops that have copies of the designers' renderings. They will scour garment districts to find fabrics that best match the designer's renderings. After fabric comes back to the shop and the muslin mock-ups are made, it will go to a cutter-draper. A costume designer's first hand (see below) will often build the initial costume and complete the fitting with the designer and the actor.

It is important to note that the stage manager is typically responsible for scheduling all actors' fittings to work out times that coordinate with rehearsals and also the designer's shop schedule. Once the fitting has been completed, the costume will proceed to the costume designer's *first hand,* or a lead stitcher, who completes the detailed sewing. Once construction is completed, in cases where costumes should not look brand-new, they are turned over to design assistants for the purpose of ***distressing,*** to make them look weathered and worn.

Distressing   Making a costume look weathered or worn.

When costumes are completed and ready for dress rehearsals and performances, they become the responsibility of the wardrobe supervisor, who makes all decisions related to costume organization and preparation in the theatre. The wardrobe crew's responsibilities begin with backstage preparation before every performance and end when the laundry is completed following every performance. In an elaborate production, there are numerous dressers from the wardrobe crew assigned to actors, especially lead actors, during rehearsals and performances. There are other areas of specialty, and artisans integral to costume design, discussed in the next section.

RELATED ELEMENTS OF COSTUME DESIGN

Makeup

A part of costume is makeup—the application of cosmetics (paints, powders, and rouges) to the face and body. With regard to age and the special facial features associated with ethnic origins, an important function of makeup is to help the performer personify and embody a character.

MAKEUP: CHANGING A FACE OR CREATING A NEW ONE

Makeup is an ancient theatre tradition. Makeup can highlight features of the face or parts of the body that might be washed out under the glare of stage lights. Makeup can also be used to alter the appearance of the face altogether. In these two photographs we see Shuler Hensley being made up for his role as the "Dreadful Monster" in Mel Brooks's musical *Young Frankenstein*. From the left: Vincent T. Schicchi, makeup prosthetics supervisor; Angelina Avallone, makeup designer; and Pam Farrow, hair and makeup supervisor. (© Greg Gilbert/The Seattle Times)

Theatrical makeup used to be more popular than it is today. In a modern small theatre, performers playing realistic parts will often go without makeup of any consequence, in which case, the actors handle their own makeup. Anything beyond the most simple makeup, however, demands an accomplished makeup designer to plan specifically what makeup actors will wear. Historical figures are frequently incorporated into realistic plays and may demand extensive use of extremely realistic prosthetic makeup. An example on Broadway was William Gibson's one-woman play *Golda's Balcony*, with Tovah Feldshuh as the former Israeli prime minister Golda Meir. Nine prosthetic noses, cast in foam latex, were required each week for the show's star.

Makeup has a long and important history in theatre, and sometimes it is a necessity—one good example being makeup to highlight facial features that would not otherwise be visible in a large theatre. Even in a smaller theatre, bright lights tend to wash out cheekbones, eyebrows, and other facial features.

Makeup is often essential because the age of a character differs from that of the performer. Suppose that a nineteen-year-old performer is playing a sixty-year-old character. Through the use of makeup—a little gray in the hair or simulated wrinkles on the face—the appropriate age can be suggested. Another situation calling for makeup to indicate age is a play in which the characters grow older during the course of the action. The musical *I Do! I Do!* with book and lyrics by Tom Jones and music by Harvey Schmidt is based on the play *The Fourposter* by Jan de Hartog. In the musical, a husband and wife are shown in scenes covering many years in their married life, from the time

MAKEUP FOR PERFORMERS IN KATHAKALI
Kathakali is a traditional form of theatre that has been practiced for many years in India. It combines song, dance, and dramatic action. It also features elaborate costumes and makeup. The makeup is extremely colorful and often takes a great deal of time to apply. In the first of these two photos, we see the makeup for a character being applied. In the second photograph, we see the performer in full makeup, as well as in costume. (© Huw Jones/Alamy)

when they are first married until they are quite old. In order to convey the passing years and their advancing age, the actress and actor must use makeup extensively.

Makeup is also a necessity for fantastic or other nonrealistic creatures. Douglas Turner Ward (b. 1930), a black playwright, wrote *Day of Absence* to be performed by black actors in whiteface. The implications of this effect are many, not the least being the reversal of the old minstrel performances in which white actors wore blackface to create stereotypical and racist depictions of African Americans. Ward was not the first to put black actors in whiteface; French dramatist Jean Genet had part of the cast of his play *The Blacks* wear white masks.

A popular musical on Broadway and on tour, Stephen Schwartz's *Wicked* portrays a green witch named Elphaba, from birth until she becomes better known as the Wicked Witch of the West. Perhaps even more amazing in *Wicked* is the makeup on the numerous flying monkeys in the production.

Asian theatre frequently relies on heavy makeup. For instance, Japanese *kabuki*, a highly stylized theatre, uses completely nonrealistic makeup. The main characters must apply a base of white covering the entire face, over which bold patterns of red, blue, black, and brown are painted. The colors and patterns are symbolic of the character. In Chinese theatre, too, the colors of makeup are symbolic: all white suggests treachery, black means fierce integrity, red means loyalty, green indicates demons, while yellow stands for hidden cunning.

When using makeup, the human face becomes almost like a canvas for a painting. The features of the face may be heightened or exaggerated, or symbolic aspects of the face may be emphasized. In either case, makeup serves as an additional tool for the performer in creating an image of the character.

Hairstyles and Wigs

Another important component of costume design includes hairstyles and wigs. When costume designers create their renderings, they include characters' hairstyles as a part of the design, which will later require a hair and wig specialist as a part of the crew. In certain periods men have worn wigs: the time of the American Revolution is one example. In England, judges wear wigs to this day.

For women, hairstyles can denote period and social class. In the middle of the nineteenth century, for example, women often wore ringlets such as Scarlett O'Hara's in the film *Gone with the Wind*. A few decades later, in the 1890s, women wore their hair piled on top of the head in a pompadour referred to as the Gibson girl look. In the 1920s, women wore their hair marcelled, a hairstyle with waves made by a heated curling iron, sometimes slicked down close to the head. In the modern period, women wear their hair in more natural styles. But again there is tremendous variety—some women have short, curly hair; others have long hair, perhaps even down to the waist. The musical *Hairspray* featured young women in the bouffant hairdos of the 1960s.

For men, too, hairstyles are significant and sometimes symbolic. A military brush cut, an Elvis Presley–style pompadour, and a ponytail each point to a certain lifestyle, but each may be interpreted in several ways.

Audiences would actually be surprised to know how often wigs are used in theatrical productions. They may not even recognize an actor or actress outside the theatre, because such a complete visual transformation can be accomplished with the use of wigs made from real hair. For a production, hair designers fashion the wigs in the shop before dress rehearsals. A hair and wig specialist is also required backstage to care for the wigs throughout the performance process to keep the hair looking exactly as the designer envisioned it. One of the most amazing uses of a wig in recent memory on Broadway was the extraordinary design by Paul Huntley for *Jekyll and Hyde the Musical*: the actor could manipulate the character's wig instantaneously, allowing him to shift back and forth between Jekyll and Hyde within the same song.

Masks

Masks appear to be as old as theatre, having been used in ancient Greek theatre and in the drama developed by primitive tribes. In one sense, the mask is an extension of the

PLAYING YOUR PART: EXPERIENCING THEATRE

1. How might what you are wearing today reveal your personality, your station in life, your character? What would lead someone to make those observations?

2. If you were a character in a play, what costume would you design for yourself to tell us the most about you? What are the key elements? Why?

3. Have you ever commented on a friend's makeup, hair, or accessories? What did your comments suggest about how you characterized your friend due to these "costume" elements?

4. Find photos of famous film stars in publications or on-line. What does the clothing they are wearing tell you about them? Why?

5. Visit the costume shop of your university or community theatre. Are there costumes available to be pulled? Are there renderings of costumes that are under construction? What types of equipment can you find in the shop?

WIGS AND HAIRSTYLES

Hairstyle indicates social status and other facts about a character; it provides information about when and where a play is taking place. Beyond that, hairstyles and wigs can make a comment. Shown here is a scene from Rodgers & Hammerstein's *Cinderella*. The actors are Harriet Harris, standing, as Cinderella's stepmother, with, from left, Laura Osnes as Cinderella, and Ann Harada and Marla Mindelle, who play the stepsisters, wearing elaborate wigs in hairstyles that exaggerate the norm even for the period. The hair and wig designs are by veteran Broadway designer Paul Huntley. (© Sara Krulwich/The New York Times/Redux)

photo essay

Masks

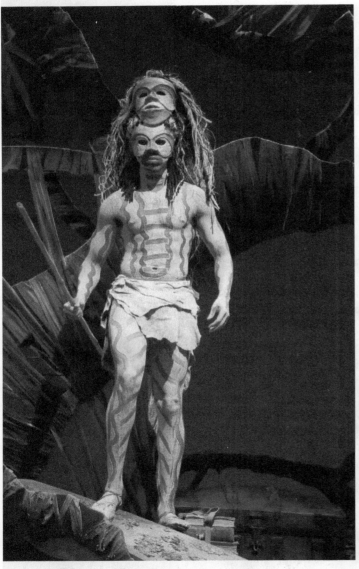

(© Geraint Lewis)

Masks are as old as theatre—they were part of ancient Greek theatre and early Asian theatre, and of ceremonial costumes in Africa and elsewhere. Masks can have a variety of uses: they can be highly decorative, but they can also convey the character and temperament of the actor wearing them. Here we see a variety of masks in old and new plays.

Atandwa Kani as Ariel in *The Tempest* by William Shakespeare, set in Africa in a production by the Baxter Theatre Centre of Capetown, in association with the Royal Shakespeare Company, directed by Janice Honeyman; Nicky Gillibrand, costume designer; Giles Cradle, set designer.

Fuenteovejuna, by Lope de Vega, directed by Julián Mesri for Repertorio Español in New York. The set, props, costumes and animal masks were designed by Leni Méndez.

(© Michael Palma)

Venetian carnival masks are worn by actors in Shakespeare's *The Merchant of Venice,* a production by the Habima National Theatre, in Hebrew, at Shakespeare's Globe in London, as part of the World Shakespeare Festival, 2012.

(© Tristram Kenton/Lebrecht Music & Arts/The Image Works)

(© T Charles Erickson)

Tristano (Pedro Pascal) and Don Bertolino Fortunato (Dick Latessa) perform the commedia play, *Pulcinella Goes to Hell*, in the Huntington Theatre Company's production of "The Miracle at Naples," by David Grimm, directed by Peter DuBois, with costumes and masks designed by Anita Yavich.

performer—a face on top of a face. Theatre masks remind us, first of all, that we are in a theatre, that the action going on before our eyes is not real in a literal sense but is a symbolic or an artistic presentation. For another thing, masks allow a face to be frozen in one expression: a look of horror, perhaps, which we see throughout a production. Masks can also make a face larger than life, and they can create stereotypes, in which one particular feature—for example, cunning or haughtiness—is emphasized to the exclusion of everything else.

Masks offer other symbolic possibilities. In his play *The Great God Brown,* Eugene O'Neill calls for the performers at certain times to hold masks in front of their faces. When the masks are in place, the characters present a facade to the public, withholding their true selves. When the masks are down, the characters reveal their inner feelings. Neutral masks are also frequently used in actors' training, to prompt them to use more dynamic physical movement without the benefit of facial expression to express character. More often today, audiences will see half masks, like those used in the *commedia dell'arte* of the Italian Renaissance, as these allow for stylized character expressions but also give the actor more freedom to speak clearly and effectively.

Characters' mask designs are also incorporated into the costume renderings and are typically built by a makeup or crafts specialist in the costume shop.

Millenary, Accessories, and Crafts

A number of the seven objectives of costume design noted at the beginning of this chapter are actually achieved through the design and use of accessories to the costumes. Accessories include items such as hats, walking sticks, jewelry, purses, and parasols. All these items instantly refer to various historical periods and also make visual statements about character and locale. Virtually every major costume shop will have a technician who specializes in millenary and crafts. Each of these pieces must be carefully designed and constructed to connect visually to the costumes and to other areas of design. It is hard to imagine a production of Shakespeare's *A Midsummer Night's Dream* without some kind of delightful donkey's headpiece or mask made specifically for the character Bottom. Theatre design and execution in all areas, including millinary, accessories, and craft, rely heavily on extensive details to make the visual world of the play compelling for audiences.

COORDINATION OF THE WHOLE

Actors and actresses would have great difficulty creating a part without costumes and accessories, and in some cases without makeup or a mask. These elements help the performer define his or her role and are so closely related to the performer that we sometimes lose sight of them as separate entities. At the same time, costumes, makeup, hairstyles, and masks must be integrated with other aspects of a production, and each demands special technical skills in order to complete the visual design.

For example, these elements are essential in carrying out a point of view in a production. Masks, for instance, are clearly nonrealistic and signal to the audience that the character wearing the mask and the play itself are also likely to be nonrealistic. Costumes suggest whether a play is comic or serious, a wild farce or a stark tragedy. Costumes, makeup, hairstyles, and masks must also be coordinated with scenery

PLAYING YOUR PART: THINKING ABOUT THEATRE

1. Think back to the last play or film you attended. How did the costume designer use color, fabric, and/or other elements to set up visual coordination and contrast among the characters?

2. Watch a historical film, like Steven Spielberg's *Lincoln*. Are there any unique accessories employed to help establish time period? What about the hairstyles? Are wigs used?

3. How are Halloween masks like theatre masks? How are they different?

4. If you have been required to read a play this semester, how might you use color and line to define one of the leading characters?

and lighting. The wrong kind of lighting can wash out or discolor costumes and makeup. It would be self-defeating, too, if scenery were in one mood or style and the costumes in another. Ideally, these elements should support and reinforce one another, and spectators should be aware of how essential it is for them to work together.

SUMMARY

1. The clothes we wear in daily life are a form of costume. They indicate station in life, occupation, and a sense of formality or informality.

2. Onstage, costumes—like clothes in real life—convey information about the people wearing them; more than that, these costumes are chosen consciously and are designed to give the audience important information.

3. The objectives of costume design are to set tone and style, indicate time and place, characterize individuals and groups, underline personal relationships, create symbolic outfits when appropriate, meet the practical needs of performers, and coordinate with the total production.

4. The designer works with the following elements: line and shape, color, fabric, and accessories.

5. Costumes can be pulled or built. When they are pulled, they are drawn from a preexisting costume collection. Building costumes means creating the complete costume: sewing and constructing the outfit in a costume shop.

6. Those working with a costume designer include a first hand (or lead stitcher) and other assistants.

7. Makeup and hairstyles are also important to the appearance of the performers and are part of the designer's concern.

8. Where called for, masks, too, are under the direction of the costume designer.

9. Often, costume, makeup, and wig assistants work with actors during a performance.

240

Lighting and Sound

11

Like scenery, costumes, and other elements of theatre, stage lighting and sound have counterparts in everyday life. For example, in real life the basic function of lighting is, of course, illumination—to allow us to see at night and indoors. But there are also many theatrical uses of light in daily life. Advertising signs often have neon lights or brightly colored bulbs. Restaurants feature soft lights, candles, and background music to help establish mood and atmosphere.

With the explosion of such handheld devices as MP3 players and smartphones, all of us carry our own sound tracks each day. In our homes, we put spotlights on special parts of a room, such as a dining-room table. Also, in our homes we frequently use a rheostat so that we can dim lights to create a mood. What home does not have projected images available through a flat-screen HD television or now even the ability to change digital images in picture frames?

STAGE LIGHTING

Lighting was historically the last element of visual design to be incorporated into theatre production—and, ironically, it is perhaps the most advanced in terms of equipment, technology, and techniques. Most of the advances have occurred in the past 100 years. Before we look at theatre lighting today, it will be helpful to have a short historical view of its development.

A Brief History of Stage Lighting

For the first 2,000 years of its recorded history, theatre was held mostly outdoors during the day. A primary reason was the need for illumination. The sun, after all, is an excellent source of light. Since sophisticated lighting was unavailable, playwrights used imagination—the handiest tool available—to suggest nighttime or shifts in lighting. Performers brought on torches, or a candle, as Lady Macbeth does, to indicate night. Playwrights also used language to indicate lighting. In *The Merchant of Venice,*

◄ *Tae Won Yi stars in* The Last Empress, *an epic Korean musical by Mun Yol Yi, presented in London. Based on a true story about the life of Queen Min, a charismatic woman in Korea's history in the mid-19th century. She struggled to forge ties with Western nations in order to keep Japan at bay, which ultimately led to her assassination at the hands of the Japanese in 1895. The director was Ho Jin Yun, with scenic design by Don Woo Park, costumes by Hyun Sook Kim, and lighting by Hyung O Choi. (© Geraint Lewis)*

Shakespeare has Lorenzo say, "How sweet the moonlight sleeps upon this bank"; this is not just a pretty line of poetry but also serves to remind us that it is nighttime. The same is true of the eloquent passage when Romeo tells Juliet that he must leave because dawn is breaking.

> Look, love, what envious streaks
> Do lace the severing clouds in yonder East:
> Night's candles are burnt out, and jocund day
> Stands tiptoe on the misty mountain tops.

Around 1600 CE, theatre began to move indoors. Candles and oil lamps were used for illumination, and the chief refinements were more sophisticated uses of these basic elements, such as those achieved in the 1770s by David Garrick, the actor-manager of the Drury Lane Theatre in London, and Philippe Jacques DeLoutherbourg (1740–1812), a French designer whom Garrick brought to the Drury Lane. DeLoutherbourg, for example, installed lighting above the stage and used gauze curtains and silk screens to achieve subtle effects with color. In 1785 an instrument known as the Argand lamp (after its inventor, Aimé Argand of Geneva) was introduced. It made use of a glass chimney and a cylindrical wick to create a steadier, brighter light.

Not until 1803, however, when a theatre in London installed gaslights, was there a genuine advance in stage lighting. With gas, which was the principal source of illumination during the nineteenth century, lighting was more easily controlled and managed. Lighting intensity, for example, could be raised or lowered. Its effectiveness, however, remained limited. In addition, the open flames of gas and other earlier lighting systems posed a constant threat of fire. Through the years there were several tragic and costly fires in theatres, both in Europe and in the United States.

In 1879 Thomas Edison invented the incandescent lamp (the electric lightbulb), and the era of imaginative lighting for the theatre began. Not only are incandescent lamps safe, but they can also be controlled. Brightness or intensity can be increased or decreased: the same lighting instrument will produce the bright light of noonday or the dim light of dusk. Also, by putting a colored film over the light or by other means, color can be controlled.

Beyond the power and versatility of electric light, there have been numerous other advances in controls and equipment over the past fifty years. Lighting instruments have been continually refined to become more powerful, as well as more subtle, and to throw a more concentrated, sharply defined beam. Also, lighting has lent itself more successfully than other theatre elements to miniaturization and computerization. Costumes must still be sewn individually, and scenes on flats or backdrops are still painted by hand. Lighting intensity, however, is controlled by electricity and therefore offers a perfect opportunity to take advantage of advances in electronics and computerization.

When applied to lighting, technological developments have allowed for increasingly complex and sophisticated controls. For a large college theatre production, 200 to 300 lighting instruments may be hung around and above the stage. For a large Broadway musical there may be 800 or many more. Each of these instruments can be hooked up to a central computer board, and light settings can be stored in the computer. By pushing a single button, an operator can, in a split second, bring about a shift in literally dozens of instruments. The resulting flexibility and control are remarkable tools for achieving stage effects.

Objectives and Functions of Lighting Design

Adolphe Appia (1862–1928), a Swiss scene designer, was one of the first to see the vast artistic possibilities of light in the theatre. He wrote: "Light is to the production what music is to the score: the expressive element in opposition to the literal signs; and, like music, light can express only what belongs to the inner essence of all vision's vision." Norman Bel Geddes (1893–1958), an imaginative American designer who was a follower of Appia, put it in these words: "Good lighting adds space, depth, mood, mystery, parody, contrast, change of emotion, intimacy, fear." Edward Gordon Craig (1872–1966), an innovative British designer, spoke of "painting with light." The lighting designer can indeed paint with light, but far more can be done. On the deepest sensual and symbolic level, the lighting designer can convey to us something of the feeling, and even the substance, of a play.

It is intriguing that today's leading lighting designers still speak of the artistic potential and aesthetics of light in precisely the same way as these early innovators did. In a sense the art of lighting has not changed, but the innovation continues, and the technology has exploded in the last twenty years. In fact, the most serious problem in lighting for the theatre today is to prevent the technology from taking over the aesthetics of the design, which is where the greatest distinction exists between contemporary lighting technicians and earlier lighting designers.

The following are the primary functions and objectives of stage lighting:

1. Provide visibility.
2. Reveal shapes and forms.
3. Provide a focus onstage and create visual compositions.
4. Assist in creating mood and reinforcing style.
5. Help establish time and place.
6. Establish a rhythm of visual movement.
7. Reinforce a central visual image, establish visual information, or both.

An experienced lighting designer will be capable of accomplishing all these functions simultaneously and will emphasize various objectives at various times during a production to help maintain a strong physical and emotional connection between audience members and the world of the play on stage.

Visibility   On the practical side, the chief function of lighting is illumination or visibility. We must be able, first and foremost, to see the performers' faces and their actions onstage. Occasionally, lighting designers, carried away with atmospheric possibilities, will make a scene so dark that we can hardly see what is happening. Mood is important, but seeing the performers is obviously even more important. It is true that unless you can see the actors and actresses, the lighting designer has not carried out his or her assignment; however, the accomplished designer will establish a balance that allows for visibility while meeting other design objectives effectively.

Shape and Form   The lighting designer must enhance the visual world of the play by revealing the objects in that world as interestingly as possible. Lighting objects from the front, with lights above the audience illuminating the stage, visually washes out all three-dimensional objects onstage, making them look flat and uninteresting. The designer must therefore enhance the actors and other visual elements of the world of the play with lighting and color from the side, top, and behind.

Focus and Composition   In photography, the term *focus* means adjustment of the lens of a camera so that the picture recorded on the film is sharp and clear. In theatre lighting, *focus* refers to the fact that beams of light are aimed at—focused on—a particular area. In stage action the director and lighting designer collaborate in creating a continually moving visual composition that always keeps the audience focused on the central action of the play. This kind of collaboration and compositional focus also allows a character to slip into position without those of us in the audience ever realizing how he got there until it is time to reveal him. Careful focus of light is integral to successful visuals onstage. Adjacent lighting and acting areas must be overlapped in focus to allow actors to move across the stage without going into and out of the edges of light beams. At the same time, the designer must control the *spill* of the light in front of and behind the actor so that it will not distract us as we watch the action of the play.

By means of focus and changes in light cues the lighting designer and director keep the audience focused on the essential action. These compositions or *looks* can vary from turning the stage into one large area to creating small, isolated areas all intended to take the audience on an interesting visual journey through the world of the play.

Mood and Style   Theatre, as a collaborative art form by definition, combines all areas of a production to establish the mood and world of the play. Once that predominant mood is established for an audience, the individual production areas can manipulate mood throughout the play, especially through lighting and sound. A production can also effectively manipulate our reaction. For example, early in a play we may see two or three romantic moments when the stage is filled with blue moonlight; then, in a later scene the look may seem the same until the action starts and we realize that the mood has changed to a cold, dark, evil situation. Action, scenery, and words, in conjunction with light, tell us exactly what the mood is. Experienced playwrights and designers know how we can be manipulated and will often take advantage of our expectations to make our journey more interesting.

In terms of style, lighting can indicate whether a play is realistic or nonrealistic. In a realistic play, the lighting will simulate the effect of ordinary sources—table lamps, say, and outside sunlight. In a nonrealistic production or a highly theatrical musical, the designer can be more imaginative: shafts of light can cut through the dark, sculpturing performers onstage; a glowing red light can convey a scene of damnation; a ghostly green light can cast a spell over a nightmare scene; a hard-edged spotlight can let the audience members know that what they are now seeing is not a realistic moment in a character's life.

Time and Place   By its color, shade, and intensity, lighting can suggest the time of day, giving us the pale light of dawn, the bright light of midday, the vivid colors of sunset, or the muted light of evening. Lighting can also indicate the season of the year, because the sun strikes objects at very different angles in winter and summer. Lighting can also suggest place, by showing indoor or outdoor light.

LIGHTING CREATES MOOD AND STYLE
Along with scenery and costumes, lighting is a key element in creating the mood and style of a production. Shown here is a scene where light criss-crosses the stage creating abstract shapes and illuminating the performers, as well as projecting colors that contrast the top section with that below. The scene is from a production of *Eurydice* by Sarah Ruhl, directed by Geoff Elliott at A Noise Within. The lighting was designed by Meghan Gray. (© Craig Schwartz)

Rhythm Since changes in light occur on a time continuum, they establish a rhythm running through a production. It is absolutely imperative that the seemingly simple lighting changes from scene to scene help establish the kind of rhythm and timing that the director needs for us to be drawn into the action. Abrupt, staccato changes with stark blackouts might unsettle us if that is called for, and languid, slow fades and gradual cross-fades can allow us a more thoughtful transition between scenes. Does the designer fade out the previous scene slowly while the next scene is beginning, thus prompting us to think about the connection? Or does the designer make the lights fade in very slowly, prompting us to ask what is to come and pulling our attention in?

photo essay

The Many Uses of Stage Lighting

(© Sara Krulwich/The New York Times/Redux)

Stage lighting can be used for many purposes: to illuminate, to highlight characters or stage areas, to create mood.

In the scene above, lighting designer Justin Townsend has used lights to highlight the couple in the center (Dashiell Eaves, and Amanda Quaid) and also the single figure at the right (Eisa Davis) in a different color and mood. The lights above add framing and atmosphere. The play is Kirsten Greenidge's *Luck of the Irish* directed by Rebecca Taichman.

Shown at the right of a scene from a production of *Desire Under the Elms* by Eugene O'Neill, directed by Dámaso Rodriguez at A Noise Within, in Pasadena, California, shows a skillful use of local front lighting: the oil lamp illuminates Abbie (Monette Magrath). Lighting by James P. Taylor; costumes by Julie Keen.

(© Craig Schwartz)

In the scene at the right *Jesus Christ Superstar,* an Andrew Lloyd Webber musical directed by Des McAnuff, lighting designer Howell Binkley has used down lighting and back lighting to isolate and highlight actor Paul Nolan in the title role.

(© Sara Krulwich/The New York Times/Redux)

At the left, lighting designer Elizabeth Harper has used lighting to create a crimson sky in the dust bowl area of the Midwest in a production of *The Grapes of Wrath* by John Steinbeck, adapted by Frank Galati, directed by Michael Michetti at A Noise Within. Note the effective use of the light to silhouette the silent actors.

(© Craig Schwartz)

Either way these changes in rhythm have an effect on our interaction with and understanding of the world of the play.

Since many lighting changes are coordinated with scene changes and changes in other production elements, it is a challenge for the lighting designer to make artistic choices that will support the director's vision, whether a change is pragmatic or solely aesthetic. Either way the importance of this synchronization is recognized by directors and designers, who take great care to ensure the proper changes—"choreographing" shifts in light and scenery like dancers' movements.

Reinforcement of the Central Image

Lighting—like scenery, costumes, and all other elements—must be consistent with the overall style and mood of a production. Over the past thirty years there has been a dramatic change in the style of writing plays. Long, extended scenes taking place in a single location are less and less common. Today's audiences are most accustomed to film and television editing, and to shorter scenes with multiple locations. Most of our contemporary plays tend to be written in a style that also cuts frequently from location to location; the actors may be on a bare stage with only the most essential props or suggested props to support the action. These kinds of changes in writing style prompt the lighting designer to provide more visual information than ever before about place and locale to allow for such simple staging. The wrong choices in lighting can distort or even destroy the effect of a play. At the same time, because lighting is the most flexible and the most atmospheric visual element of theatre, it can aid enormously in creating our theatre experience.

The Lighting Designer

The person responsible for creating, installing, and setting controls for stage lighting is the lighting designer and his or her collaborators. It is important for the lighting designer to have a background in the technical and mechanical aspects of lighting as well as a broad, creative visual imagination. The ability to translate words and actions and feelings into color, direction, and intensity comes only after much training and experience.

The Process of Lighting Design

In creating the lighting design for a production, the lighting designer first reads the script and begins to form some rough ideas and develop some feelings about the play. He or she meets with the director and other designers to discuss visual concepts. The lighting designer receives from the set designer copies of all the scenery plans and usually consults with the costume designer to learn the shape and color of the costumes.

The lighting designer will do a great deal of visual research and will also see one or perhaps several rehearsals to get the feel of the production, to see the exact location of various pieces of furniture and stage business, and to consult with the director about possible effects. Following this, the lighting designer draws a plan called a *light plot*. This includes the location and color of each lighting instrument. Also indicated is the kind of instrument called for and the area of the stage on which it is focused. When lighting instruments are moved into the theatre and hung (that is, placed on pipes and other supports), the designer supervises the focusing.

During technical rehearsals, the lighting designer works with the director to establish light cues: that is, instructions about when the lights go on and off. The designer also sets the length of time for light changes and the levels of intensity on the computer-controlled light board, which sends a digital signal to the actual dimmers to adjust the lighting instrument levels. (The actual dimmers, which allow lighting intensities to be changed smoothly and at varying rates, are located in a remote off-stage location.)

Properties of Stage Lighting   When working on the design for a production, the lighting designer knows what controllable properties of light will achieve the objectives discussed above. The lighting designer can manipulate four different properties of light for any visual change onstage: intensity, color, distribution, and movement.

Intensity   The first property of light is brightness, or intensity. Intensity can be controlled (as noted above) by devices called dimmers, which make the lights brighter or darker. A dimmer is an electric or electronic device that can vary the amount of power going to the lights. This makes it possible for a scene at night to take place in very little light and a daylight scene to take place in bright light. Since the advent of computer control systems, lighting intensities can be set at any level between 1 percent and 100 percent of full, as opposed to levels 1 through 10 on older manual controls.

Color   The second property of light is color. Color is a very powerful part of lighting, and theatre lights can very easily be changed to one of several hundred colors simply by placing colored material in slots at the front of the lighting instruments. This material is usually called a gel—short for gelatin, of which it was originally made. Today, however, these color filters are generally made of plastic, such as Mylar, or acetate.

Also in recent years, color *scrollers* have been introduced. These devices typically make it possible to change up to fifteen colors for each lighting, and the scrollers are also programmed into each light cue along with intensity and timing. Color is often mixed so that the strong tones of one shade will not dominate, since such dominance would give an unnatural appearance. Colors are most often selected to support choices made by the scenic and costume designers while still including sufficient dramatic color to support the varied action of the play. Quite often scenes will call for special effects; we expect stark shadows and strange colors, for example, when Hamlet confronts the ghost of his father.

Distribution   The third property of light that the lighting designer can use is distribution: the position and type of lighting instrument being used and the angle at which the light strikes the performers onstage. (Another term for this property could be *direction,* that is, the source from which the light comes, the type of instrument used, and the points on the stage at which a light beam is aimed.) In earlier days, footlights—a row of lights across the front of the stage floor—were used, primarily because this was almost the only location from which to light the front of the performers. However, footlights, which were below the performers, had the disadvantage of casting ghostly shadows on their faces. Footlights also created a kind of barrier between performers and audience. With the development of more powerful, versatile

THE USE OF COLOR IN LIGHTING

One of the prime elements in stage lighting is color: it can alter and transform a stage set, changing and establishing different moods. Here we see the same set from *The Underpants* by Carl Sternheim, adapted by Steve Martin, presented at the Alley Theatre, Houston. Note the stark white of the first photograph and the pink and purple hue of the second, contrasting the mood and the tone from one visual picture to another. All this is done with light. The director was Scott Schwartz, with lighting design by Pat Collins, costume design by David C. Woolard, and set design by Anna Louizos. (© T Charles Erickson)

lights, footlights have been eliminated and they are now used only when a production is trying to re-create the look and style of a classic play of the eighteenth or nineteenth century.

Today, most lighting hits the stage from above, coming from instruments in front of the stage and at the sides. The vertical angle of light beams from the *front of the house* is typically close to 45 degrees; this is an excellent angle for lighting the actor's face without creating harmful shadows, and it also gives a sense of sunlight or an overhead light source found in most locations.

There are a wide variety of lighting instruments available today, both conventional instruments and automated moving light fixtures. They all have distinctive features, and each instrument is selected for the quality of light and the design options it allows. What visual qualities or "texture" does the light produce on stage? Is it a single shaft of light, like a single beam of moonlight through the trees or a spotlight in a nightclub?

Or is the light in a pattern, such as dappled sunlight through the leaves of trees in a forest? Are the edges of the light sharp, or soft and diffused? In conventional ellipsoidal lighting instruments, light can be shaped by special shutters that close in at the edges (very few moving lights even have that capability). All these are additional tools for the designer.

Movement   The last property of light the designer can work with is movement, and in fact this is where the lighting design comes to life. On one level, the eye is carried from place to place by the shifting focus of lights: follow spots moving from one person or one area to another, automated lights changing directions, a performer carrying a candle or flashlight across the stage. The subtlest and often the most effective kind of movement of light comes with shifting the audience's focus when lights go down in one area and come up in another. Lighting cross-fades like this can shift the focus from location to location and from color to color, but even within single scenes a good lighting design will force the audience members to change their focus without even realizing it. Also, time of day, sunsets, and so on can help provide visual information for the audience.

For an example of how these properties function, consider the lighting for a production of *Hamlet*. To emphasize this play's eerie, tragic quality, with its murders and graveyard scene, the lighting would generally be cool rather than warm, but it could also have a slash of red cutting through the otherwise cool light. As for angles, if the production took place on a proscenium stage, there would be more dramatic downlighting and backlighting to give the characters a sculptured, occasionally unreal quality. In terms of movement, the lights would change each time there was a shift in locale, or a low-angle special could come on diagonally from behind the ghost of Hamlet's father. This would give a rhythm of movement throughout the play and would also focus the audience's attention on particular areas of the stage as well as support the thematic elements of the play.

The Lighting Designer's Resources   Among the resources of the lighting designer are various kinds of lighting instruments and other kinds of technical and electronic equipment.

Types of Stage Lights   Most stage lights have three main elements: a lamp that is the source of the light, a reflector, and a lens through which the beams pass. The two basic categories of lighting fixtures are conventional lighting instruments and automated or moving light fixtures. Conventional lights are fixed instruments with a single focus and design purpose. Intelligent moving light fixtures are able to alter focus, change color, project multiple patterns, rotate the patterns at varying speeds, change the size of the beam, and give a sharp or diffused focus.

Examples of common conventional lights are the ellipsoidal reflector spotlights, Fresnel spotlights, strip/cyc/flood/border lights, PARs, and follow spots:

Philips Selecon Pacific 2350 Ellipsoidal.
(Courtesy, Philips Selecon)

Philips Selecon Rama Fresnel.
(Courtesy, Philips Selecon)

1. *Ellipsoidal reflector spotlight.* This is the most widely used conventional fixture. It creates a bright, hard-edged spot. However, the edges can be softened with focus adjustment or with a diffusion filter. Lenses of different focal lengths allow for eight different standard-size beams depending on the distance from a theatre's hanging positions to the stage; this instrument is therefore useful from almost any position in the theatre. Clearly, it is the "workhorse" of contemporary lighting practice. It also has a special *gobo* slot for pattern projection. A *follow spot* is another typically hard-edged spotlight controlled by an operator that is designed to follow the leading performer across the stage. Originally, this type of light was created by igniting the mineral lime in front of a reflector in the back end of a long metal tube. The chemical reaction created a bright but slightly green light, which led to the common expression for someone who likes attention as "liking to be in the limelight."

2. *Soft-edged spotlights.* The most popular soft-edged spotlight is the Fresnel (pronounced "fruh-NEL"). It is a high-wattage spot, and the Fresnel lens helps dissipate the heat, but it can create only a soft-edged beam of light that can be focused down to a small spot or flooded to cover a larger stage area. The lens is named for Auguste Fresnel, who designed, for lighthouses, the first lenses that would not crack with intense heating and cooling. The concentric rings he cut into the lens allowed the lens to function properly while preventing the buildup of heat from cracking the lens after the light was turned off. Many lighting designers use this instrument for toplighting and backlighting and to cover a large stage area with a wash of color. The Fresnel is generally used in positions near the stage—behind the proscenium opening, or mounted close to the action on an arena or thrust stage. Another common soft-edged lighting instrument is the parabolic aluminized reflector (PAR), which emits an oval beam. *Barn doors,* with flaps that can cut off an edge of the beam, and *color changers/scrollers,* which increase the options from one color to fifteen colors on a single instrument, are common accessories used on both PARs and Fresnels.

3. *Floodlights, strip lights, and border lights.* These lights bathe a section of the stage or scenery in a smooth, diffused wash of light. Floodlights are used, singly or in groups, to provide general illumination for the stage or scenery. The light from floods can be blended in acting areas, or used to "tone" settings and costumes. They are most often used to illuminate cycloramas at the rear of the stage, or ground rows along the floor of the stage.

4. *Automated or moving light.* The moving light is the newest and most versatile instrument of the group, although there are still only a few moving lights with an independent shutter function that can be focused in a theatre like an ellipsoidal spotlight. Automated light fixtures are able to alter focus, change color using

Philips Selecon Hui Flood. (Courtesy, Philips Selecon)   Vari*Lite VL6 spot luminaire. (Courtesy of Vari*Lite)

dichroic—or two-beam—color mixing, project multiple patterns, rotate the patterns at varying speeds, change the size of the beam, and give a sharp or diffused focus. One moving light fixture used as a special can replace numerous conventional fixtures. Most contemporary lighting designers use a combination of both types of instruments. Automated fixtures are particularly useful in elaborate musical productions and are widely used in rock concerts.

Lighting Controls   Lighting design is clearly the most technologically developed element of theatre. We have already considered some of the advances in this area in terms of lighting instruments. These fixtures can now be hung all over a performance space and aimed at every part of the stage. In addition, one person sitting at a console can control the elements of these lighting instruments. New technologies have also prompted a great deal of change in the design of control systems, which now allow for remarkable computer-controlled lighting along with the ability to employ traditional methods of cue changes. Lighting control systems are extremely expensive, so the change to systems that continue to evolve technologically happens only gradually for most theatre operations.

Lighting changes—or *cues,* as they are called—are usually arranged ahead of time. Sometimes, in a complicated production (a musical, say, or a Shakespearean play), there will be from 75 to 150 or more light cues. A cue can range from a *blackout* (in which all the lights are shut off at once), to a *fade* (the lights dim slowly, changing the scene from brighter to darker), to a *cross-fade* (one set of lights comes down while another comes up) or a split cross-fade (the lights that are coming up are on a different fade count from the lights that are coming down). Thanks to computerized control, the split cross-fade is the most common.

Although light board programming is complicated and somewhat time-consuming the actual running of a show has become a fairly simple task because of well-designed computer control systems. The most critical aspect of the lighting design is the ability of the stage manager to fully understand the pacing and design aesthetic in calling the lighting and sound cues. Even the process of calling cues has been simplified in some

Cues   Any prearranged signal—such as the last words in a speech, a piece of business, or any action or lighting change—that indicates to a performer or stage manager that it is time to proceed to the next line or action.

ways by technology. In lighting for dance or for large-scale musicals it is critical to merge the lighting and sound cues. Through the use of new digital sound technology a computer-controlled sound program can interface with a computer light board and both light and sound cues can be run simultaneously with one tap of the keyboard space bar.

For instance, Strindberg's *A Dream Play* has numerous and complex scene changes—like a dream, as the title implies—in which one scene fades into another before our eyes. At one point in the play, a young woman, called the Daughter, sits at an organ in a church. In Strindberg's words, "The stage darkens as the Daughter rises and approaches the Lawyer. By means of lighting the organ is transformed into a wall of a grotto. The sea seeps in between basal pillars with a harmony of waves and wind." At the light cue for this change, a button is pushed, and all the lights creating the majesty of the church fade as the lights creating the grotto come up. In many ways stage lighting technology has finally started to catch up with, and serve, the creative ideas that artists like Strindberg and Appia had at the start of the twentieth century.

The Lighting Designer's Collaborators   As in every aspect of theatre, in lighting too there is collaboration. Those who work with the lighting designer include assistant designers and people who help create the light plot, as well as a master electrician responsible for the preparation, hanging, and focusing of the lights and all accessories (often, if not always, electricians must climb on catwalks and ladders to remote areas above, behind, and in front of the stage). One of the newer jobs is that of the moving light programmer. Until the advent of moving lights, programming light cues had always fallen to either the lighting designer or the lead associate designer. More recently, however, the complexity of programming has grown exponentially with automated fixtures and other digital accessories, thus requiring another technical specialty.

Large-scale musical productions, for example, are often so complex that even calling all the cues is impossible for one person to do. For that reason, all follow-spot cues (usually three or four follow spots in a design) are typically called by the lead spot operator. In the concert industry, this gets even more complex, as there are usually a minimum of eight follow spots and often as many as sixteen or more on a major tour of a rock musical production in addition to almost unimaginably complex moving light packages.

SOUND IN THE THEATRE

Scenery, costumes, and lighting can all be described as the visual elements of theatre. Another major design element is sound. In recent years, sound has become an increasingly important aspect of theatre, with its own artistry, technology, and designers. In fact, in 2007 the Tony Awards Committee voted to include sound design as a category beginning with the 2008 awards.

Sound Reproduction: Advantages and Disadvantages

Amplification   In the past few decades, sound reproduction has become increasingly prominent in theatre. For some audience members, it has sometimes proved to be controversial as well. The intense amplification at popular music concerts along with the availability of inexpensive personal audio systems—now in digital formats—are just two of the reasons we now expect widespread sound reproduction in the theatre. As a result, large musicals, whether presented in Broadway houses or in spacious performing art centers across the country, are now extensively amplified. Most of us, accustomed to amplified sound in many other settings, take such amplification for granted.

Some critics charge, however, that amplification in theatre is sometimes overdone, with the sound too loud, as well as too mechanical and artificial. In opera the objections are even stronger. In today's theatre, those continuing to oppose amplification appear to be the "purists." Their objections stem, no doubt, from the experience of theatergoing more than half a century ago. It may be difficult for us in the early twenty-first century to imagine, but the great American musicals of the 1940s and the 1950s—by composers like Rodgers and Hammerstein, Cole Porter, and Irving Berlin—were all produced without any sound amplification whatsoever. Today, however, electronic amplification is a way of life in theatre, and sound design has become an indispensable part of any production.

Note that the issue of amplification is less pressing in smaller venues: in "black boxes," for example, or fringe theatres in lofts or warehouses that seat perhaps 100 spectators. In such spaces, the sound component, both because of economics and because of size, is likely to be less elaborate and less noticeable. We are speaking here, therefore, of larger spaces: college or university theatres of approximately 400 or 500 seats, and professional theatres that might range from 800 to 2,000 seats.

Sound Effects Aside from the argument about the volume or pervasiveness of voice amplification, we should recognize that sound has always been an important, and necessary, component of theatre production. One aspect of this is sound effects. In earlier years—for several centuries, in fact—various devices were developed to create such sounds.

Historically, for example, a wooden drum made from slats was used to produce the sound of wind. The drum was usually two or three feet in diameter, and covered with a muslin cloth. When the drum was turned, by means of a handle, it made a noise like howling wind. Thunder was suggested by hanging a large, thick metal sheet backstage and gently shaking it. For the sound of a door slamming, a miniature door or even a full-size door in a frame was placed just off stage and opened and shut. Two hinged pieces of wood slammed shut also simulated the sound of a closing door.

A gunshot sound could also be created with these hinged pieces of wood, as well as by firing a gun loaded with blank cartridges. Live ammunition could not be used safely onstage. In some states, blank guns were (and still are) illegal. As we shall see, recorded sound, now easily digitized, makes this issue irrelevant in the contemporary theatre.

Today, of course, the developments in computer technology and digitization, which support sound design and its playback on stage, are extensive. There are many programs available on the Internet for free download as well, so it is not difficult to get started using simple sound programs. Most often these same programs have more advanced and complex capabilities that are available for purchase. You can record and play back a myriad of sound cues; if you want to interface those sound cues through a lighting control board or projection system, for creation and alteration, then you may use sophisticated software packages such as Pro Tools, Final Cut Pro, or Garage Band. Also available are SFX and CueLab computer playback systems.

There are times when sound
takes over in a production.
Of course, in most musical
productions, all the voices,
as well as the instruments of
the orchestra, are enhanced
by sound equipment. But in
many productions there are
certain moments when
sound is crucial. An
example is the scene shown
here from a production of
Summer and Smoke by
Tennessee Williams,
directed by Michael
Wilson at the Hartford
Stage Company. One of
the characters fires a gun
at another character. All
action stops; the shot
becomes the defining
event. Sound design was
by John Gromada.
(© T Charles Erickson)

The Sound Designer

The person responsible for arranging and orchestrating all the aural aspects of a production is the sound designer. Like his or her counterparts in visual design, the sound designer begins by reading the script, noting all the places where sound might be needed. For a large-scale musical, the designer also decides on the number and type of microphones to be used, the placement of speakers throughout the theatre, and all other aspects of sound reproduction.

After reading the script, the sound designer consults with the director to determine the exact nature of the sound requirements, including sound effects and amplification. The designer then sets about preparing the full range of components that constitute sound for a production. Encompassing anything from preshow and intermission music to any and all microphones to special prerecorded sound effects to preshow announcements about cell phones to live voice-overs, sound is an essential component of every theatre production.

Understanding Sound Reproduction and Sound Reinforcement

One way to classify sound design is as *sound reproduction* and *sound reinforcement*. Sound *reproduction* is the use of motivated or environmental sounds. *Motivated sounds* would be, for instance, the noise of a car crunching on gravel, a car motor turning off, and a door slamming—a sequence that would announce the arrival of a character at a house where a scene is taking place. Motivated sounds, then, are those called for by the script. *Environmental sounds* are noises of everyday life that help create verisimilitude in

PLAYING YOUR PART: EXPERIENCING THEATRE

1. How do you use lighting in your room or home for different circumstances? How do you change the lighting for those occasions? How is this similar to what is done in the theatre?

2. What sound technology do you use in your everyday life? How might this also be employed in the theatre?

3. If someone asked, "What is the soundtrack for your life?" what would your response be? How does that sound reflect who you are? How is that similar to the use of sound accompanying the production of a play?

4. On a sunny day, observe how the light shines through the leaves of a tree on your campus or near your home. What mood does the light evoke in you? Why? How?

5. What is the lighting like in your favorite restaurant? What mood does it evoke in you? Why? How?

6. Watch a film and discuss how the sound enhances the film. How is underscoring used?

7. Attend a technical rehearsal at your university or community theatre. Observe the light changes. Do you see who is operating the light and sound boards? Can you identify any of the lighting instruments and where they are hung in the theatre? Ask if you may see the computer boards that operate lighting and sound.

a production: street traffic in a city, crickets in the country, loud rock music coming from a stereo in a college dormitory. Such sounds are usually heard as background.

Sound effects are one form of sound reproduction. A sound effect can be defined as any sound produced by mechanical or human means to create for us a noise or sound associated with the play. Today, as we noted previously, sound effects are most often digitally downloaded to computers. Virtually every sound imaginable—from birds singing to dogs barking to jet planes flying—is available for digital downloading from the Internet, not only for expensive professional productions but also for college, university, and community theatres.

Sound *reinforcement* is the amplification of sounds produced by a performer or a musical instrument. With the growth of electronics and computerization in music, more and more instruments have been amplified. At any rock concert, you can see wires coming out of the basses and guitars. In an orchestra pit in a theatre, the quieter acoustic instruments such as the guitar are miked to achieve a balance of sound with the louder instruments. In today's Broadway theatres it is not unusual to have some members of the orchestra in a separate room in another part of the building with a television monitor showing the conductor. In most cases, the audience would never know about this seating arrangement. The total sound can overwhelm a singer, especially one who has not been trained—as opera singers are—to project the voice into the farther reaches of a theatre. As a result, we have body mikes on the performers.

At first, a body mike was a small microphone attached in some way to the performer's clothing. A wire ran from the mike to a small radio transmitter concealed on the performer; from the transmitter, the sound was sent to an off-stage listening device that fed it into a central sound-control system. In today's large musical productions, the microphone worn by a performer is frequently a small instrument, hardly larger than a piece of wire, worn over one ear alongside the temple or placed elsewhere near the performer's head, that carries the sound to the body transmitters.

In some musicals, the performers wear a small microphone attached to a headpiece coming around one side of the head, similar to that worn by telephone switchboard operators. Head microphones are used so that they will be as close as possible to the performer's mouth and at a constant distance away from it. (How many of us attending a musical realize that the tap dancers are frequently wearing wireless microphones near their feet, inside their dance tights?)

Still another kind of sound that must be added to the final mix is musical or other *underscoring*, which one hears between scenes or acts, and sometimes during spoken sections of a performance, to add emphasis or create mood.

Sound Technology

Microphones and Loudspeakers

In preparing the sound for a production, the designers and engineers not only must assemble all the necessary sounds but also must be certain that the appropriate microphones are used correctly and must place the speakers effectively onstage and in the auditorium.

Several types of microphones are used. A *shotgun mike* is highly directional and is aimed from a distance at a specific area. A *general mike* picks up sounds in the general area toward which it is aimed. A *body mike,* as we described above, is a wireless microphone attached to a performer's body or clothing. Microphones not worn by performers are placed in various locations. One position is alongside the downstage edge of the stage. Another position is hanging in the air above the stage. Any type of microphone must be hooked up to an amplifier that increases the electronic energy of the sound and sends it through the speakers.

The placement of loudspeakers is both an art and a science. It is necessary to determine the correct speakers for the size and shape of the theatre, and to position them so that they carry sound clearly and evenly into the auditorium—to the upper reaches of the balcony, to the side seats, and to areas underneath the balcony as well as the first few rows in the orchestra. Also, live sound from the performers must reach the sides and back of the theatre at the same time that it reaches those of us seated in the front. One problem in this regard is that sound travels much more slowly than light.

The speed of sound is only 1,100 feet per second—which means that for those of us seated at the back of a large theatre, sound from a speaker at the rear of the auditorium will be heard before the human voice from the stage. Developments in digital electronics have led to devices that process, sample, and synthesize sound for various effects, including delaying the electronic sound so that it arrives through a loudspeaker at the same time as the much slower live sound.

Sound Recordings

The process of assembling sound recordings is similar for professional and nonprofessional productions. First, a list is made of all sound required. This list is usually developed by the sound designer in consultation with the director, and possibly with a composer: for a show with a great deal of sound or music, there may be both a sound designer and a music composer. Once the list is drawn up, a master recording is made and the sounds are arranged in their order of appearance in the script. This process is called *editing*. When the production moves into the theatre, there is a technical rehearsal without performers, during which each sound cue is listened to and the volume is set. When rehearsals with the performers start in the theatre, more changes will be made. Depending on the action and the timing of scenes, some cues will be too loud and others too soft; some will have to be made shorter and others made longer.

During an actual performance of a production using sound reinforcement, an operator must sit at a complex sound console *mixing* sound or, as is becoming the norm, use a computerized playback system such as SFX or CueLab. In this way the operator blends all elements from the many microphones and from the master sound recording—so that there is a smooth, seamless blend of sound. Also, the operator must make certain not only that all sound is in balance but also that sound does not intrude on the performance or call attention to itself, away from the stage and the performers.

New Technologies in Sound   As with lighting, in recent years we have seen frequent advances and breakthroughs in sound equipment and technology. The new body microphones and a device that delays the delivery of electronic sound have already been mentioned. There are other developments as well.

Analog reel-to-reel tape decks, which were standard, are have given way to digital technology such as direct playback from a computer's hard drive. Sound is now recorded and edited at digital audio workstations, housed on personal computers. Such stations allow easier editing of sound, more complex effects, and higher-quality sound. Digital playback systems allow very easy and precise cueing of shows, as well as greatly improved sound quality.

SPECIAL EFFECTS IN LIGHTING AND SOUND

As in scene design, some effects of lighting and sound, separately or in combination, can seem unusual or even miraculous and add to the magic of live theatre.

There are several special lighting effects that can be used to create interesting visual pictures. One simple effect is to position a source of light near the stage floor and shine the light on the performers from below. This creates shadows under the eyes and chin and gives performers' faces a ghostly or horrifying quality. Another common special effect is ultraviolet light, a very dark blue light that causes phosphorus to glow; when the stage is very dark, or completely dark, costumes or scenery that have been painted with a special phosphorus paint will "light up."

The effect of slow motion—where the performers seem to be moving in jerks—is created by a strobe light, a very powerful, bright gas-discharge light that flashes at rapid intervals. As we saw earlier, technological advances in lighting have made it possible to create even more spectacular effects and to enhance these effects as well.

There are also a number of special sound effects. Sometimes speakers are placed completely around the audience so that the sound can move from side to side. Echoes can be created by a machine that causes reverberations in sound waves. Expanding audio technology also allows for more complex sound effects. Computerized noises and electronic music can be used to create special sounds for various situations, and digitization gives instantaneous access to any element of the sound design. Also, with computerized synthesizers, a few musicians can now replace a large orchestra.

Lighting and sound, therefore, like scenery and costumes, are means to an end: they implement the artistic and aesthetic aspects of a production. The colors, shapes, and lines of lighting and the qualities of sound design interact with other elements of theatre and contribute to the overall experience.

PLAYING YOUR PART: THINKING ABOUT THEATRE

1. During the last play you attended, what did you notice about the lighting? Were there lighting instruments throughout the theatre aimed at the stage? When the performance began, where did the beams of light appear to come from?

2. During that same production, what colors were created on the stage by lighting? Did you think the colors were appropriate for the production? How did the color of the lights affect your overall experience?

3. Again, during that same production, were you able to spot sound speakers? Where were they located? During the performance, did you notice if microphones were attached to the actors? Do you think there were microphones elsewhere on stage? Can you speculate as to where they were?

SUMMARY

1. Stage lighting, like other elements of theatre, has a counterpart in the lighting of homes, restaurants, and other environments in our everyday life.

2. Lighting was historically the last visual element to be fully developed for the stage but is today the most technically sophisticated. Once the incandescent electric lamp was introduced, it was possible to achieve almost total control of the color, intensity, and timing of lights. Lighting controls have also benefited from computerization, with extensive light shifts being controlled by an operator at a computerized console.

3. Lighting design is intended to provide illumination onstage, to establish time and place, to help set the mood and style of a production, to focus the action, and to establish a rhythm of visual movement.

4. Lighting should be consistent with all other elements.

5. The lighting designer uses a variety of instruments, colored gels, special accessories, and advanced dimmer controls as well as computerized control consoles to achieve effects. Electronic developments and computers have greatly increased the flexibility and control of lighting instruments and equipment.

6. Sound is taking its place alongside scenery, costumes, and lighting as a key design element.

7. Rapid advances in technology allow for sophisticated delivery in a theatre of both sound reproduction—sound effects and such—and sound reinforcement of both musical instruments and the human voice.

8. The sound designer and engineer must (a) prepare the sound track, (b) place microphones and speakers appropriately, and (c) mix recorded and live sounds during the performance to achieve the desired effects.

The Theatre Today

5

The Theatre Today

TODAY'S THEATRE: INCLUSIVE AND DIVERSE

The contemporary theatre is a rich mix of global works, new plays, experimental pieces, and revivals of classics from the past. An important component of this mixture is the musical, both new works and revivals. Seen here is a scene from the revival of *Pippin,* with Matthew James Thomas as Pippin, Patina Miller as the Leading Player, directed by Diane Paulus at the American Repertory Theatre. It was revived on Broadway, with book by Roger O. Hirson; music and lyrics by Stephen Schwartz. (© Sara Krulwich/ The New York Times/Redux)

Part Five

The Theatre Today

During the past 100 years, the world has seen unprecedented, earth-shattering changes. Discoveries and inventions have abounded, and, at the same time, war, civil unrest, unimaginable horrors, and natural disasters have marked our world.

On the positive side, we have experienced an astounding series of achievements in science, medicine, technology, communications, travel, and commerce. In medicine, for example, great strides have been made: diseases have been cured and people enabled to live much longer. Also, in information technology worldwide communication has become instantaneous, as e-mail, smartphones, and social media, such as Facebook and Twitter, allow us to reach the other side of the world in a matter of seconds. Television has brought into our homes the triumphs and disasters of this fast-paced world, shown up-close and graphically, as they occur. Media streaming has allowed us to engage with all forms of electronic entertainments.

On the other side of the ledger, in the past 75 years we have experienced World War II—in which, among other things, the Nazi regime carried out the systematic and ruthless extermination of millions of people, including 6 million Jews. In the 1960s and 1970s, the Vietnam War brought a frightening number of casualties and images of horror to the American consciousness. Civil wars and genocide took place in several African countries. There has also been the continuing, as well as regime changes and civil wars in Egypt, Libya, and Syria. Terrorist attacks took place in New York City on September 11, 2001, in Madrid in 2004, in London in 2005, and in Boston in 2013. The costly and deadly wars in Iraq and Afghanistan continued this pattern of despair and destruction.

Today's world has seen unbelievable progress and heartbreaking tragedy. Symbolic of the latter are such things as the Arlington National Cemetery honoring those in the military who have fought and died for their country. (© Eyewire/Photodisc/PunchStock)

Cell phones (most with built-in digital cameras and Internet access), laptop computers, handheld electronic devices, and digital music players have become ubiquitous. (© Ocean/Corbis)

In the midst of all this, the one thing missing from our instantaneous communication, from our digital media, from our social media, from the powerful images we see on television and film, is human contact—two groups of people in the presence of one another at the same time: the performers and the audience. As the world seems to grow more impersonal and frightening, the need for human interaction becomes more important than ever. And at the forefront of contact between people is the theatre experience.

This is a primary reason why, in spite of the multitude of challenges theatre has faced—radio, film, television, computers, digital media—it remains alive and well. In fact, in some ways it is more vital than ever. Theatre, like the best of human institutions, is all-embracing. It's safe to say that at no time in the past have audiences in the United States, in Canada, and in many other places had as wide or varied a choice of theatrical offerings as they have today. To begin with, there is an amazing multiplicity of theatrical venues: large theatres, midsize resident professional theatres, small intimate theatres, college and university theatres, community theatres, theatres with all types of audience and stage configurations. The various theatres house large spectacular productions, classics, new plays, performance art, ensemble creations, and avant-garde presentations.

The season of a resident professional theatre or a college and university theatre might include a classic from the past (the most widely produced playwright in America is William Shakespeare), an important work from the early modern period (Ibsen, Chekhov, Strindberg), a play from the mid-twentieth century (García Lorca, O'Neill, Miller, Williams, Hansberry, Albee), contemporary plays from around the world, and premieres of works by young playwrights.

A further development in contemporary theatre has been the incredibly wide range of the types of offerings: global theatre, multicultural theatre (African American, Asian American, Hispanic, Native American), gender-specific drama and theatre dealing with sexual orientation (feminist theatre, gay theatre, lesbian theatre, transsexual theatre), and political theatre, which would include feminist theatre and theatre of social commentary.

In Part Five, we look closely at the landscape of contemporary theatre: in Chapter 12, we focus on musical theatre; in Chapter 13, we examine global theatre; and in Chapter 14, we look at American theatre.

Electronic games of all types have proliferated at an astounding pace. Shown is a Nintendo Wii U touch-screen controller for the new Super Mario Bros. U video game, Japan, 2013. (© Akio Kon/ Bloomberg via Getty Images)

Controversial subjects that have been addressed in contemporary theatre include same-sex unions and other gay and lesbian issues. (© Alex Wong/Getty Images)

266

Musical Theatre

Throughout theatre history, drama has been closely associated with music and dance. In ancient Greek tragedy, choral sections were performed to the accompaniment of music and dance. Opera, which began in Italy around 1600, was originated by men who thought that they were imitating Greek drama. Shakespeare, who wrote at about the same time opera began, included songs as an important part of his comedies. The nineteenth-century term *melodrama* came from "song dramas," in which music accompanied the action onstage. In other forms of nineteenth-century theatrical entertainment, such as vaudeville and *burlesque*, singing and dancing were an important element.

It was in the twentieth century, however, that the form of musical theatre with which we are most familiar reached its highest development—for example, in *Oklahoma!*, *West Side Story*, *My Fair Lady*, *Fiddler on the Roof*, *A Chorus Line*, and Stephen Sondheim's musicals. Moreover, these musicals represent a form that came to full flower in the United States. Every other type of drama at which American playwrights and performers have excelled—such as modern tragedy, domestic drama, and farce—traces its origins to another time and another country. Though modern musical theatre has antecedents in forms such as European operetta, it is largely a product of American talent and creativity. Proof of its significance and universal appeal is the fact that it is now imitated—often quite successfully—and performed throughout the world.

THE APPEAL OF MUSIC AND DANCE

Before we look more closely at musical theatre, it will be helpful to consider the special appeal that music and dance have as part of theatre.

◀ **MUSICAL THEATRE**

During the twentieth century, American artists were important in developing musical theatre as a distinct art form, in terms of both music itself and its integration with dramatic structure. The beginnings occurred in the first three decades of the twentieth century; then there was a "golden age" of book musicals from the mid-1940s to the mid-1960s. Here we see Jan Maxwell (center) and the cast of the Kennedy Center production of Follies *directed by Eric Schaeffer, with book by James Goldman, music and lyrics by Stephen Sondheim, choreography by Warren Carlyle. (© Craig Schwartz/Center Theatre Group, Ahmanson Theatre)*

It is not difficult to understand why singing and dancing have frequently been combined with dramatic productions. First, all three are performing arts, and so there is a natural affinity among them. Second, singing and dancing have wide popular appeal. People enjoy listening to music at home as well as in the theatre. Also, in today's world, through MP3 players, tablets, and smartphones, and the ability to instantaneously download music through such services as iTunes, people hear music everywhere—while they are walking, or riding in cars, planes, or buses. When hearing music, listeners respond to rhythms and to the emotional pull of a memorable melody, especially when performed by a singer with a captivating voice and personality. Dancing can also be immensely appealing. The grace and agility of a talented, expertly trained solo dancer or ensemble and the precision of a group of dancers moving in unison provide entertainment of a high order.

Beyond their value as entertainment, singing and dancing possess an unmatched ability to capture the beauty of sound and movement and to communicate a wide range of emotions. In language there are thoughts and feelings that cannot be adequately expressed in everyday prose, and for these we turn to poetry. In the same way, there are expressions of beauty, anguish, spirituality and sheer joy that can best be conveyed in vocal and instrumental music and in dance.

OPERA

Before discussing musical theatre we should take a brief look at a close relative and predecessor, opera. Opera can be defined as a drama set entirely to music. With rare exceptions, every part of the performance is sung, including not only the arias but also the transitional sections between them, known as *recitatives*. Having begun in Florence, Italy, around 1600 as drama set to music, opera, from 1600 to 1900, spread throughout the European continent, as well as England.

During this time, it took on the characteristics that we have come to know as defining opera. Arias (strong, melodic solos), stirring duets, trios, quartets, and choruses all found their place as components of opera. The stories of opera used myth, history, and contemporary fictional and real events as source material. Also, comic opera (*opera buffa*) joined more serious opera as an option for composers. Important figures in the history of opera include the Italian Alessandro Scarlatti (1659–1725), who established the supremacy of the aria. Wolfgang Amadeus Mozart (1756–1791) brought comic opera to a peak of perfection. Richard Wagner (1813–1883), a German composer, imposed on opera his ideas of monumental works based on legends and myths, joined together in a unified theatre piece. And the Italian composer Giuseppe Verdi (1813–1901) was a superb musician with a mastery of orchestral techniques and an impressive instinct for dramatic effect.

In the late nineteenth and early twentieth centuries, Giacomo Puccini (1858–1924) composed extremely popular operas with romantic stories and appealing melodies. After that, during the course of the twentieth century, the great days of opera seemed to have passed. This was a century in which revivals of operas from earlier years became the standard repertoire. Operas continued to be composed—in the latter part of the century, many of them were commissioned by opera companies—and some found favor with audiences. Others, however, incorporated the dissonances and atonality of modern music and were not embraced by a wide public. In addition to the standard repertoire, it is not unusual for works from musical theatre to be presented by opera companies. Two examples are Gershwin's *Porgy and Bess* and Sondheim's *Sweeney Todd.* The renowned Chicago Lyric Opera announced that it will produce a musical annually, beginning with *Oklahoma* (discussed later) in 2013. Thanks to its rich heritage, opera continues to have a significant place in the performing arts.

Opera has many of the qualities of drama: vivid characters and stories with plot twists and unexpected reversals. But it has long been considered to be within the realm of music rather than drama. This is largely because the composer and the score predominate. For example, *Don Giovanni* has a libretto by Lorenzo Da Ponte, but it is never said to be "by Da Ponte." It is always "Mozart's *Don Giovanni*." Similarly, *Falstaff* is based on Shakespeare's play *The Merry Wives of Windsor,* but it is known only as Verdi's *Falstaff.* In opera, the composer reigns supreme. By contrast, musical theatre is considered to be primarily in the realm of theatre.

TYPES OF MUSICAL THEATRE

To understand modern ***musical theatre,*** it is necessary to define certain terms. Aside from *opera,* they include *operetta, musical comedy, musical theatre,* and *revue.*

Unlike opera, an *operetta* is not entirely set to music; certain portions are spoken, as in a regular drama. Operetta generally features a romantic story set in a far-off locale. An air of unreality and make-believe makes most operettas remote from everyday life. But the best ones have beautiful, soaring melodies and a plot that tells a complete story, however fanciful. Operetta features solos, duets, and trios as well as stirring choral numbers.

Musical comedy is a form of musical entertainment that emerged in the United States in the early twentieth century and that featured a light, comic story interspersed with popular music. Originally, the story was often far-fetched or even silly, but it did relate to contemporary people and events, and thus musical comedy was closer to everyday life than operetta was. The *musical,* also called *musical theatre,* evolved out of operetta and musical comedy.

OPERA

An important musical form related to musical theatre is opera, which originated in Italy at the beginning of the seventeenth century and for three centuries spread through the European continent and England. Opera stresses music: solos, duets, choruses, and other combinations of singers. Also, there is a premium on great singing rather than acting. Shown here are Ramon Vargas as Alfredo and Renée Fleming as Violetta in *La Traviata* at New York's Metropolitan Opera. (© Ken Howard/Metropolitan Opera)

Musical theatre   A type of theatre that integrates songs, spoken dialogue, acting, and dance. The story and emotions are underscored and enhanced by the music and dance which are fully integrated into the plot.

OPERETTA

Operetta stands somewhere between opera and musical theatre. There is an emphasis on the musical numbers, but scenes are also played with dialogue. Often, operetta is comic in tone, a good example being the works of the collaborators W. S. Gilbert and Arthur Sullivan in the late nineteenth century. This scene is from their operetta *The Pirates of Penzance,* presented at the Guthrie Theater, directed by Joe Dowling, with set design by Michael Yeargan and costumes by Paul Tazewell. (© Michal Daniel)

THE MUSICAL REVUE

One variation of the musical is the revue: a series of songs, sketches, and other acts strung together. In the early part of the twentieth century, the revue was a staple of American musical theatre. Singers, dancers, actors, specialty acts, and comic stars were all featured in revues. In addition, the scenic and costume effects were often extremely lavish. The subject of a recent production, *The Nance,* is the revue in the 1930s. Shown here from *The Nance* are, from the left, Lewis J. Stadlen, Cady Huffman, Nathan Lane (the star of the show) and Jonny Orsini. (© Sara Krulwich/The New York Times/Redux)

Examples of this form—*Show Boat, Porgy and Bess, Oklahoma!* and *My Fair Lady*—will be discussed in the pages that follow.

To round out the range of musical entertainment, we should note the *revue* (discussed elsewhere), in which sketches and vignettes alternate with musical numbers. The important thing to remember about the revue is that there is no single storyline that carries through from beginning to end; the scenes and songs stand alone and may have very little relationship to each other, although they often have a common theme or may be written by the same composer and lyricist.

revue

THE AMERICAN MUSICAL

Antecedents

The modern American musical had a number of antecedents in the theatre of the nineteenth century and early twentieth century. One of these was operetta; two others were vaudeville and burlesque. Though burlesque eventually became synonymous with risqué sketches and "girlie shows," for most of the nineteenth century it featured dramatic sketches and songs that satirized or made fun of other theatrical forms. Vaudeville was a series of variety acts—music, sketches, juggling, animal acts—that made up an evening's entertainment. Another form of musical production that flourished in the nineteenth century was the minstrel show, a variety show that featured white performers wearing blackface.

vaudeville and burlesque

At the same time, there was a movement toward the development of the ***book musical,*** which refers to a show with a story that traces the fortunes of the main characters through a series of adventures with a beginning, middle, and end. (The book of a musical is sometimes referred to as the *libretto,* and the person who writes it as the *librettist;* the person who writes the lyrics to a musical score is called a ***lyricist.***) By the early twentieth century, with burlesque, vaudeville, and American imitations of European operettas, the seeds of American musical comedy had been sown.

Book The storyline and dialogue of a musical.

Lyricist The author of the lyrics of the songs in a musical.

The 1920s and 1930s: Musical Comedies

Around the time of World War I (1914–1918), a truly native American musical began to emerge. The story was often frivolous, but at least it was a story rather than a series of patched-together blackout sketches, as in earlier attempts at musical shows. More important than the story—or book—was the music. A group of exceptional composers and lyricists wrote the songs for these shows. These melodies from the musical comedies of the 1920s and 1930s became known as *standards.* That is, they were so popular that they were played over and over again, and many of them are still played on radio and television and are available to the public through recordings.

Among the composers were Irving Berlin (1888–1989), Jerome Kern (1885–1945), George Gershwin (1898–1937), Cole Porter (1893–1964), and Richard Rodgers. The work of these men was fresh and innovative. Their melodies ranged from the sprightly to the haunting and featured surprising modulations and developments in the melodic line. Matching the inventiveness of the composers were the words of the lyricists. Ira Gershwin (1896–1983) wrote lyrics for many of his brother George's tunes, and Lorenz Hart teamed up with Richard Rodgers. Irving Berlin and Cole Porter wrote their own lyrics.

The lyrics were generally witty and clever, and they reflected a high order of intelligence; the rhymes were resourceful and often unexpected. For example, in "You're the Top" Cole Porter compares the singer's beloved to a wide range of superlative objects, stating that the person is the Coliseum and the Louvre Museum, comparing the loved one to a Bendel bonnet and a Shakespeare sonnet, then rhyming the tower of Pisa with the smile on the Mona Lisa.

The 1920s and 1930s: Advances in Musicals

While composers and lyricists were perfecting their art, a few shows were steps forward for the form of the musical itself. A landmark musical of this era was *Show Boat,* which opened in 1927. The music was by Jerome Kern and the book and lyrics were by Oscar Hammerstein II (1895–1960). It represented an advance over previous musicals in several respects.

Show Boat was based on a novel by Edna Ferber about life on a Mississippi riverboat. Thus the story itself was thoroughly American, not an exotic romantic fable of

SHOW BOAT: A LANDMARK MUSICAL
When *Show Boat* opened in 1927, it began a new chapter in the history of the American musical. The chorus line was eliminated, miscegenation (a romance between a white man and a black woman) was treated for the first time, and other problems facing African Americans were touched on. Also, it had a glorious score by Jerome Kern and Oscar Hammerstein. Shown here is a revival staged by Harold Prince. (© Catherine Ashmore)

the kind that was generally found in operetta. It was also a serious story, which set *Show Boat* apart from lighthearted musical comedies. In the story, Magnolia Hawks and Gaylord Ravenal, who perform on the showboat, meet and fall in love. Later, because of Gaylord's gambling, they eventually separate. Meanwhile, a subplot—a second romance, between the characters Steve and Julie—represented a first for the American musical: the love story of a white man and a mixed race (multiracial) woman. At the time, nothing like this had been shown onstage. There was further daring, and realism, in the depiction of the lives of black workers on the levees of the Mississippi, as exemplified in the song "Ol' Man River."

The score of *Show Boat* included songs that would achieve lasting fame, such as "Why Do I Love You?" "Make Believe," and "Bill." Moreover, these songs were more carefully integrated into the plot than had previously been the case. Another innovation in *Show Boat* was the elimination of a line of chorus girls, which had always been considered indispensable.

Another milestone for the American musical was passed in 1931, when *Of Thee I Sing* was awarded the Pulitzer Prize. This was the first time that a musical had been so honored and a sign that the form was beginning to be taken more seriously. With music and lyrics by George and Ira Gershwin, *Of Thee I Sing* was a satire on political and cultural institutions such as presidential elections and Miss America contests.

In 1935, eight years after *Show Boat,* another important musical opened: *Porgy and Bess,* with music by George Gershwin, book by DuBose Heyward (1885–1940), and lyrics by Heyward and Ira Gershwin. Once again, the story was powerful and realistic—even more so than in *Show Boat.* And the score by George Gershwin, which included "Summertime," "It Ain't Necessarily So," and "Bess, You Is My Woman Now," represented some of the finest compositions written for musical theatre.

Set in "Catfish Row," a black community in Charleston, South Carolina, *Porgy and Bess* deals with Porgy, a crippled man who falls in love with Bess, who has been the woman of a man named Crown. So forceful and complete is the musicalization of the story that there is some debate over whether *Porgy and Bess* should be considered musical theatre or opera. It has been performed in both theatres and opera houses, including the Metropolitan Opera in New York. A recent controversial adaptation, staged on Broadway in 2011, with the book adapted by contemporary African American playwright Suzan-Lori Parks (discussed in Chapter 14), made the work more of a musical and tried to downplay what some have considered racist and sexist stereotyping.

Meanwhile, other steps were being taken that advanced the musical. A production of 1936 called *On Your Toes* was about a Russian ballet company being persuaded to present a modern ballet. The musical score was by Rodgers and Hart, and the coauthor of the book was George Abbott (1887–1995). In addition to writing a number of the musicals of this period, Abbott was the best-known director of musicals, and was recognized for the energy, ebullience, and fast pace of his productions. The innovative aspect of *On Your Toes* was its introduction of a serious dance into musical comedy—a ballet called "Slaughter on Tenth Avenue."

In another Rodgers and Hart musical, *Pal Joey* (1940), the hero is a heel: a nightclub singer who takes advantage of women to get ahead. The presentation of an anti-hero as a leading character was a further step in the development of American musical theatre, which emerged full-blown in the 1940s and 1950s.

Musical Theatre of the 1940s and 1950s

In 1943 a musical opened that was to herald the golden era of American book musicals. This was *Oklahoma!*—which brought together for the first time the team of Richard Rodgers and Oscar Hammerstein II. Both had been involved in musical theatre since the 1920s, but they had never collaborated before.

Oklahoma! is sometimes hailed as more revolutionary than it really was. Many of the innovations it is credited with had actually appeared in earlier musicals. Set against the background of the founding of the state of Oklahoma, it tells the love story of Curly and Laurey, who are thwarted by a character named Jud. During the course of the action, Curly kills Jud onstage. Though this was considered extremely daring, several years earlier, Porgy had killed Crown onstage in *Porgy and Bess. Oklahoma!* was also praised for integrating the songs with the story, but this too had happened previously.

Even so, *Oklahoma!* in many respects offers a prime example of how complete and effective a musical can be. An important achievement was its inclusion, for the first time, of ballet as a crucial element throughout the piece. Agnes de Mille (1905–1995), a choreographer with classical training, created several dances that carried the story forward and became a part of the fabric of the musical. What's more, the entire piece—story, music, lyrics, dances—fit together to present a seamless whole. From *Oklahoma!* on, American musicals could tackle any subject, serious as well as frivolous, and present it as an integrated art form with acting, dancing, and singing masterfully intertwined. For Rodgers and Hammerstein, *Oklahoma!* was the first in a long line of successful musicals that included *Carousel* (1945), *South Pacific* (1949), *The King and I* (1951), and *The Sound of Music* (1959).

Choreography, which became such an integral part of musical theatre in the decades to follow, encompassed a number of dance forms, from the classical lifts and turns of Agnes de Mille's work to the energetic athleticism favored by Jerome Robbins (1918–1999) to the sharp, angular, eccentric moves created by Bob Fosse (1927–1987). In order to execute the many kinds of steps required, dancers became highly trained and enormously versatile, and they were able to perform everything from classical pirouettes to muscular leaps and rapid-fire tap dancing.

The outpouring of first-rate musicals in the 1940s and 1950s remains unparalleled today. Several writers who had been involved in musicals in previous decades did their best work during this period. These include Irving Berlin, with *Annie Get Your Gun* (1946), a musical version of the life of Annie Oakley; and Cole Porter, with *Kiss Me, Kate* (1948), the story of a theatre company putting on a version of Shakespeare's *Taming of the Shrew.*

In addition, a number of new composers, lyricists, and writers appeared on the scene and produced memorable musicals: Frank Loesser (1910–1969), who wrote the lyrics and music for *Guys and Dolls* (1950); Alan Jay Lerner (1918–1986) and Frederick Loewe (1904–1988), who wrote *My Fair Lady* (1956), a musical version of George Bernard Shaw's *Pygmalion;* and the composer Leonard Bernstein (1918–1990) and the lyricist Stephen Sondheim (b. 1930), who created *West Side Story* (1957), a modern version of *Romeo and Juliet.*

The 1940s and 1950s were remarkable not only for the number of outstanding musicals produced but for the range and depth of those musicals. They covered a wide variety of subjects, and the quality was impressive not only in the better-known shows but in many shows in the second rank as well. Along with composers and writers, performers, directors, designers, and choreographers were all working at the top of their form.

THE GOLDEN AGE OF AMERICAN MUSICALS

The prime of the American musical was the post–World War II period when outstanding works of all kinds—serious, comic, traditional, experimental—were created. A theatre piece in the long-standing tradition of American musical comedy, intended primarily for entertainment, is *Guys and Dolls,* with words and music by Frank Loesser. The story of a gambler who bets he can woo a Salvation Army worker, features memorable melodies that run the gamut from ballads to comic numbers. An example of the latter is a song called "Sit Down, You're Rocking the Boat," shown in this scene from a production at the Paper Mill Playhouse in New Jersey. (© Gerry Goodstein)

Musicals from the 1960s through the 1980s

Fiddler on the Roof, which opened in 1964, is believed by many to mark the end of the golden era of book musicals. *Fiddler on the Roof,* with music by Jerry Bock (b. 1928), lyrics by Sheldon Harnick (b. 1924), and book by Joseph Stein (1912–2010), tells of a Jewish family whose father tries to uphold the traditions of the past in a small village in Russia. It is in Anatevka, where the Jewish community faces persecution and a pogrom. It was directed and choreographed by Jerome Robbins, who gave it an overall style and point of view that represented the best of the American musical.

One indication of changes in the musical was the opening in 1967 of *Hair,* a celebration of the informal, antiestablishment lifestyle of young people in the 1960s. *Hair,* with music by Galt MacDermot (b. 1928) and lyrics by Gerome Ragni (1942–1991) and James Rado (b. 1932), had no real story line and represented a radical departure from the book musicals that had dominated the scene for the previous 25 years. After *Hair,* musical theatre became increasingly fragmented. In the 1970s and 1980s, fewer and fewer book musicals were written, though some successful ones continued to appear.

IN FOCUS: GLOBAL CONNECTIONS

The Theatre of Julie Taymor

The American director and designer Julie Taymor (b. 1952) is known predominately for her vibrant productions, which draw on theatrical traditions from across the globe. Her use of puppetry (adapted mostly from Indonesia) and her costume designs mark her as a designer who uses eastern traditions.

Taymor has traveled to Sri Lanka, Indonesia, Japan, and India, and her travels have allowed her to encounter the very different theatrical forms of those countries. Her experiences of Japanese nō, bunraku, and avant-garde theatre, and of Indonesian rod puppets (*wayag golek*) and shadow puppets (*wayang kulit*), were particularly influential in her later productions. In her early experiments with blending theatrical forms, she founded the theatrical company Teatr Loh, which included performers from Java, Bali, Sudan, and the West. This blending of eastern theatrical traditions has been continued through her many productions in the East and West.

Among Taymor's productions are an adaptation of a German novella set in India called *The Transposed Heads* (1984); a production of *Juan Darien* (1988, 1990), which drew on the puppet traditions of Indonesia and Japan and the music of Australia, South America, and Africa; and an opera adaptation of Igor Stravinski's *Oedipus Rex* (1992), which drew on Greek sculpture and Japanese nō costumes. However, she is best known for her productions of *The King Stag* and *The Lion King*.

The King Stag was written in eighteenth-century Italy by Carlo Gozzi and tells of King Derramo and his evil prime minister, Tartaglia. In order to ensure that his daughter will marry the king, Tartaglia tricks the king into transferring his soul into the body of a stag, with the prime minister then taking control of the king's body. By her own count, Taymor identifies nine different countries whose theatrical traditions she drew from in creating *The King Stag*. She used masks from eighteenth-century Italian *commedia*

dell'arte troupes, white ruffs from Elizabethan England, Japanese prints and colors, Taiwanese paper bird kites, Indonesian puppetry, Japanese *bunraku*, and ancient Chinese mirror stone techniques (through her use of Plexiglas puppets).

The end result was an imaginative, colorful production that could not be defined by any one theatrical tradition. Similarly, her Broadway production of *The Lion King* used elements of numerous theatrical cultures from across Asia, especially from Indonesia and Japan; also prominent was music from South Africa. Many of the scenes combine actors, masks, and puppets, illustrating once again her distinctive fusion of numerous theatrical forms. Owing to the wide range of sources, her productions are not re-creations of any one theatrical source, but rather compositions drawn from theatrical traditions across the globe.

In 2011 the spectacular musical *Spiderman: Turn Off the Dark* opened on Broadway. Taymor was the original director as well as the co-author. More recently, in 2013, Taymor directed a new production of Shakespeare's *A Midsummer Night's Dream* at The Theatre for a New Audience in Brooklyn, New York.

Prepared by Naomi Stubbs, CUNY Graduate Center.

Julie Taymor (© Jerome Delay/AP Images)

MUSICALS IN TRANSITION

After the impressive outpouring of original musicals in the years during and just after World War II, the musical entered a period of transition. Important new musicals continued to appear but added to this were new forms: concept musicals, rock musicals, "juke box" musicals. Among the new musicals which echoed the traditional musicals of the past was *A Little Night Music* with lyrics and music by Stephen Sondheim. Seen here is a scene from a Broadway revival starring Angela Lansbury (center). (© Sara Krulwich/The New York Times/Redux)

In place of book musicals there were other approaches, one being the ***concept musical,*** in which a production is built around an idea or a theme rather than a story. A pioneer in developing the concept musical was the composer-lyricist Stephen Sondheim (b. 1930). A frequent collaborator with Sondheim was the director Harold Prince (b. 1928). Two examples of Sondheim's concept musicals are *Follies* (1971) and *Assassins* (1990). The first paid tribute of the stars and music of a bygone era, but also underscored a theme of the negative effects of the passing years in terms of nostalgia and self-delusion. *Assassins* was an examination in songs and scenes of the motives and delusions of people who murdered American presidents. In addition to his concept musicals, Sondheim has also written more traditional musicals, such as *A Little Night Music* (1973) and *Sweeney Todd, the Demon Barber of Fleet Street* (1979).

Occasionally a musical came up with a variation on old formulas and appeared to break fresh ground. Such a musical was *A Chorus Line,* which presents a group of aspiring dancers auditioning for a Broadway show. *A Chorus Line,* which was directed by Michael Bennett (1943–1987), opened in 1975 and ran until 1990. It was successfully revived on Broadway in 2006.

A Chorus Line symbolized the ascendancy of dancers and choreographers in the musical. Beginning with Jerome Robbins, the "vision" of musicals was furnished more and more by choreographers who had become directors. In addition to Robbins and Bennett, these included Bob Fosse, who directed *Sweet Charity* (1966) and *Pippin* (1972); and Tommy Tune (b. 1939), a performer and choreographer who won nine Tony Awards. Among the well-known musicals for which Tune provided choreography were *My One and Only* (1983), *Grand Hotel* (1990), and *Will Rogers' Follies* (1991). For the last two he was also the director. A more recent example of an outstanding director-choreographer is Susan Stroman (b. 1954), who was responsible for such musicals as *Contact* (1999), *Producers* (2001), and *Big Fish* (2013).

Concept musical A musical that is built around an idea or a theme rather than a story.

BRITISH MUSICALS
Musicals created in Great Britain took center stage on both sides of the Atlantic in the era beginning in the early 1970s and continuing through the next two decades. The best-known composer of these was Andrew Lloyd Webber, who wrote the music for *Cats* and for *Phantom of the Opera.* Both were presented by the British producer Cameron Mackintosh. The era of the British musicals also included such productions as *Les Misérables,* shown here with Alexander Gemignani as Valjean and the cast. (© Sara Krulwich/The New York Times/Redux)

Still another trend of the 1970s and 1980s was the emergence of British composers and lyricists in the creation of musicals. The composer Andrew Lloyd Webber (b. 1948) and the lyricist Tim Rice (b. 1944) wrote *Jesus Christ Superstar* (1971) and *Evita* (1979), the story of Eva Perón of Argentina. Webber also wrote the music for *Cats* (1982), *The Phantom of the Opera* (1987), and *Sunset Boulevard* (1993). Two other large-scale British musicals of the period were *Les Misérables* (1986), originally conceived in France, and *Miss Saigon* (1989). In 2008 *Billy Elliot* and in 2013 *Matilda* arrived from Britain.

MUSICALS FROM 1990 TO THE PRESENT

In musical theatre from 1990 to the present, four trends are discernible. One is the unprecedented number of major revivals of past musical successes. One reason for the increase in revivals has been the rising cost of producing musicals, which has led producers to present tried and true musical classics that are considered

PLAYING YOUR PART: EXPERIENCING THEATRE

1. Think of a musical performance you have attended: a musical theatre piece, a rock concert, a serious choral or symphony performance. Contrast the experience of being at the event in person—the feelings, the emotions, the sensations, the thoughts—that were part of the experience that would have not been the same when watching the same performance on video.

2. Take a drama or comedy with which you are familiar (or a novel or a recent news story) and explain how you might go about translating it into to a musical performance for the stage. What characters would be involved? Where would it begin? Imagine several songs, their subject matter or titles. Would there be dancing? Of what type?

3. Discuss a stage musical you have seen. Was it a positive experience, or not? What was the high point? The low point? Which performers did you like best? Which ones did you like least? Explain your answers. If you were going to change one thing about it, what would it be?

4. Is there a song that you think might best represent a significant moment in your life? Why?

safe investments. At the same time, this is a clear indication that there has not been the same output of new work as in earlier years. On the positive side, the trend confirms that these outstanding musicals from the past form part of an important heritage and have lasting value.

A second trend—a refreshing counterpoint to the rush of revivals—has been the periodic appearance of fresh, off-beat musicals, indicating that the genre remains full of vitality. For example, *Rent* (1996), about a group of antiestablishment young people, won numerous awards, including the Pulitzer Prize and the Tony Award for best musical of the year. Another example is *Avenue Q,* a lively, iconoclastic musical featuring puppets operated by onstage characters. Two others are *In the Heights* and *Next to Normal.* Winner of the 2008 Tony Award, *In the Heights* covers three days in the lives of characters in the Dominican American section of Washington Heights in Manhattan, and features hip-hop, meringue, salsa, and soul music. *Next to Normal,* which was awarded the 2009 Tony Award, concerns a mother who is struggling with bipolar disorder and the effects her disease has on her family. As her condition worsens, other concerns surface—suicide, drug abuse, psychiatric ethics—none of which are typical subjects for a musical.

A third trend has been musicals based on films. This list would include *The Producers, Monty Python's Spamalot, Hairspray, Young Frankenstein, Billy Elliott, Once, Kinky Boots, Big Fish* and musicals presented by the Disney organization, such as *The Lion King* and *Mary Poppins.*

The fourth trend is the creation of productions out of the music of former popular stars and groups, sometimes referred to as "jukebox" musicals. The most successful of these has been *Mamma Mia!*—a story taking place in the Greek islands and based on the music of the group ABBA. The music of Billy Joel formed the basis of Twyla Tharp's dance musical *Moving Out.* In the years that followed, show after show was created by stringing together hits from one music group or another, good examples being *Jersey Boys* (2005) and *Motown* (2013). *American Idiot* (2009) creates a musical around the rock group Green Day's recording.

photo essay

The Diverse American Musical

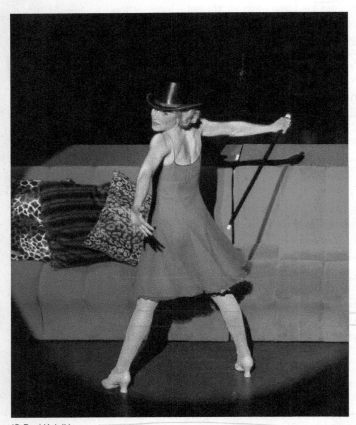

(© Paul Kolnik)

The modern American musical has covered a wide range of subjects, some lighthearted but others quite serious. Also, American musicals have embraced different styles—some reminiscent of operetta, some comic, some avant-garde. Shown here are examples of the diversity of musicals through the years.

Christina Applegate as Charity Hope Valentine in *Sweet Charity*, a traditional effervescent American musical.

A Funny Thing Happened on the Way to the Forum, by Stephen Sondheim, is based on Roman farce and so it is a musical with a classic source in the tradition of pure entertainment. This scene is from a production at the Paper Mill Playhouse in New Jersey.

(© T Charles Erickson)

A serious musical, *Fiddler on the Roof* by Jerry Bock and Sheldon Harnick, is based on the Jewish experience in czarist Russia in 1905, when Jewish tradition and even survival are put to a severe test. Here, Alfred Molina plays the lead role of Tevye.

(© Carol Rosegg)

© Sara Krulwich/The New York Times/Redux

A landmark musical was *West Side Story,* based on Shakespeare's *Romeo and Juliet,* with direction and choreography by Jerome Robbins, music by Leonard Bernstein, and lyrics and music by Stephen Sondheim and Arthur Laurents. Shown here in a revival marking the show's fiftieth anniversary is Karen Olivo, center, in the role of Anita.

PLAYING YOUR PART: THINKING ABOUT THEATRE

1. Musical theatre can be of several types: classic Broadway musicals, such as *My Fair Lady*; musicals that address serious issues, such as *Next to Normal*; musicals based on films, such as *Hairspray*; musicals resembling operettas, such as *Phantom of the Opera*; and musicals emphasizing dance, such as *A Chorus Line*. Which of these do you enjoy the most?

2. Musicals contain many different elements, including story, songs, dance, and spectacular visual effects. Is one of these more important, or should one be more prominent, than the others?

3. What is your favorite stage musical? Which element or elements make it stand out in your mind?

At the same time, original musicals have continued to appear: elaborate spectacles such as *Wicked* (2003) and *Spiderman: Turn off the Dark* (2011) as well as popular musicals such as *The Book of Mormon* (2011). There are also a number of contemporary musical theatre composers who build on the traditions of the American musical, including: Adam Guettel (b. 1964), Jeanine Tesori (b. 1961), Michael John LaChiusa (b. 1961), and Andrew Lippa (b. 1964).

It is clear that the musical theatre scene at the present time is a patchwork quilt, featuring old and new, revues and book musicals, imports and original material. All in all, the musical remains a mainstay of Broadway, and of those large theatres across the United States that feature shows with music, dance, spectacular scenery, and well-known performers.

MUSICALS IN THE NEW CENTURY

In the early twenty-first century, the American musical scene was a cross section of different types of musicals: old and new, classic and experimental, serious and comic. An example of a contemporary musical is *The Book of Mormon*, written by Trey Parker and Matt Stone, the music by Robert Lopez. Josh Gad, Nikki James, and Andrew Rannells are in the foreground in this scene. The musical featured a traditional approach mixed with irreverent subject matter.
(© Sara Krulwich/The New York Times/Redux)

SUMMARY

1. At many points in theatre history, music and dance have been combined with drama. An important art form, related to theatre, is opera, which is a drama set entirely to music.

2. In addition to opera, types of musical theatre include *operetta,* scenes of spoken dialogue alternating with songs; *musical comedy,* a light, comic story interspersed with popular music; the *musical,* also known as *musical theatre,* which evolved from musical comedy; and the *revue,* a series of individual, independent songs and comic sketches.

3. The modern musical is largely an American creation—the only theatrical form developed primarily in the United States.

4. There were many forerunners of the modern musical in the nineteenth century and early twentieth century, including operetta, vaudeville, burlesque, and the minstrel show.

5. During the 1920s and 1930s, musical comedy emerged: comic, sometimes silly stories that had glorious music with intelligent, witty lyrics, written by people like Irving Berlin, Jerome Kern, Cole Porter, Richard Rodgers, and Lorenz Hart.

6. The period from the early 1940s to the late 1960s was the golden age of the American musical, with a profusion of successful shows, many of them modern classics. These musicals integrated dancing and singing to form an overall structure that had great variety as well as unity.

7. In the past three decades, musical theatre has become fragmented: fewer book musicals are being produced; choreographer-directors rather than writers or directors have been responsible for the total vision of the show; experiments are being made with other forms, such as the concept musical; and more musicals are being imported from Great Britain.

8. Current trends in musical theatre include (a) revivals, (b) off-beat or experimental musicals, (c) musicals made from films, and (d) musicals made from the songs of a popular composer or group.

Global Theatre Today

In approaching global theatre, three points should be kept in mind. The first is that in many cultures, theatre has a long, illustrious history. Unlike American theatre, which has a relatively short history, world theatre goes back more than 2,000 years in both Europe and Asia. In Europe, preceding contemporary theatre, the theatre tradition of the past begins with Greek theatre and moves through Roman, medieval, Renaissance, eighteenth century, and nineteenth century theatre into modern theatre. In Asia, theatre in India began earlier than 2,000 years ago, and Chinese theatre a few centuries after that; Japanese theatre was established by 800 BCE.

In other parts of the world—for instance, in Africa, in pre-Columbian Latin America, and in the Native American culture of North America—there are rich traditions of rituals and ceremonies imbued with theatrical elements: costumes, song and dance, and impersonation of people, animals, and divinities.

When we look at European, Asian, and other theatres, therefore, we are looking at a tradition preceding the theatre that exists in those parts of the world today. At various points in *The Theatre Experience,* we have referred to some of these theatres and to their playwrights, stage spaces, production practices, and acting companies. In this chapter, we will concentrate on contemporary theatre throughout the world outside the United States, not just in Europe and Asia, but in Africa and other parts of the Americas as well.

A second point to be borne in mind is that beginning around 1900, Asian and other non-European theatres were influenced by developments of modern theatre in the West: the realism introduced by Ibsen, Strindberg, and Chekhov, and a number of departures from realism, such as expressionism. Thus in a country like Japan you had the traditional theatre of nō and Kabuki alongside modern theatre.

◀ **AN INTERNATIONAL CANADIAN DIRECTOR**

Robert Lepage is well known for directing both theatre and opera. A Canadian who has worked throughout Europe as well as in Canada and the U.S., Lepage is particularly well known for his creations for the theatre companies of Cirque du Soleil. A mixture of elements from many dramatic disciplines, as well as the joining of Asian and Western features together with circus elements, mark many of his productions. In 2009, Lepage presented The Blue Dragon, *a sequel to his Dragon's Trilogy twenty years later, in which he reprised the role of a Quebec artist living in China. Shown here from that production in London is Tai Wei Foo. (© Geraint Lewis)*

The third point, and in many ways, the most significant point for modern audiences, is the development of global exchanges—in communication, in ideas, in commerce, and in the arts. Thomas Friedman, in his book *The World Is Flat,* analyzes how globalization has affected business and industry in contemporary society. One can no longer tell whether a product is made by a company of a specific country, since most major corporations are multinational. The automobile industry clearly reflects the trend toward industrial globalization, as does the personal computer industry. A car created today by a Japanese, Korean, or German manufacturer may be assembled in the United States. A PC may be assembled in the United States, but the 24-hour help desk may be located in India.

The same is true in today's theatre. Many diverse groups influence one another to create the contemporary theatrical landscape. Theatre artists cross national boundaries to stage their works with artists of other countries. Popular works tour the world and cross-pollinate other theatrical ventures. International theatre festivals bring artists of various nationalities to interact with those in the host community.

The global nature of today's theatre can be seen in the offerings each summer at the International Theatre Festival at Lincoln Center in New York City. Productions from all parts of the world are presented side by side. In recent years the countries represented have included Japan, Indonesia, China, Singapore, Switzerland, Germany, Ireland, Argentina, Chile, Spain, Mexico, Italy, and France. Experimental artists appropriate the styles and techniques of traditional theatres from around the world. Artists mix and match all sorts of styles, historical antecedents, materials, and techniques.

What this suggests is that we can no longer easily classify theatre productions and artists by specific national designations. Ease of travel, electronic communication, and the commerce of theatre have all led to a blurring of national theatres. Like the global

INTERNATIONAL THEATRE FESTIVALS
A sure sign of the increasing reach and importance of global theatre is the growing popularity of international theatre festivals. In more and more countries around the world such festivals are taking a featured place on the arts scene. This scene depicts a street performance of *The Giraffes* by the French company "Off" at the International Festival of theatre, "Santiago a Mil," in Santiago, Chile, in early 2013. (© Jorge Villegas/Xinhua/Eyevine/Redux)

economy, theatre today is a global activity. In order to bring some structure to our discussion, we will organize this chapter along traditional national boundaries. However, we will frequently point to the global interplay and impact of the various theatre artists and companies.

THEATRES IN INDIA, CHINA, AND JAPAN IN THE MODERN PERIOD

The Asian continent is immense and includes roughly 40 countries and hundreds of ethnicities, languages, and theatre traditions. In the limited space of this book, it would be impossible to do justice to such diversity and multiplicity. Therefore, we will confine our discussion to three Asian countries: India, China, and Japan. In all three countries, traditional theatre continues today: *kathakali* in India, Beijing (Peking) opera in China, and *nō* and *kabuki* in Japan. But the influences of Western theatre are undeniable. As in Latin America, Asian countries were influenced in the early twentieth century by Western dramatic forms, particularly the modernist traditions of realism and departures from realism. The colonial influence also led to a weakening of the traditional forms of theatrical practice, both popular and classical.

Following World War I, there was a politicization of Asian theatres. Some theatre artists opposed Western influences and the colonial mentality. As a result, in the past half century, there has been a unique return of traditional forms blended into the sociopolitical sensibilities of Asian theatre artists. This return to traditional forms, in itself, is a rejection of colonial and postcolonial Western intrusions into the continent.

In India several changes occurred a few decades into the twentieth century. For one thing, World War I was disruptive. Perhaps more pervasive, though, was the advent of cinema. In India, film became extremely popular, from the standpoint of both producers and consumers. Films began to be produced in great numbers, and audiences flocked to them. These productions feature theatrical staging, lighting, costumes, and choreography and are often referred to as "Bollywood" films. The term combines Hollywood, the center of American cinema, with the Indian city Bombay (now Mumbai). At mid-century, this trend, and the effects of World War II, led to a decrease in professional theatre in many parts of India.

The theatre in India that emerged in the latter half of the twentieth century was primarily an amateur theatre. It is estimated that Calcutta has as many as 3,000 registered amateur theatre groups, Mumbai perhaps has as many as 500, and Madras at least 50. Many of these theatres do not have a permanent home, but some do. Also, some of them present professional-quality theatre. Moreover, these theatres keep alive plays written by Indian playwrights, past and present, as well as plays from other nations. There was also a strain of experimental theatre in India, led by such figures as Badal Sircar (1925–2011), whose plays reflect the experience of urban life in India.

In China after the civil war and Mao Zedong's rise to power following World War II in 1949, spoken drama continued to be written, but additional emphasis was given to traditional forms of popular theatre. These traditional forms were familiar in the countryside and became a medium for carrying messages from the government to remote corners of the nation. During the Cultural Revolution, which began in 1966, theatrical activity—particularly spoken drama—was more restricted; increasing emphasis was placed on a few dance-dramas, elaborately staged and performed, that had very heavy ideological or propagandistic content. For the most part, theatre artists, along with intellectuals, were seen as subversive and suffered greatly during this era in Chinese history.

Since the death of Mao, and the opening up of China to the West in the late 1970s, there has been cross-fertilization between Chinese traditions and Western drama. Theatre artists from the United States and Europe have visited and performed in China. Arthur Miller, for example, directed a production of *Death of a Salesman* in Beijing in 1983. These Western influences can be seen in plays like *The Peach Blossom Fan,* by Ouyang Yuqian (1889–1962), which tells the story of the romance between a high-class courtesan and an army general in the late Ming dynasty; and *Jesus, Confucius, and John Lennon* by Sha Yexin (b. 1939), a play about the absurdities Christ, Confucius, and Lennon encounter during their travels on the moon and around the world as representatives of God.

A CHINESE AMERICAN PRODUCTION
A prime example of international cooperation in theatre was *Cathay: Three Tales of China,* a production created jointly by the American avant-garde director Ping Chong and the Shaanxi Folk Art Theatre of Xian, China. An innovative, experimental theatre director and producer, Ping Chong has developed more than fifty productions with his company in the past three decades. *Cathay,* which featured puppet figures, was a satisfying collaboration, taking the best from two theatrical cultures. (© Richard Termine)

In addition to new drama, traditional forms, such as Beijing (Peking) opera and other forms of classic music-drama, which were repressed during Mao's rule, are becoming popular again. While much of today's Chinese drama still remains socialist in point of view and realistic in style, there have been a number of artists who push the boundaries of subject matter and style, fusing classical traditions with contemporary forms and issues. Ping Chong's puppet theatre production with the Shaanxi Folk Art Theatre of Xian, China, *Cathay: Three Tales of China* (2005), is just one example of the merging of avant-garde and traditional forms in contemporary China.

Since the end of World War II, contemporary theatre in Japan has thrived. A number of truly gifted playwrights have emerged, chief among them Kinoshita Junji (1914–2006), whose work combines social concerns with humor and, when appropriate, with elements from Japanese folk tradition. In his play *Twilight Crane,* for example, he weaves a story of greed and loss using the central image of a crane, which in Japanese culture is a symbol of long life.

In the second half of the twentieth century there were three main branches of theatre in Japan. One was traditional theatre—*nō, bunraku,* and *kabuki,* of which the most active was *kabuki.* Despite Western influences, these three ancient theatre traditions in Japan have remained vital and active today.

A second branch consisted of various manifestations of **shingeki,** a word that means "new theatre." *Shingeki* began in the late nineteenth century and in one form or another continued throughout the twentieth century. Broadly speaking, it was a modern theatre, in contrast to the traditional classic theatres. For one thing, it was more realistic than the traditional theatres. In addition, at the beginning it was influenced by such western playwrights as Ibsen and Chekhov. In the early twentieth century, *shingeki* banished the gods and the fantastic from theatre, partly because they had played such a large role in classic theatre. Later, after World War II, nonrealistic elements were admitted to *shingeki* dramas. Despite its changes and Western influences, *shingeki* remains a theatre in which the playwright is a central figure. In recent years it has included female playwrights, who were almost nonexistent in earlier times. Among Japan's contemporary playwrights are: Shoji Kokami (b. 1958), whose plays have been staged in England; Noda Hideki (b. 1955); and Keralino Sandorovich (born Kazumi Kobayashi in 1963).

Shinkgeki Modern Japanese theatre.

The third strain of modern Japanese theatre has been avant-garde or experimental theatre. A good example of this movement is the work of Tadashi Suzuki, who began his work at Waseda University in Tokyo and then developed a theatre community in the mountains at Toga. (A profile of Suzuki appears in the nearby Global Connections box.) Other theatre figures created their own brand of avant-garde work, some of it paralleling that being done in the west, but some distinctly Japanese. One example is the performance artist Issei Ogata (b. 1952), whose one-man shows underscore the humor in everyday situations: for example, an inebriated businessman attempting to catch a taxi, or a father overwhelmed by the responsibility of looking after his children.

During the past century, though at times having to overcome interruptions and censorship, theatre throughout Asia has continued to evolve to reflect political and social changes. Asian theatre today acknowledges and celebrates the traditions that established roots for the work of contemporary artists like Tadashi Suzuki and Issei Ogata, whose productions reveal and document life in Asia today.

IN FOCUS: GLOBAL CONNECTIONS

Tadashi Suzuki: Japanese Internationalist

Among important international theatre artists, a key figure is Tadashi Suzuki (b. 1939), a director, writer, and teacher who calls Japan his home but has worked with and influenced artists around the world. Suzuki first attracted attention as a part of Japan's *Shōgekijō undō,* or "little theatre movement," in the 1960s and 1970s. *Shōgekijō* was a response to what was seen as the restrictive realism and limited viewpoint of *shingeki,* the Japanese retelling of Western theatre. Like proponents of "little theatre" and avant-garde movements in the West, *shōgekijō* artists largely rejected the mainstream, preferring smaller, more adventurous audiences who were willing to engage with provocative, experimental material.

The directors Shūji Terayama (1935–1983), Shogo Ohta (1939–2007), and Yukio Ninagawa (b. 1935) were also part of this movement. Today, Tadashi Suzuki is among the world's most famous theatre directors. His Suzuki Company of Toga, in the mountains of Japan, is well known for combining stories and traditions from various cultures; this includes creating theatre pieces that remain distinctively Japanese while also entering into conversation with theatres across the globe. His work frequently comments as well on international political situations. In addition to his own company in Japan, Suzuki cofounded the SITI company in 1992, with the prominent American director Anne Bogart (b. 1951).

Exemplifying Suzuki's international work are his productions of Euripides's *The Bacchae.* In 1981, Suzuki worked with students at the University of Wisconsin to develop a dual-language version of the play, which he had been working on in Japan for a number of years. In this production, the American actors spoke English and the Japanese actors spoke Japanese, the characters responding as if they understood each other. The production also emphasized the cyclical nature of violence and power, suggesting that one tyrant dies only to be replaced by another.

Beginning in 1991, Suzuki introduced *Dionysus,* a new adaptation of the play that focused on the clash between religion and government. This production was widely interpreted as a comment on the escalating violence in the Middle East in general and on the wars between the United States and Iraq more specifically. Suzuki's actors are praised for their onstage presence and incredible athleticism. His actor-training system, the Suzuki method, combines elements of traditional Japanese theatre techniques with the experimental work that emerged from international theatre in the 1960s and 1970s. Actors spend a great deal of time focusing on their feet and the ground beneath them, building strength, flexibility, and balance through a physical connection to the earth. Many observers feel that Suzuki's most lasting impact on world theatre will be his work on actor training.

Prepared by Frank Episale, CUNY Graduate Theatre Program.

Tadashi Suzuki's *Electra,* after the Greek playwright Euripides, with Yukiko Saito in the title role. (© Jack Vartoogian/FrontRowPhotos)

THEATRES IN THE MIDDLE EAST

Although the Islamic religion has strong prohibitions against theatre, there have always been traditions of storytelling, folklore, and popular comedy throughout the Middle East, before Islamic times and since. In Turkey and Egypt, for example, religious stories were often brought to life with the use of shadow puppets. Professional storytellers would also relate tales of religious or historic events to audiences, often accompanied by musical instruments. It wasn't until the nineteenth century, however, that stage theatre was embraced as a popular means for conveying life in the Middle East. Today theatre in the Arab world is greatly affected by the politics of the region.

As in Asia and Latin America, the close of the nineteenth century and the beginning of the twentieth century saw a rise in Western colonial influence on the theatres of the Arab Middle East. The adaptation of historic events into plays became very popular. Three early playwrights are widely credited with the introduction of Western dramatic techniques into the Arab world: the Lebanese author Marun al-Naqqash (1817–1855), who combined drama with opera in his work, such as his interpretation of Molière's *L'Avare*; Abu Khalil al-Qabbani (c. 1841–1902), a Syrian who came to Egypt after his theatre was closed in Damascus; and Ya'qub Sannu (1839–1912), a Jewish-Egyptian dramatist. Western influence was particularly prevalent in the years following World War I.

After World War II and through the 1970s, there was significant development of professional theatrical activity throughout the Middle Eastern region, including Egypt, Iran, Syria, Lebanon, and Iraq. The theatres of these countries continued to be influenced by Western practices and artists, and a good deal of theatrical cross-fertilization occurred. Iran, for example, hosted the Shiraz Arts Festival through the 1970s until the Islamic revolution in 1979. The festival featured works by such notable Western artists as Peter Brook, Jerzy Grotowski, and Robert Wilson, and many of these works clearly reflected the influence of Middle Eastern theatre and literature. However, the works of many Arab theatre artists were highly nationalistic during this era and returned to traditional folk materials; examples are the works of the Iraqi playwright-director Qassim Mohammed (b. 1935).

With the rise of Islamic fundamentalism and totalitarianism in many of these countries, theatrical activities have been halted, significantly curtailed, or rigidly controlled by the state. For example, Iraq's war with Iran in the 1980s and economic hardships after the Persian Gulf War in the early 1990s severely damaged Iraq's theatrical infrastructure. The invasion and occupation of Iraq by the United States and Britain beginning in 2003 did not help matters. In Saudi Arabia, the state-sponsored Saudi Society for Culture and Arts, established in 1972, oversees much theatrical activity; however, there is great controversy over its support of theatrical art.

There are currently a number of significant theatre artists who deal with the contemporary political turmoil of the Middle East, including the ongoing battles with Israel, particularly in Egypt and in the Palestinian territories. In Jordan, the Ministry of Culture has sponsored annual theatre festivals, and there have also been independent festivals that bring together theatre artists from many parts of the Arab world.

Egyptian theatre, which has influenced and been influenced by Middle Eastern artists, is discussed in the section on Africa.

There has been Palestinian theatre since the 1850s, but historians have focused most on theatrical activities since the Israeli occupation in 1967. Many companies and playwrights have created theatrical works that express the Palestinian point of view toward Israel's control of the West Bank and, until recently, Gaza. A Palestinian company that is gaining international recognition from its visits to the Royal Court Theatre in London is Al-Kasaba Theatre, originally founded in Jerusalem in 1970 but now located in Ramallah in the occupied West Bank. In 2001, Al-Kasaba staged *Alive from Palestine: Stories behind the Headlines,* which consists of a series of monologues dealing with the intifada, the Palestinian uprising against Israel. The company's artistic director is George Ibrahim.

Two other productions that reflect the Palestinians' existence under Israeli occupation are *The Alley* (1992), a one-woman production written and performed by Samia Qazmouz al-Bakri, which focuses on the lives of Palestinian women since 1948; and *We Are the Children of the Camp* (2000) by al-Rowwad Theatre for Children in the Aida refugee camp near Bethlehem. This production, performed primarily by children, toured the United States in 2005. Among the other Palestinian theatre companies operating today are Ashtar Theatre and Freedom Theatre, founded in the Jenin Refugee camp in the West Bank.

With the recent political upheavals in many Arab Nations, known as the Arab Spring, which began in 2010, a number of young playwrights have dramatized emerging issues. They include: Mohammad Al Attar (Syria), Kamal Khalladi (Morocco), Arzé Khodr (Lebanon), Laila Soliman (Egypt), and Elyes Labidi (Tunisia).

Israeli theatre has developed since the founding of the state of Israel in 1948. Israeli drama has been influenced by the eastern European origins of many of its founders as well as the Middle Eastern traditions of those Jews who left Arab nations to settle in the Jewish state.

THEATRE IN THE MIDDLE EAST

In countries of the Middle East in recent years, theatre has often been struggling because so much of the region is in turmoil. One theatre that has remained relatively stable is the Habima National Theatre in Tel Aviv, Israel. Declared a national theatre in 1958, it has occupied a renovated theatre building at its original location since 2012. Shown here is a scene from a Habima production of Shakespeare's *The Merchant of Venice* presented in Hebrew with Jacob Cohen in the role of Shylock at Shakespeare's Globe in London. (© Tristram Kenton/Lebrecht Music & Arts/The Image Works)

One national theatre of Israel is the Habimah, which was established in Russia in the early twentieth century and settled in what was then British-controlled Palestine in 1931. The other large national theatre in Israel is the Tel Aviv Municipal Theatre, referred to as the Cameri, founded in 1944 by the director Yossef Milo (b. 1916). There are many other active Israeli theatres throughout the country—in Tel Aviv, Jerusalem, Haifa, and elsewhere. These theatres also reflect the diverse Jewish populations in Israel. For example, the Gesher Theatre, founded in Tel Aviv in 1991, consisted mostly of new Russian immigrants.

As in Europe and the United States, there are also smaller fringe theatrical groups, which experiment with avant-garde techniques, and performance artists. Most of the theatres in Israel receive some governmental subsidy. Israeli drama reflects the tumultuous history of the nation. There are also alternative theatre groups and many are showcased in the annual Acco Festival for Alternative Theatre in Acre.

Early Israeli drama dealt with the establishment of the state and nationalism. More recent dramatic works explore the complexities of Middle Eastern politics, including Israel's relationship with the Palestinians. In the 1950s, Israel's best-known playwrights were Aharon Megged (b. 1920) and the poet Leah Goldberg (1915–1970). Nissim Aloni (1926–1998), in the 1950s and 1960s, was Israel's first author to focus exclusively on theatre. In the 1970s and 1980s, Hanoch Levin (1943–1999) was a prominent playwright and director, who focused on issues of hypocrisy and self-delusion in Israel society. The most internationally recognized Israeli dramatist is Joshua Sobol (b. 1939), whose play *Ghetto* (1984) was produced throughout the world. In the 1980s, Sobol served as an artistic director with the Municipal Theatre in Haifa, frequently combining Israeli and Palestinian actors in controversial productions. Among the other Israeli playwrights who have achieved productions across the world are Motti Lerner (b. 1949) and the female playwright Anat Gov (1954–2012). Currently, the Israel Playwrights Association, which requires the production of at least two plays in professional theatres for membership, has 50 members.

AFRICAN THEATRES AND DRAMA

Early African societies had many traditional performances connected to ceremonies and rituals that employed music, song, and dance. Colorful, exotic, symbolic costumes were a key element of many rituals and ceremonies. African theatre artists in the twentieth century used these traditional forms and subverted forms of popular Western theatre in order to create works that reflected the anticolonial struggles as well as attacks against totalitarian regimes in the newly independent African nations.

Contemporary African theatre and society are divided into English-speaking Africa; French-speaking Africa; Portuguese-speaking Africa; and Arabic-speaking Africa, which includes the northern African countries Egypt, Tunisia, Algeria, and Morocco. In these nations that were originally defined by nineteenth-century European colonial powers, there are a multiplicity of cultures and languages that transcend the arbitrary colonial boundaries, and some African theatre has experimented with the indigenous languages of Africa.

In Portuguese-speaking Africa, which includes Angola, Cape Verde, Guinea-Bissau, Mozambique, and São Tomé and Principe, missionaries introduced religious drama in order to spread Catholicism. Before independence in 1975, much of the theatre in these regions was like vaudeville, although some anticolonial dramas were written as well. After independence, there was a greater focus on theatre that would arouse social consciousness, and plays followed the model of agitprop dramas; theatrical companies created collaborative works that focused on political and social issues. In Angola, for example, the National School of Theatre was founded in 1976 and staged works that focused on African liberation.

Among the best-known works from Portuguese-speaking Africa are *The Devil's Skin* (Angola, 1977) by Manuel Santos Lima b. 1935; *Bombo's Chalk Circle* (Angola, 1979) by Henrique Guerra; *The Old Man Is Untouchable* (Angola, 1980) by Costa Andrade; *Shameless* (Cape Verde, 1979) by Donald Pereira de Macedo; and plays by the Mozambican author Orlando Mendes (1916–1990).

French-speaking (francophone) Africa includes areas south of the Sahara as well as some nations in northern Africa. There is a vital theatre in the sub-Saharan nations, influenced by traditional forms of storytelling and music as well as by French theatre traditions. Many of the plays written in this part of French-speaking Africa have been produced in festivals organized in Paris. In addition, some of these African plays were also read and performed in New York during the 1990s by the off-off-Broadway Ubu Repertory Theatre. The plays of this region usually focus on historical chronicles, social concerns, and political circumstances. Among the most significant playwrights of this region are Senegal's Cheik Ndao (b. 1933), the Ivory Coast's Bernard Dadié (b. 1916), the Congo's Sony Labou Tansi ((1947–1995)) and Felix Tchicaya U'Tamsi (1931–1988), Cameroon's Guillaume Oyono-Mbia (b. 1939), and Togo's Senouvo Zinsou (b. 1946). Theatre in French-speaking Africa also received international attention when such well-known directors as Roger Blin and Peter Brook employed actors from this region in their productions.

English-speaking (anglophone) Africa, which includes Nigeria, South Africa, Kenya, Uganda, Zimbabwe, and Zambia, among others, has had a significant international impact. Anglophone theatre became more highly developed in the 1950s because of the influence of universities in this region that encouraged the work of dramatists and also organized traveling theatre troupes.

Among the influences on the theatre of English-speaking Africa are traditional forms, popular theatre, and the indigenous languages of the peoples; in fact, there has been considerable debate over whether theatre should be created in the language of the African peoples or in English. Among the leading theatre artists from anglophone Africa are the Nigerians Hubert Ogunde (1916–1990), the playwright who is often cited as the founder of modern Nigerian theatre; Moses Olaiya Adejumo (b. 1936), an actor-manager; and Olu Obafemi (b. 1951), a playwright, director, and actor. Among the leading playwrights in Zimbabwe are S. J. Chifunyise (b. 1948), Ben Shibenke (b. 1945), and Thompson Tsodzo (b. 1947).

In Kenya, the playwright Ngugi wa Thiong'o (b. 1938), who has created individual and collaborative works in Kenyan languages, was arrested by the oppressive government between 1977 and 1978 and forced to live in exile. South Africa produced many significant playwrights and theatre companies in the 1970s, including the Market Theatre, People's Space Theatre, and Junction Avenue Theatre Company; these companies frequently produced works that questioned South Africa's apartheid.

Concern for political and social equality is at the heart of the works of the South African playwright Athol Fugard (b. 1932) and the Nigerian playwright Wole Soyinka (b. 1934), and these two authors have become the most internationally renowned of all

AFRICAN THEATRE: WOLE SOYINKA

A major African playwright of the past half century is the Nigerian Wole Soyinka, who is also a poet and author. Soyinka won the Nobel Prize for Literature in 1986. Before that he had been imprisoned in Nigeria for his political views. Mixing traditional African ceremonial elements with modern themes and characters is the play shown here, *Death and the King's Horseman*. It featured Nonso Anozie (as Elesin, Horseman of the King, center) and was recently presented in London. (© Elliott Franks/ArenaPAL/The Image Works)

contemporary African playwrights. Fugard, who is white, attacked apartheid in such plays as *The Blood Knot* (1964), *Sizwe Banzi Is Dead* (1973), *Master Harold . . . and the Boys* (1982), *A Lesson from Aloes* (1987), and *Playland* (1992). Some of Fugard's early works, such as *Sizwe Banzi* and *Statements after an Arrest under the Immorality Act* (1972), were written in collaboration with black actors. His works represent the racial turmoil of South Africa during apartheid and also in postapartheid South Africa.

Another significant African playwright is the Nigerian Wole Soyinka, who is also a poet, essayist, and novelist. Soyinka began his career with the Royal Court Theatre in London in the late 1950s. His politically charged works led to his arrest in Nigeria in 1967, and to two years' imprisonment. In 1973, he adapted Euripides's *The Bacchae* for the National Theatre in England. Soyinka gained international recognition in 1986, when he received the Nobel Prize in literature. Among his best-known dramas are *The Swamp Dwellers* (1957), *The Road* (1965), *Death and the King's Horsemen* (1975), and *Play of Giants* (1985).

In recent years an important group of dramatists, writing in Arabic, has emerged in the countries of northern Africa. This group includes two Egyptian playwrights, Alfred Farag (1929–2005), the leading Egyptian playwright of the post-1952 revolution period, and Lenin El-Ramely (b. 1945), considered Egypt's leading comic dramatist. The Tunisian dramatist Jalila Baccar (b. 1952) is an author, director, and actress in films and television as well as onstage. Her Tunisian company has been featured in festivals in Europe and the United States. The Algerian playwright Abdelkader Alloula (1929–1994) was his country's leading dramatist after its independence and was assassinated by extremists in 1994. Tayed Saddiki (b. 1937) is considered the outstanding playwright in contemporary Morocco.

RUSSIA AND EASTERN EUROPE

A pivotal event for theatre in eastern Europe, as for so much else, was the fall of the Soviet Union in 1989–1991. From World War II until that time, theatre in Russia and the territories under its domination was a double-edged sword. On the one hand, there was state-supported theatre through much of the Soviet Union, which meant theatre was available as well as affordable. On the other hand, all theatrical activity was heavily censored and required to hew to the party line, with the result that experimentation, creativity, and protest were stifled if not eliminated altogether.

In the last two decades new theatrical energy has emerged throughout the region; at the same time, there has been a struggle for financial support. The two theatrical centers in Russia itself remain Moscow and Saint Petersburg. Three important traditional theatres are still very much a presence in Moscow: the Moscow Art Theatre, the Maly (Small), and the theatre of Vakhtangov. Among newer well-known theatres are the Taganka, the theatre of Oleg Tabakov, and the first gay theatre in Russia: the Roman Viktiuk Theatre.

Among the leading contemporary playwrights in Russia, Lyudmila Petrushevskaya (b. 1938) specializes in three types of drama: plays that expose the shadowy part of life, including extreme loneliness; joke plays, often based on famous literary figures; and plays exploring relationship problems. Alexander Galin (b. 1947) wrote *Retro,* the most frequently performed drama in Russia in the 1980s. The Presnyakov brothers, Oleg (b. 1969) and Vladimir (b. 1974), write plays that are extremely controversial, featuring the brutal alienation of today's world depicted in strong language. And Yevgeni Grishkovetz (b. 1967) writes, stages, and performs theatre pieces that are extremely personal and refreshingly humorous.

Among other countries formerly under Soviet domination, several have long, vibrant traditions of theatrical activity that have been rekindled. Three examples are Poland, the Czech Republic (formerly a part of Czechoslovakia), and Romania. Poland, for instance, in the twentieth century had an extremely influential pre-absurdist, experimental playwright, Ignacy Witkiewicz (1855–1939), as well as an internationally celebrated director, Tadeusz Kantor (1915–1990). During the Nazi occupation Kantor founded the underground Independent Theatre. After the war, he formed his own theatre, Cricot 2, and in the 1960s he became widely known for staging happenings. In the 1970s, Kantor began creating his own theatre pieces; the most famous of these was *Dead Class* (1970). During the next two decades, Kantor toured the world with his company and his productions, which included *Where Are the Snows of Yesteryear* (1982), *Let the Artists Die* (1985), and *Today Is My Birthday* (1990).

In the Czech Republic, Josef Svoboda revolutionized scene design in the mid-twentieth century. (See the Global Connections that profiles Svoboda in the chapter on scene design.) The playwright Václav Havel (1936–2011) challenged communist and Soviet authorities in his plays; as a result he was attacked and imprisoned, and his works were banned. In 1989, when the Czech Republic emerged as an independent nation, Havel was elected president.

In Romania, auteur director Radu Afrim reinterprets and transforms classic texts to create extremely provocative theatre pieces. His version of Chekhov's *The Three Sisters,* for example, featured the sisters as scantily clad flash dancers, and his reworking of García Lorca's *The House of Bernarda Alba* took place in a timeless location totally removed from Spain. It also transformed the matronly Bernarda of that play into a glamorous figure who engages in Olympic-style gymnastics.

IN FOCUS: GLOBAL CONNECTIONS

Ariane Mnouchkine: Théatre du Soleil

Since her founding of the avant-garde Théatre du Soleil in Paris in 1964, the French director Ariane Mnouchkine (b. 1939) has become one of the most widely admired directors in Europe and, in fact, around the world. Although strongly influenced by Copeau, Brecht, Artaud, and Meyerhold, she is also known for her effective use of non-Western dramatic techniques, especially those of Japan and India. She was born in a small town near Paris, France, and attended Oxford University in England, majoring in psychology. There, she became involved with the Oxford University Drama Society and from that point on, her interest was theatre.

In the early 1960s, Mnouchkine scraped together enough money to realize a lifelong dream of traveling to the Far East. In Japan, Cambodia, and other parts of Asia, she found a beauty of form and a sense of ritual that she considered indispensable to theatre. When she returned to Paris in 1963, Mnouchkine and several of her friends established a "theatrical community," which was to become the Théatre du Soleil (Theatre of the Sun).

The company has produced everything from loose collections of improvised materials to acclaimed versions of Shakespeare's works to a powerful 10-hour staging of the *Oresteia*, the cycle of Greek tragedies about the house of Atreus. Mnouchkine is strongly in favor of the collaborative process in creating theatrical pieces. The director, she has stated, has become all powerful. Her goal, she says, "is to move beyond that situation by creating a form of theatre where it will be possible for everyone to collaborate without there being directors, technicians, and so on." She and her company use many techniques in developing their productions. These include improvisational exercises as well as styles such as *commedia dell'arte* and various Asian rituals.

Among the best-known collectively created productions of Théatre du Soleil are *1789* (1970), which environmentally dramatized the historical background of the French Revolution; *The Age of Gold* (1975); and *Les Atrides* (1991), the adaptation of the *Oresteia*. Among her most notable productions are *And Suddenly Sleepless Nights* (1997), which deals with the plight of illegal immigrants; the two-part, six-hour *Le Dernier Caravanserail (Odysees) (The Last Caravan Stop,* 2003), which deals with the hardships of refugees. For this last piece, she and members of her troupe spent three years collecting poignant and tragic stories from refugees from all parts of the world and then wove these stories into the drama. *Les Ephemeres* (2009) consists of a series of interwoven vignettes, chiefly about middle-class life in France.

A scene from *Les Éphémères,* with Camille Grandville, left, and Juliana Carneiro da Cunha. (Ruth Fremson/The New York Times/Redux)

WESTERN EUROPE, BRITAIN, AND IRELAND

When we turn from theatre of the past to contemporary theatre in the nations of Western Europe, countries such as France, Germany, Italy, and Spain, as well as Britain and Ireland, we find that in these countries today, theatre can be divided into three categories or realms.

One realm is classic theatre. Each nation has one or more theatres that continue to produce classics from the past. France, for example, has the Comédie Française in

Paris, which was founded in 1680, more than 300 years ago. Britain has not one but two national theatres: the Royal Shakespeare Company and the National Theatre.

A second category of ongoing theatre in Western Europe and Britain is modern theatre. It began in Europe in the late nineteenth century with the plays of Ibsen, Strindberg, and Chekhov and includes both the realistic drama of those playwrights and the many who followed them, as well as the nonrealistic drama that began at the same time and the playwrights who followed this path into such departures from realism as expressionism, surrealism, and absurdism.

A third category includes the many avant-garde and experimental works, sometimes produced by directors and sometimes by acting ensembles. It should be pointed out that in Western Europe as well as Britain and Ireland, all three strands are very much alive today. What follows is a brief look at playwrights, directors, and theatre companies in this part of the world.

In Germany an important director has been Peter Stein (b. 1937), who became known in the 1970s for postmodernist productions in which he reworked classical texts to heighten ideological statements he felt were inherent in them and to express his own political viewpoints. He often used techniques of Brecht, Artaud, and naturalism. From 1970 to 1985, Stein was the artistic director of Berlin's Schaubühne Theatre.

STEIN: POSTMODERN DIRECTOR
An important modern German director is Peter Stein, who became known for postmodernist productions in which he reworked classical texts to heighten ideological statements he felt were inherent in them and to express his own political viewpoint. One such production was Stein's version of *Faust* by Goethe. Shown here is the walpurgis night scene from that presentation. (© Ruth Walz)

BROOK'S *MARAT/SADE*
In the last half of the twentieth century, a number of creative, innovative directors emerged on the European continent and in Britain. In England, Peter Brook distinguished himself, first with Shakespeare, but then with far more experimental work. One of his bold productions, influenced by the theories of Antonin Artaud, was *Marat/Sade*, shown here; it was set in an insane asylum at the time of the French revolution. (© Dennis Stock/Magnum Photos)

In the mid-1980s Stein departed from his earlier experimentation and began to stage more traditional productions. Among his important recent productions are *Faust I & II* in 2000, Euripides's *Medea* at the 2005 Epidaurus Festival in Greece, *Blackbird* in 2005 at the Edinburgh Festival in Scotland, and *The Demons* in 2010.

Among German playwrights two important figures are Heiner Müller (1929–1995) and Peter Handke (b. 1942). Müller, who began his career in communist East Germany in the 1950s, became known for the short plays he wrote in the late 1970s and 1980s— explosions of images ridiculing traditional values and institutions. His most famous play is an Artaud-like scenario, *Hamletmachine* (1977). Handke's plays—including *Offending the Audience* (1966), *Ride across Lake Constance* (1970), *They Are Dying Out* (1973), and *Slow Homecoming* (1982)—focus on the shortcomings of language as a tool for communication and are surreal and symbolic in style.

In France there were a host of important playwrights throughout the twentieth century. One of the best-known of the newer playwrights is Yasmina Reza (b. 1959), whose plays include *Art* (1995) and *God of Carnage* (2007). Among French directors a signal figure is Ariane Mnouchkine, a profile of whom appears in this chapter. Another director who works in France, Peter Brook, is emblematic of the international, global nature of today's theatre. Brook is British and began his work in Britain, but he founded a theatre in Paris some years ago and has worked there ever since. Known as the International Centre for Theatre Research, it incorporates not only European actors but a number of performers from Africa and Asia as well.

A key Italian theatre figure is the Italian playwright Dario Fo (b. 1926), known for his satirical political comedies, which attack capitalist institutions and are reminiscent of the Greek playwright Aristophanes. Fo, with his wife, the actress Franca Rame (1929–2013), has run his own theatre companies, directing and acting in his plays. Among his best-known works are *The Accidental Death of an Anarchist* (1970); *We Won't Pay, We Won't Pay* (1974); and, with Franca Rame, *Female Parts* (1981). Fo won the Nobel Prize for literature in 1997.

A Spanish director who has received international acclaim is Calixto Bielto (b. 1963), who has staged radical reinterpretations of operas and texts. In 2012, he adapted Tennessee Williams's *Camino Real* for a postmodern production at the Goodman Theatre in Chicago.

Among the significant playwrights in England is Tom Stoppard (b. 1937), who continues to write dramas emphasizing wordplay and intellectual concerns. One of Stoppard's recent dramas in his long list of intellectually challenging and stimulating

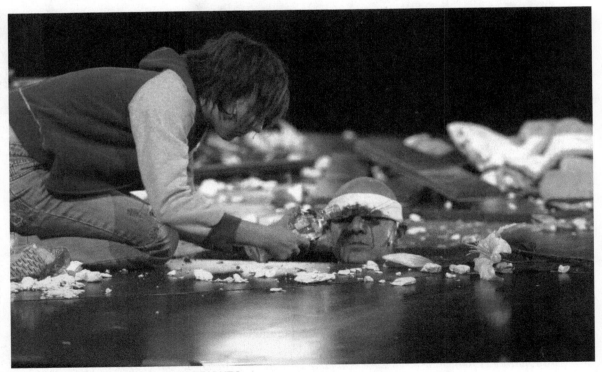

CONTEMPORARY WOMEN PLAYWRIGHTS
In the past quarter century, women playwrights have emerged throughout the English-speaking world. An award for the best new play in the English language, the Susan Smith Blackburn Prize, has coincided with this development. A play that was shocking to many people—though others applauded its honesty—was *Blasted* by Sarah Kane: it includes frank depictions of rape, torture, and cannibalism. Shown here, in a scene from a production at the Avignon theatre festival, are Katharina Schuettler and Ulrich Muehe. (The playwright hanged herself in 1999, at the age of twenty-eight.) (© Anne-Christine Poujoulat/ Agence France-Presse/Getty Images)

plays is *The Coast of Utopia,* three plays constituting a trilogy that lasts nearly nine hours and was presented in 2007 by the Lincoln Center Theatre.

A significant number of "angry" playwrights in Britain continue to attack traditional political, social, and economic institutions; among the best-known are David Hare (b. 1947) and Howard Brenton (b. 1942). More contemporary sociopolitically oriented British playwrights include Patrick Marber (b. 1964), author of *Dealer's Choice* (1995) and *Closer* (1997); and Jez Butterworth (b. 1969), author of *Mojo* (1995).

A number of female English playwrights have achieved considerable recognition, including Timberlake Wertenbaker (b. 1946) and Pamela Gems (1925–2011). Sarah Kane (1971–1999) received considerable attention after she committed suicide. Her works include *Blasted* (1995), *Cleansed* (1998), and *Crave* (1998). A British playwright who has achieved immense worldwide recognition for politically charged feminist plays is Caryl Churchill (b. 1938). Churchill, whose plays include *Cloud Nine* (1979), *Serious Money* (1987), *Mad Forest* (1990), and *A Number* (2004), has received numerous awards, including the Susan Smith Blackburn Prize, which she won twice.

A POSTMODERN ENGLISH DIRECTOR

Deborah Warner is an English director who has developed a more experimental style of production and reinterpreted texts so as to focus on feminist, gender, and other sociopolitical issues. She is best-known for the many productions she has directed starring the actress Fiona Shaw including Beckett's *Footfalls,* T. S. Eliot's *The Waste Land* (2000), *Medea* (2001), Brecht's *Mother Courage* (2009) and Colm Tóibín's *The Testament of Mary* (2013). Shown here are Shaw on the left and Warner on the right. (© Bruce Glikas/FilmMagic/Getty Images)

PLAYING YOUR PART: EXPERIENCING THEATRE

1. Have you ever found yourself in circumstances in which you were interacting with individuals who spoke only a language you did not understand? How did you negotiate that interaction? How might that have been similar to experiencing a theatre production that uses the unique traditions of a different nation?

2. Are there issues in contemporary American society that might be dramatized by playwrights of other nations in a fashion that would be different from the way in which a U.S. dramatist would represent the same issues? What might those differences be?

3. Read a play by a contemporary playwright from Latin America, Africa, or Asia. How is the play similar to U.S. dramas you have read? How is it different?

An English director who has developed a more experimental style of production, and has reinterpreted texts so as to focus on feminist, gender, and other sociopolitical issues, is Deborah Warner (b. 1959). Warner began her career with an alternative London troupe, the Kick Theatre Company, which she founded in 1980, when she was 21. She has since directed unique interpretations of the classics for the Royal Shakespeare Company and the National Theatre in London. She is best-known for the many productions she has directed starring the actress Fiona Shaw (b. 1959), including Shakespeare's *Richard III,* Beckett's *Footfalls,* T. S. Eliot's *The Waste Land* (2000*), Medea* (2001), Brecht's *Mother Courage* (2009), and *The Testament of Mary* (2013).

There is also a new generation of young Irish playwrights who dramatize social, political, and historical issues. One of the best-known is Martin McDonagh (b. 1970), whose works include *The Beauty Queen of Leenane* (1996), *The Cripple of Inishmaan* (1996), *The Pillowman* (2005), and *A Behanding in Spokane* (2010). Conor McPherson (b. 1971) has gained international attention for *The Weir* (1997), *Dublin Carol* (2000), *Shining City* (2004), and *The Seafarer* (2006).

There are many theatres in England that produce new playwrights or significant revivals, some of which are government supported, and that are internationally renowned and have toured productions globally. Among these are the previously mentioned National Theatre (which has streamed productions to film houses across the world), Royal Court Theatre, and Royal Shakespeare Company as well as the Donmar Warehouse, now under the artistic direction of the female director Josie Rourke (b. 1980), the Almeida, and the Menier Chocolate Factory.

In all the areas of Western Europe, Britain, and Ireland that we have discussed, numerous alternative theatres exist. Such theatres are also present in most major cities worldwide. In London, for example, there is an alternative to commercial theatre known as *fringe theatre,* and it is in fringe theatre that many contemporary political playwrights began their careers. The British playwrights whose work appears in fringe theatre are often in the postmodernist tradition, mixing reality with theatrical techniques and fusing concerns of high art with techniques of popular art. A British company that does site-specific works that are postmodern and interactive in style is Punchdrunk, whose adaptation of *Macbeth, Sleep No More,* was staged in abandoned warehouses in New York City.

LATIN AMERICAN THEATRES

In twentieth-century Latin America, theatre developed on many fronts: realistic drama, experimental theatre, radical sociopolitical drama, and popular forms, all existing side by side. While there have been economic, political, and social problems, including periods of censorship and governmental repression (for example, in Chile during the dictatorship of Pinochet from 1973 to 1989), all the countries in Latin America have significant theatres and playwrights. Frequently these artists have responded to the political and social turmoil in their societies.

At the beginning of the twentieth century, for instance, many comedies were written throughout Latin America—and especially in Argentina—that dealt with the unique local customs of each of the Latin American nations. In the period between the world wars, the dramatists of Latin America were clearly influenced by such European styles as surrealism and expressionism but often touched on nationalistic issues.

LATIN AMERICAN THEATRE: ARGENTINA
The Argentinian theatre group De La Guarda, in the piece *Fuerza Bruta* (*Brute Force*), has created a modern work that is part theatre, part rock concert, and part circus act. It typifies the mixing of styles and the eclecticism of much of contemporary theatre. There is no traditional stage. Performers soar through the air and, in the scene shown here, float in a transparent plastic water tank, which spectators view from below through a glass ceiling. (© Ronaldo Schemidt/AFP/Getty Images)

Following World War II, many Latin American dramatists began to focus on the unique national issues and concerns that confronted their individual countries. Some of Latin America's most developed and politically active playwrights and theatre companies can be found today in Argentina, Brazil, Chile, Mexico, and Peru. The theatre artists of these countries have fused the popular styles of their peoples with the modernist styles of modern Western theatre, including realism, expressionism, absurdism, and performance art. The most significant postwar Latin American dramatists include the Mexican Elena Garro (1920–1198), the Chilean Alejandro Sieveking (b. 1935), the Colombian Guillermo Maldonado (b. 1945), the Peruvian Mario Vargas Llosa (b. 1936), and the Brazilian Plinio Marcos (1935–1999). *Neva*, a play by the contemporary Chilean playwright Guillermo Calderon (b. 1971), was produced at New York's Public Theatre in 2013.

One of the most renowned theatre artists of the era was the Brazilian playwright, director, and theorist Augusto Boal. In the 1960s, Boal created works about historical figures, theatrical and revolutionary. Because of his Marxist point of view, Boal was forced into exile. In exile, he traveled throughout South America and other parts of the world, experimenting with different types of theatre. He became internationally known for his theoretical work *Theatre of the Oppressed* (1975), which became a manifesto for revolutionary and socially conscious theatre. (A profile of Boal can be found in the Global Connections box in Chapter 1.)

Four contemporary playwrights from Argentina are Daniel Veronese (b. 1955), Lola Arias (b. 1976), Rafael Spregelburd (b. 1970), and Federica León (b. 1970). Veronese's *Women Dreamt Horses* features a sister and three brothers at a family dinner that goes terribly wrong for all concerned; Arias's *La Esqualida Familia* is set in an arctic frontier and tells the story of a developmentally disabled orphan boy whose discovery tears apart an incestuous family; in Spregelburd's *Panic* a woman facing a financial crisis searches frantically for the key to her husband's safe deposit box; León's *Ex-Antwone* is a dreamlike fantasy in which a young man attempts to connect with a girl who has Down syndrome and has had her face replaced with a normal one. In addition to his writing, Varonese formed an important theatre company, El Periférico de Objetos, in 1989. Another important Argentine company, De La Guarda, has brought several productions to New York and elsewhere, including *VillaVilla* and *Fuerze Bruta*.

Contemporary Mexican theatre, according to a young playwright, Richard Viqueira, "wants to unburden itself from the influence of European theatrical models, and is seeking to forge its own voice. The move in new writing more and more is away from the folkloric toward the more recognizably idiomatic." Along with Viqueira (b. 1976), other recognized young Mexican playwrights include Javier Malpica (b. 1965); Sabima Berman (b. 1955), a political activist as well as playwright; Sylvia Peláez (b. 1965); and Alberto Villarreal (b. 1977).

In Cuba, the country's communist government controls most theatres. Still, there are a number of theatre companies that have been able to present works by international playwrights and contemporary authors. These include Teatro Studio (founded in 1959), Compañia Teatral (founded 1962), Compañia Teatral Humbert de Blanck (founded 1992), Teatro El Publico (founded 1992), and Argos Teatro (founded 1996). In recent years, several Cuban companies have toured internationally. For example, Teatro Buendia, an independent theatre that was established in 1986 and that stages adaptations of historically significant texts using Cuban contexts and music, performed at the Goodman Theatre in Chicago in 2010 and again in 2013.

CANADA AND AUSTRALIA SINCE WORLD WAR II

Before World War II, Canadian and Australian theatres developed commercially, presenting popular forms of entertainments that also reflected national identity. Two Australian examples are *The Squatter's Daughter,* or, *The Land of the Wattle* (1907), which focused on the Australian outlaw known as the bushranger; and the pantomime *The Bunyip,* or *The Enchantment of Fairy Princess Wattle Blossom* (1916), which included a mythological Aboriginal character. During the same period, Australia and Canada developed "little theatres"—some professional and some amateur—that presented noncommercial, and often politically charged, works. In Australia, three such companies were Sydney's New Theatre League, established in 1936; Melbourne's New Theatre Club, founded in 1937; and Brisbane's Unity Theatre, which also opened in 1937. Hart House Theatre, founded on the campus of the University of Toronto in 1919, was one example of the Canadian "little theatre" movement. It presented many of Canada's most important theatre artists in the two decades before World War II. After World War II, the Hart House became a venue for university productions, reflecting the vitality of university theatre across Canada.

Since World War II, the theatres of Canada and Australia have seen developments that parallel the complexity of international theatre. For example, in Canada in the 1950s and 1960s, many regional theatres were established. One of the most famous is the Stratford Shakespeare Festival in Stratford, Ontario. This festival, established in 1952 under the artistic direction of Tyrone Guthrie (1900–1971), continues to produce classics, musicals, and contemporary works, in multiple venues. The Shaw Festival, established in 1962, stages works by Shaw, his contemporaries, and works set during his lifetime. Australia also saw the development of theatres across the nation from the 1950s through the 1970s.

Both Australia and Canada, from the late 1960s through the present, saw the development of theatre companies dedicated to new works, experimentation, and innovative revivals of classics. In 1967, Betty Burstall (1926–2013) established Melbourne's La Mama Theatre, based on New York's famous experimental theatre. La Mama continues to function as does Company B, which was established in Sydney in 1985, and is known for presenting contemporary works and unique readings of classics. Among the stars who have recently appeared with the company are the film actors Geoffrey Rush (b. 1951) and Cate Blanchett (b. 1969). At the Sydney Theatre Company, founded in 1979, Blanchett is now the co-artistic director.

Playwrights and theatre artists have dealt with the issues related to these countries' diverse populations and concerns. In Canada and Australia, there are theatres that focus on native peoples and people of African descent. For example, the Australian musical *Bran Nue Dae* (1990) dealt with Aboriginal life. Playwrights have also dramatized issues of gender and sexual orientation in these countries. Michel Tremblay (b. 1942), who was born in Montreal, focuses on working-class Canadians and gay issues. Wadi Mouawad (b. 1968) was born in Lebanon and has written plays about

PROMINENT CANADIAN PLAYWRIGHT
A major theatre voice in Canada in recent years is Michel Tremblay, whose French language plays feature gay and lesbian issues in the world of working-class Canadians. Seen here are Eva TerraNova as Pierette, Chelsie Cravens as Rose, Jordan Novotny as Germaine, and Krista Niederjohn as Gabrielle in a production of Tremblay's *Les Belles Soeurs* at the University of Utah. (© Spencer Sandstrom/Daily Utah Chronicle)

his displaced community in Canada. Canadian Hannah Moscovitch (b. 1978) has dealt with feminist and Jewish issues in her work. The theatre company Buddies in Bad Times, established in 1979, is committed to gay and lesbian theatre. In the 1980s, feminist theatres in Australia included Home Cooking Theatre (1981) and Vital Statistix (1984). There are also playwrights who focus on universal concerns and issues, including the Australian Andrew Bovell (b. 1962), author of *When the Rain Stops Falling*.

There are also Canadian and Australian artists who present performance art, discussed earlier in this chapter, and multimedia works. The French-Canadian Robert Lepage (b. 1957) is a well-known director, creator of theatrical and operatic productions, and actor. In 1993, he founded Ex Machina, a multimedia performance center in Quebec City. Lepage is probably best-known for *KÀ*, the Cirque du Soleil production he staged in Las Vegas in 2005, and the new Metropolitan Opera production of Wagner's epic *Der Ring des Nibelungen* in 2012. Australia also has many contemporary performance artists, such as Mike Parr (b. 1945).

PLAYING YOUR PART: THINKING ABOUT THEATRE

1. In what ways does the enactment of a ritual or ceremony resemble a theatrical presentation? What elements do the two events have in common? What are the differences? What do we learn about both ceremonies and theatre by observing the differences?

2. Have you ever seen a theatre presentation of a play or production from another part of the world—from Asia, eastern Europe, the Middle East, Latin America, Canada, or Australia? What struck you about the performance: the similarities to your world, or the differences?

3. What can we learn about other countries and other cultures by seeing their theatrical presentations? How does theatre compare with news accounts for providing insight into cultures and countries other than your own?

SUMMARY

1. A number of countries in Asia and the West have theatre traditions that stretch back hundreds, and in some cases thousands, of years.

2. The modern era is marked by increasing globalization in theatre, with more and more communication and cross-pollination—a feature of much of modern society, including the arts.

3. Asian theatre has both traditional and modern branches. In places like Japan, both types of theatre remain particularly active.

4. Theatre in India today is largely produced by numerous amateur groups.

5. Despite prohibition in Muslim countries, theatre has developed in certain Middle Eastern countries. In Israel, theatre is quite active.

6. The two best-known writers of African drama are Athol Fugard and Wole Soyinka.

7. Theatres in Russia and the countries of eastern Europe have long traditions, but many of these theatres were curtailed or interrupted during the years of the Soviet Union: the 1940s until 1989–1991.

8. European and British theatre has two active components: (a) traditional and establishment, and (b) alternative. Europe and Britain are known for national theatres; strong, innovative directors; and invigorating playwrights.

9. Latin American theatre has roots in Spanish and Portuguese drama. A well-known Brazilian playwright is Augusto Boal.

10. Theatres in Canada and Australia remain active and vibrant.

Contemporary Theatre in the United States

In the early twenty-first century, theatre in the United States remains amazingly resilient, but at the same time continues to face serious challenges. One constant challenge comes from various electronic media, which proliferate year by year, not only film and television, but cell phones, tablets of all kinds, and a host of other handheld electronic devices. Computer games, too, are rivals to live theatre, particularly among young people.

Other challenges are more personal and political. Conservative politicians, for example, have succeeded in sharply reducing the appropriations given annually to the National Endowment for the Arts (NEA). From the 1960s through the 1980s, grants from the NEA to theatres, coupled with earlier gifts from large foundations, made possible the creation of the network of resident professional theatres across the country. Appropriations from Congress to the NEA, however, were drastically reduced. In 1992, the amount was $175 million; in 1997, it had dropped sharply to $99 million; in 2007, it was roughly $120 million, which, when adjusted for inflation, was not much more than the amount for 1997. In other words, after 1992 there was a precipitous drop in the NEA budget, and this was at a time when the arts most needed support. When the Obama administration came in, a portion of the budget was restored. The 2012 budget was $146 million, still not at the level of 1992.

In the United States, there has never been a tradition of government support for the arts. By contrast, in Britain and many countries in continental Europe, national, state, and municipal governments each year make generous grants to arts organizations. To

◀ A CONTEMPORARY U.S. PLAYWRIGHT

One of the most original and consistent playwrights of his generation is the comic, satirical playwright Christopher Durang. A recent drama of his entitled Vanya and Sonia and Masha and Spike *features family members whose parents named them after characters in Chekhov's plays. Set in a fictional version of a Bucks County, Pennsylvania, neighborhood, it chronicles the humorous interaction of two siblings who have remained at the family home during the visit of a successful actress sister (Sigourney Weaver). With Weaver in this scene is her brother, played by David Hyde Pierce. (© Sara Krulwich/The New York Times/Redux)* take only one example, the National Theatre in London receives the equivalent of more than $30 million per year from the British Arts Council. This grant to one theatre alone in Britain is roughly 20 percent of the entire appropriation for the NEA in the United States.

As a result of cuts in funding by the government and foundations, not-for-profit theatres have had to struggle in recent years. Among other things, there has been a shift from annual subscription sales to single ticket sales, and this together with the loss of funding has meant tighter budgets for many theatres. This, in turn, has led to fewer new plays, fewer large-cast shows, fewer musicals, and fewer plays with full-scale scenery.

Despite these very real difficulties, theatre has continued to play a vital role in the nation's art scene. Previously, we have noted the impressive variety in contemporary U.S. theatre. Audiences today can see revivals of the best theatre from the past: Greek, Elizabethan, French, and Spanish. They can see theatre from Asia, Africa, and Latin America; new plays; and avant-garde and experimental works. There are productions in translation of the best new plays from other countries. Audiences can see multicultural theatre—African American, Asian American, Hispanic, Native American—and they can see political theatre, and theatre reflecting the viewpoint of a number of minorities and special groups such as feminists and gays and lesbians. What's more, these productions can be seen in a wide variety of theatre environments. One hallmark of contemporary theatre is that all these strands exist simultaneously. As this suggests, our contemporary theatre is complex. If theatre mirrors the society in which it is produced, it is not surprising that ours is fragmented, reflecting the complexity of today's life.

One way to understand the rich assortment of theatrical organizations and theatrical venues that make up the mosaic of contemporary theatre is to look at one locality as a microcosm of theatre across the United States: the city of Chicago. In many ways what is happening in Chicago mirrors what is happening elsewhere, in the diverse types of theatre on display, as well as in the variety of theatre spaces. To begin, there are traditional Broadway-style theatres, including the Oriental, the Cadillac Palace, and the Bank of America Theatre. Not only do they offer touring Broadway shows, but in recent years they have served as tryout houses for such musicals as *The Producers*, *Spamalot*, *The Addams Family*, *Kinky Boots*, and *Big Fish*.

As for not-for-profit theatre, Chicago has a number of resident professional theatres. The largest, the Goodman, is a flagship regional theatre; it has launched several plays by August Wilson as well as other important new works. Following closely behind the Goodman is Steppenwolf, founded in 1976. The original Steppenwolf company included many actors who became stars, such as John Malkovich (b. 1953), Gary Sinise (b. 1955), and Laurie Metcalf (b. 1955), and Steppenwolf itself evolved into a leading established regional theatre. In 2007 it launched the play *August: Osage County*, which went on to win a Pulitzer Prize; and in 2009 it launched *Superior Donuts*—both by Tracy Letts (b. 1965). Another playwright featured by Steppenwolf is Bruce Norris (b. 1960).

Steppenwolf is known as an *off-Loop* theatre, meaning that it is outside the downtown commercial section of Chicago (the equivalent in New York is off-Broadway and off-off-Broadway). Other major off-Loop Chicago theatres have included Wisdom Bridge (where Robert Falls, currently artistic director of the Goodman, began his directing career), the Organic, the Body Politic, St. Nicholas, and Victory Gardens.

REGIONAL THEATRES

In the United States, regional, not-for-profit theatres are indispensable. These theatres, which emerged in the last half of the twentieth century, are spread all across the U.S., in large cities and small ones. They present the classics and plays recently produced elsewhere, but they are also often the only theatres that give encouragement and crucial exposure to new works. Shown here are Brian Dennehy as Larry Slade, left, and Nathan Lane as Hickey in a scene from Eugene O'Neill's *The Iceman Cometh* directed by Robert Falls at the Goodman Theatre in Chicago. (© Liz Lauren/Courtesy of The Goodman Theatre/AP Images)

These theatres have also introduced successful actors, including Joe Mantegna (b. 1947), and many significant playwrights. Lookingglass Theatre, founded in Chicago in 1988, has received praise for its productions of literary adaptations that use intriguing staging devices. In 2002, Lookingglass's artistic director, Mary Zimmerman, won the Tony Award for best direction, after her production of *Metamorphoses* (1998) moved to New York City.

Chicago also has the Chicago Shakespeare Theater, which is one of a number of exceptional Shakespeare theatres and festivals around the country, and which has built a reputation for staging Sondheim revivals as well as hosting global companies. (All in all, there are more than 150 Shakespeare theaters, including many outdoor spaces, in the United States, with over 30 located in California alone. Year after year, Shakespeare remains the playwright most frequently produced in the U.S.)

There are also a large number of small Equity and even smaller non-Equity storefront theatres in neighborhoods throughout Chicago. The non-Equity theatres employ actors who are not members of the professional actors' union, Equity. Both the very small Equity and non-Equity companies often present more contemporary dramas or revivals of neglected plays in remodeled spaces, which literally often are storefronts. Among the best-known small Equity theatres in Chicago is Profiles, which has built a relationship with the contemporary playwright Neil LaBute (b. 1963). A small non-Equity storefront theatre in Chicago is Theo Ubique, which is known for ingeniously staging musicals in an intimate café environment, where the performers also serve dinner to audience members prior to the start of the show.

There are also many theatres that reflect the multicultural world of Chicago. Congo Square Theatre is a company that focuses on African American drama. Teatro Vista is a theatre committed to presenting the varied works of Latino and Latino-American playwrights, while Teatro Luna is a theatre company established by Latina artists.

Along with these many diverse theatres in Chicago, there are excellent college and university theatres, such as De Paul, and Northwestern in Evanston, Illinois, which produce high-quality work. The multiplicity of theatre activity in Chicago, at so many levels, can also be found in cities large and small in almost all 50 states as well as in Canada.

NONTRADITIONAL, ALTERNATIVE THEATRE

In the twenty-first century, traditional theatre remains vital and vigorous in the U.S., as well as throughout the world. We will examine that theatre in considerable detail later in the chapter. But here, we should take note of a development that took root in the second half of the twentieth century and has become a full-blown movement in this century. It could be called nontraditional theatre, but it also goes variously by other names such as avant-garde, experimental, and postmodernist. It offers an alternative to traditional theatre, and it affords a different type of experience for theatre audiences.

A good way to begin examining nontraditional theatre is to look at what happened in the visual arts, particularly painting, in the last century. For hundreds of years painting in the Western world was representational: that is, the subject on the canvas represented something recognizable, such as a landscape or a portrait. Then, in the early years of the twentieth century other approaches to painting began to appear: abstract expressionism, collage, montage, and all manner of nonrepresentational art.

No longer were observers looking at a mountain, a seascape, or a portrait of a family or an individual. They were looking at shapes, colors, designs that did not represent anything recognizable from daily life. Geometric shapes were arranged so that, say, blue squares, yellow triangles, and red circles appeared in a pattern that was either carefully delineated or seemingly thrown together at random. The flat surface of the canvas was even broken so that sections of the painting went beyond the frame while three-dimensional outgrowths appeared on the surface.

A number of people, content with centuries of representational art, resisted this approach to painting. Those who were attracted to it, however, or curious about it, had to come to terms with a new way of communicating. This different approach to art was challenging, provocative, sometimes disorienting. A spectator had to ask: "What is the artist trying to say?" The viewer, in other words, had to make sense of this new experience and embrace it at some level other than the familiar level of recognizable places or people.

Something similar occurred in theatre in the second half of the twentieth century. There were antecedents—the auteur director Vselovod Meyerhold in the early 1900s, as well as movements such as futurism, expressionism, and surrealism. The author Antonin Artaud, in the 1930s, proclaimed that there should be "no more masterpieces," meaning that texts like the plays of Shakespeare should no longer be revered but rather treated with no more respect than a run-of-the-mill drama by a second-rate dramatist. Following World War II this movement became more widespread. In the spirit of Artaud, a central element shared by all the new experimental and avant-garde approaches to theatre was a rejection of what was called "text-based" theatre, meaning theatre based on a script written by a playwright.

Instead of beginning with dialogue and a plot created by a dramatist, the new approach originated in a number of other ways: an ensemble of actors improvised material; a group of actors joined with dancers, or perhaps incorporated film or video into their presentations; a performance artist developed a one-person show; an auteur director created a piece according to his or her personal vision. In the process, entirely new material might be utilized; or, perhaps, a classical play would be turned upside down or inside out. Frequently, too, performances took place not in a conventional theatre setting, but in an unusual or site-specific locale. One rationale for this approach is that it reflected the confused, chaotic, often irrational world in which we live. Among the developments that took hold in the post–World War II era were happenings, multimedia, and environmental theatre.

Happenings, Multimedia, and Environmental Theatre

A precursor to performance art, *happenings* were raw, thoughtfully crafted theatrical events created by painters and sculptors from 1959 to 1963. With little to no theatre training, these visual artists were part of the postmodern movement when artists explored other art forms beyond their own specific practices. Unlike the misleading title, happenings were not spontaneous or happenstance. They were intentional, organized acts that explored time and space. Performances consisted of prepared activities and tasks that were choreographed and blocked. Groups of performers engaged in pedestrian (everyday) movement or stylistic gesture with found objects or props and performed in a sculptural set. Nonsensical sounds and spoken text were used without feeling or emotion.

Identifying circumstances were removed and the senses of sight, sound, and often, scent were evoked. There was no applause or curtain call and audiences usually consisted of 40 to 50 spectators invited to the space through mailed invitations, advertising or word-of-mouth. Productions were often limited to a few performances. The first shows were performed at art galleries, in studio lofts, museums, storefronts, parking lots and other unique spaces. Happenings were produced to be an element of everyday life, eliminating the boundary of the fourth wall between performers and audience. When a performance ended, the audience often waited in the space until a performer signaled or a brave audience member initiated an exit.[1]

Multimedia is a joining of theatre with other arts—particularly dance, film, and television. In work of this sort, which is still being produced, live performers interact with sequences on film or television. The idea here is to fuse the art forms or to incorporate new technology into a theatrical event. A current form that combines theatre, dance, and media is called *performance art* and will be discussed later in the chapter.

Happenings Non-literary theatrical events, developed in the 1960s, in which the script is replaced with a scenario which provides for chance occurrences, and are performed (often only once) in such places as parks and street corners.

Multimedia Use of electronic media, such as slides, film, and videotape, in live theatrical presentations.

Environmental theatre A type of theatre, made popular in the 1960s, which attempts to eliminate the distinction between audience and acting space and which emphasizes a multiple focus for the audience rather than a single focus.

The term *environmental theatre* was coined in the 1960s by the U.S. director and teacher Richard Schechner (b. 1934); many characteristics of environmental theatre, however, had developed out of the work and theories of earlier avant-garde artists such as Meyerhold and Artaud. Proponents of environmental theatre treat the entire theatre space as a performance area, suggesting that any division between performers and viewers is artificial. For every production, spatial arrangements are transformed.

The major influence on Schechner's theories was the Polish director Jerzy Grotowski (1933–1999). Works staged by Grotowski with the Polish Laboratory Theatre from its founding in 1959 until 1970 had many characteristics of environmental theatre. For each production, the theatre space and the performer-audience relationship were arranged to conform to the play being presented. Grotowski called his theatre *poor theatre,* meaning poor in scenery and special effects. It relied on the performers for its impact.

Two experimental directors are Robert Wilson (b. 1944) and Richard Foreman (b. 1937). Their work is typically unified by a theme or point of view determined by the director, and their material is often organized into units analogous to frames in television or film. Stunning theatrical images containing the essence of the ideas that interest these directors are often the key to their work.

AVANT-GARDE AND EXPERIMENTAL THEATRE
Aside from large professional theatres, there are many smaller theatres off-off-Broadway and in cities across the United States. Some of these are minority theatres or theatres by and for special groups: gays, lesbians, or others. Alternative theatre also includes avant-garde and experimental productions. One of the foremost avant-garde directors of the past quarter century is Richard Foreman. A recent production of his—a sort of retrospective of previous work—is his *Old-Fashioned Prostitutes (A True Romance)* shown here with Rocco Sisto (right) and Alenka Kraigher at the Public Theater in New York City. (© Karli Cadel for The New York Times/Redux)

Important off-off-Broadway theatres in which avant-garde works found a home included Café LaMama, the Living Theater, the Open Theater, the Performance Group, Mabou Mines, and the Wooster Group. These theatres in New York City had counterparts all across the United States. All have experimented with physical performance techniques, improvisation, texts created by performers and directors, and environmental presentations.

Whatever the process, the result was not traditional theatre. Like their counterparts in painting, nonrepresentational theatre artists deal in images, impressions, fragments, and segments. There may be strong elements of improvisation, free association, and audience participation. Each presentation is an event, a time-based event, and it is up to the spectator to integrate its elements in some way, to determine its meaning and its impact. Another way of saying this is that viewing such theatre becomes a different kind of experience from the experience audiences are accustomed to in traditional theatre.

POSTMODERNISM

One term used to describe the nontraditional theatre we have been discussing is *postmodernism.* According to the film critic A. O. Scott, postmodernism has several attributes: "a cool, ironic effect; the overt pastiche of work from the past; the insouciant mixture of high and low styles." Although postmodernism is difficult to define specifically, it has certain distinctive facets.

For one thing, postmodernism reflects issues of power in art. Postmodernists question the idea of an accepted "canon" of classics; they also ask why certain artists (such as playwrights) and certain groups (such as white males) should have held positions of power or "privilege" throughout theatre history.

Accordingly, postmodernists rebel against traditional readings of texts, arguing that theatre productions may have a variety of "authors," including directors and even individual audience members: they argue that each audience member creates his or her own unique reading. Postmodernist directors are noted for deconstructing classic dramas and trying to represent onstage the issues of power embedded in the text. When a classic is deconstructed in this way, it may serve simply as the scenario for a production.

One of the most famous groups known for deconstruction of texts is the Wooster Group, under the artistic direction of Elizabeth LeCompte (b. 1944). In 1997, the Wooster Group presented a highly theatricalized and physical version of Eugene O'Neill's *The Emperor Jones* in a run-down theatre in the Times Square area in New York City. In 2007, it presented a version of *Hamlet* that featured various filmed scenes of *Hamlet* interspersed with live action. Postmodernists mix abstraction and realism, so that their works cannot be easily classified. Furthermore, the distinction between "high" art and popular art can no longer be clearly defined: postmodernists mix popular concerns and techniques with those of high art.

An intriguing example is the musical *The Lion King* (1997), based on a popular Disney animated film with music by the rock composer Elton John. The director of *The Lion King*, as well as the designer of the masks and puppets, is Julie Taymor, who was profiled previously. Taymor, who is a designer, director, and adapter of literature for the stage, is known for her avant-garde use of puppet techniques borrowed from Asian theatres. For example, she used puppets in staging Shakespeare's *The Tempest* (1986) at New York's Theatre for a New Audience; in her frequently revived adaptation

Postmodernism Theory that division of art works into modernist categories, such as realism and departures from realism, is artificial. Postmodernist works mix realistic and nonrealistic elements as well ass techniques from popular land traditional art.

of a short story, *Juan Darien* (1988); in a production of Igor Stravinsky's opera *Oedipus Rex* in Tokyo (1992); and in a production of *The Green Bird* (1996), an eighteenth-century comedy by Carlo Gozzi.

THEATRE IN THE UNITED STATES TODAY: TRADITIONAL AND NONTRADITIONAL

We have been describing avant-garde, experimental and other nontraditional theatre which is part of the rich mix of theatrical offerings available to today's audiences. For most of us, however, who attend the theatre, the vast majority of productions available are more traditional: revivals of well-known plays and musicals from the past as well as new dramas and musicals.

In looking at traditional types of theatre, we begin with a look at a number of playwrights who have appeared on the scene in recent decades in the United States. The period just after World War II saw the emergence of Tennessee Williams, Arthur Miller, Lorraine Hansberry, and Edward Albee; then there were other playwrights who followed the traditional style, displaying an awareness of the craft of dramaturgy and also great originality. Included in this group are Sam Shepard (b. 1943) and David Mamet (b. 1947). Like many later contemporary playwrights, Shepard and Mamet mix concerns of high art—such as the plight of the American family and the demise of the American dream—with techniques borrowed from mass entertainments such as film, popular music, and melodrama. Also, they often blur the distinction between realism and abstraction.

Sam Shepard first developed his playwriting skills off-off-Broadway with works that fused surreal and absurdist styles and abandoned traditional plot structure and development. His later dramas include *Buried Child* (for which he won a Pulitzer Prize in 1979), *Fool for Love* (1982), and *A Lie of the Mind* (1985). Shepard's plays deal with American mythology, the violence of American society, and the degeneration of the American family.

David Mamet's plays have naturalistic language and settings and some down-and-out characters whose struggles are clearly recognizable; but unlike traditional realism, they do not provide clear-cut exposition or dramatic resolutions. His plays, like Shepard's, attack many accepted ideals of American life. Among his best-known works are *American Buffalo* (1977), *Glengarry Glen Ross* (1983), *Boston Marriage* (1999), and *Race* (2009). Mamet has also written and directed a number of films.

A significant playwright bridging the twentieth and twenty-first centuries was Horton Foote (1916–2009), who wrote evocative dramas, mostly set in the South, for more than half a century. Other dramatists who made their mark in the closing decades of the twentieth century include John Guare (b. 1938), Lanford Wilson (1937–2011), Marsha Norman (b. 1947), Wendy Wasserstein (1950–2005), Donald Margulies (b. 1954), Jon Robin Baitz (b. 1961), David Auburn (b. 1969), and David Lindsay-Abaire (b. 1971). A number of other contemporary figures will be discussed later in this chapter in the sections on minority, multiethnic, and female playwrights.

THEATRE OF DIVERSITY

Before we discuss specific multicultural points of view in theatre, it should be noted that while many theatre artists wish to write from a specific ethnic or gender viewpoint, others who happen to be members of a minority group or a specific gender group, or who espouse feminism or a political outlook, do not want to be identified solely, or even primarily, on that basis. For instance, there are playwrights who are Latino or African American, but they want to be known as playwrights, without any ethnic identification. Also, there are people who are gay or lesbian, or who are strong feminists, but they want to be regarded chiefly, or even exclusively, as dramatists, not gay dramatists, lesbian dramatists, or feminist dramatists.

It is also true that theatre companies, producers, or playwrights who are identified with an ethnic or gender group may well include in their work characters and a point of view belonging to those groups, but include them as part of a larger picture. Having noted some of the variations within ethnic and minority playwriting and production, let us turn now to theatre identified with specific groups.

African American Theatre

African American theatre—also referred to as *black theatre*—is a prime example of theatre reflecting the diversity of American culture and the contributions of a particular group to that culture. African American theatre is theatre written by and for black Americans or performed by black Americans. It partakes of two important traditions. One is the Western theatre tradition, in which actors like Paul Robeson (1898–1976) and writers like Lorraine Hansberry (1930–1965) have been significant. The other is a tradition that traces its origin to theatre in Africa and the Caribbean.

African American theatre has a long history, and therefore tracing its development from its beginnings will help us understand its significance and impact on our contemporary theatre. In U.S. drama of the eighteenth and nineteenth centuries, comic black servants—who spoke a thick dialect, shuffled slowly, and wore ill-fitting costumes—were popular characters. These roles, however, were usually enacted by white performers; it was rare to see black performers on the U.S. stage in the nineteenth century.

An exception was the African Grove Theater—a black company founded in New York during the 1820–1821 season by William Brown (an African American) and the West Indian actor James Hewlett. The company was particularly noted for Shakespearean plays. Hewlett was the first black to play Othello, and the renowned actor Ira Aldridge (c. 1806–1867) made his stage debut with the company. Here, too, the drama *King Shotaway* (1823)—believed to be the first play written and performed by African Americans—was presented. The African Grove closed in 1827, however, after attacks by white audience members.

The *minstrel show* was a popular nineteenth-century form, which caricatured blacks with comic and sentimental songs, skits, jigs, and shuffle dances. The performers were usually white entertainers dressed in colorful costumes, with their faces blackened and eyes and mouth enlarged by white and red lines.

At the turn of the twentieth century, the popular syncopated rhythms of ragtime had a strong influence on the emerging musical theatre and served as a bridge for a number of talented African Americans. Bob Cole (1864–1912) and William Johnson (1873–1954) conceived, wrote, produced, and directed the first black musical comedy, *A Trip to Coontown* (1898). The comedians Bert Williams (c. 1876–1922) and George Walker (1873–1911) and their wives joined composers and writers to produce musicals and operettas such as *In Dahomey* (1902) and *Abyssinia* (1906), in which Americans for the first time saw blacks on the Broadway stage without burnt-cork makeup, speaking without dialect, and costumed in high fashion.

The early twentieth century also saw the formation of African American stock companies. The most significant was the Lafayette Players, founded in 1914 by Anita Bush (1883–1974). By the time it closed in 1932, this company had presented more than 250 productions and employed a number of black stars. Black performers and writers were also making inroads into commercial theatre in the 1920s. Twenty plays and musicals with black themes were presented on Broadway in this decade, five of them written by African Americans, including *Shuffle Along* (1921), with lyrics and music by Noble Sissle (1889–1975) and Eubie Blake (1883–1983). The decade also saw some black performers achieve recognition in serious drama, among them Charles Gilpin (1878–1930), Paul Robeson (1898–1976), and Ethel Waters (1896–1977).

The Depression forced black performers to find other ways of earning a living or to invent ingenious ways of creating their own theatre. There were a few Broadway productions of plays by blacks, such as the folk musical *Run Little Chillun* (1933) and *Mulatto* (1935) by Langston Hughes (1902–1967).

Possibly the most significant development for black theatre during the 1930s was the Federal Theatre Project, which was meant to help theatre artists through the Depression. This project formed separate black units in twenty-two cities that mounted plays by black and white authors and employed thousands of African American writers, performers, and technicians. The Federal Theatre Project created a new generation of African American artists who would develop the theatre of the 1940s and 1950s.

In 1932, *The Great Day* by Zora Neale Hurston (1891–1960) was produced on Broadway. In 1941, Orson Welles directed, for his Mercury Theater, a dramatization of the controversial novel *Native Son* by Richard Wright (1908–1960). Other important Broadway ventures included Paul Robeson's record run of 296 performances in *Othello* in 1943, and *Anna Lucasta* (1944), adapted by Abram Hill (1911–1986).

The 1950s saw an explosion of black theatre that would continue over the next five decades. *Take a Giant Step* by Louis Patterson (b. 1922) is a play about growing up in an integrated neighborhood. It premiered in 1953. In 1954, the playwright-director Owen Dodson (1914–1983)—a significant figure in black theatre since the 1930s—staged *Amen Corner* by James Baldwin (1924–1987) at Howard University. Off-Broadway, the Greenwich Mews Theater began casting plays without regard to race and also produced *Trouble in Mind* (1956) by Alice Childress (1920–1994).

Possibly the most important production of the postwar era was *A Raisin in the Sun* (1959) by Lorraine Hansberry (1930–1965). This play is about a black family in Chicago, held together by a God-fearing mother, who are planning to move into a predominantly white neighborhood where the family will be unwelcome. The son loses money in a get-rich-quick scheme and dashes their hopes, but later assumes responsibility for the family. Hansberry's play was directed by Lloyd Richards (1922–2006), the first black director on Broadway.

Richards later became head of the Yale School of Drama, where in the 1980s he nurtured the talents of the black playwright August Wilson (1945–2005), author of *Ma Rainey's Black Bottom* (1984), *Fences* (1985), *Joe Turner's Come and Gone* (1986), *The Piano Lesson* (1990), *Seven Guitars* (1995), *King Hedley II* (2000), *Gem of the Ocean* (2003), and *Radio Golf* (2005). These plays are part of an impressive ten-part series in which each individual play focuses on one decade of the twentieth century.

AFRICAN AMERICAN THEATRE

An important, irreplaceable component of U.S. theatre for the past half century has been African American theatre. The dean of this group, the towering figure, was August Wilson, who wrote ten major plays, one for each decade of the twentieth century. The scene here is from his play *Fences*, directed by Jonathan Wilson at the Hartford Stage Company. The actors are (left to right): Wandachristine, Wendell Wright and Don Mayo. (© T Charles Erickson)

The magnitude of Wilson's achievement has led a number of commentators to call him the most important U.S. playwright of the late twentieth century.

From 1960 to the 1990s, there was an outpouring of African American theatre, much of it reflecting the struggle for civil rights. Amiri Baraka (b. 1934) came to theatergoers' attention in 1964 with *Dutchman,* a verbal and sexual showdown between an assimilated black male and a seductive white woman, set in a New York subway. His plays *The Slave* (1965), *The Toilet* (1965), and *Slave Ship* (1970) also deal with the political, sociological, and psychological issues confronting blacks. Among other significant plays of these two decades were Adrienne Kennedy's *Funnyhouse of a Negro* (1964) and *The Owl Answers* (1969); Lonne Elder's *Ceremonies in Dark Old Men* (1969); Charles Gordone's *No Place to Be Somebody* (1969); Douglas Turner Ward's *Day of Absence* (1970); and Charles Fuller's *A Soldier's Play* (1981), which won a Pulitzer Prize for drama.

In 1970 the Black Theater Alliance listed more than 125 producing groups in the United States. Although only a few of these survived the decade, many had a significant impact. The Negro Ensemble Company, founded in 1967, holds the contemporary record for continuous production by a professional black theatre company. The New Lafayette Theatre, which operated from 1966 until 1972, introduced the playwright Ed Bullins (b. 1935), experimented with black ritual, and published the journal *Black Theater.* Other theatres of this period were the New Federal Theater (founded by Woodie King) and the National Black Theater (founded by Barbara Ann Teer).

In addition to the emergence of these producing organizations, another major change in the 1970s was the presence of a larger black audience at Broadway theatres, which accounted for a significant number of commercial African American productions, such as *Don't Bother Me, I Can't Cope* (1972); and *Bubbling Brown Sugar* (1976). This trend continued in the 1980s and 1990s with such hits as *Black and Blue* (1989), *Jelly's Last Jam* (1992), and *Bring in 'da Noise, Bring in 'da Funk* (1996). A later musical offering was *Fela!*—about a legendary African entertainer.

African American artists continued to make an impact on commercial and noncommercial theatre. For example, George C. Wolfe (b. 1955), author-director of *The Colored Museum* (1986), *Spunk* (1990), and *Jelly's Last Jam,* also directed both parts of the award-winning *Angels in America.* From 1993 to 2004, Wolfe was artistic director of the Public Theater, a renowned off-Broadway facility founded by the New York producer Joseph Papp (1921–1991). In 2013, Wolfe directed the Broadway play *Lucky Guy.*

Another African American director, Kenny Leon (b. 1955), in 2002 founded the True Colors Theatre in Atlanta; and in 2004 and 2010 he directed revivals of *A Raisin in the Sun* and *Fences* on Broadway. In 2011 Leon staged two Broadway productions of plays by female African American authors: *The Mountaintop,* by Katori Hall (b. 1981), and *Stick Fly,* by Lydia R. Diamond (b. 1969). Suzan-Lori Parks (b. 1964), Pearl Cleage (b. 1948), and Cheryl West (b. 1956) are also contemporary African American female playwrights whose works deal with issues of racism and feminism and have been produced in regional and alternative theatres. Two additional African American female dramatists whose works are politically charged are Kia Corthron (b. 1961) and Lynn Nottage (b. 1964). Nottage won the Pulitzer Prize for *Ruined* (2008). Thomas Bradshaw (b. 1980) is an African American playwright whose works have been staged in off-off-Broadway, off-Broadway, and regional theatres.

Asian American Theatre

Asian American theatre should be seen against its background: the long, important heritage of the theatres of Asia. The three great Asian theatre traditions—Indian, Chinese, and Japanese—all reached a high point of artistic excellence many centuries ago at a time when religion and philosophy were central in each culture; and this has kept the focus of traditional theatre allied to these realms, even though the societies themselves have modernized and changed. In addition, these three cultures created and sustained a form of theatre in which many facets of theatrical art—acting, mime, dancing, music, and text—were combined.

It is against the backdrop of these ancient traditions that contemporary Asian American theatre developed. As early as the 1850s, puppet shows, acrobatic acts, and traditional operas were imported from China to California. For most of the nineteenth century and the first half of the twentieth century, however, Asians appeared in dramatic offerings strictly as stereotypes. In films, for instance, Asian Americans played such menial parts as cooks, spies, and vamps. Leading parts—even Asian characters—were played by whites in makeup.

With the coming of more cultural and ethnic awareness in the 1960s and 1970s, this situation began to change. In 1965 several Asian American performers and directors founded the East West Players in Los Angeles. In 1973, two more groups were formed—the Asian Exclusion Act in Seattle and the Asian-American Theatre Workshop in San Francisco—and in 1977 the director-actor Tisa Chang (b. 1941) founded the Pan Asian Repertory Theatre in New York. These groups employed Asian American performers, produced dramas from the Asian cultural heritage, and emphasized new plays written by and for Asian Americans.

A number of plays by Asian American writers were produced in the 1970s and 1980s, including a memory play by Philip Kan Gotanda (b. 1951) called *Song for a Nisei Fisherman* (1982). Gotanda has continued to be an active, prolific playwright. In 2003 the American Conservatory Theatre (ACT) premiered his *Yoheen,* about the difficult relationship between an African American man and his much younger Japanese American wife. In 2007 ACT presented Gotanda's *After the War,* an epic drama about a group of people living in a boardinghouse run by a former jazzman; the characters range from an unemployed African American to a Japanese accountant to a Russian-Jewish immigrant who once lived in Yokohama.

A playwright who came to prominence in the 1980s was David Henry Hwang (b. 1957). The son of first-generation Americans who emigrated from China to California, Hwang wrote several plays that won wide recognition, beginning with *FOB,* produced in 1980; and *The Dance and the Railroad,* produced in 1981. Later in the decade, in 1988, Hwang's *M. Butterfly* opened successfully on Broadway. Based on a true story, the play deals with a French diplomat who meets and falls in love with a Chinese opera singer who he thinks is a woman but turns out to be a man and a spy. In 2003, Hwang

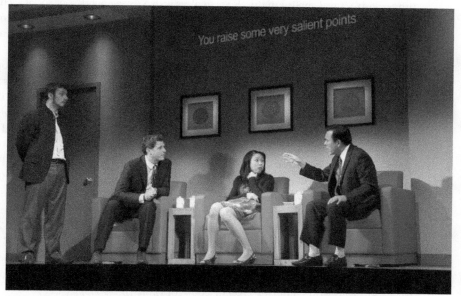

ASIAN AMERICAN THEATRE
One of the best-known Asian American playwrights is David Henry Hwang, who won numerous awards for his Broadway show *M. Butterfly.* A recent play by Hwang is *Chinglish,* shown here with (from left) Stephen Pucci, Gary Wilmes, Angela Lin, and Larry Lei Zhang. In the play, an U.S. businessman goes to China to acquire a lucrative business contract, but the deal isn't the only thing that is lost in translation when he collides with a Communist minister as well as a suspiciously attractive bureaucrat. (© Jeffrey Richards Associates, Michael McCabe/AP Images)

collaborated with the composer Philip Glass on *The Sound of a Voice*. Hwang has written many other successful works, including *Chinglish* (2011), which opened at the Goodman Theatre in Chicago and then transferred to Broadway.

The newer generation of Asian American playwrights includes Diana Son (b. 1965), Chay Yew (b. 1965), who in 2011 became the artistic director of Chicago's Victory Gardens Theatre, Han Ong (b. 1968), and Young Jean Lee (b. 1974). Son's *The Moon Please* (2002) was produced at the New York Public Theatre. Young Jean Lee has gained wide attention as a director as well as a writer. One of her plays, *Songs of the Dragons Flying to Heaven* (2006), includes video, picturing the writer being slapped repeatedly on the cheek; monologues; and a scene with Korean Americans. Later, a white couple intrudes on the action.

Latino-Latina Theatre

Contemporary Latino-Latina or Hispanic theatre in the United States can be divided into at least three groups: Chicano theatre, Cuban American theatre, and Puerto Rican or Nuyorican theatre. All three address the experiences of Hispanics living in the United States, and the plays are sometimes written in Spanish but are usually performed in English.

Chicano theatre, which originated primarily in the West and Southwest, came to prominence during the civil rights movements of the 1960s. The theatre troupe known as El Teatro Campesino ("farmworkers' theatre") grew out of the work of Luis Valdéz (b. 1940), who joined César Chavez in organizing farmworkers in California. Valdéz wrote *actos,* short agitprop pieces dramatizing the lives of workers. (The term *agitprop* means "agitation propaganda"; it was applied in the 1930s to plays with a strong political or social agenda.)

El Teatro Campesino became the prototype for other groups such as Teatro de la Gente ("people's theatre"), founded in 1967; and Teatro de la Esperanza ("theatre of hope"), begun in 1971 in Santa Barbara, California.

Valdéz's play *Zoot Suit* (1978), about racial violence in Los Angeles in 1943, opened in Los Angeles to considerable acclaim; it later moved to Broadway. Other plays about the Chicano experience followed, one of the most notable being *Roosters* (1987) by Milcha Sanchez-Scott (b. 1955), in which cockfighting is a metaphor used to explore Chicano concerns and family conflicts. Writers who have dealt with Chicano and wider themes include Arthur Giron (b. 1937), an American writer from Guatemala.

Cuban American theatre developed chiefly in Florida. The Federal Theatre Project of the 1930s resulted in fourteen Cuban American productions in 1936 and 1937. A highly regarded Cuban American dramatist who began to be produced in the 1970s was Maria Irene Fornés (b. 1930). Among the current generation of Cuban American writers who have emerged in the past quarter century are Manuel Martin (1934–2000), Mario Pena (b. 1959), Dolores Prida (1943–2013), Ivan Acosta (b. 1943), and Omar Torres (b. 1945). (Torres's work is centered in Miami and New York.) Other Cuban American playwrights include Eduardo Machado (b. 1953) and Nilo Cruz (b. 1960), who won a Pulitzer Prize in 2003 for *Anna in the Tropics.*

Nuyorican is a term that refers to Puerto Rican culture, mostly in New York but elsewhere as well. Works by playwrights with a Puerto Rican orientation began to be produced in the 1960s and 1970s by groups such as the Teatro Repertorio Español; the Puerto Rican Traveling Theatre, founded by Miriam Colon (b. 1936); and the New York Public Theater, founded by Joseph Papp. The Nuyorican Poets' Café presented plays by a number of Hispanic writers, including an ex-convict, Miguel

HISPANIC THEATRE

In the past half century, theatre from many cultures and many ethnic groups has found its way into the mainstream of theatre offerings on view. Hispanic plays, representing several branches of Hispanic theatre, have been particularly vibrant. A case in point is a joint production by the Goodman Theatre and Teatro Vista in presenting *El Nogalar,* adapted from Chevhov's *The Cherry Orchard,* by the Mexican American dramatist Tanya Saracho. The play, a scene from which is shown here, is a moving, yet comical, story about the choice between adapting to today's changing world or being left behind. From left to right, Valeria (Sandra Delagado), her sister Anita (Christina Nieves), housekeeper Dunia (Yunuen Pardo), and Maité (Charín Alvarez), the matriarch, prepare a traditional goat dinner as tensions build surrounding their beloved pecan orchard. (© Charles Osgood)

Piñero (1947–1988), whose *Short Eyes,* a harshly realistic portrait of prison life, proved to be very successful and won a number of awards in the 1973–1974 season. New Nuyorican playwrights have also come to prominence, including Yvette Ramírez, Cándido Tirado (b. 1955), Carmen Rivera, Edward Gallardo (b. 1949), and Juan Shamsul Alam. Quiara Alegreia Hudes (b. 1978) won the Pulitzer Prize in 2012 for *Water by the Spoonful,* which is part of a trilogy of plays, and also authored the book for the musical *In the Heights* (2007).

In 1971, a network of Latino theatres across the country was established. Current examples including Teatro Vista, established by two Cuban-born theatre artists, and Teatro Luna, organized by ten Latina women, including Mexican-born playwright Tanya Saracho (b. 1980), perform works by Latino artists in Chicago.

Native American Theatre

Strictly speaking, there was no Native American theatre tradition; rather, there were spiritual and social traditions that had theatrical elements. These were found primarily in ancient rituals and communal celebrations, which were often infused with cosmic significance. Also, unlike traditional Western theatre, these events had no audience as such: those observing were considered participants just as much as the principal performers.

Many of these ceremonies and the like were outlawed by the U.S. government in the nineteenth century. Thus the legacy of rituals and ceremonies, which had strong theatrical components—not to mention significant spiritual and cultural value—was lost or forced to go "underground."

The American Indian Religious Freedom Act of 1972 made it legal once again for certain ceremonies, such as the sun dance, to resume. The increased awareness of these rituals and celebrations contributed to the emergence of a Native American theatre. Two groups that led the way in the past three decades were the Native American Theatre Ensemble and Spiderwoman.

The Native American Theatre Ensemble, which was originally called the American Indian Theatre Ensemble, was founded by Hanay Geiogamah (b. 1945). (It is important to note that those familiar with Native American theatre invariably identify theatre companies and theatre artists not with the generic term *Native American theatre,* but in terms of their tribes. Thus, Geiogamah is identified as Kiowa-Delaware.) Geiogamah's organization gave its premiere performance at La Mama in New York City in 1972, and later toured widely, not only in North America but also in Europe and elsewhere.

Spiderwoman Theatre comes under the headings of both Native American theatre and feminist theatre. Founded in 1975, it is the longest continually running women's theatre in North America, as well as the longest-running Native American theatre. Three of its founding members—Lisa Mayo, Gloria Miguel, and Muriel Miguel—draw on storytelling and other theatrical traditions to celebrate their identity as American Indian women and to comment on stereotypes of women in general.

Another important Native American producing organization is Native Voices at the Autry. Randy Reinholz, a Native American, and his wife, Jean Bruce Scott, had developed a program presenting Native American drama at Illinois State University where they were on the faculty. In 2000, they were invited by the Autry Museum in Los Angeles to bring their project, Native Voices, to the Autry to become a full-time, professional producing organization. Since that beginning they have presented a series of readings, workshops, and full productions of a wide range of Native American dramatic writing.[2]

One full production was *Kino and Teresa* (2005), a retelling by the dramatist James Lujan of the story of Romeo and Juliet. The play pits people from the Taos Pueblo against their Spanish conquerors. Another production was *Super Indian* (2007), based on a radio play by Arigon Starr. This play is in comic book style and includes, among other fantastic characters, a cross-gender Medicine Woman who spins around on the ceiling.

What is important to note about Native American theatre today is that it is not primarily historical or ceremonial. Though elements of tribal traditions may be incorporated, the emphasis among playwrights and producers is really on contemporary work, fusing the problems and aspirations of today's Native Americans with their heritage. The challenges and preoccupations of young Native American playwrights are similar to those addressed by their white American counterparts.

Several Native American playwrights have published single-author anthologies of their works. These include William F. Yellow Robe, Jr. (Assiniboine); Diane Glancy (b. 1941) (Cherokee); and E. Donald Two-Rivers (1945–2008) (Anishinabe). Another important contemporary playwright is Bruce King (Turtle Clan, Haudenosaunee-Oneida).

King and Yellow Robe are also directors who have founded their own companies in the recent past and have taught playwriting and performance at the Institute of American Indian Arts in Santa Fe, New Mexico, an organization that nurtures the next generation of Native American theatre artists.

There are also many Native American theatre organizations throughout the United States, including Thunderbird Theatre at Haskell Indian Nations University, founded in 1974; Red Earth Performing Arts, founded in Seattle in 1974; and the Tulsa Indian Actor's Workshop, founded in 1993. The American Indian Community House (ACH) in New York City uses its theatre space for Native American performing artists, hosting the Indian Summer Series, a month-long festival; ACH also keeps a database of native performers.

While we have discussed many multicultural theatres in the United States, there are many other companies that reflect the ever-expanding diversity of U.S. society. For example, Noor Theatre in New York City, founded by three women of Middle Eastern descent, strives to present work from the growing Middle Eastern communities in the United States. Silk Road Rising is a Chicago theatre company that presents works relevant to the Asian American and Middle Eastern American experiences and says in its mission statement that it hopes to "advance a polycultural worldview."

Feminist Theatre and Playwrights

Feminist theatre, as we know it, is another significant movement that began in the socially active atmosphere of the late 1960s and early 1970s. It developed alongside the more general feminist movement, which stressed consciousness raising to make people aware of the secondary position women had often been forced to occupy in social and political structures. Activists in this period attempted to revise cultural value systems and

NATIVE AMERICAN THEATRE

Native American theatre, also known as indigenous theatre, is written by and for Native Americans. The participants frequently attempt to recapture not only themes and subjects appropriate to Native American culture, but also production styles and approaches of original theatrical presentations. The scene here is from a play written by William S. Yellow Robe, Jr., *Grandchildren of the Buffalo Soldiers*. It dramatizes the visit of a man, Craig Robe (James Craven), who returns to his tribe after having lived elsewhere. In this scene he is with August Jackson (Maya Washington) as part of his confrontation with his past and with the present circumstances of his people. The drama was coproduced by Penumbra Theatre Company and Trinity Repertory Company and directed by Lou Bellamy. (© Ann Marsden/Penumbra Theatre Company)

interpersonal relations in terms of an egalitarian ideology. In theatre this took the form of groups like the It's Alright to Be a Woman Theatre in New York, one of the first groups to translate consciousness raising into stage performances.

Feminist theatre developed in several directions. For one thing, there was an attempt to make women writers, past and present, more widely acknowledged and recognized. Thus historical figures like Hrosvitha, a nun who wrote plays in her convent at Gandersheim in Germany in the tenth century, and the English playwrights Aphra Behn (1640–1689) and Susanna Centlivre (c. 1670–1723) were brought to the forefront. In addition, attention was paid to several women playwrights who had made their mark in the early and middle twentieth century. One significant forerunner, for example, was the American playwright Rachel Crothers (1878–1958), who wrote and directed many successful plays from 1906 to 1937. All of Crothers's plays dealt with women's moral and social concerns, and most of them were set in urban high society. Crothers's plays are skillful, entertaining comedies, but she always focused on the issue of sexual equality. Other notable women playwrights earlier in the twentieth century were Susan Glaspell (1876–1948), Sophie Treadwell (1890–1970), and Lillian Hellman (1905–1984).

The other direction for feminist theatre was the very active writing and production that emerged in the late 1960s, when many female playwrights questioned traditional gender roles and the place of women in U.S. society. In the 1970s and 1980s, in response to the women's movement, which spurred women's playwriting and women's theatre companies, there were a number of critically and commercially successful female playwrights in the U.S. Representative works include *Fefu and Her Friends* (1977) by Maria Irene Fornés, which offered insight into female friendship and the struggles women experience in a patriarchal culture; *Still Life* (1981) by Emily Mann (b. 1952); *Painting Churches* (1983) by Tina Howe (b. 1937); and three plays that won the Susan Smith Blackburn Award, and later the Pulitzer Prize for Drama: *'Night, Mother* (1983) by Marsha Norman, *Crimes of the Heart* (1977) by Beth Henley (b. 1952), and *The Heidi Chronicles* (1988) by Wendy Wasserstein.

Although the women's movement weakened during the 1980s, women continued to write plays in increasing numbers. The playwrights who had broken new ground in the 1970s still wrote dramas, and now they were joined by other women's voices. *How I Learned to Drive* (1998) by Paula Vogel (b. 1951), about a girl's coming-of-age; and *Wit* (1998) by Margaret Edson (b. 1962), about a college professor who wrestles with a fatal illness, are examples of women's ongoing exploration of new subjects and new forms. Both plays won the Pulitzer Prize.

There are many contemporary U.S. female playwrights. Earlier in this chapter, we mentioned four significant African American female playwrights: Suzan-Lori Parks, Pearl Cleage, Kia Corthron, and Lynn Nottage. We also noted that there are feminist Latina American, Asian American, and Native American playwrights. Among other current female playwrights whose works deal with feminist and broader social issues are Sarah Ruhl (b. 1974), Theresa Rebeck (b. 1958), Rebecca Gilman (b. 1965), Carson Kreitzer, and Amy Herzog (b. 1979). Sarah Ruhl was awarded the Susan Smith Blackburn Prize in 2004, an award given annually to a woman who writes for the English-language theatre, and was the recipient of a MacArthur "genius" grant. Ruhl's play *The Clean House*, a Pulitzer Prize finalist, concerns a Brazilian maid who turns out to be a comedian and who refuses to clean the messy house of her disorganized employers. A recent play by Ruhl, on Broadway in 2009, was *The Next Room*. Among recent works by Herzog are *After the Revolution*, *4000 Miles*, and *Belleville*.

POLITICAL THEATRE: A FEMINIST PERSPECTIVE
A well-known contemporary woman playwright is Sarah Ruhl. In her play *In the Next Room (or The Vibrator Play)*, she presents a feminist point of view about the circumstances of women in the late nineteenth century when society was dominated by men, and women's feelings of sexuality were often suppressed. In such a society, sexual fulfillment for some women could be found only indirectly and infrequently. Shown here are Maria Dizzia and Michael Cerveris as patient and doctor in a scene from the play. (© Sara Krulwich/The New York Times/Redux)

A successful writer for television, Theresa Rebeck in her play *The Scene* wrote a sharp, pointed satire about today's television industry. Her play *The Water's Edge* transplanted the Greek story of Agamemnon, the returning warrior, to modern times and developed a seriocomic drama that mixes a tragic situation with amusing observations. A more recent play by Rebeck is *Seminar*. Carson Kreitzer has written several plays about women who are driven to kill. One of these plays—*Self-Defense, or Death of Some Salesmen*—was the story of Aileen Wuornos, a prostitute in Florida who became a serial killer. Kreitzer's *The Love Song of J. Robert Oppenheimer* concerns the soft-spoken man responsible for developing the atomic bomb.

Some scholars estimate that more than 100 feminist companies have been founded in the United States; these companies include At the Foot of the Mountain, Women's Experimental Theatre, and Omaha Magic Theatre, founded by the playwright Megan Terry. One company, Split Britches, was started in 1981 by Lois Weaver (b. 1949), Peggy Shaw (b. 1944) and Deborah Margolin (b. 1953) as an offshoot of Spiderwoman Theatre. Split Britches became well-known for its production of *Belle Reprieve* (1991), which made satiric references to Tennessee Williams's *A Streetcar Named Desire* and was created collaboratively with an English gay company, Bloolips. Many of the feminist companies that were started in the 1970s and 1980s, at the height of the women's movement, have closed. But several still remain, including Women's Project and Productions, which was founded in 1978 by Julia Miles. And new feminist companies have developed in recent years. Rivendell Theatre, founded in Chicago in 1995, is, according to its mission statement, committed to presenting audiences with "artistically challenging, thought provoking plays that explore the female experience." Feminist theatre companies continue to urge audiences to reexamine their own gender biases and those of their society.

WOMEN PLAYWRIGHTS EMERGE
An important development in recent years has been the emergence of women playwrights after many years of male domination among American dramatists. Today women playwrights are coming to the forefront in impressive numbers, and among them is Amy Herzog. In her play *Belleville* a young couple have abandoned the stability of their life in the U.S. for a life in bohemian Paris where their marriage unravels, at the same time that many lessons are learned. Playing the couple in this scene at the New York Theatre Workshop are Maria Dizzia and Greg Keller. (© Sara Krulwich/The New York Times/Redux)

Gay and Lesbian Theatre

Lesbian theatre groups can be part of feminist theatre, but gay and lesbian theatre is also a distinct movement. A number of plays and performers introduced gay and lesbian themes into theatre before the 1960s. For example, in the nineteenth century and the early twentieth century there was a considerable amount of cross-dressing in performances: men often appeared in "drag" and women in men's clothing, raising questions about sexual and gender roles. Also, some plays included material on this subject; one example is Lillian Hellman's *The Children's Hour* (1934), in which a presumed lesbian relationship between two schoolteachers was presented.

Though considered too stereotypical by some, the play that first brought gay life to the attention of mainstream audiences was *The Boys in the Band* (1968), by Mart Crowley (b. 1935). Crowley depicted a group of men living an openly gay life. In the years that followed, complex gay characters were presented unapologetically. Plays in the 1970s and 1980s included *The Ritz* (1975) by Terrence McNally (b. 1939), Jane Chambers's *Last Summer at Bluefish Cove* (1980), and *Torch Song Trilogy* (1983) by Harvey Fierstein (b. 1954). Since then, more and more plays have dealt expressly with gay issues. In these dramas, not only is the lifestyle of gays and lesbians presented forthrightly, but frequently a gay or lesbian agenda is also put forward.

In addition to a general concern for gay and lesbian issues, there was a sense of urgency engendered by the AIDS crisis and gay rights issues. This led to a number of

GAY AND LESBIAN THEATRE

Among the many alternative theatres that emerged in the last part of the twentieth century was theatre centering on the gay and lesbian experience. An important drama in this category was *The Normal Heart*, a largely autobiographical drama by Larry Kramer. The play, about the beginning of the AIDS crisis in the early 1980s, pits two characters against each other, one urging a full-throated confronation with the public calling attention to the epidemic and the other talking a more measured approach. A 2011 revival of the play featured the performers shown here: Ellen Barkin, John Benjamin Hickoy and Joe Mantello. (© Sara Krulwich/The New York Times/Redux)

significant dramas, including *The Normal Heart* (1985) by Larry Kramer (b. 1935), *As Is* (1985) by William M. Hoffman (b. 1939), *The Baltimore Waltz* (1992) by Paula Vogel (b. 1951), Tony Kushner's two-part play *Angels in America* (1993–1994), Terrence McNally's *Love! Valour! Compassion!* (1995), and Richard Greenberg's *Take Me Out*, which won a Tony Award in 2003. The continuing push for gay rights equality, including gay marriage, is also reflected in many popular recent Broadway productions that contain gay themes and references, including Douglas Carter Beane's *The Nance* (2013) and the musical *Kinky Boots* (2013).

"Gender-bender" groups such as the Cockettes and the Angels of Light in San Francisco and Centola and Hot Peaches in New York are an offshoot of gay and lesbian theatre. An important company in New York was the Theater of the Ridiculous, founded by John Vaccaro, which developed an extraordinary writer and performer— Charles Ludlam (1943–1987). Ludlam rewrote the classics to include a good deal of wild parody and frequent cross-dressing; he also created the long-lived Ridiculous Theatrical Company. Another important group was the Five Lesbian Brothers, a collective of five women, including the solo performance artist Lisa Kron, who were based in New York City and staged plays parodying mainstream attitudes toward gender and sexuality. Chicago's About Face Theatre, founded in 1995, has as a mission: "to be Chicago's celebrated center for lesbian, gay, bisexual, transgender, queer and ally (LGBTQA) arts."

Though a number of groups have not survived, individual performers and playwrights in gay and lesbian theatre remain very much a focus of attention.

POLITICAL THEATRE

Political theatre concerns itself with political ideas, causes, and individuals. It can run the gamut from dramas that take a strongly partisan point of view to those with a more even-handed probing of ideas and causes. It can attack a target, espouse a cause, or engage in satire to expose what the dramatist considers a wrongheaded regime or a wrongheaded approach to a problem. Many dramatists of the past, such as George Bernard Shaw and Bertolt Brecht, have incorporated a clear political agenda into their work.

In the United States, there was a marked increase in political drama during the period of the Vietnam War, with such plays as Megan Terry's *Viet Rock,* Barbara Garson's *MacBird,* and the musical *Hair.* In the 1970s, the militant black power movement also created a number of plays that had a strong political purpose.

A number of the plays we have discussed in the previous sections of this chapter qualify as political plays, in addition to their other concerns or focus. Many of the plays in the multiethnic group—African American, Hispanic, Asian American, and others—have a political as well as an aesthetic purpose. These plays serve to speak up for the rights and for the recognition of a particular ethnic group. The same could be said of feminist theatre and of gay and lesbian theatre: the playwrights who focus on these concerns are often passionate about a particular political position that is clearly reflected in their work. Examples include the plays dealing with AIDS by Kramer, Vogel, and Kushner mentioned above. Another play with strong political implications was *The Vagina Monologues* (1996) by Eve Ensler (b. 1953), a dramatic presentation of actual women's stories of intimacy, vulnerability, and sexual affirmation.

In a reaction against the administration of George W. Bush and many of its policies, there was an outpouring of essentially political plays. To indicate the type and range of political plays presented during the Bush years, we will mention three pieces. The first is *Baghdad Burning: Girl Blog from Iraq* (2005), about everyday life in Iraq during the war; it was based on the blog of a girl living there, and actors read entries telling of both routine and horrific incidents leading to the girl's disappointment. Another is *The Treatment* (2006), Eve Ensler's dramatization of post-traumatic stress disorder as revealed in scenes between a male U.S. war veteran and a female military psychologist. A third play was *My Trip to Al Qaeda* (2007), written by Lawrence Wright (b. 1947) based on a book by Wright, *The Looming Tower: Al Qaeda and the Road to 9/11.*

Other political plays do not deal directly with a particular party or administration, but nevertheless have a strong political component. *Nine Parts of Desire* by Heather Raffo is a powerful portrait of a cross-section of Iraqi women: their problems, their plight, and their distant hopes. Another political play is *Exonerated* by Jessica Blank and Erik Jensen, which includes actual transcripts of trials and other testimony of people who had been sentenced to death but were later proved to be innocent.

PERFORMANCE ART

The antecedents of performance art include earlier avant-garde experiments of the twentieth century, such as dada, surrealism, and happenings, each of which stressed the irrational and attacked traditional artistic values and forms. Other antecedents were the theories of Antonin Artaud and Jerzy Grotowski and popular forms, such as clowning, vaudeville, and stand-up comedy. Throughout the years the term *performance art* has been applied not just to theatre, but to a number of diverse artistic endeavors such as "action painting." In the 1970s, one branch of performance art emphasized the body as an art object: some artists suffered self-inflicted pain, and some went through daily routines (such as preparing a meal) in a museum or in a theatre setting. Another branch focused on site-specific or environmental pieces in which the setting or context was crucial: performances were created for specific locations such as a subway station, a city park, or a waterfront pier. One hallmark of all these presentations has been to challenge various types of mainstream arts and invite new ways of experiencing them.

In the theatre, the term *performance art* has been applied to different activities at different times. In some of the earliest forms of performance art, story, character, and text were minimized or even eliminated. The emphasis was not on narrating a story or exploring recognizable characters but rather on the visual and ritualistic aspects of performing. This type of theatre was often the work of an individual artist who incorporated highly personal messages, and sometimes political and social messages, in the event. The overall effect was often like a continually transforming collage. As might be expected, there was, as mentioned earlier, an affinity between this kind of theatre—with its emphasis of the visual picture formed onstage—and painting. Often, stage movement in performance art was also closely related to dance, as in the work of Martha Clarke (b. 1944).

In more recent years performance art has often been associated with individual artists who present extended autobiographical monologues or one-person shows in which they portray various characters through interconnected monologues. There are also some performance artists who stage presentations that feature clowning and other popular slapstick techniques borrowed from the circus and other popular arts. Several such artists—Karen Finley (b. 1956) was one of the most visible—became a center of controversy when their work was seized on by conservative groups and members of Congress as a reason to oppose funding the National Endowment for the Arts. These artists often espoused such causes as feminism and civil liberties for lesbians and gays. Often nudity and other controversial representations of sexuality or sexual orientation were used to confront audiences. Such was the case in *Alice's Rape* (1989), in which Robbie McCauley performed nude as her great-great-grandmother, a slave on the auction block.

Two artists who began performing solo pieces in alternative spaces but later received commercial productions are Spalding Gray (1941–2004) and Bill Irwin (b. 1950). Gray, a monologist who discussed issues that ranged from his own personal concerns to politics, was reminiscent of ancient storytellers who created a theatrical environment single-handedly. Irwin's performances are mime-like, and he uses popular slapstick techniques to reflect on the contemporary human condition. Anna Deavere Smith (b. 1952), an African American performance artist, won considerable acclaim

Performance art
Experimental theatre that initially incorporated elements of dance and visual arts into performance. Since performance art often is based on the vision of an individual performer or director rather than playwright, the autobiographical monologue and solo performance have become popular performance art forms.

PLAYING YOUR PART: EXPERIENCING THEATRE

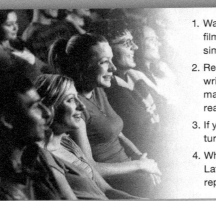

1. Watch one of the one-person shows by Spalding Gray or John Leguizamo that has been filmed. In what ways is this work different from traditional theatre? Are there any similarities?

2. Read a play by a twenty-first century African American, Latino American, or feminist playwright. What are the specific themes the play focuses on? How are the themes and dramatic techniques unique to the playwright? How are they similar to other plays you have read?

3. If you were to create a one-person monologue about your life, what events would you capture? Do you think it could be successful as a performance art work?

4. What films or television shows have you seen that represent either African Americans, Latino Americans, Asian Americans, women, or gays and lesbians? Do you believe these representations are accurate? Why? Why not?

in the early 1990s for pieces dealing with racial unrest. In her works, she portrays numerous real people she has met and interviewed. For example, her *Twilight: Los Angeles 1992* presented people affected by the uprising that followed the acquittals in the first trial of police officers charged with brutalizing Rodney King.

Other well-known monologists are Eric Bogosian (b. 1953), Danny Hoch (b. 1970), John Leguizamo (b. 1965), Mike Daisey (b. 1973), Lisa Kron (b. 1961), and Sarah Jones (b. 1973). Ping Chong (b. 1946) is an Asian American performance artist who mixes multimedia into his works. One constant in performance art is that it has generally featured solo performances. However, there have been, and continue to be, exceptions. For example, the works of certain ensembles that often mix movement, sound, and multimedia, such as the Blue Man Group, have also been categorized as performance art.

A number of spaces have become recognized for their presentation of performance artists. These include two in New York City: PS 122, a converted public school in the East Village in Manhattan; and the Kitchen, also located downtown. In addition, many museums throughout the United States are known for presenting series of performance artists, including the Walker Museum in Minneapolis and the Museum of Contemporary Art in Chicago. The fact that performance art is most often presented in converted, found spaces, or museums again reflects the eclectic nature of the form and its relationship to earlier avant-garde movements and the visual arts.

TODAY'S THEATRE: GLOBAL, ECLECTIC, DIVERSE

As we have pointed out, perhaps at no time in theatre history has there been such a wide-ranging group of live theatre events available to audiences. Despite the ever-present competition from electronic media— films, television, computers, and numerous handheld devices—live theatre remains very much a presence in our lives. It is truly global and international, with influences and exchanges from every corner of the world. Productions can regularly be seen not only in larger Broadway-style emporiums, but in excellent regional theatre and first-rate university and college productions. The kinds of theatre available range from the finest classics—Shakespeare is the most

GROUP PERFORMANCE ART

In most cases performance art involves one person who appears, generally, in an unusual setting and may combine his or her performance with story telling, dance, or art. A troupe called llotopie is an exception in that it is a group effort that bills itself as performance art. Their piece *Water Fools* has been performed in many locations around the world and is shown here at the Oceans Festival in Lisbon, Portugal. As part of the spectacle, everyday objects become mythical creatures, cars pull caravans, gods march into battle, while a fifteen-foot Queen watches over the entire magical kingdom. (© Nacho Doce/Reuters/Corbis)

widely produced playwright in U.S.—to the most cutting-edge, postmodern presentations. In short, the opportunities today for rewarding experiences in the theatre are truly global and diverse on all sides.

When we turn from the theatre of today to the theatre of the future, a question arises: Where will theatre go from here? It is impossible, of course, to answer with any certainty. We can assume, though, that the trends described in this chapter and Chapter 13 will continue. Theatre of the future will no doubt continue to present new works alongside a rich mixture of plays from the past. In both writing and production, theatre will draw on many sources. We cannot know whether or not new plays will attain the greatness of the past, but playwrights show no sign of abandoning theatre, despite the larger financial rewards offered by film and television.

We can be sure that theatre will survive in a vigorous form, no matter what challenges it faces from electronic media. At the same time, modern technology will play an important role in theatre: in lighting effects, with the use of computerized lighting boards, in the shifting of scenery, and in other ways. There will also, no doubt, continue to be multimedia experiments, fusing theatre with film, digital media, dance, and computer-generated media.

PLAYING YOUR PART: THINKING ABOUT THEATRE

1. Explain why some theorists might categorize a stand-up comedian as a performance artist.
2. Discuss why a film or television show you have seen might be categorized as postmodern.
3. Discuss key changes in communication that have had an impact on global theatre.
4. Discuss why a film or television show that you have seen might be categorized as a documentary drama.
5. How do you think theatre will be affected by new digital technologies? Explain your answer.

With all its innovations, however, theatre of the future will be an extension of theatre of the past. Theatre will continue to be enacted by women and men in person before an audience, and the plays they perform will deal with the hopes, fears, agonies, and joys of the human race.

It is clear that the complexity of the modern world will result in a heterogeneous theatre. Ongoing exploration of the diversity of contemporary society means that diverse theatres will continue to spring up. There is no question that in the twenty-first century theatre will be as complex and fragmented as the world in which it exists.

SUMMARY

1. Contemporary U.S. theatre is a reflection of and a reaction to the complexity of modern times.
2. The city of Chicago, with its many types, levels, and sizes of theatres, offers a microcosm of U.S. theatres across the country.
3. An important development of the past half century has been the emergence of non–text based theatre, sometimes referred to as postmodernist. Rather than being initiated by a dramatist, a theatre event is created by an auteur director, an acting ensemble, a performance artist, or some combination of these.
4. Avant-garde and experimental theatre, which grew out of earlier approaches, is alive and well in the United States.
5. Multiethnic theatre in U.S. is vibrant, with a number of facets: (a) African American theatre, (b) Asian American theatre, (c) Hispanic theatre, and (d) Native American theatre.
6. There are many active minority theatres and theatres with special points of view, including (a) feminist theatre, (b) gay and lesbian theatre, and (c) political theatre.
7. An important form of theatre today is performance art.
8. Much of the new theatre activity today is a reflection of the theories of postmodernism.

Plays That May Be Read Online

The following is a list of plays that are used as examples to highlight key concepts in *Theatre Experience,* 13th edition, and that can be read online. Any play in this edition that can be found on the Internet is highlighted in blue typeface. Should you want to read any of these plays, or if your teacher has assigned one, you can refer to this list and find an online version.

Abraham and Isaac http://www.wwnorton.com/college/english/nael/noa/pdf/13BromePlay_1_12.pdf

Adding Machine, The (Elmer Rice) http://www.scribd.com/doc/25952449/Elmer-Rice-The-Adding-Machine

Alchemist, The (Jonson, Ben) http://www.gutenberg.org/ebooks/4081

All For Love (Dryden, John) http://www.gutenberg.org/ebooks/2062

All's Well That Ends Well (Shakespeare, Wiliam) http://www.gutenberg.org/ebooks/1125

Antigone (Sophocles) http://classics.mit.edu/Sophocles/antigone.html

Antony and Cleopatra (Shakespeare, William) http://www.gutenberg.org/ebooks/2268

Arms and the Man (Shaw, George Bernard) http://www.gutenberg.org/ebooks/3618

Bacchae, The (Euripides) http://www.gutenberg.org/ebooks/35173

Birds, The (Aristophanes) http://www.gutenberg.org/ebooks/3013

Blood Wedding (Lorca, Federico Garcia) http://www.poetryintranslation.com/klineasbloodwedding.htm

Brand (Ibsen, Henrik) http://archive.org/details/cu31924026309199

Busy Body, The (Centlivre, Susana) http://www.gutenberg.org/ebooks/16740

Caesar and Cleopatra (Shaw, George Bernard) http://www.gutenberg.org/ebooks/3329

Candida (Shaw, George Bernard) http://www.gutenberg.org/ebooks/4023

Chantecler (Rostand, Edmond) http://www.gutenberg.org/ebooks/10747

Cherry Orchard, The (Chekhov, Anton) http://www.gutenberg.org/ebooks/7986

Cid, The (Corneille, Pierre) http://www.gutenberg.org/ebooks/14954

Clouds, The (Aristophanes) http://www.gutenberg.org/ebooks/2562

Comedy of Errors, The (Shakespeare, William) http://www.gutenberg.org/ebooks/23046

Country Wife, The (Wycherley, Willliam) http://archive.org/details/countrywifecomed00wych

Cymbeline (Shakespeare, William) http://www.gutenberg.org/ebooks/1133

Cyrano de Bergerac (Rostand, Edmond) http://www.gutenberg.org/ebooks/1254

Doctor in Spite of Himself, The (Molière) http://archive.org/details/dramaticworksofm01moliiala

Doll's House, A (Ibsen, Henrik) http://www.gutenberg.org/ebooks/2542

Dream Play, A (Strindberg, August) www.archive.org/details/playsbyaugustst00bjgoog

Electra (Euripides) http://www.gutenberg.org/ebooks/14322

Electra (Sophocles) http://classics.mit.edu/Sophocles/electra.html

Emperor Jones, The (O'Neill, Eugene) http://archive.org/details/emperorjones00onegoog
Enemy of the People, An (Ibsen, Henrik) http://www.gutenberg.org/ebooks/2446
Eumenides, The (The Furies) (Aeschylus) http://www.gutenberg.org/ebooks/8604
Every Man in His Humour (Jonson, Ben) http://www.gutenberg.org/ebooks/3694
Every Man Out of His Humour (Jonson, Ben) http://www.gutenberg.org/ebooks/3695
Everyman http://archive.org/details/everyman00newy
Faust (Goethe, Johann Wolfgang von) http://www.gutenberg.org/ebooks/14460
Frogs, The (Aristophanes) http://www.gutenberg.org/ebooks/7998
Great God Brown, The (O'Neill, Eugene) http://gutenberg.net.au/ebooks04/0400091h.html
Ghosts (Henrik Ibsen) http://www.gutenberg.org/ebooks/8121
Government Inspector (The Inspector General) (Gogol, Nikolai) http://www.gutenberg.org/ebooks/8121
Hairy Ape, The (O'Neill, Eugene) http://www.gutenberg.org/ebooks/4015
Hamlet (Shakespeare, William) http://www.gutenberg.org/ebooks/1524
Heartbreak House (Shaw, George Bernard) http://www.gutenberg.org/ebooks/3543
Hedda Gabler (Ibsen, Henrik) http://www.gutenberg.org/ebooks/4093
Henry IV, Pt. 1 (Shakespeare, William) http://www.gutenberg.org/ebooks/2251
Henry IV, Pt. 2 (Shakespeare, William) http://www.gutenberg.org/ebooks/1117
Henry V (Shakespeare, William) http://www.gutenberg.org/ebooks/1119
House of Bernarda Alba, The (Lorca, Federico Garcia)
http://www.poetryintranslation.com/PITBR/Spanish/AlbaActI.htm
Importance of Being Earnest, The (Wilde, Oscar) http://www.gutenberg.org/ebooks/844
Julius Caesar (Shakespeare, William) http://www.gutenberg.org/ebooks/2263
King Lear (Shakespeare, William) http://www.gutenberg.org/ebooks/2266
King Stag, The (Gozzi, Carlo) http://www.epc-library.com/freeview/F_1814.pdf
Libation Bearers (Aeschylus) http://records.viu.ca/~johnstoi/aeschylus/libationbearers.htm
Life is a Dream (Calderon de la Barca, Pedro) http://www.gutenberg.org/ebooks/2587
Little Clay Cart, The (Sudraka) http://www.gutenberg.org/ebooks/21020
London Merchant, The (Lillo, George) http://archive.org/details/londonmerchanto00lillgoog
Love's Labours Lost (Shakespeare, William) http://www.gutenberg.org/ebooks/1109
Lysistrata (Aristophanes) http://www.gutenberg.org/ebooks/7700
Macbeth (Shakespeare, William) http://www.gutenberg.org/ebooks/1129
Major Barbara (Shaw, George Bernard) http://www.gutenberg.org/ebooks/3790
Marriage of Figaro, The (Beumarchais, Pierre)
http://oll.libertyfund.org/?option=com_staticxt&staticfile=show.php%3Ftitle=1563&Itemid=27
Master Builder, The (Ibsen, Henrik) http://www.gutenberg.org/ebooks/4070
Measure for Measure (Shakespeare, William) http://www.gutenberg.org/ebooks/1126
Medea (Euripides) http://www.gutenberg.org/ebooks/35451
Menaechmi, The (Plautus) http://www.perseus.tufts.edu/hopper/text?doc=Perseus:text:1999.02.0101
Merchant of Venice, The (Shakespeare, William) http://www.gutenberg.org/ebooks/2243
Merry Wives of Windsor (Shakespeare, William) http://shakespeare.mit.edu/merry_wives/full.html
Midsummer Night's Dream, A (Shakespeare, William) http://www.gutenberg.org/ebooks/1514
Misanthrope, The (Molière) http://archive.org/details/comedies00molirich

Miser, The (Molière) http://www.gutenberg.org/ebooks/6923

Miss Julie (Strindberg, August) www.gutenberg.org/ebooks/14347

Mrs. Warren's Profession (Shaw, George Bernard) http://www.gutenberg.org/ebooks/1097

Much Ado About Nothing (Shakespeare, William) http://www.gutenberg.org/ebooks/2240

No Exit (Sartre, Jean Paul) http://archive.org/stream/NoExit/NoExit_djvu.txt

Oedipus the King (*King Oedipus*) (Sophocles) http://classics.mit.edu/Sophocles/oedipus.html

Othello (Shakespeare, William) http://www.gutenberg.org/ebooks/1531

Peer Gynt (Ibsen, Henrik) http://archive.org/details/peergyntadramat01ibsegoog

Phaedra (Phedre) (Racine, Jean) http://www.gutenberg.org/ebooks/1977

Pirates of Penzance, The (Gilbert, W.S. and Sullivan, Arthur) http://www.gutenberg.org/ebooks/808

Prometheus Bound (Aeschylus) http://www.gutenberg.org/ebooks/8714

Pygmalion (Shaw, George Bernard) http://www.gutenberg.org/ebooks/3825

Richard II (Shakespeare, William) http://www.gutenberg.org/ebooks/1111

Richard III (Shakespeare, William) http://www.gutenberg.org/ebooks/2257

Rivals, The (Sheridan, Richard Brinsley) http://www.gutenberg.org/ebooks/24761

Romeo and Juliet (Shakespeare, William) http://www.gutenberg.org/ebooks/1513

R.U.R. (Capek,Karel) http://ebooks.adelaide.edu.au/c/capek/karel/rur/

Saint Joan (Shaw, George Bernard) http://archive.org/details/SaintJoan

School for Scandal, The (Sheridan, Richard Brinsley) http://www.gutenberg.org/ebooks/1929

School for Wives, The (Molière) http://archive.org/details/comedies00molirich

Sea Gull, The (Chekhov, Anton) www.gutenberg.org/ebooks/1754

Second Shepherds' Play, The www.calvin.edu/academic/engl/215/ssp.htm

Servant of Two Masters, The (Goldoni, Carlo)
http://gutenberg.ca/ebooks/goldonident-twomasters/goldonident-twomasters-00-h.html

Shakuntala (Kalidasa) http://www.sacred-texts.com/hin/sha/index.htm

Sotoba Komachi (Zeami) http://etext.virginia.edu/toc/modeng/public/WalSoto.html

Six Characters in Search of an Author (Pirandello, Luigi) http://www.ibiblio.org/eldritch/lp/six.htm

Tamburlaine (Marlowe, Christopher) http://www.gutenberg.org/ebooks/1094

Taming of the Shrew, The (Shakespeare, William) http://shakespeare.mit.edu/taming_shrew/full.html

Tartuffe (Molière) http://www.gutenberg.org/ebooks/2027

Tempest, The (Shakespeare, William) http://www.gutenberg.org/ebooks/23042

The Great God Brown http://gutenberg.net.au/ebooks04/0400091h.html

Three Sisters, The (Chekhov, Anton) http://www.gutenberg.org/ebooks/7986

Tragical History of Dr. Faustus, The (Marlowe, Christopher) http://www.gutenberg.org/ebooks/779

Troilus and Cressida (Shakespeare, William) http://www.gutenberg.org/ebooks/1790

Twelfth Night (Shakespeare, William) http://www.gutenberg.org/ebooks/1526

Two Gentlemen of Verona (Shakespeare, William) http://www.gutenberg.org/ebooks/1108

Uncle Vanya (Chekhov, Anton) http://www.gutenberg.org/ebooks/1756

Volpone (Jonson, Ben) http://www.gutenberg.org/ebooks/4039

Way of the World, The (Congreve, William) http://www.gutenberg.org/ebooks/1292

Would-Be Gentleman, The (Molière) http://archive.org/details/comedies00molirich

Glossary

Above Upstage or away from the audience.

Acting area One of several areas into which a stage space is divided in order to facilitate blocking and the planning of stage movement.

Ad lib To improvise lines of a speech.

Aesthetic distance Physical or psychological separation or detachment of audience from dramatic action, usually considered necessary for artistic illusion.

Allegory Symbolic representation of abstract themes through characters, action, and other concrete elements of a play.

Amphitheatre Large oval, circular, or semicircular outdoor theatre with rising tiers of seats around an open playing area; *also,* an exceptionally large indoor auditorium.

Antagonist Opponent of the protagonist in a drama.

Apprentice Young performer training in an Elizabethan acting company.

Apron Stage space in front of the curtain line or proscenium; also called the *forestage.*

Arena Stage entirely surrounded by the audience; also known as *circle theatre* or *theatre-in-the-round.*

Aside In a play, thoughts spoken aloud by one character (often, to the audience) without being heard or noticed by others onstage.

At rise Expression used to describe what is happening onstage at the moment when the curtain first rises or the lights come up.

Audition A tryout by performers before a director for a role in a play or musical.

Automated light Piece of lighting equipment that can change the direction, focus, color, and shape of the lighting beam by remote control. Made possible by advances in electronics and computerization.

Backdrop Large drapery or painted canvas that provides the rear or upstage masking of a set.

Backstage Stage area behind the front curtain; *also,* the areas beyond the setting, including wings and dressing rooms.

Ballad opera Eighteenth-century English form that burlesqued opera.

Basic situation Specific problem or maladjustment from which a play arises.

Batten Pipe or long pole suspended horizontally above the stage, on which scenery, drapery, or lights may be hung.

Beam projector Lighting instrument without a lens, which uses a parabolic reflector to project a narrow, nonadjustable beam of light.

Below Opposite of *above;* toward the front of the stage.

Biomechanics Vsevolod Meyerhold's theory that a performer's body should be machinelike and that emotion could be represented externally.

Black box A theatre space that is open, flexible, and adaptable, usually without fixed seating. The stage-audience configuration can be rearranged to suit the individual requirements of a given production, making it both economical and particularly well suited to experimental work.

Blackout Total darkening of the stage.

Blocking Pattern and arrangement of performers' movements onstage with respect to each other and to the stage space, usually set by the director.

Book (1) Spoken (as opposed to sung) portion of the text of a musical play. (2) To schedule engagements for artists or productions.

Bookholder Prompter who gave actors their lines in Elizabethan theatres.

Border Strip of drapery or painted canvas hung from a batten or pipe to mask the area above the stage; *also,* a row of lights hung from a batten.

Bourgeois or domestic drama Drama dealing with problems—particularly family problems—of middle-and lower-class characters. There are serious and comic domestic dramas.

Box Small private compartment for a group of spectators built into the walls of a traditional proscenium-arch theatre.

Box set Interior setting using flats to form the back and side walls and often the ceiling of a room.

Build To create a costume from scratch in a costume shop.

Burlesque A ludicrous, comic imitation of a dramatic form, play, piece of literature, or other popular entertainment.

Business Obvious, detailed physical movement of performers to reveal character, aid action, or establish mood.

Capa y espada ("CAH-pah ee ehs-PAH-dah") Literally, "cape and sword"; Spanish play about intrigue and duels of honor.

Casting Choosing performers to play specific roles in a play or musical. Usually performers are chosen who suit the part in age, gender, and other features, but at times there is "casting against type."

Catharsis ("kuh-THAR-sis") Greek word, usually translated as "purgation," which Aristotle used in his definition of tragedy, referring to the vicarious cleansing of emotions in the audience through their representation onstage.

Catwalk Narrow metal platform suspended above the stage to permit ready access to lights and scenery hung from the grid.

Cazuela ("cah-zoo-AY-lah") Gallery above the tavern in the back wall of the theatres of the Spanish golden age; the area where unescorted women sat.

Center stage Stage position in the middle acting area of the stage, or the middle section extended upstage and downstage.

Choregus ("koh-REE-guhs") Wealthy person who financed a playwright's works at an ancient Greek dramatic festival.

Chorus (1) In ancient Greek drama, a group of performers who sang and danced, sometimes participating in the action but usually simply commenting on it. (2) In modern times, performers in a musical play who sing and dance as a group.

City Dionysia ("SIT-ee digh-eh-NIGH-see-uh") The most important Greek festival in honor of the god Dionysus, and the first to include drama. Held in the spring.

Climax The high point in the development of a dramatic plot.

Comedia ("koh-MAY-dee-ah") Three-act full-length nonreligious play of the Spanish golden age.

Comedy In general, a play that is light in tone, is concerned with issues that point out the excesses and folly of human behavior, has a happy ending, and is designed to amuse.

Comedy of ideas A comedy in which the humor is based on intellectual and verbal aspects of comedy rather than physical comedy or comedy of character. A drama whose emphasis is on the clash of ideas, as exemplified in the plays of George Bernard Shaw.

Comedy of manners Form of comic drama that became popular in the English Restoration, that is set within sophisticated society, while poking fun at its characters' social pretensions, usually through verbal wit.

Commedia dell'arte Form of comic theatre, originating in Italy in the sixteenth century, in which dialogue was improvised around a scerario involving a set of stock characters, each with a traditional costume, name, and often mask.

Comic premise Idea or concept in a comedy that turns the accepted notion of things upside down.

Compañias de parte ("cōhm-pa-NYEE-ahs day PAHR-teh") Acting troupes in the Spanish golden age, organized according to a sharing system.

Complication Introduction, in a play, of a new force, which creates a new balance of power and entails a delay in reaching the climax.

Computer-assisted design (CAD) Designs created by computer. All features of a set design, including ground plans, elevations, and walls, can be indicated by computer, and variations and alternations can be easily created and displayed.

Concept musical A musical that is built around an idea or a theme rather than a story.

Conflict Tension between two or more characters that leads to a crisis or climax; a fundamental struggle or imbalance—involving ideologies, actions, personalities, etc.—underlying the plot of a play.

Constructivism Post–World War I movement in scene design, in which sets—frequently composed of ramps, platforms, and levels—were nonrealistic and intended to provide greater opportunities for physical action.

Corral Theatre building of the Spanish golden age, usually located in the courtyard of a series of adjoining buildings.

Counterweight Device for balancing the weight of scenery in a system that allows scenery to be raised above the stage by ropes and pulleys.

Crew Backstage team assisting in mounting a production.

Crisis A point in a play when events and opposing forces are at a crucial moment, and when the course of further action will be determined. There may be a series of crises leading to the definitive climax.

Cross Movement by a performer across the stage in a given direction.

Cues Any prearranged signal—such as the last words in a speech, a piece of business, or any action or lighting change—that indicates to a performer or stage manager that it is time to proceed to the next line or action.

Cue sheet Prompt book marked with cues, or a list of cues for the use of technicians, especially the stage manager.

Curtain (1) Rise or fall of the actual curtain, which separates a play into structural parts. (2) Last bit of action preceding the fall of the curtain.

Curtain-raiser In nineteenth-century theatre, a short play presented before a full-length drama.

Cyclorama Permanent fixture or curved drop used to mask the rear and sides of a stage, usually representing sky or open space.

Dada Movement in art between the world wars, based on presenting the irrational and attacking traditional artistic values.

Denouement ("deh-noo-MAHN") Point near the end of a play when suspense is satisfied and "the knot is untied."

Designer (front) elevations Drawings that indicate the total, exact details of a set as seen from the point of view of the audience.

Deus ex machina ("DEH-oos eks MAH-kih-nah") Literally, "god from a machine," a resolution device in classic Greek drama; hence, intervention of supernatural forces—usually at the last moment—to save the action from its logical conclusion. In modern drama, an arbitrary and coincidental solution.

Dimmer Device for changing lighting intensity smoothly and at varying rates.

Dim out To turn out lights with a dimmer.

Director In American usage, the person responsible for the overall unity of a production and for coordinating the work of contributing artists. The American director is the equivalent of the British producer and the French *metteur-en-scène*. ("meh-TURR ahn SENN").

Distressing Making a costume look weathered or worn.

Dithyramb ("DITH-ih-ramb") Ancient Greek choral song describing the adventures of a god or hero.

Double entendre ("DOO-bluh ahnTAHN-druh") Word or phrase in comedy that has a double meaning, the second often sexual.

Doubling Term used when a performer plays more than one role in a play.

Downstage Front of the stage, toward the audience.

Dramaturg *Also,* literary manager. On the staff of a theatre, a person who consults with and advises authors and directors, writes program notes, and edits scripts.

Drapers Technicians who pattern, pin, and drape the fabric to fit the actors in a production perfectly.

Dress rehearsal The first full performances of a production before performances for the public.

Drop Large piece of fabric—generally painted canvas—hung from a batten to the stage floor, usually to serve as backing.

Ellipsoidal reflector spotlight Sharp, powerful light used at some distance from the stage.

Emotional recall Stanislavski's exercise, which helps the performer to present realistic emotions. The performer feels a character's emotion by thinking of the conditions surrounding an event in his or her own life that led to a similar emotion.

Ensemble playing Acting that stresses the total artistic unity of a group performance rather than individual performances.

Entrance Manner and effectiveness with which a performer comes into a scene, as well as the actual coming onstage; *also,* the way this is prepared for by the playwright.

Environmental theatre A type of theatre, made popular in the 1960s, which attempts to eliminate the distinction between audience and acting space and which emphasizes a multiple focus for the audience rather than a single focus.

Epilogue Speech by one of the performers to the audience after the conclusion of a play.

Exit A performer's leaving the stage, as well as the preparation for his or her leaving.

Exposition Information necessary for an understanding of the story but not covered by the action onstage; events or knowledge from the past, or occurring outside the play, which must be introduced so that the audience can understand the characters or plot.

Expressionism The attempt in drama to depict the subjective state of a character or group of characters through such nonrealistic techniques as distortion, striking images, and poetic language.

Farce A subclass of comedy with emphasis on exaggerated plot complications and with few or no intellectual pretensions.

Flashback In a narrative or story, movement back to a time in the past to show a scene or an event before the narrative resumes at the point at which it was interrupted.

Flat A scenic unit consisting of canvas stretched on a wooden frame often used with similar units to create a set.

Flood, floodlight Lighting instrument without lenses which is used for general or large-area lighting.

Fly loft Space above the stage where scenery may be lifted out of sight by ropes and pulleys.

Follow spot Large, powerful spotlight with a sharp focus and narrow beam which is used by an operator to follow principal performers as they move about the stage.

Footlights Row of lights in the floor along the front edge of the stage or apron. Almost never used in contemporary theatre.

Forestage See *Apron.*

Found space Space not originally intended for theatre, which is used for theatrical productions. Avant-garde artists often produce in found spaces.

Fourth wall Convention, in a proscenium-arch theatre, that the audience is looking into a room through an invisible fourth wall.

Freeze To remain motionless onstage, especially for laughs or in a tableau.

Fresnel ("fruh-NEL") Type of spotlight used over relatively short distances with a soft beam edge, which allows the light to blend easily with light from other sources; *also,* the type of lenses used in such spotlights.

Front of the house Portion of a theatre reserved for the audience; sometimes called simply the *house.*

Futurism Art movement, begun in Italy about 1905, which idealized mechanization and machinery.

Gallery In traditional proscenium-arch theatres, the undivided seating area cut into the walls of the building.

Gauze See *Scrim.*

Gel Thin, flexible color medium used in lighting instruments to give color to a light beam.

Genre A French word meaning type or category. In theatre, genre denotes the category into which a play falls: for example, tragedy, comedy, or tragicomedy.

Grid Metal framework above the stage from which lights and scenery are suspended.

Groove system System in which tracks on the stage floor and above the stage allowed for the smooth movement of flat wings on and off the stage; usually there were a series of grooves at each stage position.

Ground plan A blueprint or floor plan of the stage indicating the placement of scenery, furniture, doors and windows, and the various levels of the stage, as well as the walls of rooms, platforms, etc.

Hamartia ("hah-MARH-tee-ah") Ancient Greek term usually translated as "tragic flaw." The literal translation is "missing the mark," which may suggest that hamartia is not so much a character flaw as an error in judgment.

Hanamichi ("hah-nah-MEE-chee") In kabuki theatre, a bridge running from behind the audience (toward the left side of the audience) to the stage. Performers can enter on the hanamichi; important scenes may also be played on it.

Hand props Small props carried on- or offstage by actors and actresses during a performance, such as canes, umbrellas, or briefcases. See also *Props.*

Happenings Nonliterary theatrical events, developed in the 1960s, in which the script is replaced with a scenario that provides for chance occurrences, and are performed (often only once) in such places as parks and street corners.

Hashigakari ("ha-shee-gah-KAH-ree") Bridge in nō theatre on which the actors make their entrance from the dressing area to the platform stage.

Heroic drama Serious but basically optimistic drama written in verse or elevated prose, with noble or heroic characters in extreme situations or unusual adventures.

Hireling Member of an Elizabethan acting troupe who was paid a set salary and was not a shareholder.

House See *Front of the house.*

Hubris ("HEW-brihs") Ancient Greek term usually defined as "excessive pride" and cited as a common tragic character flaw.

Imitation To simulate or copy behavior observed in real life.

Inner stage Area at the rear of the stage that can be cut off from the rest by means of curtains or scenery and revealed for special scenes.

Irony A condition the reverse of what we have expected or an expression whose intended implication is the opposite of its literal sense.

Kill To eliminate or suppress; for example, to remove unwanted light or to ruin an effect through improper execution.

Lazzi ("LAHT-zee") Comic pieces of business repeatedly used by characters in Italian commedia dell'arte.

Left stage (also referred to as stage left) Left side of the stage from the point of view of a performer facing the audience.

Living newspapers In the United States, the Federal Theatre Project's dramatizations of newsworthy events in the 1930s.

Long run Term used in commercial theatre when a drama is performed for as long as it is popular.

lyricist The author of the lyrics of the songs in a musical.

Magic if Stanislavski's acting exercise, which requires the performer to ask, "How would I react *if* I were in this character's position?"

Managing director In nonprofit theatre organizations, the individual who controls resources and expenditures.

Mask (1) To conceal backstage areas or technical equipment from the audience by means of scenery. (2) Face or head covering for a performer, in the image of the character portrayed.

Masking Scenery or draperies used to hide or cover.

Melodrama Dramatic form made popular in the nineteenth century that emphasized action and spectacular effects and also used music to underscore the action; it had stock characters, usually with clearly defined villains and heroes.

Minstrelsy Type of nineteenth-century production usually featuring white performers made up in blackface.

Mise-en-scène ("miz-on-SEHN") Arrangement of all the elements in a stage picture at a given moment or throughout a performance.

Multimedia Use of electronic media, such as slides, film, and videotape, in live theatrical presentations.

Multimedia theatre Presentations in which theatrical elements are combined with other art forms, such as film, video, art, or dance. Frequently, several media are combined in a single production.

Multiple setting Form of stage setting, common in the Middle Ages, in which several locations are represented at the same time; also called *simultaneous setting*. Used also in various forms of contemporary theatre.

Musical theatre A type of theatre that integrates songs, spoken dialogue, acting, and dance. The story and emotions are underscored and enhanced by the music and dance, which are fully integrated into the plot.

Naturalism Attempts to put on stage exact copies of everyday life; sometimes also called *slice of life*.

Nonrealism Also known as departures from realism, means all types of theatre that depart from observable reality.

Objective Stanislavski's term for that which is urgently desired and sought by a character, the long-range goal that propels a character to action.

Obstacle That which delays or prevents the achieving of a goal by a character. An obstacle creates complication and conflict.

Offstage Areas of the stage, usually in the wings or backstage, that are not in view of the audience.

Onstage Area of the stage that is in view of the audience.

Open To turn or face more toward the audience.

Orchestra (1) In American usage, ground-floor seating in an auditorium. (2) Circular playing space in ancient Greek theatres.

Pace Rate at which a performance is played; *also,* to perform a scene or play to set its proper speed.

Pantomime A form of theatrical presentation that relies on dance, gesture, and physical movement without speech.

Parabasis ("puh-RAB-uh-sihs") Scene in classical Greek Old Comedy in which the chorus directly addresses the audience members and makes fun of them.

Parados ("PAR-uh-dohs") In classical Greek drama, the scene in which the chorus enters; *also,* the entranceway for the chorus in Greek theatre.

Parterre In French neoclassical theatre, the pit in which audience members stood.

Patio In theatre of the Spanish golden age, the pit area for the audience.

Pensionnaire ("PON-see-oh-NARE") Hireling in a French acting troupe.

Performance art Experimental theatre that initially incorporated elements of dance and visual arts into performance. Since performance art often is based on the vision of an individual performer or director rather than playwright, the auto-biographical monologue and solo performance have become popular performance art forms.

Periaktoi In Greek theatre, vertical three-sided column that could be rotated to show three different scenic pictures.

Period Term describing any representation onstage of a former age (e.g., *period costume, period play*).

Perspective Illusion of depth in painting, introduced into scene design during the Italian Renaissance.

Pit Floor of the house in a traditional proscenium-arch theatre. It was originally a standing area; by the end of the eighteenth century, backless benches were added.

Platform Raised surface on a stage floor serving as an elevation for parts of the stage action and allowing for a multiplicity of stage levels.

Platform stage Elevated stage with no proscenium, sometimes called a *trestle stage*.

Plot As distinct from story, patterned arrangements of events and characters in a drama, with incidents selected and arranged for maximum dramatic impact.

Point of attack The moment in the story when a play actually begins. The dramatist chooses a point that he or she judges will best start the action and propel it forward.

Pole and chariot Giacomo Torelli's mechanized means of changing sets made up of flat wings.

Postmodernism A contemporary concept suggesting that artists and audiences have gone beyond the modernist movements of realism and departures from realism and such categories as "high art" and "popular art."

Preparation (1) Previous arranging of circumstances, pointing of characters, and placing of properties in a production so that the ensuing actions will seem reasonable. (2) Actions taken by an actor or actress in getting ready for a performance.

Previews Tryout performances of a production before an audience, preceding the official "opening" performance.

Private theatres Indoor theatres in Elizabethan England.

Producer In American usage, the person responsible for the business side of a production, including raising the necessary money. (In British usage, a producer for many years was the equivalent of an American director.)

Prologue Introductory speech delivered to the audience by one of the actors or actresses before a play begins.

Prompt To furnish a performer with missed or forgotten lines or cues during a performance.

Prompt book Script of a play indicating performers' movements, light cues, sound cues, etc.

Prop Properties; objects that are used by performers onstage or are necessary to complete a set.

Proscenium ("pro-SEEN-ee-um") Arch or frame surrounding the stage opening in a box or picture stage.

Protagonist Principal character in a play, the one whom the drama is about.

Public theatres Outdoor theatres in Elizabethan England.

Pull To choose a costume from an inventory owned by a theatre company or costume warehouse.

Rake (1) To position scenery on a slant or at an angle other than parallel or perpendicular to the curtain line. (2) An upward slope of the stage floor away from the audience.

Raked stage Stage floor that slopes upward away from the audience toward the back of the stage.

Realism Broadly, an attempt to present onstage people and events corresponding to those in everyday life.

Regional theatre (1) Theatre whose subject matter is specific to a particular geographic region. (2) Theatres situated in theatrical centers across the country.

Régisseur ("ray-zhee-SUHR") Continental European term for a theatre director; it sometimes denotes a dictatorial director.

Rehearsal Preparation by a cast for the performance of a play through repetition and practice.

Rendering a complete drawing of a set, usually in color.

Repertory, or repertoire Acting company that at any time can perform a number of plays alternately; *also,* the plays regularly performed by a company.

Restoration drama English drama after the restoration of the monarchy, from 1660 to 1700.

Reversal Sudden switch of circumstances or revelation of knowledge, which leads to a result contrary to expectations; called *peripeteia* ("peh-rih-puh-TEE-uh") or *peripety* ("peh-RIP-uh-tee") in Greek drama.

Revolving stage Large circular turntable in a stage floor on which scenery is placed so that, as it moves, one set is brought into view while another one turns out of sight.

Right stage (also referred to as stage right) Right side of the stage from the point of view of a performer facing the audience.

Ritual Ceremonial event, often religious, which takes place in a prescribed sequence.

Role playing In everyday life, the acting out of a particular role by copying the expected social behavior of that position.

Romanticism Nineteenth-century dramatic movement that imitated the episodic structure of Shakespeare, and thematically focused on the gulf between human being's spiritual aspirations and physical limitations.

Satire Comic form, using irony and exaggeration, to attack and expose folly and vice.

Satyr play One of the three types of classical Greek drama, usually a ribald takeoff on Greek mythology and history that included a chorus of satyrs (mythological creatures who were half-man and half-goat).

Scaena ("SKAY-nah") Stage house in a Roman theatre.

Scene (1) Stage setting. (2) One of a series of structural units into which a play or acts of a play are divided. (3) Location of a play's action.

Scrim Thin, open-weave fabric, which is nearly transparent when lit from behind and opaque when lit from the front.

Script Written or printed text—consisting of dialogue, stage directions, character descriptions, and the like.

Set Scenery, taken as a whole, for a scene or an entire production.

Set piece Piece of scenery that stands independently in a scene.

Shareholders In Elizabethan acting troupes, members who received part of the profits as payment.

Sides Script containing only a single actor's lines and cues. Elizabethan actors learned their roles from sides.

Simultaneous setting Medieval tradition of presenting more than one locale onstage at the same time.

Skene ("SKEE-nee") In ancient Greek theatre, the scene house behind the orchestra.

Slapstick Type of comedy, or comic business, that relies on ridiculous physical activity—often violent in nature—for its humor.

Soliloquy Speech in which a character who is alone onstage speaks inner thoughts aloud.

Spill Light from stage-lighting instruments that falls outside the area for which it is intended, such as light that falls on the audience.

Spine (1) In the Stanislavski method, a character's dominant desire or motivation; usually thought of as an action and expressed as a verb. (2) *Also*, the "through-line" or general action that runs through a play from beginning to end.

Stage convention An established theatrical technique or practice arbitrarily accepted through custom or usage.

Stage door Outside entrance to dressing rooms and stage areas that is used by performers and technicians.

Stage house Stage floor and the space around it to the side walls, as well as the space above it up to the grid.

Stage right right side of the stage from the point of view of a performer facing the audience.

Stage left left side of the stage from the point of view of a performer facing the audience.

Stage manager Person who coordinates all aspects of a production related to the director and actors, both during the rehearsals and during the run of the show; he or she ensures that the director's artistic choices are maintained during performances.

Standing room only (SRO) Notice that all seats for a performance have been sold but standees may be accommodated.

Stanislavski method Konstantin Stanislavski's techniques and theories about acting, which promote a naturalistic style stressing (among other things) psycho-physical action as opposed to conventional theatricality.

Stitchers The technicians who sew all of the costumes for a production.

Stock characters Two dimensional, stereotypical characters

Stock set Standard setting for a locale used in every play which requires that environment.

Storm and stress Antineo-classical eighteenth-century German movement, which was a forerunner of romanticism; in German, *Sturm und Drang.*

Strike To remove pieces of scenery or props from onstage or to take down an entire set after a final performance.

Subplot Sometimes referred to as parallel plot, a secondary plot that reinforces or runs parallel to the major plot in an episodic play.

Subtext Meaning and movement of a play below its surface; that which is not stated but implied.

Summer stock Theatre companies operating outside major theatrical centers during the summer, often producing a different play every week.

Symbol A sign, a visual image, an object, or an action that signifies something else; a visual embodiment of something invisible. A single image or sign stands for an entire idea or larger concept—a flag is a symbol for a nation; a logo is a symbol for a corporation.

Symbolism Movement of the late nineteenth century and early twentieth century that sought to express inner truth rather than represent life realistically.

Teaser Short horizontal curtain just beyond the proscenium, used to mask the fly loft and, in effect, to lower the height of the proscenium.

Technical Term referring to functions necessary to the production of a play other than those of the cast and the director, such as functions of the stage crew, carpenters, and lighting crew.

Technical director Staff member responsible for scheduling, construction, and installation of all equipment; he or she is responsible for guaranteeing that designs are executed according to the designer's specifications.

Tetralogy In classical Greek theatre, four plays—three tragedies and a satyr play—written by one author for a festival.

Theatre of the absurd Twentieth century plays expressing the dramatists' sense of absurdity and futility of human existence through the dramatic techniques they employ.

Theme Central thought of a play; the idea or ideas with which a play deals and which it expounds.

Thespian Synonym for "performer"; from Thespis (sixth century BCE), who is said to have been the first actor in ancient Greek theatre.

Thrust stage Stage space that thrusts into the audience space; a stage surrounded on three sides by audience seating.

Tragedy Dramatic form involving serious actions of universal significance and with important moral and philosophical implications, usually with an unhappy ending.

Tragicomedy During the Renaissance, a play having tragic themes and noble characters but a happy ending; today, a play in which serious and comic elements are integrated. Many plays of this type present a comic or ironic treatment of a serious theme.

Tragic flaw The factor that is a character's chief weakness and makes him or her most vulnerable; it often intensifies in time of stress.

Trap Opening in a stage floor, normally covered, which can be used for special effects or allows for a staircase ostensibly leading to a lower floor.

Treadmill Belt or band, usually 3 feet to 5 feet wide, that moves across the stage, on which scenery, props, or performers can move on- or offstage. Generally moves parallel to the front edge of the stage. Operated electronically today, with safety devices to avoid injuries to performers.

Trilogy In classical Greece, three tragedies written by the same playwright and presented on a single day; they were often connected by a story or thematic elements.

Unities Term referring to the preference that a play occur within one day (unity of time), in one place (unity of place), and with no action irrelevant to the plot (unity of action).

Unity A requirement of art; an element often setting art apart from life. In drama, the term refers to unity of action in structure and story and to the integrity and wholeness of a production.

Upstage At or toward the back of the stage, away from the front edge of the stage.

Wagon Low platform mounted on wheels or casters by means of which scenery is moved on- and offstage.

Well-made plays Type of play popular in the nineteenth century and early twentieth century that combines apparent plausibility of incident and surface realism with a tightly constructed, highly causal, and contrived plot.

Wings (1) Left and right offstage areas. (2) Narrow standing pieces of scenery, or "legs," more or less parallel to the proscenium, which form the sides of a setting.

Work lights Lights arranged for the convenience of stage technicians, situated either in backstage areas and shaded or over the stage area for use while the curtain is down.

Yard Pit, or standing area, in Elizabethan public theatres.

NOTES

Chapter 1

1 Walter Kerr, "We Call It 'Live Theater,' but Is It?" *New York Times,* January 2, 1972. Copyright 1972 by the New York Times Company. Reprinted by permission.
2 Jean-Claude van Itallie, *The Serpent: A Ceremony,* written in collaboration with the Open Theater, Atheneum, New York, 1969, p. ix.
3 Richard Nelson, interview in *Lincoln Center Theater Review,* Spring 2013, pp. 4–7.
4 Bernard Beckerman, *Dynamics of Drama: Theory and Method of Analysis,* Knopf, New York, 1970, p. 129.

Chapter 2

1 Notes on *King Lear* are from G. K. Hunter's edition of Shakespeare's *King Lear,* Penguin, Baltimore, 1972, pp. 243–244.

Chapter 3

1 The Performance Group, *Dionysus in 69,* Noonday, Farrar, Straus, and Giroux, New York, n.d.
2 Ibid.
3 Material on the proscenium, arena, and thrust stages was suggested by a booklet prepared by Dr. Mary Henderson for the educational division of Lincoln Center for the Performing Arts.
4 Antonin Artaud, *The Theater and Its Double,* Grove, New York, 1958, pp. 96–97.

Chapter 4

1 Konstantin Stanislavsky, *An Actor Prepares,* Theatre Arts, New York, 1948, p. 73.
2 Jean Benedetti, *Stanislavski,* Routledge, New York, 1988, p. 217.
3 David Bridel, "In the Beginning Was the Body," *American Theatre,* January 2011.

Chapter 8

1 Albert Camus, *Le Mythe de Sisyphe,* Gallimard, Paris, 1942, p. 18.
2 From the book *Waiting for Godot* by Samuel Beckett. Copyright 1954 by Grove Press; renewed copyright 1982 by Samuel Beckett. Used with the permission of Grove/ Atlantic, Inc.

Chapter 9

1 Robert Edmond Jones, *The Dramatic Imagination,* Theatre Arts, New York, 1941, p. 25.

Chapter 14

1 Discussion of happenings prepared by Professor Susan Pfeffer.
2 The material on Native Voices at the Autry is based on reporting by Sarah Lemanczyk in the March 2007 issue of *American Theatre.*

Index

The Theatre Experience, in its most flexible role ever!

Mc Graw Hill Education create™

Create what you've only imagined at www.mcgrawhillcreate.com.

Choose only the content you want. Skipping the musical theatre chapter? Build a book that contains only the chapters you want, in the order you want. Or, incorporate chapters from other McGraw-Hill texts. Create will even re-number the pages for you.

Add plays or other readings. Use our Special Collections to include additional readings right in the text.

- Choose from our library of works by great playwrights, including Sophocles, Henrik Ibsen, Molière, Oscar Wilde, Eugene O'Neill, Susan Glaspell, and many more.
- 35 plays by William Shakespeare are available by Act and all are available as eBook Option.

For a complete list of available works, visit www.mhhe.com/wilsonte13e/xxxxxxxxxx, or browse the entire collection at www.mcgrawhillcreate.com.

Include your own content. Add your syllabus, course requirements, department information, or other content that you've created specifically for your Theatre Appreciation course!

Choose your format. Print or eBook? Softcover, spiral-bound, or loose leaf? Black-and-white or color? Perforated, three-hole punched, or regular paper? No matter the format, Create has the best fit for you and your students.

Customize your cover. Pick your own cover image and include your name and course information right on the cover. Students will know they're purchasing the right book—and using everything they purchase. *The Theatre Experience,* **in its most flexible role ever!**